THE COMPLETE BOOK OF

BICYCLING

All New Fourth Edition

by EUGENE A. SLOANE

A FIRESIDE BOOK
Published by Simon & Schuster
New York   London   Toronto   Sydney   Tokyo   Singapore

Simon and Schuster/Fireside Books
Published by Simon & Schuster Inc.
Simon & Schuster Building
Rockefeller Center
1230 Avenue of the Americas
New York, NY 10020
Simon and Schuster/Fireside and colophons are registered trademarks of Simon & Schuster Inc.
Designed by Irving Perkins Associates
Manufactured in the United States of America
10   9   8   7
Library of Congress Cataloging in Publication Data
Sloane, Eugene A.
    The complete book of bicycling.

    Rev. ed. of: The all new complete book of bicycling. 3rd totally rev. and updated ed. c1980.
    "A Fireside book."
    Bibliography: p.
    Includes index.
    1. Cycling.   2. Bicycles.   I. Sloane, Eugene A.
All new complete book of bicycling.   II. Title.
GV1041.S55   1988   629.2'272   88-404
ISBN 0-671-65803-4
ISBN 0-671-65802-6 (pbk.)

Grateful acknowledgment is given for text, artwork, and photographs reprinted with permission
of Shimano American Corporation, Michelin Tire Corporation, SunTour U.S.A., Inc., and Wy'east
Color, Inc.

ACKNOWLEDGMENTS

So many people have contributed their time and talent to this book that I hardly know where to begin. Friends in the bicycle industry have been more than generous in sending me background data and test products. The wizards who answered my technical questions are paragons of patience and ability. If I have omitted anyone who helped with this book, please accept my gratitude anyway and understand that the omission was not intentional.

Credits to the Bicycle Industry

From the bicycle industry I especially want to thank Tom Franges, Paul Brobeck, Andy Toohey, Chris Allen, and Barry Ladd of SunTour U.S.A. and SunTour management for permission to use their excellent technical drawings which you will find throughout this book.

John Uhte, the answer man at Shimano Corporation, not only answered my many queries about product maintenance, adjustment, and installation, but also granted permission to use his company's fine technical drawings which I used throughout this book.

6   ACKNOWLEDGMENTS

Paul Chess and Frank Brilando of Schwinn Bicycle Company were most helpful, especially in providing me with the test data on front-wheel quick-release retention in Chapter 2. Julian Edwins, who builds elegant custom bicycles, and Douglas Hayduk are talented metallurgists; they both made major contributions to Chapter 1 on frame materials.

Tony Garafolo, when he was with Trek Bicycle Corporation, and his secretary Barbara Brickham, were generous with both their time and test products. Steve Zeoli, Brian Foley, Dave Campbell, and Dave Hogan of Cannondale Corporation were most helpful.

I also wish to thank Greg Siple of BikeCentennial for the many excellent photos he provided; Bill Wilkinson, the executive director of the Bicycle Federation of America, for sound data on bicycle sales; Mark Williams of Bell Helmets, Inc., and Kevin Gallagher of Mountain Safety Research for useful data on bicycle helmets and for test samples; Chris Anderson of Jim Blackburn Designs for samples and data on bicycle carriers and bike workstands.

For sound counsel and product samples I am grateful to Hal Davis and Dr. Roberto Luchino of Campagnolo Corp.; Richard Goodwin, Mavic, U.S.A.; and John Temple, TI Sturmey-Archer of America.

To Howard Hawkins, the president of Park Tool Company, who has designed more and better bicycle tools than anybody, special thanks for all his help. Thanks, too, to Walt Jarvis, publisher of *Bicycle Dealers Showcase* magazine; Frank Berto, West Coast editor of *Bicycling* magazine; Angel Rodriguez and Glenn Erickson, the "R" and "E" of AR&E Cycles, Seattle; and George DeLap, the owner of Hazel Dell Bike Shop, Vancouver, Washington.

For excellent data on bicycle safety, special thanks to Joel I. Friedman, National Injury Clearinghouse, U.S. Consumer Product Safety Commission; Barbara Carraro, in charge of statistics for the National Safety Council; Ed Blodgett, traffic engineer at the Washington State Department of Transportation; V. R. Hodgson, director of the Biomechanics Laboratory, Department of Neurosurgery, Wayne State University; and David Fife, M.D., Dade County, Florida.

A very special note of thanks to Dion and Trish Reynolds, the talented photo team, for many of the product photos in this book.

Phillip Dochow and Kelly Sibley wrote most of Chapters 3 and 11, and for that they get this paragraph all to themselves.

A special "thank you" to copy editor Jeff Klein who did a yeoman job of helping clarify my manuscript in areas that were clear to me but not necessarily to the bicycle novice.

Thanks, too, to my wife Carol and to her sons John and Paul for their encouragement and support during the long hours of writing. John's hi-tech talents were of immense help in bringing me up to speed on a computer and word processing program that was strange, new and mysterious to me.

Last, and far from least, I wish to thank my editor, Herb Schaffner, for a truly superlative job of creative criticism and constructive help and encouragement. Herb, you were great!

Eugene A. Sloane
Vancouver, Washington

CONTENTS

INTRODUCTION

"Hey, sonny, what's your mommy gonna buy you for Christmas *next* year?"

Those were the derisive words screamed at me from the open window of a taxi. The year was 1967. The month was December. The day was cold. The place was Detroit. I was bicycling to my job as a magazine editor from my suburban home. Clearly I was no child. But bikes were, for the most part back then, a child's toy to the men in the cab. They obviously saw an adult on a toy as a figure to be ridiculed. A day or so later I heard a child, about ten, say to his mother as I cycled past, "Mommy, Mommy, look at that man on the bike!"

Times, indeed, have changed since 1967. Today there are nearly 80 million bicycles in use. About 39 million adults ride them. It may be a small shock to any chauvinists out there, but those riders are 55 percent female. Nowadays, some 12 million people ride a bike at least once a week. That's a cheering thought.

Today, cycling is a family affair as well as a solo activity. I see couples tootling along on single bikes and on tandems. Some carry kids on a child carrier or tow them along in a trailer. One recent summer day on the Oregon Coast, for example, I

11

stopped to admire the ocean scene. I noticed a couple on their bikes coming down the road. The man was towing two children in a trailer. His wife's bike, as well as his own, carried bulging bike packs. I just had to lean over from my bike to talk to them as they approached. Seems they were en route to San Francisco from Anchorage, Alaska. Which dramatically illustrates another great way to bike that really is unique to this latter part of the 20th century—bicycle touring and camping. Certainly at no other period in our history have so many cyclists so enthusiastically taken to the open road. Parts of many campgrounds are set aside for cyclists. These sections are called "wilderness" or "remote" sites, and you can bike right up to most of them. The peace and quiet of these remote campsites is a far cry from the noise and the smoky 24-hour campfires to which auto and van campers seem addicted.

More and more people are also riding their bikes to work. For example, one recent survey noted that nearly two million of us commute by bicycle. That's great. Studies show that in major cities served by mass transportation, you can get to work as fast or even faster on a bike. For example, at one time I lived in suburbia, 12 miles north of my office in downtown Chicago. To catch a train, I had to walk about half a mile to the station, which took about 20 minutes if I hustled. When I got there I usually had to wait five or ten minutes for the train to arrive. It took the train about 35 minutes to get to the station in the Loop. It took another ten minutes to walk from the station to my office. That's one hour and fifteen minutes travel time. I could (and did) easily cover that same distance, in the same time, by hopping on my bike and pedaling through city streets and on a bike trail along Lake Michigan. I arrived at the office exhilarated from the ride. Other commuters sat in stuffy, uncomfortable trains or buses, a chore I found tiring and stressful. Since I could bike to work at least 200 days a year, even in winter, I saved $3.50 daily in train fare, which paid for my bike during the first year. My bike used no gas or diesel fuel, did not pollute the atmosphere with carcinogens and lead, and took up little space in congested downtown Chicago. Someday we're going to have complete urban gridlock, the ultimate city traffic jam. When that day comes I hope the bicycle is accepted as the solution to urban transport I know it to be. Bikes sure got a lot of people to work in New York City when a widespread electrical failure halted train service on two occasions and a railway strike halted service on yet another. The press, television, and radio were full of pictures and stories about people who made their way on bikes over the Brooklyn Bridge and through the streets of Manhattan. I will never forget the day fellow workers left our hotel at 57th Street and Park Avenue for an office on Wall Street about nine miles away. They took a taxi, I rode my bike. I was there sitting in the office when they showed up 20 minutes after I arrived. I mentioned the old saw about cabbing in Gotham: "Shall we walk, or do we have time to take a cab?" Biking is better.

Besides health aspects, I think another reason for the growth in popularity of bicycling can be laid to the media, which have widely reported on this country's bicycle successes at the Olympic games in Los Angeles, and more recently, on Greg LeMond's dramatic win in the world-famous Tour de France in 1986—the first time an American finished first in this historic race. LeMond's feat surely makes us all aware that the bicycle is no toy, but a dynamic and fun way to get around. These days we have people like champion Lon Haldeman and his wife Sue Notorangelo tearing across the U.S. from coast to coast in something like nine and a half days on a tandem.

Sure, bicycling is nostalgic, bringing us back to our childhood. The kids of the 1960s are the young adults and even parents of today. When they were young, bicycling was beginning a boom in popularity equalled only by the bike boom of the late 1890s and early 1900s. Children in the 1960s saw their parents, and older adults, embrace bicycling as an enjoyable way to exercise and maintain good health. Today these young adults, influenced by their parents' enthusiasm for cycling, are creating another bicycle boom, with sales again reaching an estimated 11.4 million bikes in 1986. There were also 11.4 million cars sold in 1986. I like to think that everyone who bought a car that year also rushed out and bought a bike the same day. It's a happy thought, anyway.

At a more leisurely pace, thousands of cyclists are touring on the road, and commuters bike to work every day. Even two *new* breeds of bikes have been specially designed for both activities. I'll review the new breed of "commuter bikes" or "city bikes," plus the latest in all-terrain bicycles, in Chapters 1 and 4. The commuter bike is great for commuting, for getting around town, going shopping or to the library. The all-terrain bike can whiz you silently along a mountain trail, taking you 25 miles into the wilderness in four hours or so, leaving nothing behind but the imprint of its fat tires on the trail itself. There's even a bike made for triathlon events, in which competitors swim 2.4 miles, bike 112 miles, and then run 26.2 miles. There's much more about these and other types of bikes in this book, including how to buy a bike, how to fit it to your body dimensions, and how to repair and maintain them.

Perhaps you've heard of the "runner's high." Well, you can get the same effect from cycling. Exercise promotes the release of substances called "endorphins," which are said to bring a feeling of well-being, euphoria, and greater resistance to pain, at least temporarily.

Cycling is a stress-free way to good health in that you can put as much energy into cycling as you wish. Cycling does not demand maximum energy output at any time. You can loaf along or speed up, depending on your physical condition. Doctors recommend bicycling as a good way for people who have had heart surgery to get back in shape. Cycling is much easier on muscles and knee joints, which is one reason why runners and joggers are turning to bikes these days. Cycling reduces stress because the vigorous exercise leaves you feeling so darn good after a hard, healthy ride to the office or to home. I've left work bone-tired and after a few miles discovered my body coming alive again as I cycled home.

So get out on that bike as soon as you can. This book will tell you how to cycle safely, how to keep your bike in tip-top condition, and how to find the bike that's just right for you. Happy cycling!

Gene Sloane
Vancouver, Washington

ONE

HOW TO BUY THE BIKE
THAT'S RIGHT FOR YOU

If you don't own a bike, this chapter will help you select the one that's just right for you. If you do own a bike but want to upgrade to a better method, there's help here for you too. Whether you want a bike to take on cross-country tours, around town, or to ride on remote mountain trails, I've compiled criteria here to help you make your selection.

In this chapter you'll also learn how to check a bicycle for safety, all about the newest types of frame tubing, how to order a custom bike tailor-made to fit you, and what basic accessories you will need. There are tips about tandems, help for the handicapped—and most important, how to select a bike that will fit your bodily dimensions, and how to adjust saddle and handlebar height for comfort and safety.

Let's start with what *not* to buy, and where not to buy it. I strongly advise against buying a bicycle anywhere but in a good bike shop. Bike store mechanics usually do a competent job of taking a bike out of its factory shipping carton and assembling it so you can ride it safely. If you buy a bike in any other type of outlet, chances are more than even that the assembler will be a stockroom clerk who is not trained to assemble and adjust a new bike so it's safe and reliable to ride.

15

 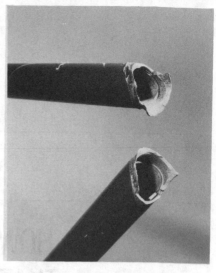

Fig. 1-1: Inexpensive bikes have poor welding which can result in tube separation if the bicycle hits a bump or a curb.

Fig. 1-2: These are the top and down tubes of the bike in Fig. 1-1.

If you buy an el cheapo $69.96 special, and you buy it in a discount store, you're really asking for trouble. Aside from the high probability of poor assembly (usually by an untrained stockperson), the bike itself may be only marginally safe for anything but the most casual of slow rides on a flat surface where there is absolutely no traffic. I've found such bikes to have poor brakes which may stop you at slow speed, but may not bring you to a safe stop in an emergency situation, or let you hold speed to a safe level on steep hills.

Bikes much under $200 usually have poorly made frames of low-quality steel. Frame tubes may be poorly welded. Under stress they may come apart and cause an accident and injury. Fig. 1-1, for example, shows just such a frame. Here tubing has indeed simply parted company, leaving the frame in two pieces. Fig. 1-2 shows the top and down tubes as they broke off from the head tube in Fig. 1-1.

The el cheapos also have thin dropouts, as shown in Fig. 1-3. This happens to be a three-speed model, but such dropouts (where the wheel axle is fitted) also appear on inexpensive ten-speed models. Here the dropouts are simply pushed into frame tubing, the frame tubing is pressed, and the dropouts are welded to the tubing ends. Such a design makes accurate frame alignment difficult and contributes to frame whip, which can cause loss of control. A high-quality dropout, found on better bikes, is shown in Fig. 1-4. Other problems with cheap bikes are caused by poor quality control at the factory, which can lead to improperly adjusted and installed derailleurs, loose wheel or bearing assemblies and out-of-line wheels, loose wheel hubs, and loose headsets—all of which can cause an accident and injury. Misaligned wheels affect braking and steering control. Machining of head tube ends and fork crowns may be inaccurate, making accurate adjustment of headset bearings impossible. Headset bearings can become loose and cause wheel shimmy, loss of control, and, ultimately, an accident. You'll find fewer such quality-control defects as the price of the bicycle goes up. The better the factory assembly, the better the bike itself.

We'll discuss the hazards, causes, and elimination of wheel shimmy at greater length in Chapter 2. Later on in this chapter you'll learn how to check out a new bike so it will be safe to ride. Right now, let's concentrate on buying the right bike for your needs.

Fig. 1-3: Hallmark of a cheap bike is the dropouts. Here the rear wheel dropout is simply a stamped piece of low-carbon steel clamped and welded into the stays.

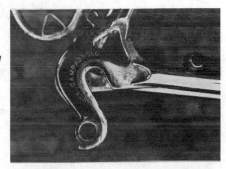

Fig. 1-4: Here's the kind of high-quality dropout that marks a good bike.

DIFFERENT BIKES FOR DIFFERENT USES

So often people buy what they consider to be a really expensive bike, say for around $150, then decide, after a year or so of comparison shopping, to upgrade to a $500 bike. You'll usually find top-line components on bikes that cost $500 and up. If possible, I'd start with the best bike you can possibly stretch your budget to buy. In future years you'll be glad you did. Back in 1958, when I first started cycling as an adult, I just wanted to get a little exercise. My mind was tuned to heavy, heavy coaster-brake models, so that's what I bought. Then, one day, an old geezer whizzed by me on a strange-looking contraption with funny-looking handlebars. I caught up to him at a stop-light, with great difficulty, even though I was at last 20 years his junior. I asked how he liked that thing he was riding. He looked at me pityingly and with a slight aura of contempt, and suggested I should look into a lightweight, ten-speed, high-performance bicycle. He said that the cheapest ten-speed would be a lot easier to pedal than the most expensive coaster-brake or three-speed bike on the market. Of course, wanting only the very best for myself, I hotfooted it down to one of the few places in town that catered to ten-speeders and bought one for what seemed to me to be an exorbitant price: $85. I was hooked, bitten by the bug of cycling, although I didn't realize it at the time. But within a month I was back at the bike shop to upgrade, and this time I spent $250 for the best stock touring bike in the store. Today that bike would cost around $1,200. Mine is still alive, though it has had much face-lifting. The frame has been repainted, and all the components have been replaced, several times; but that old frame still rolls on, as comfortable and as responsive as ever. It looks great, too, in its new clothes.

City Bikes for Around Town

If you want a good general-purpose bike to use around town, and don't plan to use it for long-distance cycle touring and camping trips, I heartily recommend a new breed of bike, known as a "city bike" or "commuter bike." By whatever name, they combine the comfort and durability of the old Schwinn and Columbia bikes of the 1930s with the pedaling efficiency and strong materials and components of the modern light-weight.

A typical city bike (Fig. 1-5) costs anywhere from $200 to $450. It has 26-inch wheels with fat tires that absorb road shock and give excellent traction on a wide variety of surfaces. These tires are also less prone to flats from street debris than the skinny tires found on road bikes. (More about road bikes later.) The city bike's flat handlebars put you in a more upright position than you find with downturned racing-type handlebars, so you have better visibility in traffic without having to strain your neck to look up. Handlebar-mounted brake and shift levers are easy to reach, and brakes are more than adequate when prop-erly adjusted.

The city bike is ideal for commuting. You can install bike packs and carriers to carry the packs, so you can bring along a change of clothing, rainwear, your briefcase, and extra tubes in case of a flat. The wider tires can keep you upright should you have to veer to the right onto gravel, grass, or a bumpy strip, or to jump a curb to avoid a collision. City bikes usually come

Fig. 1-5: Excellent example of a high-quality commuter or city bicycle. Note the upright handlebars, fat tires, and more than adequate gearing. A fine bike on which to commute to work.

with adequate gearing so you can climb hills more or less easily. (See Chapter 4 for data on gearing and gear ratios.) Most city bike pedals do not come equipped with toe clips and straps. Without them, you can get your feet on and off the pedals quickly and easily when you take off and stop. However, toe clips and straps can be added to most city bike pedals.

All-Terrain Bicycles

All-terrain bicycles are just that. Almost anywhere two wheels can go, ATBs can take you. On the highway, off the road on remote mountain trails, even through snow (with care). ATBs (Fig. 1-6) resemble city bikes, but true ATBs have wider, knobbier tires, a wider gear range for negotiating steep mountain trails at low speed, a more self-correcting, forgiving steering

Fig. 1-6: An aluminum-frame all-terrain bicycle combines strength with lightness. This is the type of bike to take on remote mountain trails.

geometry, and a stronger frame that's safe going downhill on bumpy terrain.

You can use an ATB for commuting and city riding, but in my opinion a city bike isn't really suited for off-road use. The city bike may be less expensive than a good ATB, but the frame is often not as sturdy, nor are its components designed for hard use on bumpy wilderness trails.

You can get a reasonably good ATB for around $300. However, if you are serious about riding in the wilderness, I urge you to spend another $500 or so for a high-quality ATB that will get you there and back. Remember, 25 miles into the wilds of a mountain trail is an unlikely place to find a bike shop to replace a broken fork, bent axle, or busted spokes. For serious off-road riding you need the best you can afford. Think of an all-terrain bicycle as you would a fine backpack, good canoe, sturdy tent, or warm sleeping bag. When your comfort and possibly even your well-being depend on the equipment you use, the best is never too good.

For more information on all-terrain bicycles, please let me refer you to my latest book, *Eugene A. Sloane's Complete Book of All-Terrain Bicycles*. There's so much to know about these great bikes that I can't compress everything you need to know in one chapter. I can tell you, though, that all-terrain bikes are, right now, the hottest-selling, most popular bike on the market, judging from reports I get from bike dealers and from the manufacturers I talked to at the major bicycle trade conventions in California and New York. Four or five years ago all-terrain bikes were virtually unknown in this country except to a small band of dedicated bikees in California. Then the ATB share of the bike market was infinitesimal. Today, ATBs account for over 20 percent of all bike sales, and their share of the market is climbing fast.

Why have ATBs suddenly become so popular? The answer is simple. These bikes are just so darned comfortable. They seem to glide over the ruts and bumps of city streets; hitting a bump at speed does not tear the handlebars out of your grasp. And not only are they forgiving, but, as I noted earlier, they are truly all-purpose. You can ride them on city streets or bikeways (Fig. 1-7), over wilderness trails (Fig. 1-8), and while touring and camping over paved roads. ATBs are truly today's beasts of burden, which is why they are favored by those intrepid riders of the mean streets of major cities, messenger people.

Fig. 1-7: An all-terrain bicycle is also useful on city streets. Its upright stance gives good visibility and less neck strain. The fat tires are less prone to flats.

Fig. 1-8: Trail riding on an all-terrain bicycle can get you 25 miles out into the wilderness in a few hours, a trip that would take all day for a backpacker.

Women appreciate the stability and the upright stance of ATBs. These bikes are especially suited to carrying children, as well as camping gear or what-have-you (Fig. 1-9).

Fig. 1-9: It's hard to beat an all-terrain model for safety and stability when carrying a child on a bike.

Road Bicycles for Long-Distance Touring and Bike Camping

Road bicycles have been the most popular type of bicycle for general-purpose riding for the past 40 or 50 years. Today these bikes (Fig. 1-10) are still favored by experienced bicyclists who want a machine that combines high performance with comfort. You won't be quite as comfortable on a road bike as you would be on an ATB. But the road bike, with its narrower tires and lighter weight, does make long-distance touring a bit easier than on an ATB. For one thing, road bikes are around three to five pounds lighter than a comparable quality ATB. For another, the dropped handlebars let you lean farther to increase streamlining (wind constitutes some 80 percent of the resistance to pedaling). The rolling resistance of the skinnier high-

Fig. 1-10: A road bike with its skinny tires and strong but light frame, such as this one, is great for long-distance touring on paved roads.

pressure tires of a road bike is about 10 percent less than that of the fatter, knobby tires on an ATB.

With road bikes, as with all bikes, you get pretty much what you pay for these days. If you're really serious about hitting the road and cruising the byways of rural America, I urge you to spend at least $500 for a road bike. That way you'll be assured of getting top-quality frame construction and design, high-quality tubing, and reliable components. Moreover, such a bike, like all good bikes in that price range, will be a lifetime investment (unless it's stolen; see Chapter 4 for a rundown on good locks).

Bicycles Built for Two

Tandems are a great way to go. They offer many advantages over a single bike. For example, a high-quality tandem (Fig. 1-11) weighs only around 40 pounds, compared with a single road bicycle of similar quality, which weighs around 25 pounds. Two riders on a tandem only have 20 pounds of bike each, a total weight savings over a single bike of five pounds per rider. You may think five pounds isn't much, but just try carrying a five-pound sack of potatoes on the back of your single bike, uphill, and you'll see what I mean.

Another major advantage of a tandem is that it faces far less wind resistance than two single bikes. About 80 percent of your pedaling energy on a single bike goes into overcoming wind resistance. Even when the wind is not blowing hard, air is an

Fig. 1-11: A tandem bicycle requires less strength for two to pedal than one each on a single bike. It also makes communication easy between the riders.
(Bikecentennial photo)

Fig. 1-12: Safest way to carry a child is in a trailer, whether the bike is a tandem or a single road bike as shown here. While you can carry everything you need for a long-distance camping trip in a trailer, that might be a problem on a tandem.

invisible brake that slows you up. On a tandem, only the front rider (called the captain) faces the wind. The rear rider (called the stoker) is hidden behind the captain and faces very little wind resistance. Two riders on a tandem can leave a single rider far behind. Tandem cyclists can pedal about 20 percent farther than a single cyclist, given the same road conditions and strength of the three riders. To be sure, uphill climbs are slower on a tandem than on a single, but on a downhill run the tandem is hell on wheels. Uncontrolled, a tandem can easily get up to 40 to 50 miles per hour on even a mild, four-degree grade. Which is why better tandems have disk brakes. They need them, believe me.

Tandems are ideal for touring. As I said earlier, tandems can cover more territory faster and easier than a single bike. Biking 100 miles a day or more is possible even for riders of modest strength. Tandem riders are close enough so they can carry on a conversation during the ride and so share the pleasures of the trip.

There are a few disadvantages to a tandem, which I consider to be minor compared to the pluses they offer. For example, a tandem has less room to carry bike packs than two single bikes. However, the two riders on a tandem can easily tow a bike trailer (Fig. 1-12) to carry all the equipment needed for long-distance bike touring and camping. On city streets, the tandem, because of its longer wheelbase, is not as maneuverable as a single bike. However, this is merely my observation. I've never heard any complaints from tandem enthusiasts on this point, but that's been my experience. Also, good tandems cost a bundle. You can get a good tandem for as little as $1,500, and the best ones cost upward of $2,500 or even more. Still, consider the price of two single bikes of comparable quality. A reasonably good road bike costs around $500. Better road bikes cost around $750 to $2,500, and one make can be had for $6,500. The more exotic bikes, made of space-age tubing such as titanium or carbon fiber, will dent your bankroll by at least $4,000 on up to $12,000 for a complete tandem. We'll get into these fancy machines later in this chapter. I've no idea what the four-person tandem shown in Fig. 1-13 costs, but you can bet that a new subcompact car wouldn't cost much more. This elongated tandem is really more a curiosity than a practical bike. But with strong riders it sure must be unbeatable on the flats.

Beware of the el cheapo tandem. These heavy clunkers may

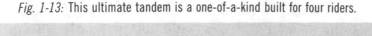

Fig. 1-13: This ultimate tandem is a one-of-a-kind built for four riders.

Fig. 1-14: All-terrain tandems are also available, such as this model with a short wheelbase designed for twisty mountain trails.

only cost around $350, but they weigh 70 to 80 pounds, have low-grade components, including brakes, and are awkward to handle. They ride like a truck. The cheap tandem is fine, though, as a rental unit for resorts, or for manhandling by two strong teenagers who only ride around town.

Notice that gender has not entered into this discussion. Old-time tandem makers, in fact, were pretty sneaky about where the stoker sat. If you look at turn-of-the-century models, you'll see the lady up front all right. Here she seems to be the captain. But if you look closely, you'll see that the bike is steered from behind, by the rear-riding captain, who is always male. See Chapter 13 for details.

You can also buy an all-terrain tandem (Fig. 1-14). However, I'd be inclined to use that tandem on more or less straight roads and stay away from narrow mountain trails with sharp corners, deep ravine dropoffs, and logs you could hop over only with a single ATB.

Bikes for the Triathlete and Road Racer

Road-racing and triathlon bikes are so similar as to be the same bike. I'm not talking the Olympics, the Tour de France, or other exotic, merchandisable events here. Bikes used in these events are handmade machines that can cost more than $40,000. No, I'm just talking about racing bikes used by your average racer who enjoys the competition of the road races run in accordance with the rules of the governing body of racing in this country, the United States Cycling Federation. You can buy custom-made bikes, tailored to your bodily dimensions, for racing or any other type of cycling, for that matter. There's more about custom bikes later in this chapter. For now, off-the-shelf road-racing bikes (Fig. 1-15) are the subject.

Road-racing bikes, also used for triathlon events, have a shorter wheelbase, steeper frame angles, and a less forgiving frame geometry (Fig. 1-16). These bikes have extremely stiff frames, so all your energy translates into forward motion and as

Fig. 1-15: Here's a typical road-racing bicycle. It has a short wheelbase, very responsive steering, and close-ratio gears. It's for the racing athlete. The stiff frame would give the average touring cyclist too hard a ride.

Fig. 1-16: For the triathlete, this bicycle has a short wheelbase and quick steering, with a very stiff frame.

little as possible is lost in frame whip. Which means bikes built for road racing are a butt-busting, harsh ride. But their frame geometry and short wheelbase make them extremely maneuverable.

One problem with these short-wheelbase bikes is that the front wheel is much closer to the downtube than on any other kind of bike except track-racing bikes; if you turn a sharp corner when a pedal is at the three o'clock position, your toe could hit the front wheel and cause a spill.

Racing bikes also have a very close-ratio gear setup. The difference between the high and low gears of these bikes may give snappy gear shifts for the strong road-racing athlete. But if you're not in shape, the lowest gear on these bikes may have you walking up any hill much steeper than a 6 percent grade.

Track bikes (Fig. 1-17) are a breed apart. They have fixed gears. There's no freewheel. If the wheel turns, so do the pedals. There are no brakes. You slow down or stop by backpedaling. Racers can even come to a complete stop on the track, and, with both feet on the pedals, balance, stay upright, and outwait a rival doing the same thing.

There's a special type of track bike used in time-trial racing, which is a race against the clock. The rider attempts to cover a given distance in a shorter time than anyone else, or at least quicker than competitors at that event. Time-trial bikes are made for just one thing, speed, speed, and more speed. Frame, wheels, and components are as light as possible. If you tried to ride a time trial on any surface rougher than a smooth racing track, the wheels would very likely collapse at the first bump.

I'm sure not telling racing cyclists anything they don't know. Just thought *you'd* like to be informed, in case the racing fever overtakes you. In which case, see Chapter 12.

Fig. 1-17: Track bikes have fixed gears so maximum thrust goes into the wheels. Racers can balance the bikes in one fixed position, holding still until the moment is ripe for a take-off. Track bikes do not have brakes.

Fig. 1-18: A folding bike like this one can be stashed away in your car trunk, apartment closet, or your boat. It folds down to about half the size you see here.

Folding Bikes

Folding bikes (Fig. 1-18) are great for stowing where space is at a premium, such as on sailboats, in the trunk of a car, or stashed away in a closet in a tiny apartment. I take mine along when I travel by air on business. I can usually find a few hours in the evening to unwind on my folding bike before fear of strange city streets drives me back to the hotel. Airlines charge upward of $25 to accept any bike, even a tiny folding one, if they know it's a bike. So do what I do: Pack it in a sturdy cardboard box, label it "machinery," hand the box over to the ticket agent, and sign the airline's disclaimer for liability. No charge.

The trouble with foldups is that they weigh about as much as an ATB. Some have only three speeds, but five- and ten-speed models are available. They offer a good way to get exercise while exploring strange territory. You can buy one for around $250.

Recumbents

The advantages of recumbents include excellent components and high-quality frames, because they are all either mostly handmade or of limited production (Fig. 1-19). You get high quality for the price. Since the bike is low to the ground, the rider is laid back. Therefore, recumbents are more aerodynamically efficient than more upright road bikes. On the other hand,

Fig. 1-19: A recumbent lets you sit back, allowing you to better use your stomach and leg muscles for go-power.

the lower profile of a recumbent may make them harder for automobile drivers to spot. I use a flag on a five-foot plastic pole to make drivers aware of my presence. Leg, back, and shoulder muscles all contribute to pedaling power because your back is braced against the seat. Recumbents are incredibly comfortable. When riding them myself, I hardly notice road bumps that bounce me around even on my ATB. One model even lets you use your hands as well as your legs to get power to the rear wheel. Because your body sits upright, as you do in a car, you have excellent visibility.

The design of these bikes varies quite widely from builder to builder. Right now there are eight or nine small firms that make recumbents, which explains the relatively high price of these machines. They cost from $800 to $2,500.

If you're handy with a brazing torch, you can build your own recumbent from an old BMX bicycle, or make one from scratch. Plans for the BMX conversion are $5, for the recumbent, $20. For an additional $10 you get blueprints for the recumbent. All plans come with a bill of materials. From Alternative Bikestyles, P.O. Box 11344, Bonita, CA 92002.

BMX Bicycles

BMX means "Bicycle Motocross." These are the little 20-inch-wheel machines you see kids on, pulling wheelies up curbs and over obstacles real or imaginary, becoming airborne briefly down small hills. There are three levels of BMX bikes. The most common make is the $75 special available from discount stores. These are the kind kids destroy fairly rapidly, sometimes banging themselves up in the process. Then there are the better bikes, which can cost up to $150. They are still street bikes, unsuitable for much else than play. Most of these bikes are single-speed. Some have caliper brakes on both wheels, others only on the rear wheel. And they are heavy—boy, are they heavy! Kids think they can go like the wind on them, and for a block or two they can actually keep up with me. It gives me great joy to leave them behind. But first I point out that if they want to keep up with a ten-speed, they will have to dump the truck they're riding and get a bike like mine. Heft a BMX sometime, and compare its weight with a ten-speed road bike in the same price range. However, for children up to 12, BMX bikes—the better ones, at least, with gussetted reinforced frames—are virtually indestructible. And the frames are small enough so kids can ride them safely. Just don't buy them a BMX or any other kind of bike with "ram's horn" handlebars, which are hi-rise, or semi-hi-rise bars. If the child should fall off the bike, and at the same time the wheel turns so that one end of the handlebar strikes him in the stomach area, he could suffer serious injury. It's happened.

A more costly BMX is made for BMX track racing. These bikes have highest-quality steel-frame tubing (see discussion on frame tubing later in this chapter), reinforced at critical frame junctures. Components are first-class. These bikes can cost as much as $850 or even more, and are used primarily in

Fig. 1-20: BMX bikes let kids do stunts like this.

Fig. 1-21: Kids can jump over 2-foot-high hills separated by up to 25 feet!

Fig. 1-22: In a BMX race, riders routinely clear double-jump hills.

BMX track events. The bikes must be strong enough to with-stand the impact of airborne jumps over small hills as far apart as 27 feet (Figs. 1-20, 1-21, and 1-22), slamming around curbs (berms), banging into bumps, and into each other. BMX races are held all over the U.S. under the aegis of two sponsoring organizations. (See Chapter 12 for more data on BMX racing.) Unless your child is serious about BMX racing, buying him a competition model at great cost would be a waste of money, in my opinion. The mid-range bikes costing between $150 to $250 are very sturdy little machines. They will serve your child well until he or she is old enough to appreciate the advantages of a good all-terrain or road bike.

Here is a special warning about BMX bicycle pedals. Some BMX bicycles have cranks that are about a half-inch longer than the pedals on adult road bikes. This long a crank is not a prob-lem in itself. But most BMX bikes come with pedals that have sawtooth serrated edges. There are cases on record in which children have had a foot fall forward off the pedal, jam between the pedal and the frame or ground, and, with the bike still moving forward, having their Achilles tendon cut by the saw-tooth edge of the pedal. The foot slips off the pedal on these bikes when they hit a bump hard, moving the child's entire body forward. You might consider filing off these teeth or re-placing them with road pedals, which do not have these teeth.

Bikes for the Handicapped

If you're confined to a wheelchair but have the use of your arms, you can get out into the fresh air and get aerobic exercise on a high-performance self-propelled machine. If you have lim-ited mobility, for whatever reason, it's possible there's some form of self-propelled transportation available to you. At the very least, if you are using a stock, heavy wheelchair, there are lighter, more efficient, easier-to-use conveyances already on the market.

For example, several firms make racing wheelchairs, com-plete with brakes. Paraplegics use them in races in the Special Olympics. There are wheelchair racing events held throughout the U.S. At least one firm, Access Designs, makes an arm-

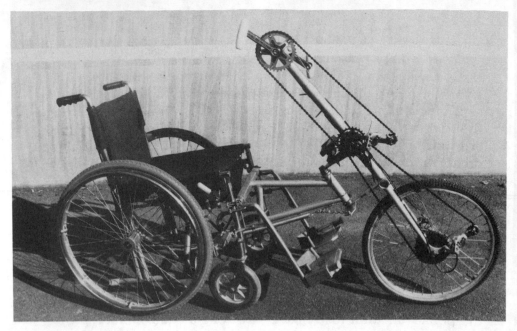

Fig. 1-23: The contraption in the front of this wheelchair helps the handicapped person travel faster and climb hills more easily.

Fig. 1-24: Some of the 24 gears in the front end of the wheelchair adapter shown in Fig. 1-23.

Fig. 1-25: The wheelchair rider can use arm power to pedal and steer at the same time for greater speed and mobility.

powered pedal adapter kit for wheelchairs (Figs. 1-23, 1-24 and 1-25). The kit is a 24-speed derailleur system, with gearing from 10 to 80.28 inches. This super-low gear should bring at least moderate hills within the capability of a moderately strong wheelchair person. The kit comes with a Sturmey-Archer Elite ST brake activated by backpedaling. For details, write to Access Designs, 627 S.E. 53rd, Portland, OR 97215, or a publication called *Spokes 'N Sports*. Their January-February 1987 edition has a listing of manufacturers of a wide variety of self-propelled devices for the handicapped. The editors, Cliff and Nancy Crase, said a reprint of this information is available. Write to them at 5201 N. 19th Ave., Suite 111, Phoenix, AZ 85015. The Crases also publish *Paraplegic News*.

Tailor-Made, a Bicycle Built for You!

Back in 1970 there were very few custom bike builders in this country. Most were in Europe. Today there are hundreds of excellent frame builders who handcraft a bicycle to fit the exact body dimensions of a rider. If you've ever had a tailor custom-fit your clothing, you can begin to imagine how well a custom-fit bike will fit you. A custom, handmade bike (Figs. 1-26, 1-27, and 1-28) takes your arm, leg, and torso lengths, weight, strength and even the type of riding you do, into consideration.

A custom bike really makes sense for two reasons. First, if your arms, legs, or torso are longer or shorter in proportion to the norm, then a custom frame is well worth the money. If you're very tall, say over six and a half feet, or very short, under five feet, then you really should consider a custom frame. Second, if you are an ardent bicyclist you will appreciate the fit of a custom frame in terms of comfort and performance. You'll be able to reach the handlebars without strain or neck pain. You'll be able to use muscles more effectively because the seat tube angle will put the saddle at the correct position over the bottom bracket. You can specify the braze-ons you want so you can bolt, rather than have to clamp on, such extras as a pump holder, carrier or rack fittings, water bottle cage(s), and light mountings. You can have the bike designed for touring, road or track racing, time trials, criteriums, triathlons, or off-road trail riding.

Fig. 1-26: This custom, hand-made bicycle fits its owner like a glove. If you have longer or shorter body dimensions than the norm, a custom-built bike is the (expensive!) answer to getting a machine that will be the most comfortable for you.

Fig. 1-27: Detail of a very fine hand-made custom bicycle frame. The tubing in this frame is made of the new Excel composite material described later on.

Fig. 1-28: This is the kind of quality construction you get in a custom frame. This model is an aluminum-frame bike that sold for around $6,500 as a complete machine.

You can specify exactly the gearing, types of brakes, or any other accessory you want.

Of course a custom bike is expensive. They start at around $1,000 and can go as high as $6,500. We're not talking professional racing bikes here, either, which can, as noted earlier, reach the astronomical cost of $40,000 or more. There's a lot of information on fitting a bicycle to you in the next section of this chapter. There's a list of good frame builders in the Appendix of this book.

Not everyone needs a custom bike. Bikes today come in a wide range of frame sizes. Adjustable components—such as stems, handlebars, seat posts, and brake levers—can be used to tailor an off-the-shelf bike closely to your specific needs. Remember, stock off-the-shelf bikes are designed to fit the majority of people. But some women have longer arms on a shorter torso and need a bike specially made for them.

Bikes for Women

There is an off-the-shelf bike made just for women, designed and built by a woman. It's the Terry bike (Fig. 1-29). These bikes come in as small a frame size as 16 inches, to fit a woman four feet, 11 inches tall. Table 1 gives the full range of her frame sizes (Georgena Terry, Terry Bicycles, 140 E. Despatch Dr., E. Rochester, NY 14445).

Fig. 1-29: This is a bike built by a woman, for a woman. Note the small front wheel, which permits a short frame for a short person.

Table 1-1

TERRY BIKE FRAME SIZES, AS DETERMINED BY WOMAN RIDER'S HEIGHT
(All seat tube, straddle height, and top tube dimensions in inches)

HEIGHT	SEAT TUBE	STRADDLE HEIGHT*	TOP TUBE
less than 4'11"	16	26.1	18.9
4'11"–5'1"	17	27.3	19
5'1"–5'3"	18.5	28.7	19.3
5'2"–5'4"	20	30.3	19.5–21
5'4"–5'7"	21.5	31.8	21
more than 5'7"	23	33.2	21.5

* A function of inseam measurement and bottom bracket height above the ground.

Note: Terry does not, at this writing, make all-terrain bicycles. However, all-terrain bikes have higher bottom-bracket ground clearance, allowing you to roll over obstacles such as branches, rocks, stumps, etc., without bottoming out. If, for example, a 20-inch road bike fits you, then a 19- or even 18-inch all-terrain bike would be right for you (Fig. 1-30). The ultimate criterion is top-tube clearance. Men and women should have about a one-inch clearance between their crotch and top tube on a road bike. On all-terrain bikes men and women both need a two-inch clearance, because the rider may come down pretty hard on the top tube if he or she has to straddle the ground with both feet to stay upright (see How to Ride an ATB in the next chapter). You should be able to move your body forward off the saddle, take your feet off the pedals, place them on the ground, and still not have your crotch area make contact with the top tube. If you do not have sufficient clearance for this maneuver, the bike is too big for you. For example, in an emergency-stop situation, you may have to get both feet on the ground in order to stay upright. Top-tube clearance must be adequate to avoid pain should you have to execute such a maneuver.

Fig. 1-30: This sloping top-tube all-terrain model is another route to a shorter bike. Here the rear wheel is smaller than the front wheel.

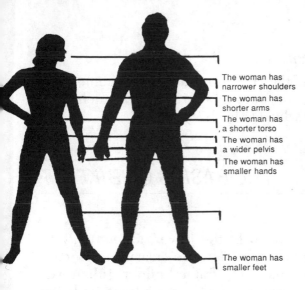

The woman has narrower shoulders

The woman has shorter arms

The woman has a shorter torso

The woman has a wider pelvis

The woman has smaller hands

The woman has smaller feet

Fig. 1-31: While leg length is about the same for both men and women, other body dimensions are different, which is why a bike designed just for a woman makes sense.

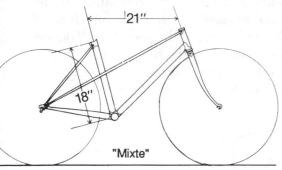

21"

18"

"Mixte"

Fig. 1-32: This "mixte" woman's frame is an attempt to arrive at a bike a woman can use with comfort. These frames are more flexible, so some pedaling energy is converted to frame whip, rather than going to the wheels.

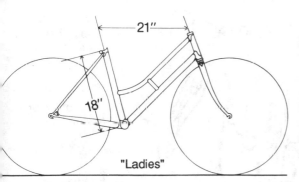

21"

18"

"Ladies"

Fig. 1-33: Like the mixte in Fig. 1-32, this heavy clunker is another attempt at a "woman's" bicycle. Moreover, like the mixte, cable lengths for the rear brake and derailleur are longer, making the rear brake less efficient and the rear derailleur harder to shift.

In her sales literature, Ms. Terry notes: "Women have shorter torsos, shorter arms and smaller hands than a man with the same leg length [Fig. 1-31], therefore the top tube must be shorter on a woman's bike. Since diamond frames can't be built under 20 inches without compromising frame dimensions, most small women have had to ride mixte [Fig. 1-32] or traditional 'girls' bicycles, [Fig. 1-33]. Neither of these frames solve the problem of the distance from the saddle to the handlebars."

From Table 1 you can see that Terry builds a small frame with a 16- or 17-inch seat tube. She does this by using a 24-inch front wheel and a 27-inch rear wheel (Fig. 1-29).

THE BASICS OF BIKE FIT

Since custom bikes are built to fit the buyer, a good way to review the basics of bike fit is to review the measuring process used by custom bike builders. A top frame builder, Julian Edwins, wrote, "An accurate measurement of the human body [as shown in Fig. 1-34] is essential to the custom frame builder. To start with, the builder needs the length of the foot, the distance from floor to knee (flat-footed), and length from knee to femur (greater trochanter). These dimensions determine the seat tube angle. They are also important because they involve the 12

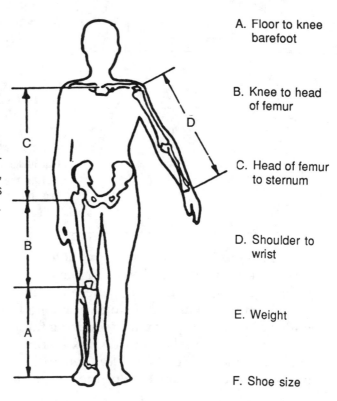

A. Floor to knee
   barefoot

B. Knee to head
   of femur

C. Head of femur
   to sternum

D. Shoulder to
   wrist

E. Weight

F. Shoe size

Fig. 1-34: When you order a custom frame built just for you, these are the body dimensions the frame builder needs to have.

MUSCLES THAT COME INTO ACTION DURING PEDALLING

The thicker area of each line indicates greater activity by the muscle

1 Gluteus maximus, medius and minimus
2 Rectus femoris
3 Vastus lateralis and medialis
4 Sartorius
5 Tensor fascia latae
6 Biceps femoris

7 Peroneus longus
8 Gracilis
9 Tibialis anterior
10 Soleus
11 Gastrocnemius
12 Iliopsoas (iliacus, psoas major and minor)

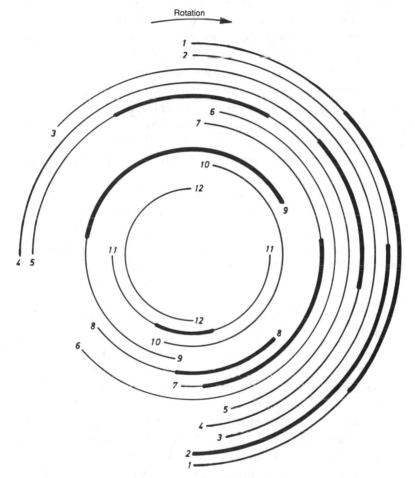

Fig. 1-35: A custom bike that fits you perfectly helps you make the most of these muscles used in cycling.

muscles and muscle groups involved in turning the crank [Fig. 1-35]. For all these muscles to perform at peak efficiency (assuming they are in top condition), they must be correctly positioned in relation to the bottom bracket and the pedal axle.

"Correct position, seated on the bike, your *knee* is directly above the pedal axle when the crank is parallel to the ground (one crank should be at the three o'clock position). If you try to obtain this position by moving the saddle rearward or frontward, you will change the distance of reach to the handlebars, in which case you may be asking for neck and back pain as you strain to see ahead, or have to bend over to reach the handlebars. If the bike is too short and you try to compensate with a very long stem, you'll have more body weight over the front wheel. This is bad for three reasons. First, excess weight over the front wheel makes for poor steering control. Second, the longer stem changes steering response by the rider, because a longer stem gives greater leverage. Third, more weight on the front wheel reduces rear-brake effectiveness. This could lead to an end-over if the front brake is grabbed hard, pitching the rider headfirst forward off the bike as the rear wheel comes up in the air.

"The correct position is best achieved by the seat-tube angle that's compatible with your body dimensions. Such a fit helps you get not only more efficient use of your muscles, but also gives you a good balance between back and stomach muscles. This balance also prevents pelvic tilt, which in turn provides the femur with a fixed pivot point, rather than an unstable one that would reduce efficiency.

"Sending the builder accurate, correct measurements also means that top tube and handlebar stem lengths are right for you. Measurements from the head of the femur to the top of the sternum (breast bone) and the length of the arm from shoulder to wrist combine to determine top tube and handlebar stem lengths."

Your author recommends that if your build and bodily dimensions are unusual (and that includes your weight), be sure to mention them to your builder, who needs all the data he can get. Remember: a custom frame, built to your accurate bodily dimensions, will give you comfort and efficiency. You'll have a frame that will make the best possible use of your own athletic ability. Be sure to let the builder know what you intend to use the bicycle for. For example, do you want a touring bicycle, an all-terrain machine, or a special racing model? If you tell him, the builder can design the bicycle with the correct frame angles for the specific use you have in mind.

Fig. 1-36: A Julian Edwins custom-built touring bicycle.

Fig. 1-37: A Julian Edwins track-racing bicycle with fixed gears, no brakes.

Julian Edwins was himself a racing cyclist and has a background in metallurgical engineering and machine design. His custom frames (Figs. 1-36 and 1-37) and complete bicycles are used by cyclists who enjoy competitive events, as well as by touring cyclists. Julian will be happy to answer your specific questions on frame design. He can be reached at Edwins Cycle Co., P.O. Box 81, Owen Sound, Ontario, Canada N4K 5P1, or 519-376-2852.

Saddle and Handlebar Adjustments

Of course you don't need to spend a bundle on a custom frame to get a bicycle that's reasonably close to your body dimensions, style, and type of riding you plan. All you need to understand are the basics of bike fit, as explained above. Now that you know that moving the saddle fore or aft or changing stem length may affect the fit of the bike, you can start from here. If the bike is too small for you—that is, if you have much more than an inch of crotch clearance above the top tube—an extra long seat post isn't the answer to getting you up high enough. Look at Fig. 1-38. Visualize that saddle being raised another two inches. Look at the seat tube. It's at an angle with the top tube. If the saddle is raised, the seat tube angle continues because the seat post is at the same angle as the seat tube. Raising the saddle by using an extra long seat post (they are available) simply puts your body back farther toward the rear wheel, your knees back farther from the bottom bracket and your hands

Fig. 1-38: The tubes of a bicycle. Note that as the seat tube is raised, the rider would be placed farther back from the handlebars and the bottom bracket.

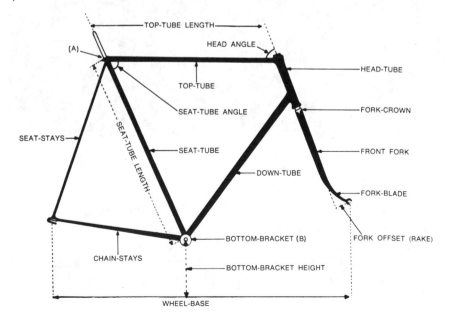

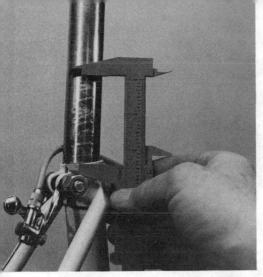

Fig. 1-39: At least 2.5 inches of the seat tube *must* be inside the seat tube. Otherwise the seat tube could break under stress, perhaps causing an accident.

back farther from the handlebars. You can raise the saddle up or down no more than an inch, if the frame otherwise fits, but I can't advise much more saddle height adjustment than that. If you do raise the saddle up, *be sure to leave at least 2½ inches of the seat post inside the seat tube* (Fig. 1-39). Otherwise, with more seat post showing, the post could snap off and cause an accident and/or injury. The seat post binder bolt should be tightened to a torque of 132 inch/pounds (see Chapter 5 for a definition of torque).

Saddle Height Adjustment

The correct saddle height, for most people, is found by sitting on the bike while someone holds it upright. Then, wearing the shoes you will use for cycling, move the crank arm so it is straight up and down. The pedal should be at the 12 o'clock position. If the saddle is at the correct height, your knee should be slightly bent. You may have to readjust the saddle later, but before you do, ride at least five miles before making the readjustment. You should be able to put your foot down on the pedal at the 12 o'clock position to absorb road shock. If the saddle is too low, you won't get full leg extension. Orthopedic surgeons tell me prolonged pedaling when the saddle is too low can put undue pressure on the knee and its associated muscles, tendons, and cartilage, straining these parts of your leg.

Another way to adjust saddle height is by measuring your inseam length while standing on the floor in stocking feet and

Fig. 1-40: There should be around a 1- to 1½-inch clearance between you and the top tube on a road bike, as shown here, and 1½ to 2 inches between you and the top tube of a commuter or all-terrain bicycle. The all-terrain bicycle has a higher ground clearance, so the seat tube is shorter than on a comparable size road bike. Correct saddle height is measured from the saddles to the centerline of the bottom bracket axle, "A" in photo.

adding 10 percent to this measurement. For example, if your inseam measurement is 30 inches, the correct saddle height would be 33 inches from the centerline of the bottom bracket spindle (axle) to the top of the saddle (Fig. 1-40).

What all this means is that even when you find a bike you can straddle in comfort, that does not necessarily mean the bike is going to fit your body. Different manufacturers use different seat tube angles or different top tube lengths for the same size bicycle. If you feel the "reach" from the handlebars is too long for you, look for another bike. If your knees, as you straddle the bike with someone holding the bike upright, seem too far back from the centerline of the bottom bracket, or too far forward, look for another bike. But before you do look, make sure the saddle is at the right height for you.

Another saddle adjustment is tilt, the angle the saddle assumes relative to the top tube. You can adjust saddle tilt by loosening the adjustment bolt (Fig. 1-41) located just under the saddle. There are many makes and varieties of seat post adjustment bolt sizes, but they all work on the same principle. The seat post head, where the saddle wires are clamped, has serrations that lock the saddle at whatever tilt you set it. Adjust the saddle tilt by loosening the seat post bolt, grabbing the saddle firmly by the nose and rear and moving it up or down. I like the saddle nose pointed just slightly downward. Too much downward tilt thrusts my body weight too far forward, with my weight being supported by my arms and hands on the handlebars. This weight exacerbates a basic problem all cyclists share, the pain created by pressure on the ulnar nerve located in the palm. This means good cycling gloves and a soft handlebar cover are important, especially on a long trip (Figs. 1-42 and 1-43). Women often seem to prefer the saddle flat, parallel to the top tube. The seat post saddle binder bolt should be tightened to a torque of 132 inch/pounds.

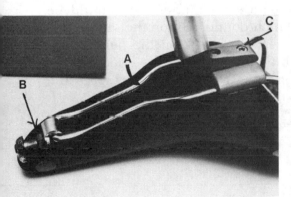

Fig. 1-41: This saddle is upside down to show you where to adjust the saddle tilt. The Allen bolt "C," when loosened, permits you to tilt saddle up or down. This leather saddle will stretch eventually; you can reduce stretch by turning bolt "B" clockwise. "A" shows the saddle wires.

Fig. 1-42: A soft handlebar cover helps prevent pain in the palms of your hands.

Fig. 1-43: Padded leather gloves such as these also help prevent pressure pain on the ulnar nerve in your hand. Gloves also protect hands in the event of a fall.

Handlebar Height

If the handlebars are too high or too low for you to reach comfortably, you can also move the stem up or down. But again, *you should have at least two inches of the stem in the head tube* (Fig. 1-44). Otherwise the stem could snap off (Fig. 1-45), especially as strain on the handlebars increases as you pedal up a steep hill. When buying and fitting an all-terrain bicycle, remember that moving handlebars up or down also requires an adjustment of the front brake. Your dealer should know this. However, if you decide to move your handlebars up or down yourself, you will find complete instructions on front brake readjustment in Chapter 5. The stem binder bolt should be tightened to a torque of 180 inch/pounds. Sit on the saddle in a comfortable crouch and place both hands on the handlebars. You should be able to reach them and reach the brake levers. There's a wide range of stem lengths on the market, so if the

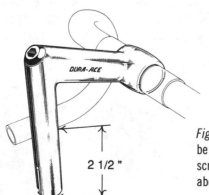

2 1/2 "

Fig. 1-44: At least 2.5 inches of the stem should be inside the head tube. Some stems have a line scribed in the metal. This line should not show above the headset locknut.

Fig. 1-45: If more than 2.5 inches of the stem shows above the headset locknut, stress can cause the stem to break, as shown here. When that happens, you can't steer the bike, and an accident can occur.

bike fits you o.k., but if you have very short arms or unusually long arms, you might think about having the dealer change the stem to a shorter or longer length unit.

Check pedal and fender clearance. Sit on the bicycle saddle while a friend holds it upright and move a pedal so it comes as close as possible to the front wheel as you turn it. Make sure that the toe of your shoe, as it rests on the pedal, comes no closer than 1 inch to the wheel. If you plan to have fenders installed, allow 1½ inches for this clearance. Then check again when your fender is installed. You can ride 90 percent of the time without getting your foot knocked off the pedal or jammed between the pedal and the frame. But if a sharp turn of the wheel coincides with a maximum forward position of the pedal, and there's not enough room for the pedal to clear the wheel or the front fender, you could be in for a spill.

HOW TO CHECK OUT A NEW BIKE

Check how well your new bicycle has been designed, built, and store-assembled right where you bought it. Before you leave the store, make sure the bicycle is in safe, reliable operating condition by following these steps. (For safety, it is also important you make all these checks every 500 miles you ride the bike and before every long trip.)

Brakes

Pull each brake lever (Fig. 1-46) in turn as hard as you can. The brake levers should not come closer than 1 inch to the handlebars. If they move closer, the brakes will be unsafe, for two reasons. First, brake cables and even brake components normally stretch as you apply the brakes. This stretch prevents you from applying full stopping power to the brake shoes. Second, with repeated braking, the brake cables will stretch permanently, so that even less stopping power can be applied to the brake shoes. You can adjust your brakes to remove cable stretch as necessary (see Chapter 5), but the dealer should make an initial brake adjustment on your new bike if, as stated, brake levers can be squeezed down to less than an inch from the handlebars. Otherwise, you will leave the shop on a bicycle that may not have the stopping power you need in an emergency or for controlling speed on fast downhill runs.

If the bicycle has extension levers (Fig. 1-47), have the dealer remove them before you leave the store. The dealer should also install a shorter brake lever spindle because with the extension levers removed, this longer spindle will project from the side of the brake housing, where it can come in contact with your hand. See Chapter 5 if you want to do this yourself. Extension levers are very dangerous, even when brakes are properly adjusted, because they may not give you the stopping power you need in an emergency. You can check this for yourself by pulling the *main* levers hard. Notice where they stop. Then pull

Fig. 1-46: Test brakes by pulling hard on brake levers. Brake arms "A" should show little or no flex. Cables should be tight in binder bolts "B."

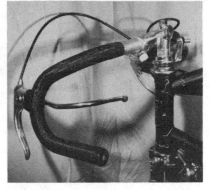

Fig. 1-47: Extension levers should be removed. They are dangerous because they may work where little braking power is needed, but may not stop you in an emergency. See text for details.

the *extension* levers hard. Notice where they stop. You will see that the main levers still have travel, but the extension levers have either hit or have come so close to the handlebars that when the cables stretch they *will* hit the handlebars. This means that extension levers provide less stopping power. Extension levers may work in standard braking situations—when approaching a stoplight, for example—but won't stop you when you must brake hard to avoid an accident. I have persuaded at least one nationally known bicycle outlet chain to issue instructions to their mechanics to remove these levers from any new bikes that still have them. It didn't take much persuasion. All I did was suggest that only one costly product liability lawsuit resulting from a bicycle accident could send insurance costs sky high. Better brakes do not come with extension levers. Lower-grade brakes that use them have more flexible components. Such flex *also* reduces braking capacity by translating brake-lever pull energy to brake parts instead of to the wheel rims.

Now check the brakes themselves for tightness and flexibility. Squeeze the front (left) brake lever hard and hold it, while straddling the bike with both feet on the floor. Rock the bike back and forth. Watch the brake arms and brake shoes. If the brake arms (Fig. 1-46) move a lot as you rock or push the bike back and forth, they may be too flexible for sufficient emergency braking power. If the brake is indeed loose, check to see whether the binder bolt holding the brake in the fork crown is loose, or the hole drilled through the crown is larger in diameter than the binder bolt. In any case, what you do *not* need are flexible brakes. Repeat this test on the rear brake.

Because all-terrain bicycles have more powerful brakes, you can exert greater pull and thus more force on the main brake cable. If this cable is not securely tightened in the cable binder bolt, it could slip out of the binder bolt and leave you without

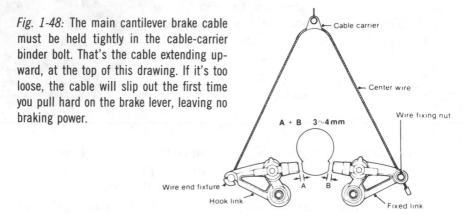

Fig. 1-48: The main cantilever brake cable must be held tightly in the cable-carrier binder bolt. That's the cable extending upward, at the top of this drawing. If it's too loose, the cable will slip out the first time you pull hard on the brake lever, leaving no braking power.

that brake. Fig. 1-48 shows where the main brake cable is held in the cable binder bolt. The cable binder bolt is on the cable carrier, and another, smaller cable rides in this carrier and connects to the brakes. Make this check in both the front and the rear on all-terrain bike brakes. As you squeeze each brake lever *hard*, make sure that the main brake cable does not slip in the cable binder bolt. It's happened to me and to other all-terrain bike owners on the very first ride on a brand-new bike. So do check these cables, front and rear, to make sure the main cable is held firmly in the carrier. I'll say it again: *Warning! If the cable slips out of the carrier fixing bolt, you will lose braking power!*

Again, because all-terrain bicycle brakes are so powerful, brake shoes can slip when brakes are applied, unless the shoes are securely tightened, accurately positioned, and correctly adjusted. If the brake shoes (Fig. 1-49) should slip, they can dive

Fig. 1-49: Cantilever brake shoes must be held tightly in the clamp "A." If they are loose, the shoes can slip under the rim, either locking the wheel by tangling in the spokes or bringing about total loss of braking power.

under the wheel rim and may tangle in the spokes. Before leaving the bike shop, make sure that brake shoes are tight, correctly positioned, and that any cable slack is removed (see Chapter 5). This applies to the cantilever brakes I noted above, and to newer types of brakes such as U-brakes and cam action brakes.

Fork Bearings

The fork bearings, shown in Fig. 1-50, must be properly adjusted for steering control. If the bearings are too tight, steering will be harder and the bearings will wear out faster. If the bearings are too loose, you can experience front-wheel shimmy. Make these checks of fork bearing adjustment. Lift the front wheel off the ground and rotate the handlebars from side to side. The handlebars should move easily, without binding or tightness. If you sense tightness, the bearings are too tight and should be readjusted. Next, straddle the bike with both feet on the ground and grip the front brake lever hard. Rock the bike back and forth. Loose headset bearings can cause wheel shimmy. If the headset bearings are loose, you will hear metal-

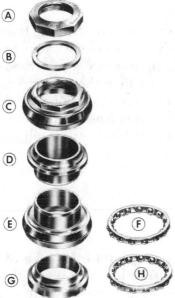

Fig. 1-50: If the headset bearings adjustable cup is too loose, the fork will be loose. As a result you may have wheel shimmy at high speed, which could cause loss of control.

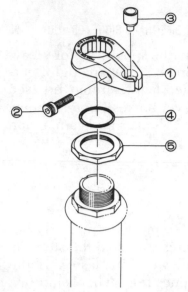

Fig. 1-51: This locknut replaces the locknut "A" in Fig. 1-50 and helps prevent headset adjustable cup "C" from loosening under the stress of bumpy roads.

lic clicking sounds from the bearings or feel looseness in the fork as you rock the bike back and forth. Shimmy usually starts when your front wheel hits a bump, or even a shallow depression in the road. The wheel is lifted upward just enough to let the shimmy start. Front-wheel shimmy is dangerous, particularly on a fast downhill run, because with each oscillation of the wheel the shimmy becomes faster, wider, and within seconds more difficult or impossible to control. You wind up quickly losing control, dumping the bike, and getting hurt. I know, it's happened to me.

All-terrain bicycle headsets take an even greater beating than road bike headsets, which is why they've become notorious for working loose and causing wheel shimmy. Only a few thousandths of an inch of bearing wear can cause the headset to become loose and out of adjustment. I recommend you install, or have the dealer install, a replacement headset locknut with an Allen screw lock; this will help prevent the headset adjustable cup from working loose. SunTour makes such a unit (Fig. 1-51).

Wheel Bearings

Check both wheels for bearing adjustment. Hold the bike off the ground and wiggle each wheel sharply left to right. If the wheel shows any sidewise movement or looseness, there's a problem. The danger here is that loose wheel bearings, *and* lose fork bearings, will work together to produce front-wheel shimmy. Either condition alone can lead to shimmy. Together, shimmy is more likely to occur. Shimmy usually starts when your front wheel hits a bump or even a shallow depression in the road. The wheel is lifted upward just enough to start to shimmy. After that, it takes over with a life of its own. The end result can be far from pleasant, believe me.

Wheel Alignment

Spin each wheel in turn, with the wheel off the ground. You can usually detect badly out-of-alignment wheels by eyeballing the wheel as it passes a brake shoe. Or hold a pencil firmly against the fork—or, for the rear wheel, the seat stay—and watch for this lateral misalignment. This type of wheel wobble is dangerous. First, it makes accurate adjustment of brake shoes virtually impossible. If brake shoes are to be adjusted to the correct ⅛-inch from the wheel rim (Fig. 1-52), shoes will rub on one side or the other of a badly untrue wheel. Braking can be uneven and erratic. (Chapter 5 has details on brake adjustment.) Before leaving the bike shop, have the dealer true up the wheels. (Chapter 10 shows you how to true your own wheels when road use causes them to become untrue.)

Fig. 1-52: Wheels should be true, not wobble from side to side, permitting brakes to contact rim evenly for maximum braking power.

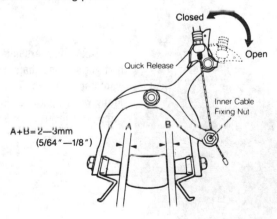

Check for loose spokes. The wheel may be true, but if any of the spokes are loose, that trueness will last no longer than the first 100 miles, at best. Pluck each spoke. They should all feel tight. If you find one loose spoke, have the dealer check them all and retrue the wheel. Check all spokes again. Repeat as necessary.

Stem Binder Bolt

Check the stem binder bolt for tightness by holding the front wheel firmly between your knees while you twist the handlebars from side to side. If the handlebars turn but the wheel doesn't, the stem bolt needs tightening.

The stem expander binder bolt (Fig. 1-53), when properly tightened, holds the stem firmly in the fork steering column. If this bolt is too loose, it may be possible for the wheel to turn but the handlebars stay put. This can be an especially hazardous condition when it occurs in an all-terrain bicycle. ATBs usually travel slowly when traversing a mountain trail. Lots of steering pressure is needed to keep the bike going where you steer it—through mud, over fallen trees, through water. If the stem bolt is loose, it is quite possible to turn the handlebars without the front wheel following this direction. It's even more hazardous on a fast downhill run over a rough trail, especially when sharp turns have to be made. (See Chapter 9 for more information.)

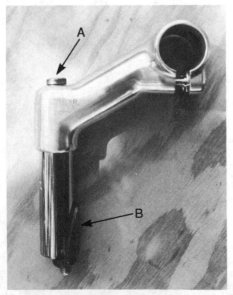

Fig. 1-53: Stem expander bolt "A" must be tight so handlebars will turn when you want them to turn. This bolt holds stem firmly when tightened. Expander nut "B" grips stem inside steering head tube.

The Saddle

Make this saddle check before you leave the bike shop. Grasp the saddle firmly and see if you can twist it from side to side, in a circular motion. If the saddle moves, the seatpost binder bolt is too loose (Fig. 1-54). Have the dealer tighten it to a torque of 132 inch/pounds. (See Chapter 5 for definition of torque.)

Fig. 1-54: Seatpost binder bolt must be tight to keep saddle from moving.

Check Shifting

With the bike on a work stand, run through all the gears. If you are not familiar with how a derailleur multi-speed system works, this is a good time to learn. There's more on gear shifting in Chapter 2. Also, please see Chapter 6 for details on derailleur adjustment and maintenance.

For now, all you need do is check to make sure the chain will shift through all the gears smoothly and, above all, accurately. *Check the rear derailleur first.* As you turn the cranks, shift from the smallest freewheel cog up to the largest cog. The chain should not override the large cog (Fig. 1-55) and fall to the left where it can get jammed between that cog and the spokes. Fig.

A

Fig. 1-55: Rear derailleur should be properly adjusted so that it cannot be shifted so far to the left that it falls off the large rear cog "A" and locks up the rear wheel by jamming between that cog and the spokes. "B" points to the chain well to the left, jammed between the big cog and the spokes.

Fig. 1-56: Spokes shown by arrows have almost been cut in half after the chain fell between the spokes and the large rear cog.

1-56 shows what happens to spokes when this happens; spokes can actually get cut all the way through. But that's not the real hazard. The big danger is that when the chain jams between the freewheel and the spokes, the rear wheel can lock up. If the wheel locks, the bike will skid sidewise, and can fall over. If the chain jams while you're pedaling hard, your foot could slip, you could lose balance, and lose control of the bicycle. You could be dumped and hit the pavement, hard (which is why you should *never* leave home on a bike without wearing a helmet. More on helmets in Chapter 2). If the bike falls into traffic, you could be run over.

Shift the chain down from the largest to the smallest freewheel cog. The chain should come to rest accurately on that cog. Make sure that the chain does not travel so far to the right that it falls off and jams between the small cog and the chainstay (Fig. 1-57). If this happens, you could have wheel lock-up or lose your balance as the chain suddenly jams.

Check the front derailleur (Fig. 1-58). Make sure it too shifts smoothly and accurately from one chainring to the other. If the chain falls off to the left, off the small chainring, you will have a sudden pedal skip that could cause loss of balance and control. If the chain gets caught between the chainwheels, pedals can lock up and cause loss of balance and control. If the chain falls off the large chainwheel, to the right, it could jam between that chainwheel and the front derailleur body as you pedal. Again, a potentially hazardous loss of control and balance can occur.

Fig. 1-57: When you shift to the smallest rear cog, chain "A" should not move so far to the right that it falls off the small cog and jams between that cog and the chainstay "B," locking up the rear wheel and causing an accident.

Fig. 1-58: Make sure front derailleur cage is parallel to the largest chainwheel, and that the chain can't jam between the cage and that chainwheel. Chain should also not fall off small chainwheel to the left when shifting to that gear. Chain should shift smoothly onto all three (or two) chainwheels.

Make sure the dealer has demonstrated not only how to shift all gears, but that such shifting can be accomplished smoothly and accurately. Index shifting systems, such as that made by Shimano, SunTour, and Campagnolo, can prevent accidents caused by inaccurate shifting. These derailleurs move the chain by click stops, so you don't have to feel your way from one gear to another. Indexed shifting takes the guesswork out of changing gears. Once adjusted they are great! (See Chapter 6 for adjustment instructions.) But if it's a choice of a bike at a given price with or without indexed shifting, I recommend the one with the index system.

Check Bottom Bracket Bearings and Pedals

Grasp each crank or pedal (each through the frame) and briskly move them from side to side. If you feel any looseness, the bottom bracket bearings should be readjusted. (See Chapter 8.)

Check pedals by moving them from side to side. Inexpensive pedals quite often have sideplay even when brand new. But if the bike you're contemplating costs much more than $200, pedals should have no sideplay at all.

About Toe Clips and Straps

Better road bikes usually come equipped with toe clips and straps (Fig. 1-59) on the pedals. The clips and straps are actually a safety device, in my opinion, because they keep your feet on the pedals when you're straining hard uphill or pushing hard on the flats. If your foot should slip off the pedal when you're pushing hard, you could lose your balance and even dump the bike. See Chapter 2 for information about the safety aspects of toe clips and straps.

Fig. 1-59: If the bike has toe clips and straps, practice getting feet in and out of them in an empty school playground before attempting to ride in traffic. Keep straps loose in traffic.

Accessories

I consider some bike accessories a *must*. If you contemplate bicycle touring and camping, or riding an ATB in the wilderness, a pump is an absolute necessity. Tires have a habit of going flat far from the nearest service station. The pump can be the self-mounting kind, or require a special fitting that clamps on the frame (Fig. 1-60). Some pumps can simply be compressed slightly so they hold themselves in the frame (Fig. 1-61). These pumps are available in different lengths to fit your size frame without a paint-scarring clamp. However, given the rough use of all-terrain bikes on the trail, I recommend you clamp the pump to the frame. If you hit a hard bump, or knock the pump with your leg accidentally, you sure don't want to jar the pump loose and have it tangle in the spokes or chainwheel.

Fig. 1-60: Some pumps require a clamp to hold it in the bike frame.

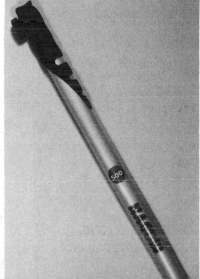

Fig. 1-61: A better idea is to buy a pump that fits your bike frame. The handle is spring-loaded so it can compress together and hold itself in the bike frame. Pump handle is curved to fit contour of bike frame.

There are two types of pumps. One has a head to fit a U.S. Schraeder valve stem (Fig. 1-62), the other has a head to fit skinny European Presta stems (Fig. 1-63). You need a tire wrench and a patch kit (or a spare tube) so you can fix a flat. A small handlebar-mounted tinkle bell can alert other bikes, hikers, and pedestrians of your presence.

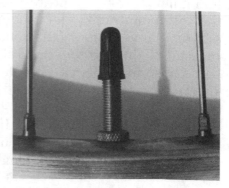

Fig. 1-62: American Schraeder valve stem.   *Fig. 1-63:* European Presta valve stem.

If you plan on commuting or cycle touring, you need carriers and bike packs. I like the Blackburn alloy carriers for strength and lightness (Fig. 1-64). If you ride at night, front and rear lights can save your life. Some states require them. I like generator or rechargeable-battery-powered quartz halogen lights that throw a powerful beam (Fig. 1-65). A helmet for your noggin is an absolute must. Do not ride too fast without donning one. See the helmet data in Chapter 2 and Chapter 4 for more information on accessories.

Fig. 1-64: These lightweight aluminum carriers can be mounted on your bicycle to carry panniers for long-distance bike tours.

Fig. 1-65: If you plan to ride your bike at night, a good headlight and taillight are *musts* for safety. This rechargeable light set has quartz halogen bulbs and works even when the bike is stationary.

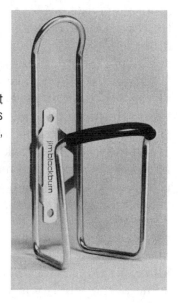

Fig. 1-66: For any bike tour, you should also have at least one, preferably two, water-bottle cages like this one, bolted or clamped to a frame tube, and, of course, water bottles.

Finally, you will need at least one water bottle cage to hold a water bottle. The cage (Fig. 1-66) can be clamped on the frame. Or, if your frame has brazed-on bosses, the water bottle cage can be bolted in place.

Now, let's briefly review frame tubing, including the new space-age bicycle frame tubing that has recently appeared on the market.

Steel, Aluminum, Magnesium, Titanium or Carbon Fiber Composites?

Bicycles frames are now available with tubing of steel, aluminum, magnesium, titanium, and carbon fiber composites. Here's an explanation and a brief review of the pros and cons of each of these materials and the ways in which they are joined. Since I am not a metallurgical engineer, I asked one to write this portion of the chapter. He is Douglas Hayduk, of Boulder, Colorado. He is the author of *Bicycle Metallurgy for the Cyclist.* He will be happy to send you a copy for $8.95. Write him at 604 Marine St., Boulder, CO 80302.

Doug notes that "up to around 1974, the choice of material for bicycle frames was simple. It was either steel or nothing. Today, however, you can find bikes made of a wide variety of materials. Some of the more exotic, low-production frames alone can cost upwards of $800. That's just for the frame. By the time you stick on wheels, cranksets, handlebars, and all the other components, the cost can be in the thousands of dollars and that's for an off-the-shelf bike.

"There is a lot of misunderstanding about the pros and cons of various frame materials. Here are a few popular misconceptions: aluminum is too soft and brittle. It's light but not strong. If an aluminum frame is welded, it's weak at the weld. If it's glued together, it's weak at the glued joints. If it's screwed and glued, it's stronger but may still break at the joints. Magnesium is too brittle. Titanium is too flexible. Titanium frames will waste energy in frame whip that should go into forward movement of the entire bike. Carbon fiber composites may decompose, come apart, crack. *All of these statements are false!* Steel, aluminum, titanium, magnesium, and carbon fiber composites all have similar strength-to-weight ratios. [Fig. 1-67 shows some of the labels you will find on frames made of these materials.]

Fig. 1-67: A few of the dozens of labels you will find on bike frames made of high-quality steel tubing.

Only the Top Tube, Seat Tube and Down Tube of a frame with this transfer are made from REYNOLDS 531 Tubing—plain gauge.

The Top Tube, Seat Tube and Down Tube of a frame which bears this transfer are REYNOLDS 531 BUTTED tubing.

All the tubing in a bicycle with this transfer is REYNOLDS 531 — Frame Tubes, Chain & Seat Stays & Fork Blades, but it is all plain gauge tubing.

This transfer signifies that the bicycle is an aristocrat, a thoroughbred — made throughout of REYNOLDS 531 tubing BUTTED for lightness with strength.

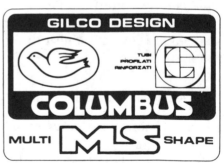

"Other misconceptions relate to how steel frames are fastened together. Lugged frames [Fig. 1-68] are thought to be stronger than unlugged frames [Fig. 1-69]. That's totally wrong. Cheap lugged mass-produced frames are usually weaker than a carefully brazed-up lugless frame. Well-made frames have tubing ends accurately mitered so they butt tightly up against the tube to which they are welded, brazed, or lugged. Inaccurately mitered tubing [Fig. 1-70] makes for a weak joint, whether it's lugged or not. Electrically welded steel frames of cheap bikes are at least as susceptible to fatigue and impact breakage as any other type of frame. Thermal inert-gas welded frames, known as T.I.G.-welded [Fig. 1-71], can be as strong as the best hand-brazed frame. T.I.G.-welded frames are also less expensive than hand-brazed frames because the joining is done by machinery, eliminating a lot of hand labor.

Fig. 1-68: High-quality lugged frame. Two of the lugs are shown by arrows.

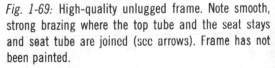

Fig. 1-69: High-quality unlugged frame. Note smooth, strong brazing where the top tube and the seat stays and seat tube are joined (see arrows). Frame has not been painted.

Fig. 1-70: Inaccurately mitered tubing makes for a weak joint. You can see gaps where the top tube and down tube are spot-brazed to the head tube, made prior to finish brazing.

Fig. 1-71: This is a high-quality, T.I.G.-welded frame. Not as pretty as the lugged or smoothly brazed lugless frames, but just as strong.

Three Grades Of Steel

"There are three types of steel used in bicycle frames today. Plain carbon steel is used for tubing of bicycles that sell for around $100. Low-alloy steel is used for more expensive bicycles. Super-high-strength steel is used for specialty racing bikes and a few super-expensive high-end bikes. Let's start with low-carbon steel.

Low-Carbon Steel

"Low- or plain-carbon steel is also called '1020' steel, or 'high-tension' steel. You'll see decals on inexpensive bikes bearing one or the other of these names. This seam-welded tubing, unless further treated, can have a weakened section in the vicinity of the seam. Plain-carbon steel is inexpensive, at least compared with better steels, because it contains only iron alloyed with small amounts of carbon (usually 0.2 percent) and manganese. This steel is not as strong as the steel used in better bikes. To make up for its weakness, manufacturers use tubing with heavier walls that are quite thick compared to more costly tubing. The result is a heavier and 'deader' feeling, but you get a lower-cost bicycle. These bikes feel sluggish, without the spirited liveliness associated with a truly lightweight frame. The ride will be harsh, so these bicycles are not suited for long-distance touring. The plain-carbon steel tubing in these bikes is also straight-gauge, which means that the tubing is the same thickness for its entire length.

Low-Alloy Steel

"The steel used to make the tubing of higher-priced bicycles is generically called low-alloy steel, or just alloy steel. This steel is an alloy of iron, carbon, and small amounts (5 percent or so) of manganese, molybdenum, vanadium, and/or nickel. Most of this tubing is seamless, which eliminates the weakened zone where seamed tubing is welded. However, seamed tubing of low-alloy steel can be just as strong as seamless tubing if it is heat-treated after welding. Such tubing is made by True Temper Sports, the only bicycle tubing manufacturer in the U.S.

"Low-alloy tubing is made even stronger by a process called 'butting,' in which tubing walls are thin in the middle and thickened at the ends. [Fig. 1-72]. You'll see decals on bikes made with tubing that say 'double-butted' (such as Reynolds).

Fig. 1-72: Highest quality, strongest steel frames are made of double-butted steel. Tubing walls are thin in the middle and thickened at the ends, where added strength is needed at the joints.

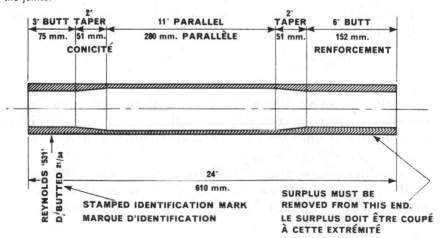

Better frames have double-butted main tubing as well as double-butted forks and stays. The double-butted ends provide added strength where tubes are brazed or welded together, where the heat of such joining may weaken the tubing. Another type of tubing which has thicker ends is called 'tapered gauge.' It has a tapered wall thickness throughout most of its length.

Very High-Strength Steel

"Examples of the highest-strength bicycle tubing are Reynolds 753, Vitus 983, and Tange Prestige. This tubing is processed to higher strengths than Reynolds 531, and Columbus SL and SP tubing. Very high-strength steel tubing is carefully heat-treated and worked to combine lightness (thin walls) with strength. However, Reynolds 753 takes a very skilled and specially trained person to braze it. It's costly, with virtually paper-thin walls that are not generally recommended for most bicycles. It is best suited for specialty bikes, such as racing machines where cost is not a factor and where the weight saved, even if only a few ounces, can make the difference between winning and losing a race or establishing a new time-trial record.

"Tange Prestige and Vitus 983 tubing is not quite as strong as Reynolds 753. Wall thickness of this tubing approaches that of other conventional steel tubes. You will also find this tubing used in the most expensive bicycles where a lighter, yet strong frame is desired.

Non-Ferrous Frame Materials

"Here's a quick review of bicycle frames made of materials other than steel. Let's start with aluminum.

Aluminum Frames

"Aluminum bicycle frames are not new. They've been made since the late 1890s. What is new is that aluminum frames made today compare very favorably with all-steel frames in strength, durability, and ride. Most bike makers include at least one aluminum bicycle in their line.

"Aluminum tubing used today is an alloy of other metals as well as aluminum. Some of these alloys are heat-treatable for higher-yield strengths. Other alloys rely on mechanical hardening (cold-working) for strength. Both types of aluminum alloys are used.

"For example, Alan and Vitus bicycles use aluminum-alloy tubing that has the same diameter of steel tubing, 1⅛ inches. For strength, these alloys use very thick wall tubes.

"Other aluminum-alloy bicycles obtain strength by using larger-diameter tubing, up to 1⅓ inches. Bicycles with this tubing include Cannondale [Fig. 1-73], Trek [Fig. 1-74], and Klein [Fig. 1-75]. In my opinion, this fatter tubing permits a bicycle design of greater strength combined with lighter weight than offered by the smaller-diameter, thicker tubing.

"It's been claimed that aluminum bikes absorb road shock better than steel bikes. The Alan and Vitus bikes do offer a more comfortable ride than some good steel frames. The stiffer frame design of Klein and Cannondale frames, however, provides about the same comfort in terms of road-shock absorption as comparably priced steel frames. Aluminum bicycle frames are also generally lighter than steel bicycle frames, although this weight advantage is marginal in the highest price lines, especially compared with super-high-strength steel frames.

"One advantage possessed by aluminum-alloy frames is that they can be anodized. Anodizing is a hard, thick protective-finish layer of oxide formed by chemically treating the tubing in an acid bath. Nearly any color can be added to the anodized

Fig. 1-74: Trek aluminum frame detail.

Fig. 1-73: Cannondale aluminum frame detail.

Fig. 1-75: Klein aluminum frame, all-terrain bicycle.

layer for an attractive finish that is much more durable and scratch-resistant than any paint finish. Not that you're going to leave your good bike out in the rain, but it may be some comfort to know that aluminum frames won't rust.

Magnesium

"Magnesium bike frames have very recently entered the market and are now being mass-produced in England by Kirk Precision, Ltd. The chief advantage of this frame is low cost. The frames can be die-cast in minutes, after which it has to be machined for the fork and bottom bracket units. The overall quality of the fully assembled bicycle is comparable to a steel-frame bike in the $400 range, as a preliminary guess. At this writing these frames are so new there has been little opportunity to ride or lifecycle-test them. The Kirk frame, however, appears to be well designed. It has had extensive testing on the road as well as in the laboratory, according to the manufacturer.

"Magnesium is much like aluminum, with only two-thirds the density (weight for an equivalent volume of metal) of aluminum alloys. Thus the strength and stiffness of magnesium is less than that of aluminum, and more magnesium is required to produce a frame that's strong and stiff. Because of the additional magnesium required, the weight of these frames approaches that of steel frames. The magnesium used in the Kirk frames is an alloy of magnesium, aluminum, and zinc.

"There are a few drawbacks to magnesium. One is its very poor corrosion resistance, lower than that of steel. Corrosion-preventing coatings on magnesium bike frames is vital. Kirk uses a corrosion-protective coating that I believe eliminates this corrosion problem. Certainly the price is right.

Titanium

"Titanium has been used successfully in the aerospace and marine vessel industries. The metal is lighter than steel, but heavier than aluminum. Its strength and rigidity are about midway between steel and aluminum. Titanium's corrosion resistance is very high, so it doesn't need to be painted or anodized. Its major drawback is still cost. Premium frame builders have apparently solved frame design problems that plagued Speedwell and Teledyne. Titanium bicycles are very competitive as to strength, rigidity, durability, and shock absorption with the best frames of any material.

Composites

"The use of composites is one of the most exciting developments in bicycle technology today. Composite material is simply a combination of high-strength reinforcement fibers surrounded and held together in a matrix of epoxy or polymer resin. If you're familiar with tennis racquets, golf clubs, fishing rods, ski poles, or Corvette auto bodies made of composites, you have an idea of the composites used for bicycle frame tubing. However, instead of glass fibers in an epoxy matrix, the composites used in bicycle frame tubing are graphite fibers embedded in an epoxy or polyester matrix and formed into bicycle tubes.

Carbon-fiber bicycles appeared in the early 1970s with the appearance of the Exxon Graftek bicycle. This bike was quite popular among racing cyclists. However, it had a number of construction and design problems, and suffered a fairly early demise.

"Today, however, carbon-fiber bicycle-frame development appears to have eliminated the Exxon frame deficiencies. Composite frames made today are very strong, rigid, and resistant to impact and fatigue damage. The most attractive feature of these frames is that they are as much as two pounds lighter than their lightest steel-frame counterpart. The only drawback is their price, several hundred dollars more than other top-of-the-line stock frames. For example, the frame alone is around $950. The complete bike will cost around $1,800 minimum. Complete composite-frame bicycles are currently being produced, at this writing, by Trek, Peugeot, Eclipse, Guerciotti, Nishiki, Alan, Look, and Vitus.

Combinations

"Some frame designers feel that a combination of materials will give desirable characteristics to a frame. For example, Raleigh's Technium line of bicycles [Fig. 1-76] uses a combination of aluminum and alloy-steel tubing. The three main tubes (top, down, and seat tubes) are adhesive-bonded into the lugs. Seat-stays and chainstays are of chrome-moly tubing, brazed into the lugs and dropouts. Raleigh claims that the bicycle has the best characteristics of both metals, strength, and lightness.

"Still another new and at this time unique combination of materials is the Excell CSK tubing, made by Excell of France. This tubing consists of a very thin-walled, high-strength steel tube with a carbon and Kevlar fiber-reinforced epoxy composite tube inside the steel tube for added strength. This tubing is lightweight, very rigid, and can be brazed together like a conventional steel frame. The CSK tubing is only available, at this writing, in custom-built frames. It is also *very* expensive."

Fig. 1-76: Raleigh Technium aluminum frame bicycle detail.

Chrome-Plating Problems

Chrome-plated bicycle tubing makes for a shiny, attractive bicycle. The finish is highly scratch-resistant. There are, however, several drawbacks to a chrome plate finish. If the chrome gets scratched, rust can develop that can work its way between the chrome plating and the bicycle tube. The bicycle then has to be rechromed, or the scratch covered with paint. But few paints adhere well to chrome. Doug Hayduk discusses another, more serious problem with chrome plating:

"During the plating, hydrogen atoms may enter the steel and make it more brittle and liable to severe cracking. However, such hydrogen embrittlement is fairly rare and easily prevented by baking the chromed tubing right after plating at 350 degrees.

"A more serious problem may arise when frame tubes are immersed in an acid bath to clean the steel prior to plating. If any acid is left in the tubing and is not rinsed out, it will eat away the tubing wall from the inside. Later, the frame tubing may fracture or break at the acid-thinned spot. Rinsing the frame in an alkaline bath would neutralize any trapped acid and prevent such tubing failure.

A Word About Frame Failure

"Bicycles built today are usually well designed so as to avoid stress-risers, places where stress can concentrate, eventually causing the tubing to weaken and break. This is not to say that failure due to improper design, quality-control failures in heat treating, welding, or brazing do not occur. Such failure does happen, but as I noted, it is rare compared with other types of frame failure.

"These other types of frame failure are caused by impact, by running into curbs, hopping off small hills, and stunting with a bike not designed for that great an impact. Other types of frame failure can result, as noted above, from inadequate joint design, improper assembly such as welding, brazing, adhesive bonding, etc. Metallurgists are quite good about coming up with a reason for a frame failure. The detective work in finding the cause of frame failure has been well established. Just by looking at a metal fracture surface, a metallurgist can often tell just how the metal failed. They can determine, for example, if the failure was due to fatigue, overload, impact, or hydrogen embrittlement."

I agree with Doug Hayduk's analysis of current frame materials. In years past, though, your author has ridden several titanium frames, including the ill-fated Speedwell and the now defunct Teledyne makes. I can report that the Speedwell titanium frame was so flexible that it felt like I was riding a rubber bike. With every stroke of the pedal I could see the bottom bracket flex to the right or to the left at least a half inch. I quickly returned this bike to its British manufacturer while I was still in one piece. The Teledyne was much better, but still had more flex than I like. Aside from flex, both bikes had a millionaire's price tag. Better you shouldn't know. Both bikes were poorly designed, in my opinion. As I noted earlier, excellent titanium bicycles have been made by Cecil Behringer and used by European bicycle racing teams. Cecil's price tag? Around $10,500 for just the frame.

The Raleigh composite Technium I have ridden certainly is light, responsive, and quite comfortable. Prices range from around $250 to around $600, depending on the quality of the steel in the stays and the quality of the components. The $600 model is a good compromise between the stiffness of a road-racing bike and the shock absorbency of a touring bike, and for that reason it should be ideal for triathlon events. I have given the new Trek composite bike a tough workout on long trips and it too has stood up well and offered a comfortable, responsive ride.

I saw the Kirk magnesium frame bike at a bike show and was impressed by its quality appearance and especially by its low price. If Kirk's factory in England can spit out a frame every few minutes and has eliminated the corrosion problem noted above, their impact on the bike market is going to be major.

I have bounced both Cannondale and Klein aluminum bikes up and down rough mountain trails and have watched others do the same. The bikes withstood these rigors with ease. Relatively new materials, like composites, titanium, high-grade steels, aluminum, and magnesium, promise to bring new comfort, responsiveness, and, in many cases, lower prices to high-grade bicycles.

I hope by now that you have learned how to select a bicycle that will fit your needs, and how to make a safety check before taking the bicycle home. In the next chapter, we will discuss how to ride a bicycle safely through city traffic, on the highway, and over mountain trails.

Chapter

TWO

HOW TO RIDE IN COMFORT
AND SAFETY

Safety awareness is what brings you back from a bike trip all in one piece, unscathed and happy. Sometimes, as I ride down a city street, the thought goes through my mind, like an old refrain, "the alert cyclist is the safe cyclist." In this chapter, I'll try to explain what I mean by the word "alert," because in that word lies a host of survival skills. After hundreds of thousands of miles of bicycling in city and country, I exercise most of these skills almost subconsciously. I know, for example, that if I don't make eye contact with the car driver at an intersection, that I can't be sure I've been seen. I also know, without thinking about it, that even if I'm sure the driver has seen me that he or she won't run into me. There are literally hundreds of safety-related decisions you *must* make every time you take a bike trip.

These decisions must be based on accurate information. What will that driver do now? Can I escape into a ditch? Jump a curb to get away from a car or even a pedestrian? How should I cross this intersection? Will that driver coming out of the shopping mall driveway wait until I pass? Is this a safe road for me? How can I tell by the driver's actions if the car coming from behind will pass me safely on this narrow two-lane road? What am I doing on this narrow two-lane road in the first place? As an experienced cyclist I ask myself these and dozens of similar questions as I pedal along, because I'm aware that I'm more vulnerable on a bike than in a car. This chapter will review these and other road dangers, tell you how to avoid them, and what to do if you can't. You may have just seconds to identify a hazard and take preventative measures almost instinctively. Because if you have to stop to think about what you must do in a particular situation, it may be too late. Remember, even at the slow speed of 10 miles per hour you are traveling almost 15 feet per second. A car moving at only 25 miles per hour is covering almost 37 feet per second. Split-second action is often the only way to avoid an accident on a bicycle. It doesn't help much to reflect that the skills you learned as a car driver can save you on a bicycle. In 1985, 30 percent of bicycle-accident fatalities involved cyclists between the ages of 15 and 24, and 34 percent involved cyclists who were over age 25. There are, indeed, special skills you need as a cyclist that no amount of driving experience will give you. That's what this chapter is all about: getting out there and back, safely, on your bicycle.

Most bicycle accidents are avoidable. They simply do not have to happen. In this chapter you will learn how to avoid an accident and keep from becoming one of those mind-numbing injury and fatality statistics. Before we get into the specifics of accident prevention, here is a summary of what causes them. Each basic cause will be explained in detail later in this chapter, along with preventative measures. Here are the major causes of bicycle accidents:

1. Rider error (I think this is a conservative estimate): 75%
2. Vehicle driver error (bicyclist could not escape): 10%
3. Poor bicycle maintenance (see maintenance and adjustment chapters in this book): 5%
4. Defective bicycle trail design or dangerous road condition: 3%
5. Defective bicycle owner's manual (inadequate instructions): 3%
6. Defective bicycle assembly at retail level: 2%
7. Defective bicycle (assembly or design of frame or component): 2%

Wear a Helmet at All Times!

I would not go two feet on my bicycle without a helmet on my head. Studies have clearly shown that fatal head injuries of bicyclists involved in an accident are at least 60 percent more likely to occur to the rider who is *not* wearing a helmet.* Your brain is the most complex and impact-vulnerable part of your body. An impact that would only bruise an arm or a leg could kill you if it involved your head instead.

Helmets are cheap. Good ones only cost around $45 to $55. How valuable is your head? Certainly it's worth more than the price of a helmet. I know of accidents that occurred when the bicycle was standing still, the rider lost balance, struck his head on a curb and, helmetless, died from the impact.

Good helmets are shown in Figs. 2-1 through 2-9. Helmets should have a label inside that says it meets the A.N.S.I. Z90-4 standards (Fig. 2-10). Children in particular should wear helmets. Bell makes an excellent child's helmet, Fig. 2-9.

* see p. 136 for references.

Fig. 2-1: An excellent helmet for the cyclist. Note the reflective stripes and the air vents.

Fig. 2-2: This is the helmet used by racing cyclists in many events, with extra wide air vents to keep the head cool.

Fig. 2-3: This MSR helmet is a cyclist's version of an excellent rock climber's helmet, with high resistance to penetration.

Fig. 2-4: The inside of the MSR helmet is lined with deep Styrofoam-type padding.

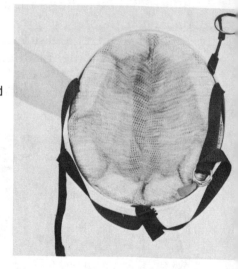

Fig. 2-5: This Bailen helmet was designed by a physician. It has excellent retention, ventilation, and an eyeshade.

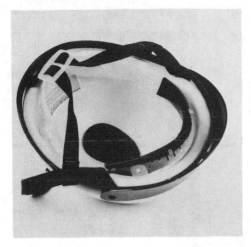

Fig. 2-6: Inside of the Bailen helmet. Note that this helmet, like most other helmets, has an adjustable strap inside for a good fit.

Fig. 2-7: The Targa helmet, with aerodynamic scoop air vents and a built-in eyeshade, is designed for the touring cyclist.

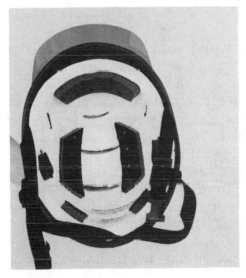

Fig. 2-8: The Targa helmet features removable foam pads inside for fitting to your head. Strap retention is excellent.

Fig. 2-9: Bell also makes a child's helmet in various sizes. Your child should also always wear such a helmet. Note the padded child seat with safety bar, an excellent way to carry a child.

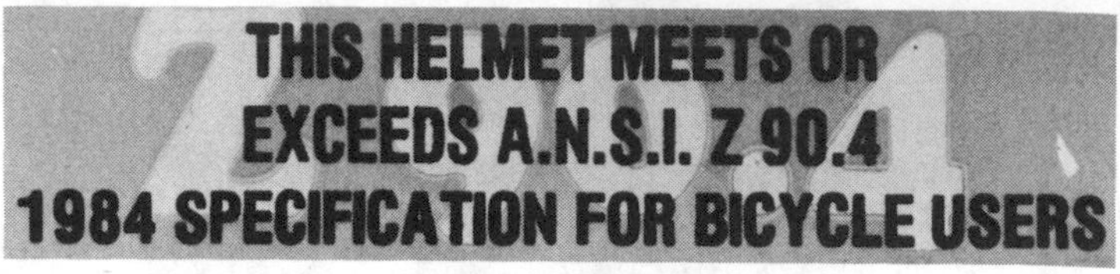

THIS HELMET MEETS OR EXCEEDS A.N.S.I. Z 90.4 1984 SPECIFICATION FOR BICYCLE USERS

Fig. 2-10: Any helmet you buy should bear this emblem. This is your assurance that the helmet meets specifications as to impact and penetration resistance and has straps that will keep the helmet on your head in the event of an accident.

How to Carry a Child Safely

The best way to carry a child safely on a bike is to put him or her in a trailer (Fig. 2-11). A child can weigh from 15 to 45 pounds or more. That much weight on the bike can reduce the bike's stability, accuracy of steering, and balance. However, if a trailer isn't available, the next best way is to use a good child seat *over the rear wheel,* as is shown in Figs. 2-9 and 2-12. The child carrier should have a restraining strap for the child and protectors so the child can't get a foot caught in the rear-wheel spokes. You can carry two children, or one child and camping gear, in most trailers. Modern trailers, available in most bike stores, add amazingly little drag. They also can come with covers and even see-through windshields so little tots won't feel shut in, and can always see a parent from the trailer.

Fig. 2-11: The safest way to carry a child is in a trailer. The bike will be better balanced and the children will be more comfortable.

Fig. 2-12: Here both parent and child are wearing helmets, and the child, even though asleep, is held safely in the child carrier. Note the wet gear. *(Greg Siple photo)*

Be as Bright as a Pinwheel

You should also make yourself as visible as possible. Wear a road worker's reflective vest over your jacket or shirt. You can find them in most bike stores. They have holes so they breathe and won't cause you to overheat on a hot day. The brightest Day-Glo orange clothing, ugly as it may seem to you, may mean the difference between being seen and being invisible to a motorist. Whether you're riding a recumbent or a conventional bike, a flag, waving at the tip of a plastic rod (Fig. 2-13), is an eye-catcher to a motorist.

Fig. 2-13: The more visible you are, the safer you will be. These touring cyclists are dressed in bright clothing, and the man on the recumbent has a bright red flag waving from atop a plastic rod for even greater visibility. *(Greg Siple photo)*

A FEW IMPORTANT SAFETY FACTS

I am going to start with a few bicycle accident statistics. Now I know statistics are boring. What I hope to do is breathe some life into these numbers by telling you how to avoid becoming one of them, even though the first statistic relates to bicycle accident fatalities. Yes, there's cheering news in these somber statistics.

According to the 1986 edition of *Accident Facts,* published by the National Safety Council, in 1940, for every 100,000 bicycles in use, there were 9.59 bicycle-accident-related deaths. By 1985, this figure had dropped by more than 90 percent! For every 100,000 bicycles in use in 1985, there were 0.93 bicycle-related fatalities. Now *that's* an improvement! Had 1985 bicycle accidents occurred at the 1940 rate, some *10,372* cyclists would have been killed, instead of the 1,000 that were killed. I am sure that this encouraging decrease in the rate of bicycle fatalities during this 45-year period is due to increased awareness of bicycle safety among bicyclists, as well as among motorists (who themselves may be bicyclists). Civil authorities have helped educate bicyclists and have provided alternative bike routes and bicycle trails far from the madding crowd of motorized traffic.

How Bicycle Accidents Occur

Sloane's rule of survival on a bike is to **give the right-of-way to anyone who wants it, any time he or she wants it!** On a bike is no place to be macho, to argue with a behemoth of a car or truck, or even another bicyclist or a pedestrian, about who should go first or who is in the right. Better to be safe. You can always get mad later, when you're back home, safe and sound. I advise against cussing out or giving the finger to a motorist who has come too close to you, particularly if he's in a pickup truck. Some of these rednecks have backed up and run over cyclists, or punched them out. Unless you're an expert in self-defense, save your anger for later. If possible, tell the police about the situation and give them the car's license plate number.

A review of actual typical bike accidents, and how they could have been avoided, will I hope demonstrate how you can avoid becoming such a statistic in the annals of accident reporting.

The data that follows comes from the "A Two-Year Bicycle Accident Survey," July, 1981 through June, 1983, made in Palo Alto, California, by Diana Lewiston. I use this study because I believe it to be typical of all such studies. For example:

Time of day: 89 percent of bicycle accidents reported to police occur between 7 a.m. to 7 p.m. Accidents peak between 7 to 9 a.m., 11 a.m. to 1 p.m., 3 p.m. to 7 p.m.

Traffic: This may seem strange at first, but think about it. The Palo Alto study reported that there were fewer bicycle accidents on streets with high traffic counts than there were on streets with lower traffic counts. One can only conclude that cyclists on busy streets were the more skilled and experienced, and/or that the alertness of cyclists on less busy streets was dulled by the lower volume of cars on the road.

Lesson 1: Be alert 100 percent of the time, no matter where you ride.

Injuries: About 84 percent of all reported accidents resulted in injury. Legs were the most frequently injured. More seriously hurt cyclists suffered multiple injuries.

Intersections: Most accidents occur at intersections. Of 200 such accidents in Palo Alto, 35.5 percent were at right-turning intersections, where both motorist and cyclist were going straight. Most of these accidents occurred where the cyclist was traveling at a right angle to the motorist (Fig. 2-14). The cyclist was almost always riding *into* or *against* the flow of traffic, usually on a sidewalk. If the traffic, for example, was going north, the cyclist was riding south. Most of these accidents were at a crosswalk. Most involved a cyclist 17 or under. At such intersections 11 percent of the accidents occurred at business intersections (shopping malls, etc); 42.5 percent of the intersections had stop signs, 27.5 percent had right-on-turn signal lights.

Lesson 2: Never ride against the flow of traffic, even if you're on the sidewalk. Be doubly careful as you approach driveways, especially at shopping centers. Watch out for pedestrians and especially for small children.

Right-turning intersections where the car and cyclist were traveling parallel (in some cases both cyclist and motorist had a green stoplight), accounted for 28 percent of the accidents in this study. In Fig. 2-15, the car and cyclist collided at the intersection. There are three situations that could have contributed to this accident. First, the cyclist on the street was located in the motorist's blind spot. Second, the driver assumed that the cyclist would stop at the intersection so he could safely turn right. Third, the cyclist assumed that the motorist knew he wanted to cross the intersection and would wait for him to do so. The cyclist on the sidewalk evidently made the same assumptions.

Lesson 3: Never make any assumptions about anything, even if you have made eye contact and believe the motorist sees you. He does not know what you have in mind, either.

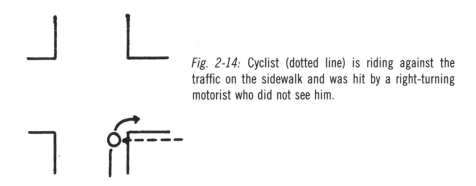

Fig. 2-14: Cyclist (dotted line) is riding against the traffic on the sidewalk and was hit by a right-turning motorist who did not see him.

Fig. 2-15: Even though both cyclists (dotted lines) are proceeding in the direction of traffic, they did not stop to let a vehicle conclude a right turn and were struck at the intersection.

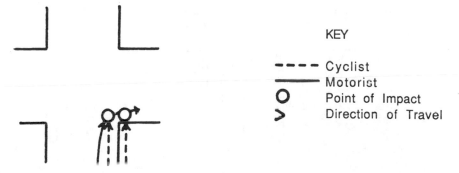

KEY

- - - - Cyclist
——— Motorist
O   Point of Impact
>   Direction of Travel

Lesson 4: If you ride on the sidewalk, be aware that motorists may not see you at an intersection because they are watching the road and not the sidewalk, or because their view is obstructed by a vehicle in front of them. Also be aware that unless the sidewalk is a designated bike lane, it may be illegal to ride on it. (If pedestrians, particularly children, are on a sidewalk bike lane, be ready to take evasive action to avoid running into them. A tinkle bell on your bike can warn them of your presence.) If you feel the road is too dangerous, and the sidewalk is illegal, I urge you to find a safer road.

Lesson 5: As you approach an intersection you wish to drive through, whether or not there's a stoplight or stop sign, pedal to the right and behind the left rear wheel of the vehicle in front of you (Fig. 2-16) before you reach the intersection. Stay about six to eight feet behind the car. If you keep this position both the driver behind and the driver ahead can see you and neither can turn into you on a right turn, because you are not

Fig. 2-16: The safest way to approach an intersection is to ride into the left tire lane of the car ahead, so you can proceed through the intersection without the car behind turning into you. If you need to make a left turn, this is also the safest, most visible position at the intersection, particularly in a left-turn-only lane. To make a left turn on a four-lane highway with two lanes going in each direction, you should ride behind the left tire of the car in the left lane ahead of you.

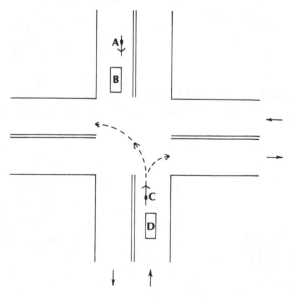

positioned in a place where they can do so. Oncoming cars, or cars to the left or right, can see you. In Fig. 2-16, bicycle "A" is located behind vehicle "B," and can be seen in that vehicle's rear-view mirror. Bicycle "C" is in the best position, in the left side of the vehicle lane, to make either a left or a right turn, after, of course, waiting until oncoming vehicle "B" has cleared the intersection. If bike "C" was in the right side of the vehicle lane, vehicle "D" could pass to the left of the bicycle and collide with it in an attempt to make a right turn. Believe me, it's quite common for a motorist to blithely ignore the presence of a bicycle and make a right turn as though the bike were not on the road at all. If you should find yourself by the curb lane at an intersection with a vehicle on your left, wait to see that the vehicle proceeds straight or completes a turn to the right before you go straight through the intersection. Never ride parallel to a vehicle, especially on the right (blind) side as you approach and go through an intersection.

With the bicycle and vehicle driving parallel (Fig. 2-17), these cyclists made two errors. They assumed, obviously incorrectly, that the motorist had seen them and would let them turn left. You can see the point of impact, at "O," where car "A" ran into the bicycles.

Fig. 2-17: Here both cyclists are in danger. The foremost cyclist, just ahead of car "A," wanted to turn left from the curb position. He turned left all right, right in front of the vehicle, where he was struck. The cyclist who was struck by car "B" also tried to get in front of that car from the curb in the right lane. Both bikes started their turn from the motorist's right blind spot.

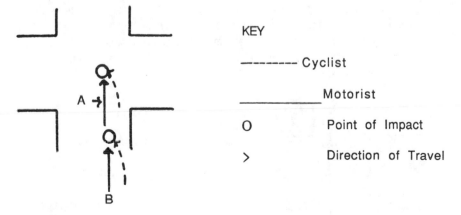

KEY

-------- Cyclist

_____ Motorist

O   Point of Impact

>   Direction of Travel

Lesson 6: Don't try to speed ahead of a vehicle and try to turn left in front of it. Instead, let the vehicle pass, make sure all's clear, *then* make your left turn.

Lesson 7: The bicyclist was riding in the curb lane, to the right of the vehicle in its blind spot. The cyclist decided to make a left turn, speeded up as he approached the intersection, turned in front of the vehicle and was hit by car "B." The cyclist could have avoided being hit in two ways. First, he could have stopped at the intersection, and when traffic permitted, signaled and made a left turn diagonally across the intersection, as a car would. Or, he could have slowed enough to position himself behind the left rear wheel of the car that had been on his left, first making sure that traffic from the rear would permit this maneuver. Then, when the light changed (if there is a stoplight) and traffic permitted, he could have turned left more safely from this position because he would be more visible to motorists. The cyclist also assumed that the motorist would know that he wanted to turn left—a violation of Sloane's second rule of bicycle safety, which states that you should never assume what a motorist will do.

Failure to Yield or Obey a Stoplight Signal: When bicyclists ignore a red stoplight signal they violate both traffic regulations and common sense. In Fig. 2-18 a cyclist pedaled up to an intersection, looked in all directions and thought he had time to go through the red light and the intersection before a car came too close. Again, note the cyclist on the sidewalk. The

Fig. 2-18: Here the bike on the right was struck by car "A" because he did not wait for that car to clear the intersection. The cyclist was struck by car "B" even though he had the right of way. Here, his mistake was to assume that because he was almost across the intersection the motorist would not charge out at him. You can never be sure that a vehicle will not run a yellow or stop signal.

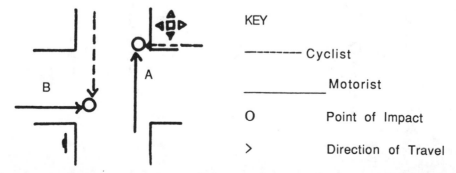

KEY

- - - - - - - Cyclist

_____ Motorist

O   Point of Impact

>   Direction of Travel

motorist had proceeded when the stoplight was yellow, though the cyclist assumed he would stop. The vehicle hit the bicycle at the crosswalk.

Lesson 8: Always obey stoplight signals and stop sign warnings. Even if the stoplight has turned green in favor of the bicycle, it's always safer to wait until all traffic has stopped at the red light before attempting to cross the intersection at a right angle to traffic. Bicycle "B" in Fig. 2-18 had the green light, but it turned yellow when the bike was almost across the intersection. The motorist did not yield and hit the bike.

Lesson 9: This accident was an error of judgment on the part of the driver. However, had the cyclist been more alert or more skilled, he might have steered to the right and around the vehicle. This is a very dangerous situation, which, like many, means a virtually unavoidable accident created by the motorist's own poor judgment, lack of understanding of the limitations of a bicycle, and the knowledge that inside that steel cocoon *he* won't be the one who's hurt in a collision with a bicycle.

Four-Lane Right and Left Turns: In Fig. 2-19, bicycle "A" is in the wrong position to make a left turn, but in the correct posi-

Fig. 2-19: Bicycle "A" is in the wrong position for a left turn but in the correct position to turn right. Bike "C" is in the correct position for a left turn from this four-lane highway. Bike "C" is also in the correct position for a left turn from a mandatory left-arrow signal.

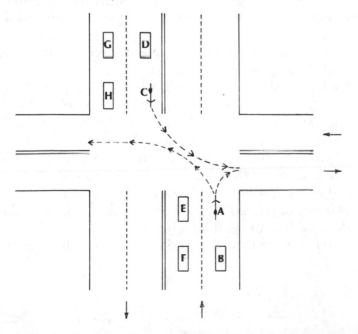

tion for a right turn. Car "B," behind the bike, may assume that the cyclist will either go straight or turn right. If the cyclist turns to the left, car "B" could decide to switch to avoid the bicycle, in which case the car would hit the bike in the center of this intersection.

Lesson 10: When making a left turn on a four-lane street, always start the turn from your left lane. Bike "C" has the right idea, positioning himself in front and to the left of car "D," in the left side of that lane. Car "D" must swing to the right lane *around* the bike, or wait until the bike has made its left turn. Bike "C" would also have to wait until oncoming traffic had cleared, unless the bike is in a mandatory right-turn lane and has a right-turn arrow, which means that oncoming traffic has a red signal and is blocked from proceeding. In fact, bike "C" is the safest one when making a mandatory left turn at a stoplight. Cars "G" and "H" can proceed straight ahead or turn right without hitting bike "C." But if bike "A" tries to turn left, it will be in imminent danger of being hit by cars "E" or "F," the drivers of which might very well assume that the cyclist would not risk a turn in front of them.

Compounded Errors of Judgment: Look at Fig. 2-20. The motorist did not yield to the bicyclists, and the cyclists did not let the vehicle pass—and they had the right-of-way. But as I said earlier, it's not important who has the right-of-way. It's who doesn't get hit that's important. In my opinion, both cyclists should have seen that the vehicle was already more than half-way through its left turn and let the car pass before crossing the intersection.

I prefer to ride my bike on streets where parked cars are permitted. That's because those streets usually have an extra half-lane so people can open their car doors to get in and out of the car without interfering with passing vehicles. This gives you a special lane to bike without using the vehicle traffic lane. It's also safer because on streets where parked cars are not allowed you *must* ride next to the curb, with little room for cars to pass you on your left, while to the right, there's that curb.

Parked cars present three hazards. As you can see in Fig. 2-21, the driver of parked car "A" has suddenly opened the driver's side door into the path of a bicycle.

Lesson 11: As you pass a parked car, look through the rear

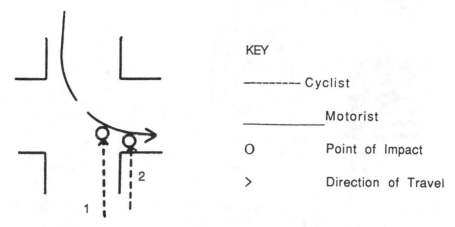

KEY

------- Cyclist

_____ Motorist

O   Point of Impact

>   Direction of Travel

Fig. 2-20: Here the vehicle may not have signaled his left turn intention, or the cyclists did not notice him start this turn. Both cyclists were struck.

Fig. 2-21: Streets with parked cars have an extra lane so motorists can open a left-side door without striking passing cars. If you're cycling in that lane, be aware that someone may open a door in front of you. Car "B" is illegally parked in a clearly marked bike lane, which is not at all unusual in cities.

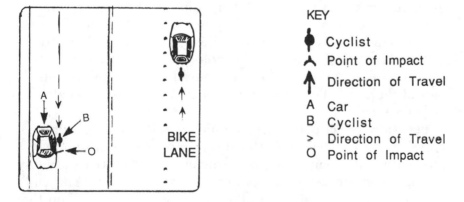

KEY

● Cyclist
⅄ Point of Impact
↑ Direction of Travel
A Car
B Cyclist
> Direction of Travel
O Point of Impact

window and/or the left side-view mirror to see if anyone is in the driver's seat. If so, assume the door is about to open. Slow to a crawl. Look back over your left shoulder, check to make sure that oncoming traffic will let you veer out in the vehicle lane if you have to avoid a suddenly opened car door in front of you. Keep your fingers on the brake levers to save precious seconds if you *do* have to stop suddenly.

A guide sign used for marking officially designated Bikeways.

The "diamond lane" gives preference to certain vehicles such as bicycles.

Used to warn motorists of a midblock bike path crossing.

Fig. 2-22: Signs like these seem to be invisible to motorists so don't depend on them to denote a safe place to bicycle. Keep a wary eye on traffic even when you are in a designated bike lane.

Watch for the second hazard, shown in Fig. 2-21, of a car parked in a clearly marked bike lane. You should be able to see car "B" in plenty of time to go around it, carefully. First check traffic from behind to make sure there's room for you to do so. Remember, a yellow line on the road, along with a sign that says "Bike Lane" or a similar warning (Fig. 2-22), does *not* mean motorists will pay one bit of attention to it. I well remember when, after months of lobbying, we cyclists finally persuaded Chicago's city council to designate appropriate streets as bike lanes. For a few weeks motorists (with the notable exceptions of cab and bus drivers) steered clear of the bicyclist's part of the road. Then the signs became invisible, and all was as before.

The third hazard of parked cars often goes unrecognized. Here's what can happen (as it did to me). As you ride along a nice wide suburban street, pedaling away, a motorist suddenly swoops in front of you, pulls to the curb and parks. You can't stop, except by running into the car's rear bumper. When that happened to me, I hit it so hard I broke a nice new expensive Schwinn Paramount touring bike in half. The front wheel stayed true and held tight in the fork, which was more than I did—I suffered a badly sprained wrist. As I crawled out from under the rear of the car I saw a woman standing over me. I'll never forget her words. She said, "*What* are you doing under my Cadillac?" I think I'd have felt better if she had just said "car," since that was the second Caddy I had tangled with in

15 years of cycling on city streets. She did have the grace to take me to a hospital and to put my two-piece bike in her trunk until I could come back to pick it up.

Lesson 12: If parked cars are allowed on a street, never cycle next to the curb. Instead, stay to the right of the vehicle lane, where you would be if cars were parked.

Black cars, parked at night on a street on which no parking is allowed, present a similar hazard. One winter evening I was wearing battery-heated socks because the temperature was down around zero. I noticed my feet were getting cold so I looked down for a second to check the battery connection, which was prone to corrosion. Before I could look up I found myself sprawled on the roof of yet another Cadillac. I suffered no harm, but my bike's frame and fork were totalled. In both of these cases, although my front wheel hit first, it stayed true and was transferred to another bike. That's a credit to the strength of a well-laced wheel.

About Extended Rear-View Mirrors

Bicyclists have been hurt, and in some instances even killed, by extended rear mirrors (Fig. 2-23) that project from the right side of pickup trucks, campers, and cars towing house trailers or boats.

Fig. 2-23: The extended left-side rear-view mirror (arrow) has killed cyclists in the past. Here, at least, the driver of this car has had the courtesy and good sense to give these cyclists a wide berth. But don't you count on it.

Lesson 13: Be alert and aware of vehicles coming behind you. If you see one with a projecting right side-view mirror, move as far to the right as you can. If necessary, pull a wheelie and hop over a curb.

Use Sign Language

Signal your intentions as shown in Fig. 2-24! You can't depend on a motorist seeing or understanding what you're trying to tell him, but it's safer if you try. An arm straight out to the left means you intend to make a left turn. An arm straight up means a right turn. An arm straight down means you are coming to a stop. Holding your arm down and waving it means you are slowing down.

TURNING   TURNING   SLOW or
LEFT   RIGHT   STOP

Fig. 2-24: Use hand signals to let motorists around you know what you intend to do. Arm straight out means left turn. Arm upraised means right turn. Arm straight down means you intend to stop or to slow down.

Bike Trails—Use With Caution!

A bike trail (Fig. 2-25) takes you far from the madding crowd of motor vehicles. The better trails wind through woods, pass by lakes and streams, offer peace and quiet and solitude. However, many trails aren't paved but gravel-surfaced, as in Fig. 2-25. Be aware that gravel can be slippery, and if you come to a cement sidewalk across the trail, watch for gravel kicked up on the sidewalk, particularly if you have to make a turn as you cross it. I have found that trails in city, county, or state parks are poorly marked. On some trails, for example, the cyclist turns a corner and suddenly finds himself going down a steep hill and then discovers that the trail turns sharply to the left or to

Fig. 2-25: Bike paths far from highways offer serenity and freedom from trafffic.

the right, narrowing for some inexplicable reason from 10 feet to 8 feet wide. Trail designers should erect signs warning the cyclist of all trail hazards; they should be placed at least 50 feet from the hazard to give the cyclist plenty of warning. Such hazards include steep hills, bumps on the trail, narrowing of the trail, sharp hidden corners and turns, upcoming crosswalks with pedestrian traffic, and upcoming highways with vehicular traffic.

Fig. 2-26: Here this bike path parallels a highway in the Netherlands, not far from Amsterdam.

Some trails parallel roads, as in Fig. 2-26. These trails are certainly a lot safer than any city or even country road. But they do have their safety problems, which include children weaving around on small bikes or skateboards, pedestrians, and in Europe, mopeds and small motorcycles.

Rear-View Mirrors

Up till now I have urged you, when appropriate, to look back over your left shoulder to be aware of traffic behind you. But you can now buy a small clip-on rear-view mirror that fastens to your eyeglasses or your helmet to give you a surprisingly wide view of the scene behind you. And since the mirror is used by only one eye, you can still see the road ahead with the other eye. While these mirrors (Figs. 2-27 and 2-28) are suitable for riding on the highway, I really can't recommend them for off-road trail riding on all-terrain bicycles since projections on the trail—rocks, tree, branches, etc.—can bump you off the bike. This relatively harmless fall can become serious if the mirror is pushed into your eye.

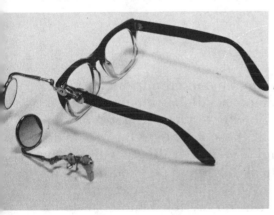

Fig. 2-27: Rear-view mirrors can clip on eyeglasses.

Fig. 2-28: If you don't wear glasses, there's a rear-view mirror you can fasten to your bike helmet.

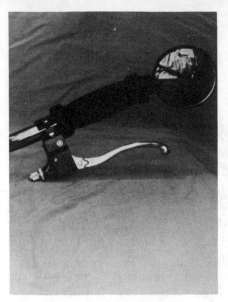
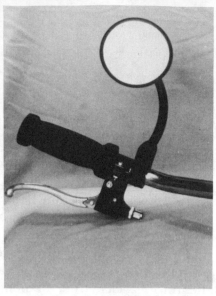

Fig. 2-29: This mirror fits right into the end of handlebars, except the aluminum handlebars of all-terrain bikes. This direct attachment minimizes mirror "bounce."

Fig. 2-30: This mirror clamps onto the end of any handlebar, but since it's mounted on a stalk, it is less stable than the mirror in Fig. 2-29.

I have used eyeglass and helmet-mounted mirrors for years, but lately I have come to prefer a handlebar mounted mirror. This way I can glance down quickly to check traffic from behind. There are three types of these mirrors. One make fits directly into the handlebar end (Fig. 2-29). This type of mirror does not wobble from road shock like the type fixed on a stalk (Fig. 2-30). You can also buy a wide-angle rear-view mirror. I have a normal-perspective mirror on my left handlebar and a wide angle on the right. That way I can keep track of both oncoming lanes behind me if I'm on a four-lane road. The wide-angle mirror is particularly valuable when riding on the shoulder of an interstate freeway, because a cyclist can check traffic from on and off ramps as well as the highway itself. Mirrors are also a great way to keep in touch with cyclists behind you. You don't want to leave a friend too far behind.

A warning about rear-view mirrors: These little mirrors only give you monocular vision. This means you can't be sure *how fast* traffic is coming from behind, or even exactly *how far away* a truck or a car is behind you at any given moment. The optic computer in your head can't accurately gauge distance when processing a monocular image. You'll see what I mean by closing one eye and guessing how fast a car behind you is moving. Now try both eyes. See the difference? I learned this lesson the hard way. I depended on a rear-view mirror to check whether or not I could make a left turn. I saw a little VW bug coming up from behind me, but it seemed far enough away that I had time to make a left turn in front of it. As soon as I started the turn that VW was right on top of me. It had been moving much faster than I thought. The driver had to swerve to the left to miss me, and did so with much screaming and blowing of his horn. He was not pleased, and I don't blame him.

Bicycling on Interstate Highways

Your first reaction to biking on interstate highways or freeways was probably the same as mine, the first time I contemplated it. "No way!" But if you want to travel the mountains or many other areas out west, only interstate highways take you where you want to go. If there are roads, many are too narrow for safe cycling, with no shoulders for cyclists to escape passing cars, pickup trucks, logging trucks, or camp trailers. If you want to cross over the mountains of the west, traveling by the interstate may be your easiest, safest route.

But in many states cycling on the shoulder of an interstate highway is illegal. In California, Oregon, Washington, and other states, it is legal to ride on the shoulder of many interstate highways, except for those near big cities, where there are alternative roads. The traffic on interstate highways near cities such as Portland, Seattle, and other major cities of the west is too dense for safety, and I refer both to the number of vehicles as well as to some of the drivers.

I see many bicyclists on Washington and Oregon Interstate routes 1-205 and 1-5, for example, going both north and south, headed for Canada or California or someplace in between. The shoulder of many interstate highways is a nice, comfortable ten feet wide. It's paved, usually smooth and free of debris. If you ride on the right side of the shoulder you have a good eight feet between you and the nearest vehicle. The grades of interstate highways are usually far less steep than two-lane side roads. There are reasonably spaced rest stops for calls of nature, and generous landscaped areas to stop for snacks without leaving the highway.

As you might have guessed, I have a few safety tips about cyling on interstate highways. *First, never ride on them at night!* Whether you're sporting a reflective vest, have reflectors, and a good taillight or not, a fatigue-dulled driver may still wander onto the shoulder. This may happen during the day, of course, but if you keep a careful watch on upcoming traffic you can see a recklessly meandering driver and escape by riding off the shoulder into the landscape. In some five years of daytime cycling on interstate highways I have yet to come nearly as close to being hit by a vehicle as I have when cycling on other roads.

Second, be aware of the push-pull effect of big trucks! Big trucks push a bubble of air in front of them, which tends to push you to the right as the truck approaches you. The truck then creates a partial vacuum behind it as it displaces air, which pulls you to the left. Such displacement is known in physics as the Bernoulli effect. Once aware of the effect—which is usually quite mild—I counteracted it easily by leaning a bit to the left as the truck approached and a bit to the right after it passed. This push-pull effect, however, can dump you if it's compounded by high winds from any direction. Fortunately I have never had this problem. In fact, I discovered that the suction effect of big trucks actually pulled me along no matter which way the wind was blowing. When I was cycling into a stiff headwind, big trucks always turned the wind around or reduced its intensity as they passed. There are so many trucks on the highway that I nearly always found my way eased by them when the wind was not going my way.

Third, be especially cautious as you approach on and off ramps! As you arrive at an off-ramp, where traffic on your left may exit and cross in front of you, you *must* stop. Do *not* depend on a rear-view mirror to check how far away or how fast traffic is coming up from behind you. Traffic is *always* going faster than you think it is. Take a look at Table 2-1. You can see that from a block away a vehicle traveling 75 miles per hour takes only 2.5 seconds to reach you. You would never make it if you decided to beat it across the intersecting on-ramp. Even if you were pushing 20 mph, it would still take you two full seconds to go 15 feet, and that's just cutting it too darned close. Wait—you're worth it.

As you approach an off or exit ramp (Fig. 2-31), stop and look

Fig. 2-31: When you cycle on interstate highways and you approach an off-ramp where traffic is leaving the highway, stop at the spot marked "X" on this photo. Look at the highway behind you. When you are sure oncoming traffic is not going to exit and cut in front of you, proceed as fast as possible to get across this ramp (arrow).

Table 2-1

SECONDS TO TRAVEL A STANDARD CITY BLOCK OF 280 FEET

MILES PER HOUR	FEET PER SECOND	SECONDS PER BLOCK
5	7.3	38
10	14.7	19
15	22	13
20	29	10
55	81	3.5
60	88	3.2
70	102	2.7
75	110	2.5

back. Only when you are positive that traffic coming in the right lane is not going to exit should you proceed across the ramp. If you see an oncoming vehicle with its right turn signal blinking, of course you know enough to stop and let it turn off before you cross the ramp. But the cars that exit the freeway *without* a turn signal really worry me. I have looked back hundreds of times at five miles of straight road on a clear day to see a car three or four blocks away. By the time I counted off ten seconds, that car would be next to me. Even at a quarter of a mile away, a car going 70 miles per hour will reach you in 13 seconds. Practice counting the seconds it takes for a car to reach you as you wait to cross an exit ramp. It won't take long until you can estimate, with a comfortable margin of safety, how long you need to get across that ramp.

On-ramps (Fig. 2-32) are a little safer for cyclists than exit ramps. When you're entering the highway you don't have to cross an exit ramp the long way, parallel to the traffic, because vehicles will be moving slower than they do on the highway. As Fig. 2-32 shows, what you do is stop at the point where the on-ramp merges with the highway. When traffic coming down the on-ramp is clear (i.e., when you see no cars on the ramp), simply take a straight cut to the right, across the ramp, and turn left down the ramp's shoulder. You can then safely merge with the highway shoulder at the base of the off-ramp.

One final note about interstate highways. If you plan to use them, check with the state department of transportation to make sure you can do so legally. Then, check again with the state highway patrol. I was stopped by a Washington State highway patrol officer recently and told I had to get off Interstate Highway 205, because "it was illegal for me to be cycling on the shoulder of that road." I did not argue. The next day I called the Washington State Department of Transportation, which assured me that it was legal. At my request they sent me correspondence between the D.O.T. and the state police headquarters, together with a bicycle map of the entire state interstate road system, showing where bicycling was legal and where it was not. Then I wrote a letter to the chief of the Washington State Highway Patrol and sent copies to the governor, my state senator, the officer that stopped me, and his boss, the lieutenant of his barracks, together with copies of this correspondence from the D.O.T. to his department, plus my

Fig. 2-32: Stop where you see the "X" on this picture to check traffic coming down an on-ramp. When no traffic is in sight, cut across the ramp at a 90-degree (arrow) angle to get to the other side, then bike down the on-ramp's shoulder until it meets the highway shoulder.

own background in bicycling. In about a week I had letters from all these people, plus a visit from the lieutenant, who was very nice, as was the chief. The lieutenant said he asked his officers if they knew that it was o.k. for cyclists to ride on the shoulder of some 90 percent of the state's interstate highways. Half of them said it was their understanding that it is illegal to bicycle on the shoulder of any interstate highway, which documented the stories I had been getting from local bike shops and bicyclists. Seems the police had been routinely stopping and ordering cyclists off the freeways. I am sure many long-distance cyclists had their plans cut short by such police action, because side roads are not always available. And those side roads that are available at many off-ramps are narrow with no shoulders, have high-speed local traffic, and are far more hazardous than the interstate highway. As I noted, however, the Washington State Highway Patrol people were most cooperative once they understood the situation.

How to Use Your Brakes

At least 80 percent of your braking power comes from your front brake. That's a basic fact to always keep in mind. An easy way to visualize what happens when you brake is to take a book, put it on the table, push one edge of the book with one hand, and hold it back with the other. You will see that the end of the book you are pushing tends to rise up in the air, and the end you are holding tends to dig into the surface. That's precisely what happens when you depress both brake levers. The kinetic energy stored in the bike as forward momentum, plus the weight of you and your bike, is transferred to the front wheel. The rear wheel tends to rise up off the ground.

Emergency stops: Now that you understand why some 80 percent of your total braking power comes from the front wheel, let's discuss how to come to a safe, controlled stop, even in an emergency situation. Suppose you're cycling down a city street and suddenly a truck appears in front of you. You *must* stop. You have no time to turn or take evasive action. What to do? Grab *both* brake levers and squeeze them as hard as you can. If time permits, you should also move your body as far toward the rear of the bike as possible. Both of these maneuvers give you maximum braking power and help prevent an "endo" (a bike term that means that the rear wheel goes up in the air and the rider is pitched head forward over the handlebars with a distinct possibility of landing on his head). If you grab just the front brake, or apply it first, an endo is very likely. If you grab just the rear brake, the rear wheel can lock up and cause the bike, with you on it, to skid sideways but still slide forward on the ground. How far it slides in that position depends on how fast you were going in the first place.

Keep downhill speed under control: If you're biking down a long hill, it's tempting, I know, to let 'er roll at full speed. I know it's fun to see the astonishment of drivers as you pass them at 40 mph going downhill. But my advice is: don't do it! Don't let speed build up so fast that you can't stop in a reasonably quick time for any surprises you find on the road. When you come to a curve, be aware that around that curve may be a trailer truck jackknifed across the width of the road. Can you see the road ahead of you clearly?

Control your downhill speed by using first one brake and then the other. Alternating the use of the brakes gives rims—overheated from the friction of brake pads—time to cool off. If your wheel rims get too hot, heat will be transferred to the air in the tubes, and as air heats, it expands. Many riders have suffered blowouts due to overheated rims, with subsequent loss of control and bodily injury. Tubular tires cannot only blow out, but are held on the rim with a cement that can soften under heat; when the cement softens, the tire will not only slide around the rim until the valve stem breaks off and the tire deflates, but the tire may slide right off the rim to one side or the other. If you worry that the rim is overheating, stop and feel it. I remember the day I was tending some bikes outside a store in Vermont. My fellow cyclists were in the store, shopping for lunch. It was a hot day in August. The sun was beating down on the bicycles. Suddenly I heard a series of pops. At first I thought someone was shooting at me. Then I realized that the tires were exploding as the overheated air in the tubes expanded from the sun's heat. Air can expand and blow a hole in tubes no matter whether the heat comes from brake shoe friction or from the sun's rays.

Plan an escape route: Try to anticipate surprises and know where you can make a quick turn-off or stop if need be. As I said in the previous chapter, always look for an escape route. Suppose a child darts out in front of you. Had you thought about an "escape route," you would know, for example, that you either could turn into the next left lane (you should keep an eye on oncoming traffic with your rear-view mirror or an occasional rearward glance), or to the right, jumping up over the curb by pulling up on the handlebars hard so the front wheel clears the curb by three or four inches. Say you're riding down a country lane. To your right there's a shallow ditch, and to the right of the ditch there's an open field. That ditch and that open field are your escape routes if you have to turn off the road to avoid a collision. So you're much more likely to make a good emergency decision if you think ahead about how you will avoid a collision in any particular biking situation.

Above all, *avoid head-on collisions.* If you have to, dump the bike on its side, but don't hit anything or anyone head-on. Say you're biking toward an intersection shielded by bushes on your right. You won't be able to see the traffic from that road until you pass the bushes. You should now take two precautions. First, slow down to a crawl, say two or three miles an hour. Keep your hands on the brake levers so if a car appears, you can stop before you travel too far into the intersection. As a second precaution consider what you would do if, despite your caution, a car suddenly appeared on a collision course with you. I routinely (traffic permitting) swing my bike over to the left side of the lane as I approach the intersection. From this position I have room to make a sharp right turn toward the curb, or if necessary into the intersection itself to avoid a collision from a car coming from my right.

Use your brakes sparingly as you make a turn. Your bike rides at a greater angle to the ground when you are turning than when you are riding straight. On a turn, greater side forces exert themselves at the point where the tire makes contact with the ground. If the ground is at all slippery (gravel, wet leaves, etc.) when you brake, the bike could dump on its side. Be especially wary of braking around sharp corners at high speed. Slow down before you arrive at the turn if you're not sure how slippery the surface will be or what is around the other side of the curve.

More about wheel shimmy: A few years ago, while on a bike tour of Austria, I was leading some 40 American bicyclists down a steep mountainside. The road was long and straight, with two lanes. A loaded Mercedes logging truck was approaching in the opposite lane. An unprotected drop-off of about 1,200 feet gaped to my right. As I reached about 30 miles per hour, my handlebars and front wheel suddenly began to move violently from side to side. With every turn of my wheels, the shimmy increased in width and frequency. Within a few seconds after the shimmy started I realized it was only going to get worse. Nothing I could do—gripping the handlebars or braking or both—could stop the shimmy from increasing in intensity. I realized I was losing control, that the bike was going to fall over to one side or the other. I did not want to hit the logging truck. Falling 1,200 feet did not appeal to me, either. So I shifted my weight until the bike fell over, with me on top of it, and slid down my side of the road. It all happened so suddenly that the cyclists behind me had no chance to take evasive action, and three or four of them fell on top of me and each other. Fortunately no one was hurt beyond losing a little skin here and there, which is a hazard you learn to ignore, at least until you pour antiseptic on the abrasions. The endorphins you earn as a hard-pedaling cyclist, however, are themselves a mild form of anesthesia. Cuts and bruises never seem to hurt as much at the time they occur as they do later on, as you soak in a hot bath or shower. Back at the camp, we went over my bike minutely, but could find nothing that would have caused the shimmy. Finally I checked the fork blade alignment. Sure enough, one blade was slightly bent, but not enough to be obvious to the naked eye. The blade was bent during the airline shipment from the U.S. to Austria. I should have braced the fork dropouts —and the rear dropouts—with a dummy axle or piece of wood for shipment.

A bent fork blade is not the only cause of front-wheel shimmy. Other shimmy problems can be traced to loose head-set bearings, loose wheel bearings, poor weight distribution, or loose carriers and panniers. See Chapters 8 and 9 for information on headset and wheel-bearing adjustment. Poor weight distribution makes your bike hard to balance and steer accurately. I shudder when I see bike tourists with heavy items such as a tent and sleeping bag strapped down on top of the carrier so the load is higher than the top of the saddle. It's much safer to distribute the load between two rear- and two front-mounted carriers (Fig. 2-33). To keep weight distributed

Fig. 2-33: A safely loaded bicycle has the weight evenly divided fore and aft, as shown here. Practice riding with a loaded bike until you get used to the changed handling, steering, and braking.

Fig. 2-34: Check carrier mounting bolts before every trip. Bolts are shown by arrows "A" and "B."

Fig. 2-35: This rear carrier has six mounting bolts which should be checked for tightness before a trip.

evenly over both wheels, load rear panniers so they weigh about the same, and load front panniers the same way. That way the bike will be balanced, steer more accurately and, with more weight on the front wheel, less likely to shimmy. Loose panniers can contribute to wheel shimmy. Strap them down so they don't bounce, or fall off the carriers. Check all carrier mounting bolts (Figs. 2-34 through 2-37) before every trip, and on the road, each day.

A fully loaded bicycle is much harder to handle. Steering on a fully loaded bike (Fig. 2-33) is sluggish. You won't be able to make quick, sharp turns. Your balance will be off and the bike will seem to have a will of its own. Practice riding your fully loaded bike before taking off down the road. You'll find that after 25 miles or so handling the bike becomes more comfortable—getting on and off, starting and stopping, turning and

Fig. 2-36: Some carriers are clamped to seat stays. These clamp bolts are more apt to work loose than carriers bolted to brazed-on fittings as in Figs. 2-34 and 2-35.

Fig. 2-37: Here is the strut of the rear carrier shown in Fig. 2-36. Again, check clamp and strut mounting bolts for tightness before every long trip. A loose strut could catch in spokes and cause an accident.

braking will begin to feel natural. Be aware that braking power is drastically reduced as you load up the bike! Remember to use greater pressure as you pull the brake lever to control speed, and to be especially careful as you travel downhill. Control your speed!

Braking is adversely affected when you're towing a loaded bike trailer. Take sharp turns slowly so you don't turn the trailer over. Fig. 2-38 shows a trailer loaded with everything but the kitchen sink. Note that most of the load is not securely tied down. I know who sent this photo—it was taken just for laughs. Don't use this as an example of how to load a trailer. However, stowing a spare trailer tire under the front, as was done here, is a good idea, because trailer tires are a different size than bike tires.

Fig. 2-38: Carry your camping load with a bike trailer. This cyclist has enough stuff for 10 people, or so it appears. This cyclist has not tied his load down, which is not the healthiest way to go. The picture was set up to show how not to load a trailer. Note the spare tire is under the front of the trailer, which *is* a good idea. *(Bikecentennial photo)*

Watch out for storm sewer gratings, bridge expansion joints, and railroad tracks! The bars in some sewer gratings (Fig. 2-39) are spaced far enough apart that bike tires can drop down in them if the bike crosses the grating at a parallel. You can imagine what will happen. The bike will come. to a sudden stop, the rear wheel will lift up and you might be pitched forward over the handlebars onto your head.

Some bridge expansion joints, like sewer gratings, can be wide enough to trap your wheel. As you cross any bridge, watch out for the place where the bridge roadway meets solid ground, or, if it's a long bridge, watch for an expansion joint about midway across. These joints look like steel interweaved fingers. They let the bridge's structural members expand and contract without damage to the bridge as the outside temperature varies and as the sun heats up the road surface. Cross such joints and railroad tracks at angle to avoid catching a wheel in them.

Fig. 2-39: The bars in storm sewer gratings are often spaced wide enough to catch a tire and cause an accident. Steer around such gratings. Cross bridge expansion joints and railroad tracks at an angle to avoid catching a wheel in them.

Check the road surface: Get in the habit of paying attention not only to the traffic around you, but also to the surface of the road on which you are riding. Watch out for potholes, particularly those more than two inches deep. You should be able to ride over shallower potholes, particularly if you see them before you hit them. Steer around deeper potholes (after first checking to see if traffic permits such a detour). If you ride after a rainfall, deep potholes and chuckholes can be filled with water and so appear shallow.

You can't avoid every bump. Learn how to take them with maximum comfort to you and minimum harm to your tires. As you watch the road, you'll know when a bump is coming up that you can't avoid. As you approach the bump, keep both pedals flat, so the cranks are parallel to the ground, as shown in Fig. 2-40. Here the rider has his weight off the saddle, and is absorbing the road shock with his legs and arms. The bike in this picture is an all-terrain model, so the posture is more exaggerated than that of a road bike, but I think you get the point.

Fig. 40: Take road shock when riding over bumps or potholes by lifting off the saddle with feet on both pedals, as shown here. This rider is on an all-terrain bike, but use this method on road bikes too, although in not quite so exaggerated a form.

If You Get Hurt

Sooner or later you'll most likely fall off your bike. Most falls result in little more than a few scratches or minor bruises. If you know how to fall, you can minimize damage to your body.

How to Fall: Don't practice falls, but if you see you are losing control think about how you are going to land. Experienced cyclists try to assume a *tuck.* They tuck their head down, pull their knees up and try to land on their shoulder, absorbing road shock as they roll forward. If you land with your arms extended straight out to absorb road shock—instinctive with most people —you're asking for a bad wrist sprain or a broken arm. If you aren't wearing padded bike gloves (Fig. 1-42) you may lose a little skin from the palm of your hands as they hit the pavement. In any event, remember that the last part of your body you want to hit the pavement first is your head! Even with a helmet on your noggin. A helmet protects against abrasion and offers impact resistance. But no helmet can fully protect against a very hard shock. If you should land on the top of your head, though it is unlikely, you could suffer a compression fracture of the spine, which could make you a paraplegic or quadriplegic. It's happened.

Type medical information on a card for your wallet. Include the date of your last tetanus shot, blood type, and any special data a doctor should know such as diabetes, heart problems, and allergic reactions to medications.

If you should fall off your bike and get hurt, here's what to do and what not to do:

1. Don't be a hero and try to ride home. An attorney friend of mine fell off his bike, then got up and rode home. In an hour his neck began to hurt unbearably, so his wife drove him to a hospital emergency room. X-rays revealed that he had broken his neck. This man was a weight lifter as well as a bicyclist, so he had excellent musculature which supported his head to a degree after his accident. But, had he wiggled his head the wrong way just once, the nerves of his spinal column could easily have been severed and he would have been an instant paraplegic or quadriplegic. He's fine today, but it was a close call.

Don't assume you're o.k. after you fall off your bike. You may be fine, but you can't be sure. A hard impact on cement can shake up the best of minds. You may very well be seriously injured and not know it. If you're in the line of traffic, crawl out of it if you can. Better, have someone help you. If you're not in a traffic lane, lie still until the paramedics come and take you to the hospital, especially if you think you have broken a bone or hurt your spine.

2. If you landed on your head, ask your doctor about being alert during the next few weeks for dizziness or headaches that could mean brain injury, and what you should do about it.

3. Try to get the names, addresses, and phone numbers of witnesses. Or have someone else do it for you.

4. Have someone call the police so an accident report can be filed.

5. Sequester your bicycle. *Lock it up.* Do not ride it, do not get it repaired, do not let anyone else ride it. Your bicycle may very well be your best witness if a defect in design, manufacturing, or assembly caused or contributed to the accident. You can't be absolutely sure nothing is wrong with your bike until an expert examines it.

6. Look up the original owner's manual that came with the bike, your bill of sale or receipt for payment of the bike, and all subsequent repair receipts, and have them ready for use.

7. Keep the clothing you were wearing at the time of the accident. Wrap them up, including your helmet if you were wearing one, and your shoes. They could be important later on.

8. As soon as possible, have someone go out to the exact scene of the accident and photograph the roadbed and surrounding scenery.

9. Consult a good personal injury attorney. As you check the attorney's references, try to find out if he or she has had any experience with bicycle accident cases, and what was the disposition of the litigation. After you review the case with the attorney, find out if he or she will take your case on a contingency basis. That means that the attorney will not charge you for work he does in preparing your case, and in exchange for this investment of his professional time he gets 30 percent of whatever amount is recovered for you. However, you may have to pay certain out-of-pocket expenses such as the fee of an expert witness and any laboratory work

such as a metallurgical analysis of the bicycle or its components. If the attorney won't take your case on a contingency-
fee basis, that tells you what that counsellor thinks of it. You
could then discuss the case with other attorneys.

How to Keep a Quick Release From Quick Releasing!

In many accidents the rider claims that when he or she hit a
bump, the front wheel came off, which dumped the bike and
caused serious personal injury. The type of wheel-retention
device involved in most of these alleged accidents is the quick-
release mechanism (Fig. 2-41). I use the word "alleged" because these devices are safe, if properly used. The problem
often comes from improper adjustment, either because the
owner was careless, his owner's manual did not instruct him
adequately as to the correct use of this mechanism, or because
someone else played with and loosened this mechanism without his knowledge. Let's first review how to use the quick-
release mechanism.

    If you look closely at part No. 4 in Fig. 2-41 you will see that
I have added an arrow labeled "A." The arrow points to a fat
part of the quick-release lever shaft. This is called a cam. A
close-up of this cam is shown in Fig. 2-42. The wheel hub axle
(14) is hollow. The quick-release skewer (3) goes through the

Fig. 2-41: Quick-release skewer must be properly closed for safety. Please see text for
details.

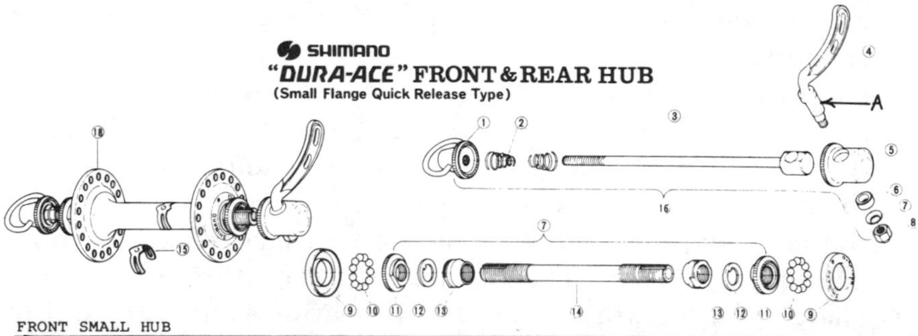

SHIMANO
"DURA-ACE" FRONT & REAR HUB
(Small Flange Quick Release Type)

FRONT SMALL HUB

ITEM NO.	PART NO.	DESCRIPTION	ITEM NO.	PART NO.	DESCRIPTION
1	233 9001	Nut for Mounting Stud	11	233 1700	Locking Nut
2	233 2100	Volute Spring	12	233 1600	Key Washer
3	233 0800	Mounting Stud	13	233 1500	Cone
4	233 0400	Cum Lever	14	233 1800	Axle (M9x108mm)
5	233 0300	Body Cum Lever	15	233 1200	Oil Cap
6	233 0700	Bushing	16	233 9002	Complete Quick Release Unit
7	233 0500	Coned Disc Spring	17	233 9003	Complete Axle Unit
8	233 0600	Cap Nut	18	235 41100	COMPLETE FRONT HUB (28H)
9	233 1400	Dust Cap		235 61100	COMPLETE FRONT HUB (32H)
10	000 0125	Steel Balls 3/16"		235 81100	COMPLETE FRONT HUB (36H)

Fig. 2-42: Greatly enlarged section of a quick-release cam. When you turn the quick-release lever the cam rotates, tightening wheel axle in dropouts.

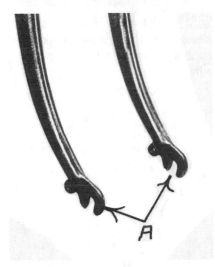

Fig. 2-43: The quick-release locks wheel axle in place at "A."

hub's hollow axle. When the quick-release lever (4) is turned toward the tightening position, its cam (Fig. 2-42) also turns. When it turns, it forces the nut (1) and the cam body (5) together. This cam action then squeezes down on the axle and holds it securely in the dropouts (Fig. 2-43).

You can tell when the quick-release skewer is safely and properly tightened when you see "teeth" marks on the face of the dropouts, as shown in Fig. 2-44. In fact, if the wheel has been removed more than once, you should see multiple, overlaid "teeth" marks, not just one set of them. These indentations or teeth marks are caused by the serrated sawtooth edges of the quick release nut (1) and lever body (5) shown in Fig. 2-41 and in Fig. 2-45. Some hubs also have locknuts with serrated edge teeth, as in Fig. 2-46. If your hubs have such locknuts, you should also find the serrations on the inside of the dropouts on both front and rear wheels.

Fig. 2-44: If the quick-release has been properly adjusted and tightened you should see overlapping "bites" in the steel of the dropout, like these.

Fig. 2-45: The inside faces of the quick-release have sharp serrations like these that bite into and grip the wheel axle firmly in the dropouts.

Fig. 2-46: Better hubs have sawtooth serrations (arrows) that leave "teeth marks" or bite marks on both sides of dropouts, which indicate a better and safer grip.

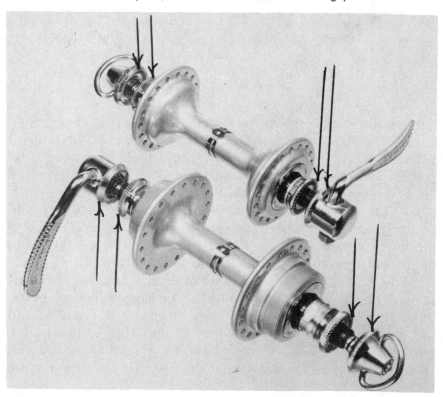

Adjusting the quick-release mechanism is simple, once you understand that it is a cam-action device and not a nut-and-bolt device. Some people think the quick-release is just another nut-and-bolt gadget. I hope by now you know it's a cam-action mechanism. To tighten it correctly, you first make sure it is correctly adjusted so the cam works safely. You adjust the quick-release as follows:

1. Turn the quick-release lever so that it's perpendicular (straight out) from the dropouts, as shown in Fig. 2-47. Holding this lever with your right hand, turn the adjusting nut clockwise with your left hand until you feel it tighten and you can turn it no farther by hand. *Do not tighten this nut with a tool!*
2. Turn the quick-release lever all the way so it faces toward the rear of the bicycle. As the lever passes the six o'clock position (Fig. 2-47), facing out from the bike, you should begin to feel resistance. As you force the lever toward the rear of the bike, this resistance will increase. It should take considerable force to move this lever all the way toward the

Fig. 2-47: The first step in adjusting the quick-release is to move the lever (right) perpendicular to the bike frame. Hold the lever and tighten the adjusting nut (left) snug. Do not use a tool on the adjusting nut.

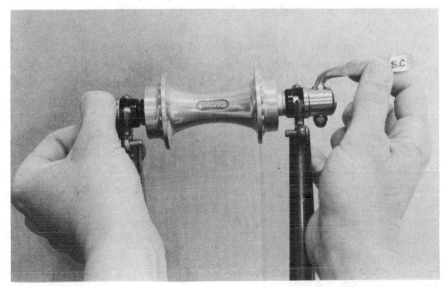

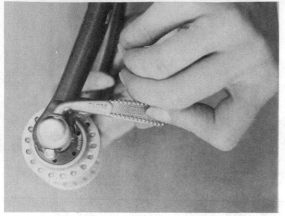

Fig. 2-48: When the quick-release adjusting nut has been positioned as shown in Fig. 2-47, you will feel resistance as you turn the lever toward the closed position. It should take considerable pressure to move the lever all the way to the closed position, shown here, pointing toward the rear of the bike.

Fig. 2-49: When quick-release is closed, the word CLOSE should be visible, as shown here.

rear of the bike. With the lever in that position (Figs. 2-48 and 2-49), you should see the word CLOSE, if it's engraved on the lever.

3. Turn the quick-release lever so it faces toward the *front* of the bicycle, as shown in Figs. 2-50 and 2-51. Most quick-release levers will have the word OPEN engraved on the lever, as in Fig. 2-50. Now you should be able to remove or insert the wheel hub axle into the dropouts.

Schwinn wheel retention test: The Schwinn Bicycle Company has made a lab test of the force required to pull a front wheel out of the dropout when the quick-release mechanism was in various stages of being tightened. When the lever was in the closed position, *it took nearly 500 foot-pounds of pressure to pull the wheel out of the dropout.* What this means is that allegations of a properly tightened front wheel "falling" out of the dropout and causing an accident have to be sheer hogwash. Even if the bike hit a pothole and the front wheel popped into

Fig. 2-50: Wheel can be removed when quick-release lever is in the open position, pointed toward front of bike.

Fig. 2-51: OPEN on this quick-release lever shows when lever is in the open position.

the air two or three inches, the wheel would stay in the drop-outs. No road has fingers or grippers that are going to grab a bike wheel and pull it out of the dropouts to the tune of 500 foot-pounds. A foot-pound is that amount of energy or force that will move a given weight a given distance. I can illustrate how well a properly adjusted quick-release mechanism holds a wheel in the dropouts by an accident I had (one of only three over 25 years). I was going about 15 miles per hour when my front wheel was caught by the interlocking fingers of a bridge expansion joint. The sudden stop threw me forward over the handlebars and buckled the fork and the top and down tubes. The wheel stayed in the dropouts.

In conclusion, remember to inspect the quick-release of both wheels every time you get on the bike. Never assume that safely tightening them on your last ride means they are safe now.

Some bicycles have solid axles that are bolted on. These should be tightened to a torque of at least 300 inch-pounds. See

Chapter 5 for a definition of torque, and Chapters 5 through 10 for detailed maintenance instructions on every moving part of a bicycle. Review Table 2-2 below for periodic maintenance data and refer to the appropriate chapter for details.

Table 2-2

PERIODIC MAINTENANCE AND SERVICE*

PART	SERVICE	FREQUENCY	CHAPTER
Axle nuts	Check tightness	Monthly	7
Bottom bracket	Disassemble, lubricate, adjust	Yearly	8
Brake cables	Check for worn, frayed strands	Six months	5
Brake cables	Replace if frayed or worn	As needed	5
Brake levers	Check tightness of mounting bolts	Six months	5
Brake pivot nut	Check tightness	Two months	5
Brake shoes	Check wear, adjustment, nut tightness	Four months	5
Carriers	All mounting bolts and nuts	Four months	4, 9
Chain	Clean, lubricate	Two months	8
Chainwheels	Clean. Check bolt tightness	Two months	8
Cranks	Check spindle nut tightness	Four months	8
Derailleurs	Check shifting. Adjust	Four months	6
Derailleur cables	Check for frayed strands	Four months	6
Derailleur cables	Replace worn cables	As needed	6
Fenders	Check mounting nuts	Four months	4, 9
Frame	Clean, wax, retouch paint	As needed	11
Freewheel	Clean, lubricate. Check cog wear	Four months	8
Headset bearings	Clean, lubricate, adjust	Four months	9
Hubs	Clean, lubricate, adjust	Six months	8
Pedals	Clean, lubricate	Six months	8
Seat post	Check tightness of binder bolt	Four months	9
Shift levers	Check mounting bolt tightness	Six months	6
Spokes	Check tightness. Replace as needed	As needed	10
Stem bolt	Check tightness	Four months	9
Tires	Check pressure, wear, cuts, gouges	Weekly	8
Wheels	Check alignment, retrue as needed	Four months	10

* Frequency of maintenance varies depending on use of bicycle. These frequencies are based on average use.

About Toe Clips and Straps

Most better road bikes, some all-terrain bikes, and all true road- and track-racing bikes come with toe clips and straps (Fig. 1-59). You can also install them yourself (see Chapter 8). Since you can pull one pedal up while you push the other one down, toe clips and straps add about 40 percent to your cycling efficiency, compared to cycling without them. If you have never used pedals with toe clips and straps, practice the steps below until you can do them without looking down or taking your eyes off the road.

1. *Starting:* Keep toe straps loose. Straddle the bike. Pull a pedal up to about the 2 o'clock position. Insert your foot into the pedal, push down on that pedal and at the same time get up on the saddle.
2. As you coast, tip the other pedal up with your toe so you can slide your foot into it.
3. *Stopping:* To get your feet out of the pedals, pull one foot back and up when the pedal is at about the 6 o'clock position (Fig. 2-52). Continue pulling your foot up (Fig. 2-53).

Fig. 2-52: Pull up and back to remove your foot from a pedal with a toe clip and strap.

Fig. 2-53: Tilt your heel up as your foot moves partway off the pedal.

Fig. 2-54: Tilt your heel up even more sharply to release your shoe (or shoe cleat) from the pedal frame.

Fig. 2-55: Hold the strap buckle open to loosen the toe strap.

When your foot is almost free, tilt your heel up so your shoe (or shoe cleats) won't catch on the pedals (Fig. 2-54). Stop the bike and with your free foot on the ground, remove your other foot from the pedal.

4. Keep toe straps loose in traffic so you can get your feet out of the pedals quickly in an emergency. If toe straps are so tight you can't get your feet out of the pedals, you have two options. One, anticipate the need, reach down (without taking your eyes off the road), press the buckle release lever (Fig. 2-55), and pull the strap up by the buckle to loosen it. Two, lift your heel and *jerk* your foot upward. Again, *never tighten toe straps so tight that you can't get your feet out of the pedals at any time.*

Drafting Is O.K. if You Do It Right

"Drafting" means letting the cyclist ahead break the wind for you. You do this by staying about a half bike length to the rear and to one side of the rider in front. Don't get so close that you can't stop if the rider in front has to stop quickly. Stay slightly to one side, like the cyclists in Fig. 2-56, so that if he does stop, you will have clearance to get past him. Racing cyclists take turns drafting each other all the time, and they know how to do it. Drafting is especially helpful when you're riding into a stiff wind.

Fig. 2-56: The rider on the left in this photo, next to the shoulder stripe, is "drafting" behind the rider in front of her. She is also in the safest position, a bit to the side of the front rider.

Slippery Roads

With good tires (Fig. 2-57) you can ride on snow up to about three inches deep. I routinely pedaled over snowy roads when I commuted to work 12 miles from my suburban home to downtown Chicago. I only quit when the streets became snow-packed, or when it had snowed over ice. Freshly fallen snow provides a surprising amount of traction. Of course, an all-terrain bike (Fig. 2-58) with its fat, knobby tread tires (Fig. 2-59), is much better for riding in the snow than road bikes with skinnier, smoother tires (Fig. 2-57). You can even take a road bike through water, though I prefer to do this with an all-terrain bike (Fig. 2-60). In autumn, be careful about riding on leaf-strewn streets, especially right after a rainfall. Wet leaves are almost as slippery as ice.

Fig. 2-57: You *can* ride in snow, but it's not easy.

Fig. 2-58: This rider was riding on snow until the grade became too tough. He's crossing Oregon's McKenzie Pass on Route 242, altitude 5,342 feet, in July! *(Bikecentennial Photo)*

Fig. 2-59: Use this knobby-tread tire on your ATB for traction in snow.

Fig. 2-60: You can also pedal through water, but be prepared to shift down before you hit liquid—and be ready to fall if you don't have enough speed up when you hit.

Radios Are a No-No

Don't mix bicycling with those handlebar-mounted radios or the kind you clamp over your ears. They prevent you from hearing traffic noises around you, such as warning honks from motorists and sirens from emergency vehicles that alert you to danger. These radios also distract you from paying close attention to the myriad street hazards I have discussed in previous pages, such as potholes, kids darting into the street, or doors of parked cars opening in front of you, to name just a few. If you're listening to the radio you won't be alert to sounds from your bicycle that warn of impending mechanical failure, such as the ping of a broken spoke, the tap of embedded glass in a tire, the grinding of a mis-shifted chain. Some states recognize the hazards of radios on bicycles and have made them illegal. With a radio blaring in your ears, you also miss the music of the wind, the rustle of leaves, rippling sounds of waves, the songs of birds —in short, all the lovely sounds of the great outdoors.

What You Should Know About Dogs and Other Animals

I like dogs. I have one, an endearing little cocker spaniel whose joy in life is chasing anything that moves—bikes, other dogs, cats, cars, birds, rabbits, you name it. If the cyclist dismounts, my dog wags his tail and becomes very friendly. But other dogs may not be so playful. I've been chased down rural roads by big German shepherd farm dogs, aching to bite me or my bike. On the flats I could outrun them, but on a hill they are a problem. The literature of bicycling has many examples of dogs that have caused serious bicycle accidents, either by running into the bike or by biting the cyclist after he has stopped.

For whatever reason, dogs of any size or shape may attack a cyclist. In particular, be *very* suspicious of Doberman pinschers, bulldogs, weimaraners, German shepherds, pit bulls, and all black dogs. The friendliest of some family pets can turn into attack animals as you cycle past. Friends who have been bitten tell me that the owner usually says: "Why, I can't understand why Fido would bite you. You must have aggravated him

terribly. The children all love him, he's so gentle and friendly!"
So is a mother grizzly bear to her cubs.

Dogs often attack silently. If you hear hard breathing and the
patter of rapidly moving feet from behind, it's going to be a dog
on the attack. Dogs cheat, too. They will wait until you start a
hill climb and then chase after you. Or, if they're in a yard,
they'll cut at an angle across the lawn to get to you.

Here's how to prevent being bitten or knocked off your bike
by a dog:

1. Most dogs can run up to 15 miles an hour but only for a very
   short distance. So if you can outrun it, that's your best bet.
2. If you can't outrun the animal, stop and dismount. Analyze
   the dog's body language. If it avoids eye contact, looks to
   one side, exposes its body by lying upside down, seems to
   grin at you, keeps its body close to the ground and its tail
   down or wagging, chances are it means to be friendly. Until
   you get back on the bike, after which the chase may start
   again.
3. However, never look the animal straight in the eye. If his
   body is tense, ears up, teeth bared in a snarl, and he growls,
   urinates, and paws the ground with a front foot, he is after
   your blood. You might try easing the tension by speaking
   softly. Don't extend your hand if you want it back. Be sub-
   missive, even though that thought is anathema to all cyclists.
   If the beast wants to come up and sniff you, let him do so,
   but don't sniff back.
4. If it looks as if the dog is really going to attack, I recommend
   you spray it with Halt, which is a relatively harmless dog
   repellent carried by postal carriers, meter readers, and delivery people. A chemical spray called Mace is much more
   effective than Halt.
5. If you carry and use either Halt or Mace and any of the spray
   falls on a person, especially a child, you could be in for a
   lawsuit. If you'd like to carry a non-chemical dog repellent,
   try the small hand-held electronic sound generator, called
   the Dog Chaser (Fig. 2-61). I loaned mine to my postal carrier, who reported that it did, indeed, deter dogs from an
   attack. The Dog Chaser, according to the manufacturer,
   "emits a high-frequency sound that causes extreme discomfort to the attacking dog. Dogs simply cannot stand the high-

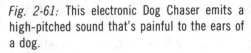

Fig. 2-61: This electronic Dog Chaser emits a high-pitched sound that's painful to the ears of a dog.

pitched sound, and the closer they come, the greater the degree of pain." I think that this gadget, if widely used by cyclists, would soon train dogs to keep away. It's not inexpensive at $61, but it lasts for years, with an occasional change of batteries. Pressurized sprays, on the other hand, have a limited shelf life and may be lifeless when you need them most. The Dog Chaser is available from Spencer Aircraft Industries, Inc., 8410 Dallas Avenue South, Seattle, WA 98106.

6. Don't try to strike a dog while you ride. You may not stop the dog and it could cause you to lose control of the bike.

If you are bitten, try to track the dog home so it can be checked for rabies. Treatment for rabies these days is much less painful than it used to be, but still, it would be nice to know whether or not you have been exposed to the virus. You should notify the city or county health authorities as soon as possible, so they can hold the dog for as long as it takes to check it for rabies. If you are badly hurt, you need a good attorney who can instigate litigation on your behalf. I urge you to take such action, because dog owners are reluctant to restrain their animals and further attacks are very likely.

All-terrain cyclists who travel on trails into the wilderness face a few special hazards from animals. Never pet or approach a wild animal. If you're going into the wilderness, carry a snake-bite kit and know how to use it. I'll never forget the time I was riding my ATB on a narrow, twisting mountain trail. Around one sharp corner I saw a rattlesnake sunning itself in the middle of the trail. I couldn't avoid it—the trail was too narrow. So I pulled my front wheel up and wheelied over the snake. My rear wheel did go over it, but the snake had no chance to bite me, or I don't think it did.

Larger mammals can be a hazard to cyclists, particularly if you happen upon them unexpectedly, especially if the animal is a female bear with cubs, for instance. If you run into a bear, rangers and wildlife authorities instruct that outrunning it is the safest action. But, they warn, a bear can run up to 30 miles per hour for a short distance. A black bear may simply walk away if you wait patiently, but they can climb trees, so don't try to escape them that way. Grizzly bears can't climb trees, so keep that in mind in the *extremely* rare event that you would be confronted by one on the trail. As a last resort, authorities also direct that you lie down and play dead, an action the implications of which leave me somewhat less than enthusiastic. But if that's your only recourse, do it. For more information on riding in the wilderness, I urge you to read my book *Eugene A. Sloane's Complete Book of All-Terrain Bicycles.*

Children's Plastic Trikes

Children's little plastic tricycles (Fig. 2-62) can be hazardous to kids and adults. They have no brakes. Their low profile makes them hard to see from the driver's seat of a vehicle. I have

Fig. 2-62: These little plastic trikes can be dangerous. Their low profile makes them hard to see from the driver's seat of a vehicle.

Fig. 2-63: Children on plastic trikes can get up to 8 to 10 mph on these things.

Fig. 2-64: Young children may not pay attention to street traffic or look right and left before proceeding. Let them ride only with adult supervision, or in a playground or other safe area.

timed children at speed on them and can report that they can get up to eight miles per hour. Stronger kids can probably do ten mph for a short time.

Children cannot be depended on to stop, look both ways, and then cross the street on these trikes, as shown in Figs. 2-63 and 2-64. I know of two cases in which children on these trikes have been hit by cars and now, tragically, are quadriplegics. If your child has one of these trikes, stay with him or her while riding, or restrict riding to a supervised play area.

Miscellaneous Safety Tips About Riding

On a downhill run keep your speed under control and grip the top tube between your knees. This will help to keep both your body and the bike from wobbling, and may prevent wheel shimmy if your bike is so inclined.

As you approach a hill, shift to a lower gear before starting your climb. If you delay shifting until the going is hard, you may find it difficult or impossible to shift down. You may either have to ease off pedaling pressure by turning from one side of the road to the other (not the safest of procedures), or stop, lift up the back wheel, twirl the pedals, shift down, and start up again. Manufacturers of the latest wide-range derailleur systems claim you can shift while climbing steep hills. My experience tells me otherwise.

One hazard of shifting while hill climbing is that the chain may not shift accurately, so it lies partially on one gear and partly on another. The chain may not grab the teeth of the rear or front cogs and may slip. If the chain slips while you are exerting pedal pressure, the pedal will slip forward and you could very well lose your balance and fall off the bike, or inadvertently steer to the left into another cyclist or into a vehicle.

About "Slick" tires: "Slick" (totally bald) tires (Fig. 2-65) are a recent innovation. These tires come in sizes for both road and all-terrain bicycles. Manufacturers claim that because the tire has a smooth layer of rubber instead of a patterned tread, they grip the road better because there's more rubber on the road. I'm not sure where this story will end. All I can say now is that at least one serious injury has occurred to a cyclist whose bike

Fig. 2-65: "Slick" or bald treadless tires are new to the bicycling scene. They come in sizes to fit both road and all-terrain bikes. It's claimed that the slicks, like the tire at the left, give greater road adhesion because there's more rubber on the road than with conventional or knobby tires (right).

slid sideways on his first ride with the slicks. He had changed from knobby tires on his all-terrain bike to the bald tires. On his first sharp turn, the rear wheel skidded and the bike fell. He had been making the same turn, on the same road, with the same bike with knobby tires for years. This is a statistically insignificant sample of one, so we'll see what time brings.

The next chapter will tell you all about the health aspects of cycling and review what you should know about diet and the prevention of injuries and what to do about them if you are injured.

References: WEAR A HELMET AT ALL TIMES!
1. Lewiston, Diana: *Two Year Bicycle Accident Survey, July, 1981, Through June, 1983,* Palo Alto, CA.
2. Karlson, Trudy A., M.S.: *The Incidence of Hospital-Treated Facial Injuries From Vehicles:* Center for Health Systems, University of Wisconsin, Madison, WI.
3. Hodgson, V. R., Director, Gurdjian-Lissner Biomechanics Laboratory, Department of Neurosurgery, Wayne State University, Detroit, MI: *Improving Head Crash Protection.*
4. Fife, Daniel, MD., et al: *Fatal Injuries to Bicyclists: The Experience of Dade County, Florida.* The Journal of Trauma, vol. 23, No. 8.

Fig. 3-1: These are the leg muscles of a dedicated cyclist.

Chapter

THREE

BICYCLING YOUR WAY TO A HEALTHIER YOU

Bicycling is *great* exercise! It keeps your body flexible, muscles firm, and belly tight. Best of all, cycling is a stress-free way to lifelong health. You can tailor a workout to fit your physical condition and age, without risk of overdoing it or of damage to joints and muscles. You can pedal slowly if you're just beginning a physical fitness program, or faster if you're already in good shape and want to stay that way. Bicycling strengthens your heart, reduces blood pressure if it's too high, improves the ability of lungs to deliver oxygen to your muscles, and keeps your energy level up all day. Combined with a sensible diet, bicycling is a terrific way to lose weight and stay slender. Here's why bicycling is good for your heart, muscles (Fig. 3-1), and lungs.

WEIGHT CONTROL

You can lose weight by combining a sensible low-calorie diet with cycling exercise. For example, let's say you weigh 180 pounds, 30 pounds more than the slimmer you of a few years ago. You'd like to lose those 30 pounds, permanently. If you have a sedentary job, you need about 15 calories per pound of body weight, or 2,700 calories a day ($15 \times 180 = 2,700$) just to stay at your 180 pounds. If you ride a bike ten miles per hour for one hour, you'll consume 350 of your unwanted calories. Drop your daily caloric intake to 2,450 and you'll save another 250 calories—that's a daily total of 600 calories. Since each pound of body fat is equivalent to 3,500 calories, you need to lose, over time, 105,000 calories to reach 150 pounds. Diet plus biking can do it in about six months ($105,000 \div 600 \div 30 = 5.8$ months). By then your ticker will be stronger, your blood pressure down, your energy level up, and you'll be able to ride your bike farther and faster than you ever thought possible.

OTHER BENEFITS OF CYCLING

The heart becomes a more efficient pump: Because it is strengthened and enlarged, the heart beats more forcefully. It pumps more blood with each beat. So, more oxygen is delivered to the extremities, where it's used to fuel muscle activity. The heart beats slower, both at rest and during exercise, because it works more efficiently. The heart of a trained cyclist can pump the same amount of blood with one-third fewer beats than the heart of someone who is out of shape. That makes for less wear and tear to the heart over the course of a lifetime.

Lung capacity increases: Conditioned cyclists need to take fewer breaths and their hearts can deliver more oxygen to the muscle with less effort at any given level of activity.

Blood pressure is reduced: Blood pressure rises less during exercise, and is also lower at rest. Exercise helps reduce the blood pressure of people who suffer from hypertension. High blood pressure contributes to the incidence of heart attacks and strokes.

The blood's clotting mechanism is affected: Vigorous cycling dramatically increases the blood's anti-clotting activity, inhibiting the formation of clots that can clog blood vessels and precipitate heart attacks and strokes.

Cholesterol deposits in the arteries are reduced: Vigorous cycling helps to clear away cholesterol deposits, which can lead to clogged and hardened arteries, and may eventually cause a heart attack or stroke.

A program of vigorous exercise can't guarantee you will never develop cardiovascular disease. That ultimately depends on a host of risk factors, including your diet, the amount of stress you commonly work under, and your hereditary predisposition to the disease. However, vigorous cycling can certainly reduce the risk of heart attacks and strokes.

A WAY OF FITNESS FOR EVERYBODY

If you are just starting a program of physical fitness, remember that it never pays to overdo it. Exercise physiologists stress that you should always give your body a day's rest after a bout of strenuous exercise. This allows time for the muscles to get rid of metabolic waste products that are left over after a hard workout. It also gives time to repair and replace muscle tissue that is torn during vigorous exercise. Athletes in training live by the adage, "no pain, no gain." That's because they can only reach peak performance by continually pushing beyond their present physical limits. If you're not a conditioned athlete, however, pushing too hard could give you injuries that may plague you for a long time to come.

Get to know your physical limits, and push against them a little at a time. Don't expect to go from being a slouch to an example of prime fitness overnight. If you do too much at first, you will either wear yourself out and won't want to exercise anymore, or you will hurt yourself and be put out of commission altogether. Pain is the surest sign that you are going too far. When you reach that threshold, back off. Once you have committed yourself to a fitness program, improvement occurs so quickly that you really won't have to push it. Moreover, those in the worst shape due to years of inactivity will witness the most dramatic improvement as they exercise.

Here's a word of caution for people over 35 who want to get fit. If many years have passed since you regularly exercised, or if your family has a history of heart problems, you should consult a doctor before beginning a program of strenuous exercise. This should include an electrocardiogram, which determines the presence of any irregularities in heart activity. People over the age of 50 should probably have this examination regardless of their previous level of activity. People over the age of 60 should choose less vigorous kinds of exercise, unless they have exercised regularly for years or can gradually condition themselves in a fitness program that is supervised by their doctor. People over 60 should also get a regular physical exam, including an electrocardiogram, every year.

Cycling Tailors Exercise to Ability

Cycling gives you the option of working out at any level of activity. If you are out of shape to begin with, you can start with short rides at a relaxed pace. Over the course of several weeks, maybe even several months, you should increase the duration and the pace of your rides. Eventually, long daily rides at moderate speed should form the basis of your program. Try to cover five to ten miles at a pace of ten to 12 miles per hour, depending upon your own level of fitness and the amount that you feel you can "push" yourself without strain. Avoid using excessively high gears. It's likely to give you an injury. Try to maintain a cadence (the number of pedal revolutions per minute) of about 70 rpm.

Real aerobic training begins as you intersperse workouts of 45 minutes to one hour of fast-paced riding in the exercise routine described above. Fifteen miles per hour or more would be a fast pace. That means you would be covering ten miles in

40 minutes or less. For most riders, such a level of activity would tax the heart and lungs to the upper range of their capacities. To collect the full aerobic benefit for your cardiovascular system, take fast-paced rides regularly, but no more than three or four times per week. In fact, if you really work out hard one day, it would be best to do less than your normal moderate ride on the following day. Or you could give yourself a break and take the next day off altogether.

How long it takes to work up to a fast-paced routine depends on your physical condition at the outset, as well as your sense of dedication. It may take some people months of exercise just to be able to ride several miles every day at any pace. The important thing to remember is that you are trying to develop an active lifestyle, and that this lifestyle will be yours for a long time to come. You need to develop an exercise routine that you can practice every day, without becoming bored. Too many people have jumped headlong into a newly active life, only to burn out from overexertion early on.

Staying in Shape All Year Long

Here's another good reason to make cycling the core of your exercise routine: Cycling is a reliable and energy-efficient form of transportation. It can be difficult to fit regular exercise periods into your working day. But, with cycling, you can get a daily workout as you commute back and forth to your job. At one time I commuted eight miles by bike every day. Even though I had to fight traffic, I could make it in the same time it took to drive my car, find a parking place, and walk the last few blocks to my destination. It was a 35-minute ride on most days, and some days I even beat my average time by car. That's quite enough for good aerobic training.

Of course, for those of us living in the "moderate" climate of North America, there comes a time each year when the weather can make riding difficult, if not downright dangerous. Still, you don't need to let it keep you from exercising regularly. In the winter months, when cycling outdoors becomes impractical, a number of activities can be used to maintain your fair-weather level of fitness.

Stationary Cycling

Stationary cycling is one of the most popular forms of winter exercise for the cyclist. Cycling indoors provides exercise with total convenience. With a cycling machine, or with your bike on a windtrainer (Figs. 3-2, 3-3) or rollers (Fig. 3-4), you can have all the benefits of a gym in your own home. An extra half-

Fig. 3-2: Exercise on a trainer like this APX Blackburn Designs windtrainer. Your bike installs and removes from this sturdy windtrainer quickly and easily. The blower under the rear wheel simulates pedaling resistance, which can be as little or as great as you like, depending on the gear you're in. This rider is warming up before going outside to ride (you won't need cycling togs or helmet for inside riding).

Fig. 3-3: This compact Pacer-mate indoor windtrainer can be stored in a closet when you're finished exercising.

Fig. 3-4: Bike rollers are a bit tricky to master but you can get a workout while you learn to balance.

hour to 45 minutes every morning is all it takes to maintain an optimal level of physical conditioning throughout the year. Before you leave for work, you can already have finished a daily workout, an activity which most people find revitalizes them for the day ahead.

The main disadvantage of indoor cycling is that it tends to get rather boring after a while. However, there are ways to compensate for this. You can take advantage of the time you spend exercising to improve yourself in other ways. Take the time to really concentrate on something. Turn on the radio or TV, tune in to the morning news, and find out what is happening in the world. Set a stand (Fig. 3-5) in front of yourself and read some good literature. Or put the bike in front of a window and relax as you watch the world come to life for another day.

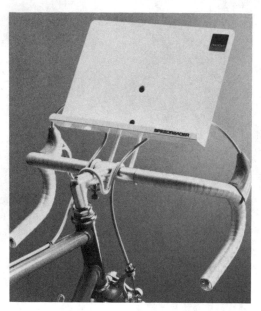

Fig. 3-5: Relieve the monotony of indoor training by watching TV or reading a book on a reading stand like this one from Blackburn Designs. The stand is sturdy and clips on and off the handlebars quickly.

Using the Heart-Rate Target Zone

Whatever technique you use, it's important to find a way to keep motivated in a program of stationary cycling. Many people find that the most successful technique is to keep track of the progress they are making. This is where indoor cycling has an advantage over cycling outdoors. It allows you to determine precisely how long and how hard you need to exercise.

You can use a simple formula to determine the level of exercise needed to attain cardiovascular fitness. Physiologists say that you need to work out until your heart is beating at 75 percent of its maximum rate. The maximum rate for you depends on your age. For example, start with a heart rate of 220 beats per minute and subtract one beat for every year of your age. Multiply by .75 to get your 75 percent maximum heart rate (Fig. 3-6). So, for a 20-year-old person the value would be

$$220 - 20 = 200$$
$$200 \text{ x } .75 = 150 \text{ beats per minute.}$$

Others recommend exercising within a target zone of 60 percent to 85 percent. Remember that your maximum heart rate

Fig. 3-6: When you exercise, work out hard enough to reach your heart-rate target zone. For example, if you're 40 years old your heart rate should be between 125 and 150 beats per minute.

also depends a lot on your physical condition. If you have any doubts, see your physician.

Several of the stationary cycling machines on the market have devices that monitor your pulse rate as you cycle. Some are even equipped with onboard computers that are programmed to give an electronic signal, like a light or a beep, when your exercise level has dropped below the target zone. When you find that you need to be working out harder, you can increase the pedaling resistance on the cycling machine.

If you use your own bike on a windtrainer, you can use gadgets that keep track of your heart rate. There are some high-tech devices on the market that can be worn like a wristwatch and automatically read your pulse. Another style straps or clips to the handlebars, and measures the pulse in your finger or your earlobe. The latter varieties are relatively inexpensive, unlike the wireless watch types, which can cost several hundred dollars.

Use the pulse meter to monitor your pace over the course of your exercise session. The chart (Fig. 3-7) shows the typical target zone exercise pattern for the average 40-year-old man.

Fig. 3-7: Warm up gradually, as shown by this chart. Don't try to reach your heart-rate target zone immediately, and cool down gradually toward the end of your exercise period.

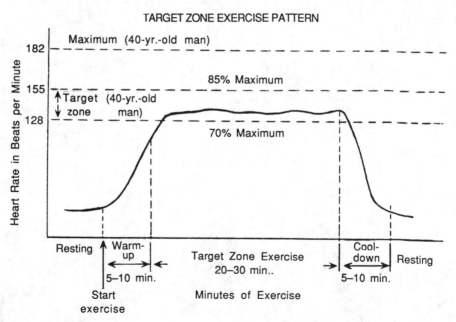

Set the pedaling resistance low, and begin pedaling with a ten-minute warm-up phase. The warm-up will prevent painful leg cramps, caused by pedaling too fast. Gradually increase the resistance until you work up to your 75 percent heart rate maximum. Continue to exercise with your heart rate at the desired level for 20 to 25 minutes, maintaining a cadence of about 80 to 85 rpm. To determine cadence, use a watch with a second hand and count the number of times your right or left leg reaches the top of its stroke in one minute. At the end of 25 minutes of strenuous workout, decrease the resistance and keep pedaling at a relaxed pace for another five to ten minutes. This helps to rid the muscles of lactic acid, which can make your legs stiff and sore.

Until you get used to it, you are likely to think the pedaling is too easy and the resistance should be increased. However, you need to remember that you are not working against the resistance of the road on your tires or the wind on your body as you would while riding on the street. Neither are you taking advantage of the bike's forward momentum to coast. Resist the temptation to turn up the resistance or shift to a higher gear too early. The constant movement of your legs on the pedals is enough to get your heart working and the blood pumping hard in a very short time. At all times you should pay attention to the body's vital signs, such as heart rate, respiratory rate, and how hot you feel or how much you are sweating. *If at any time you begin to experience dizziness, extreme shortness of breath, irregular heart action, or pain, stop exercising immediately. Consult your doctor.*

Compatible Exercises

If you try everything and indoor cycling is still a bore, you might turn to another aerobic exercise to fill the winter cycling void. Actually, any vigorous exercise can be used to maintain aerobic capacity throughout the year, so long as it is practiced regularly. In order to prepare yourself for cycling, however, you should be conscious of what kind of workout your body is getting. Running, cross-country skiing, and speed skating are three activities highly compatible to cycling in terms of their aerobic potential, as well as the muscle groups that are used.

PHYSIOLOGY OF THE CONDITIONED CYCLIST

Proper physical conditioning significantly improves a cyclist's ability to perform. Oxygen supply to the muscles is the crucial factor. The rider who is in top physical condition (Fig. 3-8) has more wind. The reason for this should be obvious by now. Under stress, our hearts beat faster, and we begin to breathe hard because the muscles are demanding more oxygen. Conditioned riders have lower heart rates to begin with, larger lung capacities, and better developed cardiovascular systems. They don't need to huff and puff so much to get the oxygen they need. In this way, their bodies conserve energy, and they go farther before wearing out.

Fig. 3-8: This healthy woman is a good example of what regular cycling exercise can do.

A stronger heart and circulatory system can more easily get oxygen to muscle tissue, where it's used to burn the body's fuel. Mostly, our bodies use fatty acids and glucose for fuel. In the presence of oxygen from the blood, these substances undergo a complex chemical transformation. During metabolism, fuel and oxygen are converted into water and carbon dioxide, and energy is released. Without enough oxygen, the process won't be complete. Other waste products will be left over and less energy will be generated. The same kind of thing happens when the carburetor on your car isn't working as it should to mix air and gas together. The car goes half the distance with less power on the same amount of gas and puts out clouds of black smoke, which is actually unburned or only partially burned fuel.

Fatty acids and glucose are derived from the digestion of fats and carbohydrates. After digestion, glucose and fatty acids enter the bloodstream, where most are used as fuel for working muscles, nervous system activity, and other bodily functions. Food that is not immediately used for energy is converted into body fat, and used later for meeting the body's energy needs.

Excess glucose is also converted by the liver and the muscles into glycogen. Sometimes called animal starch, glycogen is a complex structure of several glucose molecules. Glycogen is stored in the liver and muscles for future energy use. When blood sugar drops too low, liver glycogen is reconverted to glucose and released into the bloodstream, primarily to provide glucose to the brain. Muscle glycogen is used when glucose and fat in the blood can no longer supply the energy demands of the exercising muscle.

As energy demand increases through exercise, the muscle's energy source changes. At rest, the energy used by muscle tissue is minimal. Most of the resting muscle's energy needs are met by fatty acids in the blood. During light exercise, blood sugar is utilized along with fatty acids for energy. Little or no muscle glycogen is used until the body is exercising quite vigorously. During maximal aerobic output by the muscles, energy is derived almost totally from muscle glycogen stores.

These are all examples of aerobic metabolism, that is, metabolism occurring in the presence of oxygen. During extremely strenuous physical activity, as in a sprint, energy demand can completely outstrip the body's ability to supply oxygen to working muscles. When this happens, a process called anaerobic metabolism occurs. The oxygen-starved muscles are capable of performing at very high levels of energy output for short periods of time. However, there is a drawback. Anaerobic metabolism is an inefficient process. Since it occurs without oxygen, complete metabolism of glycogen into carbon dioxide and water cannot occur. Large amounts of waste products, especially lactic acid, are produced during anaerobic activity. Build-up of lactic acid in the muscles is one of the reasons you can feel very stiff the day after a real workout.

The accumulation of lactic acid contributes to the onset of fatigue, since increased acidity of the blood interferes with nerve and muscle function. The depletion of glycogen stores and blood sugar eventually culminates in the "wall" or the "bonks," a point at which the body can't sustain further vigorous activity. A cyclist hitting the wall may drop from exhaustion. In effect, the brain is telling the body to stop, because any remaining glucose will be needed to keep the brain going.

Since oxygen delivery to the muscles is higher for the conditioned cyclist, metabolism is more likely to be complete. More energy is produced from the same amount of fuel, and fewer waste products accumulate. Greater blood flow clears lactic acid from the muscles more rapidly. Conditioned cyclists also use more fatty acids for fuel, which helps to conserve glycogen stores. Since the depletion of glycogen stores and the build-up of lactic acid are primary causes of fatigue, conditioned riders can perform longer before fatigue sets in.

The Importance of Diet

You can own one of the most sophisticated and finely tuned racing machines in the world, but you won't win any races if you run it on low-octane gasoline. The same goes for the amazing machinery of the human body. If you expect it to perform, you have to provide it with high-quality fuel. Unfortunately, it isn't so simple as a choice between good and bad food. It's more a matter of balance, and in order to achieve that balance you should know how the body uses the food you put into it.

Tests have been conducted to determine what kind of diet results in the highest level of athletic performance. In one study, the subjects were fed a mixed diet of protein, fat, and carbohydrates. Then they worked out on stationary bikes until they became exhausted. They were able to exercise for an average of 1 hour and 54 minutes before they had to quit. After three days of eating a high-protein, high-fat diet, they got back on the bikes. This time they exercised only 57 minutes before they became exhausted. Finally, the group ate a carbohydrate-rich diet for three days. When they got on the bikes again, they were able to exercise continuously for 2 hours and 47 minutes.

In spite of all the folk beliefs about protein, it isn't an important source of energy. Protein is used by your body to maintain muscle and other body tissue. Use of protein for energy is minimal, however, and only plays a significant role during starvation, when nothing else is available and the body begins to consume itself in order to stay alive. The long-term need of the exercising cyclist for protein is what's important here. You need your muscles in order to move, and you need more protein than the sedentary person to keep those muscles in good shape. But the task of keeping them fueled goes to other nutrients altogether.

Carbohydrates are the most important source of energy to the exercising muscle. Fats come in second, only because it is harder for the body to release energy from them. It takes twice as much oxygen to get the same amount of energy from fat as it does from carbohydrate. At the same time, fat provides concentrated energy. One gram of fat produces twice the energy of one gram of carbohydrate. So, since it takes longer to metabolize, fat is better fuel for the long haul.

As activity level rises and falls, the body's dietary needs change. During periods of high physical stress, like on a long bike tour, you should have a large daily intake of carbohydrates. Eat plenty of bread, grains, beans, fruits and vegetables to ensure that you have plenty of fuel to burn. When you are vigorously exercising every day, you need more calories, and fat provides concentrated energy. However, it's important to be aware of two things. First, excess carbohydrates and protein are converted into body fat. You don't have to eat much fat to meet bodily needs. Second, the average American diet is entirely too high in fat. Currently, Americans get 40 percent of their calories from fat. A figure of 30 percent or less is considered ideal. Diets rich in fat have actually been shown to decrease athletic performance.

If you follow an intense program of physical conditioning, you will be putting a lot of wear and tear on muscle tissue, and will also have greater protein needs. However, here again you need to use caution. Foods like red meat, eggs, and cheese are concentrated sources of protein. But they also contain large amounts of fat and cholesterol. Foods high in fat generally take longer to digest. Eating protein-rich foods that are also low-fat, like fish and beans, will help keep your fat intake down. Plant sources contain lower-quality protein, but by combining beans with bread and grains, or with small amounts of meat, fish, and dairy products, you can get all the protein you need, with plenty of carbohydrates too.

In general, the best diet would contain about 58 percent carbohydrates, 12 percent to 15 percent protein, and 30 percent or less fat. It is also better to eat complex carbohydrates, like bread, rice, pasta, and potatoes, than to eat refined carbohydrates like sugar or honey. Beyond their use for quick energy, refined sugars have little or no nutritional value. Furthermore, complex carbohydrates are digested and absorbed more slowly, so they will provide you with energy over a longer period of time. A diet high in complex carbohydrates helps the cyclist to avoid the dreaded "bonks."

Dieticians stress that as long as you eat a balanced diet, you will get all the vitamins and minerals your body needs. However, there is a lot of debate about this subject within medical and sports nutrition circles. Some researchers claim that vitamin supplements increase vitality and are helpful in preventing illness. Others believe that the risks outweigh the benefits. They point out that the fat-soluble vitamins—A, D, E, and K— can be toxic if taken excessively. If you decide to take vitamin and mineral supplements, remember that more is not always better.

Eat a variety of foods to get vitamins and minerals in balanced proportion. Eat food as fresh as you can get it, to be assured that it contains the highest possible vitamin content. Some vitamins are lost during storage; processing, overcooking, and time also contribute to the loss of vitamins in food. A number of minerals can be lost through sweat during strenuous activity. The greatest mineral losses are of salt, potassium, calcium, magnesium, and iron. Make up these losses through the food you eat, if possible. Vitamin and mineral supplements may be advisable if you are under heavy physical stress and do not have access to good meals.

If you are taking up cycling in order to lose weight, you are making a good choice. The average cyclist riding at six miles per hour, a fairly easy pace for most people, can burn about 200 calories in one hour. Increase your pace to 13 miles per hour, and you are using up to 500 calories per hour! Just remember: If you are working out regularly, your body has a constant energy demand that can only be filled by a steady caloric intake. Don't try to work out on a 1,000 calorie, high-protein diet. Your body is going to need carbohydrates to keep up with the higher energy expenditures. And don't be discouraged if after you lose some weight, you begin to put it back on. What's probably happening is that you are building muscle, which weighs more than fat.

A Word About Cholesterol

Interestingly enough, the best diet for athletic performance is roughly the same as that recommended by the medical community to reduce your risk of developing heart disease and cancer. Both the U.S. Department of Agriculture and the American Cancer Society say that we eat too much fat, red meat, and refined sugars for our own good. They recommend eating more carbohydrates, more fruits and vegetables, and more foods high in dietary fiber. Research suggests that a diet like this helps stem the development of heart disease and cancer.

The link between excessive consumption of cholesterol and heart disease is well known. We hear so many warnings about eating this stuff that the very sound of the word has become something evil in itself. So, it may surprise you to hear that cholesterol is essential for maintaining your health. The body uses cholesterol to make certain hormones. It is an ingredient in bile salts, which aid in food digestion. And cholesterol in the membranes that cover the body cells keeps them from being dissolved by our bodily fluids.

The problem comes when we eat too much of it. 80 percent of our entire bodily need for cholesterol is met by the liver, where it is produced. Only 20 percent comes from the food we eat. The consumption of too much fatty food results in elevated levels of cholesterol in the blood, where it has the potential for inflicting serious harm. When too much cholesterol is present in the blood, particles of it become lodged in the artery walls. Over time, deposits of cholesterol can grow and obstruct the passage of blood.

Blood clots form around the obstructions. Clots may get too big, or else break loose, and completely block the flow of blood. When the clot lodges in one of the coronary arteries that carry blood to the heart, oxygen is cut off to the area supplied by the clogged artery. This kills muscle cells in the area, in what we commonly call a heart attack. If a clot obstructs an artery in the brain, a stroke results. Either condition can be permanently debilitating. And, as we all know, they are often fatal.

The good news is that cycling can help reduce cholesterol deposition in the arteries. Maybe you have heard lately about something called "good" cholesterol. What that really means is that the cholesterol-carrying substances in our blood can roughly be divided into two types, called high-density lipoprotein (HDL) and low-density lipoprotein (LDL). HDL is believed to be able to clear deposits of cholesterol from the blood vessels and help the body to excrete it. In a study involving cyclists in the Boston area, exercise was shown to increase the ratio of HDL to total cholesterol in the blood. Those riders who averaged 77 miles per week showed favorable blood levels of HDL. In effect, regular cycling cut their risk of heart attack in half.

Warm Up Before You Work Out

If a dog or cat lives at your house, watch it the next time it gets up from one of its many naps. It won't go anywhere without a good stretch of the back and legs first. Animals seem to know intuitively something that most of us forgot long ago. For one, they relax every chance they get. But more important, they know that muscles and joints have to be loose before they can move as they should.

You should know it too. Placing undue stress upon muscles that have not been properly warmed up is a common cause of sports- and work-related injuries. Muscles that have grown tight through disuse and habitually poor posture are a contributing factor to a host of ailments, including headaches and back pain. Stretching is so important that if you are planning a regular exercise program, you should begin by establishing a daily routine of stretching first. Preferably it is something you should do every morning if you can. It is something you must do immediately before and after a heavy workout.

Here's why. Muscles are composed of many intercrossed fibers. When they have been inactive for some time, all those intercrossing fibers get a little stuck together. That's the reason you usually feel stiffest in the morning when you first wake up. The only way to get them unstuck is to warm them up, and you do that best by pumping warm blood through them. If they aren't warmed first, muscle fibers are likely to tear and cause painful injuries, as anyone who has "pulled" a muscle in their back or neck can tell you.

You need to ease into your exercise routine with some gentle stretching exercises. Then, when you start cycling, begin at an easy pace for the first five to ten minutes to make sure that muscles are fully supplied with warm blood. Include about a five- to ten-minute cooldown period at a relaxed pace toward the end of your ride. When you finish the workout, repeat some of the major stretches. This does two things. It helps to loosen up muscle fibers that have shortened and tightened up during the workout. It also helps to prevent lactic acid build-up, which can make your muscles sore.

Whatever you do, don't bounce when you stretch. Bouncing only heightens nerve impulses and causes muscle to contract, just the opposite of what you are trying to accomplish. Remember: Slow and sustained elongation of muscle fibers is what does it. Stretch as far as you can without feeling undue pain. As you get into better shape, you will be able to stretch more fully with less discomfort. Here's a description of a few of the most important stretches to do before riding.

Neck and Shoulders (Fig. 3-9): Cyclists are particularly prone to neck and shoulder pain, because they spend a lot of time hunched over the handlebars. Loosen these muscles with a few minutes of neck rolls at the beginning of your stretching routine. First move in one direction, then reverse and roll your head around the opposite way. Move your head around slowly, feeling the muscles stretch one at a time. If you work at a desk,

Fig. 3-9: Prevent neck and shoulder muscle pain with a few minutes of neck rolls at the beginning of your stretching routine. Roll your head around, first on one side, then on the other side. Feel how your muscles stretch as you move your head. If you sit at a desk this exercise will keep your neck and shoulder muscles flexible.

or do something else that requires a lot of concentration and little movement, you will probably be surprised at the stiffness you feel when you do this simple stretch.

Quadriceps and Lower Back (Figs. 3-10, 3-11): The powerful quadriceps muscles in the upper leg are prone to painful cramping (the infamous "charley horse") if not stretched properly before exercise. Muscles in the back must be kept supple

Fig. 3-10: The powerful quadriceps muscles in the upper leg are prone to painful cramping (the infamous "charley horse") if not stretched properly before exercise. To stretch the quads, sit down on your buttocks with both legs drawn up close to your sides. Move either foot around from underneath and place it flat against the opposite knee. Repeat with the other foot.

Fig. 3-11: Prevent lower back pain by keeping back muscles supple. Place both hands on the floor behind you, lift your buttocks up off the floor and twist your lower back as shown. Hold this position for ten seconds. Repeat with the other leg.

to avoid lower back pain. To stretch both muscle groups in one position, sit down flat on your buttocks with your legs drawn up close to your sides. Move either your left or right foot around from underneath and place it flat against the opposite knee. With your hands directly behind you, lift your buttocks off the ground and twist your lower back as shown. Hold for a count of ten. Repeat. Then do the same for the other side. You should be able to feel the stretch in the large muscle on top of your thigh, and in the muscles of your lower back .

Hamstrings (Fig. 3-12): This is an important stretch to do both before and after a workout. Tension in the hamstrings is a common cause of lower back pain. Sit flat on the ground with your legs straight out before you. Draw one leg up close to your body and place the foot against the opposite leg, as shown. Stretch your arms forward to the foot of the outstretched leg, as far as you can go without feeling undue pain. Hold for a count of ten. Repeat. Then do the same for the other leg.

Fig. 3-12: Prevent tension in hamstring muscles with this stretch routine before and after exercise. Sit on the floor with your legs straight out. Draw one leg close to your body and place the other foot against your leg as shown. Stretch your arms forward to the foot of the outstretched leg as far as you can. Hold for ten seconds. Repeat with the other leg.

Calf and Achilles Tendon (Fig. 3-13): This stretch will help you avoid injury to the vulnerable Achilles tendon. Lean forward on the back of a chair as shown, or else against a wall with your

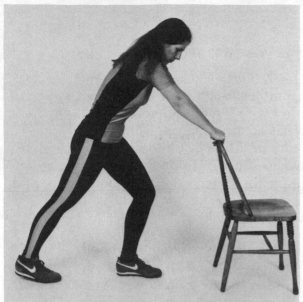

Fig. 3-13: This stretch helps avoid injury to the vulnerable Achilles tendon. Lean forward on the back of a chair as shown, or else against a wall with your hands at shoulder height. Bend forward at the knee to bring it as close to the wall or chair as you can. Hold for 15 seconds. You should feel a good stretch in the back of your lower leg.

hands at shoulder height. Bend forward at the knee to bring it as close to the wall or chair as you can. Hold for a count of 15. You should feel a good stretch in the back of your lower leg.

COMMON CYCLING-RELATED INJURIES: PREVENTION AND CURE

One of the advantages of cycling as a form of physical conditioning is that it keeps most cyclists relatively free of the kind of stress injuries suffered by people who practice other popular sports. Bike riders can and do develop problems in their knees, ankles, and other joints at times. Proper stretching before each

Fig. 3-14: Another stretch for the hamstrings which also helps loosen the hip joint. Grasp the foot and ankle as shown and rotate it ten times in each direction. Repeat for the opposite leg.

ride may ease or prevent such injuries (Figs. 3-14, 3-15, 3-16). However, cycling doesn't pound the cartilage in the joints as other forms of exercise will. A strenuous ride of 45 minutes can work the heart and lungs just as hard as an equal period of running on concrete and asphalt can, without its bone-jarring effects.

Fig. 3-15: Another good quadriceps stretch. Try to keep the back straight and hold for 15 seconds on each leg.

Fig. 3-16: This stretch exercise for the calf and Achilles tendon also loosens the shoulders. This is a particularly good exercise after a ride. Hold this bend for 15 seconds, straighten up and repeat.

Most serious cycling-induced injuries involve parts of the legs—the knees, hips, and ankles. It is understandable that a cyclist might develop problems in these areas. Especially if you ride often, your legs need to work as they should through thousands of revolutions of the crank on every ride. Sometimes problems occur when the rider is using a bike of improper frame size, or one where saddle and stem height has not been properly adjusted (see Chapter 1 for information on frame sizing). Wobbling and side-to-side movements of the legs and ankles during pedaling is another principal cause of cycling injuries. Overexertion can result in chronic injury. This can be a matter of considerable frustration to racing cyclists and serious long-distance riders.

Knees, Hips, and Ankles

Let's begin by looking at the knee (Fig. 3-17). The knee joint works on a hinge between the two major bones of the leg: the femur, or thigh bone, and the tibia. The knee allows a range of leg motion between squatting (flexion), and standing tall (ex-

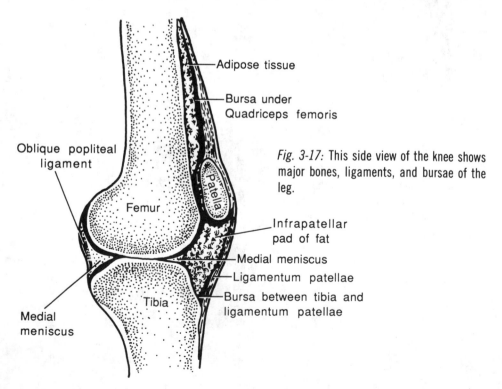

Adipose tissue

Bursa under
Quadriceps femoris

Oblique popliteal
ligament

Patella

Femur

Fig. 3-17: This side view of the knee shows major bones, ligaments, and bursae of the leg.

Infrapatellar
pad of fat

Medial meniscus

Ligamentum patellae

Bursa between tibia and
ligamentum patellae

Tibia

Medial
meniscus

tension). The bones of the leg also articulate to allow rotational movement. A complex system of ligaments ties the upper and lower leg together. They give stability to the joint, both backward and forward, as well as from side to side. The patella, that small oval disk of bone at the front of the knee, checks overextension of the joint. Cartilage, which separates the major bones of the knee, prevents bone-to-bone contact. Fluid-filled sacs called bursae line the parts of the knee and provide frictionless movement.

Bursitis: Bursitis, or inflammation of the bursae, is a common knee complaint of cyclists. It should be stressed, however, that in ordinary circumstances, the bursae never become inflamed. It is only when pedaling action is forced or prone to excessive lateral movement that bursitis is likely to develop. The patella bursae are particuarly prone to athletic injury. Symptoms include pain behind the kneecap and painful swelling of the joint. Occasionally, bursitis may have to be treated by surgically draining the joint. This is a relatively simple procedure that is virtually painless.

Tendinitis: More common than bursitis is tendinitis, an inflammation of the tendons and ligaments caused by excessive stress on the knee. Tendinitis causes tenderness and pain on either side of the patella, and may be accompanied by a grating sensation during movement. Both bursitis and tendinitis are best treated through rest. Take a few days off from riding. Use a lower gear when you start up again, and check your pedaling for any lateral movements of the legs.

Cartilage Injuries: Injuries to the cartilage can be far more serious. Chondro-malacia is a degenerative ailment that usually affects the cartilage behind the kneecap. Direct trauma, caused by using gears too high for the grade being climbed, may contribute to the onset of the disease. Overextension of the knee caused by a saddle set too high, because it drives the patella against the femur, may also be a cause. Chondro-malacia also produces a grinding sensation in the joint. The disease will eventually break down the cartilage. If you suspect that this may be the cause of problems in your knee, see a specialist.

Leg Wobble: Lateral movement of the leg at the top of the pedaling stroke is a common cause of problems in the knee. If you suspect leg wobbling as the cause of leg or knee pain, have

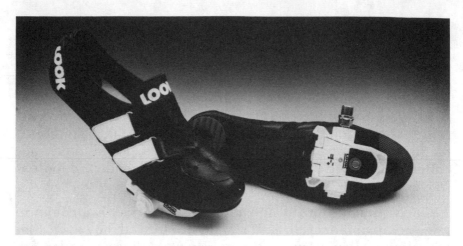

Fig. 3-18: These Look bike shoes and pedals can be adjusted for individual lateral movement of the leg and foot in pedaling. If you've been cycling for some time, look at your shoe soles. If the imprint from the pedals angles across the sole, you need the angle adjustment these shoes and pedals can give.

someone watch for it as you ride. You can often correct a wobbly stroke by using a pair of cleated cycling shoes (Fig. 3-18). Cleated shoes are made to attach securely to a specially designed pedal and will help reduce side-to-side movements. Another problem may be leg length differences, which will lead to unbalanced pedaling and could give you hip pain as well. This can be remedied by using a shorter crank arm on the side with the longer leg. Your bike dealer will have crank arms of varying length. See Chapter 7 to change the crank arm yourself.

Hip Injuries: Serious injuries to the hips are more rare. Leg length differences or a wobbly stroke can cause pain in the hip. Hip pain will often be felt in the main muscle at the front of the leg, right at the point where it attaches to the pelvis. Hip pain can give you more trouble off the bike than on, since problems in the hip can interfere with walking. Solutions to hip problems are pretty much the same as those for knee injuries. To begin with, get some rest. Then, before you get back on the bike, make sure that you have corrected any leg wobble and properly adjusted your saddle's height.

Achilles Tendinitis: Another common complaint of cyclists is a painful inflammation called Achilles tendinitis. The Achilles tendon is massive in comparison to most other tendons in the body, so it takes longer to loosen it up. The Achilles tendon is subject to extreme forces through movement of the ankle. If irritated it will easily become inflamed. Generally, it is side-to-side movement of the ankle in pedaling which irritates this tendon. Use of cleated cycling shoes will usually correct side-to-side movement. Simple overuse is another common cause of Achilles tendinitis. Rest is the best cure for inflammation of the Achilles tendon. Be sure to stretch the Achilles tendon before you start to ride, and warm it up slowly through a relaxed starting pace.

Muscle Pain and Stiffness

Lower back pain: This can be a problem on long rides, though cycling isn't generally a cause of chronic back problems. When you are touring, be sure to keep your lower back muscles supple by stretching frequently, especially in the morning and again at the end of the day's ride. Switch hand positions frequently to alleviate strain on the back. If you are really bothered by lower back pain, check your body's position as you lean into the handlebars. You may want to try another style of handlebars to reduce the stress on your back. Randonneur bars (Fig. 3-19)—dropped handlebars which tilt upward at the out-

Fig. 3-19: The upswept design of these Randonneur handlebars helps relieve neck and shoulder strain while touring.

side edge—are preferred for touring. They let you shift more weight onto the saddle. See Chapter 9 for instructions on changing handlebars. People who have chronic lower back problems shouldn't be discouraged from cycling. Indications are that cycling actually helps to strengthen the lower back.

Neck and shoulder pain: This can really be crippling on long rides. Most riding positions make you tilt your head back. The weight of your body leaning forward on the handlebars produces constant tension and fatigue in the neck and shoulder muscles. As you ride, change the position of your hands on the bars. Get off the bike from time to time and keep those muscles loose by stretching frequently. If neck and shoulder pain really bothers you, move the stem up until it is no more than an inch below the saddle level. This will lift the weight of your torso off the bars a bit, and reduce the bend in your neck. You can also try a different stem length, which can shift some of your weight from the handlebars. See Chapter 9 for a disussion of stem height and length.

Coping With the Numbs

Numbness isn't usually a serious problem for cyclists, though it can be annoying all the same. It often afflicts a cyclist's fingers, toes, and crotch, because constant pressure is placed on the hands, feet, and buttocks during countless hours of riding. Many riders find that numbness doesn't go away after a good night's sleep, but continues to plague them for weeks after a long-distance ride. Numbness is caused by the continuous pressure of bone on nerves.

Numb hands: This is caused by the compression of nerves running out to the finger through pressure on the mid-hand where it wraps around the handlebars. Dropped handlebars allow the rider to change hand positions frequently, thereby relieving prolonged pressure on any one point. Try to rest your weight on the fleshy part of the palm, from just below the thumb across the base of the hand. A good pair of padded cycling gloves can help, as will padded handlebar covering.

Numbness in the feet: Particularly the big toe, this is caused by pressure on the bones of the feet against the hard steel of a rattrap pedal. You can cure this problem by making small shifts in the position of toe clips or by loosening the straps on the clips. You can also get a pair of cycling shoes with a stiffened sole that protects your foot from hard pedal edges (Fig. 3-20).

Numb crotch: This results from compression of nerves running along the base of the pelvis. This can be a source of major discomfort, especially during long bike tours when all you can do is tough it out to the end of the trip. If you feel numbness in the crotch, it's best to get off the bike and wait for feeling to

Fig. 3-20: These Nike shoes have stiff soles which spread foot pressure on ATB pedals. They're also great for road cycling.

return before continuing your ride. Adjust the position of the saddle, tilting it forward slightly. This will allow you to shift more of your weight to the buttocks, taking pressure off the mid-crotch area where the nerves run. You can also try moving the saddle forward a bit or raising the stem to shift your weight toward the back of the saddle. Stand up on the pedals from time to time to relieve the pressure periodically and get the blood flowing through the area again. If all else fails, you might try a wider saddle.

Saddle Soreness

Saddle burn is another common and painful problem experienced by many long-distance cyclists. The problem is complicated by riding in hot, humid weather. Here, sweating increases the slipping of the crotch across the saddle. Loose shorts will scrape the skin raw and eventually injure the area to the point where bacteria from sweat can cause an infection of the irritated skin. The skin may abscess if the infection is not checked soon enough. If the condition progresses this far without treatment, it's sure to knock you out of the saddle until it heals.

Any measure that reduces friction on the skin of the crotch reduces your chance of getting saddle sore. Talcum powder or Vaseline helps reduce friction. Talc also counteracts the slipperiness caused by sweating. Be sure to wash the affected area at night. As you sleep, leave it open to the air, which helps heal raw skin. Most cycling shorts are designed to reduce friction caused by saddle pressure against the skin. Try to find shorts with a seamless crotch made of soft cotton or chamois. These materials will help to absorb excess sweat. Make sure that they fit snugly and do not bunch up in the crotch. It's also best not to wear underwear, because it tends to chafe the skin. Saddle soreness is easier prevented than treated. Take measures at the beginning of your ride to make sure you don't develop problems before it's too late.

KEEP AN EYE ON THE WEATHER

In the small town where I live in the wet, mild climate of the Pacific Northwest, there is a man who uses his bike to go everywhere. I don't see him much when the rain is really pouring down, but most days he is on the bike, in good weather and bad. His costume is always the same: shorts, sneakers, helmet, and a fishnet shirt. Usually, I shiver just to look at him.

The body has a remakable temperature regulation system. Even when it is exposed to ambient temperatures ranging between 50°F and 150°F, the body's internal, or core, temperature may vary as little as 2°F. Cyclists have an advantage over people waiting for the bus in the rain, or someone sitting in the shade as they bear out the heat of the day. When it's cold, the heat generated by stepped-up metabolism helps keep you warm. When it's hot outside, exercise makes you sweat. Sweat cools you when it's evaporated by the wind on your body. Still, those long, hot summer days, like the cold, dark days of winter, can spell big trouble for the cyclist. We can't all enjoy the kind of conditioning that lets the man in the fishnet shirt be so indifferent to the weather. Show the weather the respect it's due. Don't start your ride in very hot or very cold weather without taking some precautions first.

Guard Against Heat Disease

Everybody knows how a workout in the heat can leave you exhausted. In extreme cases it can kill you. These are the mildest and the most serious examples of what might be called heat disease. You should learn to recognize the symptoms of heat disease, and know the measures needed to counteract it.

At the lower end of the scale, heat disease is a simple problem of dehydration and electrolyte loss. Heat cramps in the muscles of the legs, arms, and trunk result when profuse sweating lowers the level of electrolytes—such as sodium, potassium, and magnesium—in the blood. Cramps in the legs can be extremely painful, and debilitating if you are on a long ride. More serious dehydration will result in heat exhaustion, the symptoms of which can include pallor, profuse sweating, rapid and uneven heartbeat, muscle cramps, dizziness, and fainting. Heat exhaustion occurs when body fluids have become so depleted that the body's built-in cooling system can't work efficiently. Leg cramps and heat exhaustion respond favorably to rest and fluid replacement.

Heat stroke is the deadly form of heat disease. Since people often suffer heat stroke in areas far from places of treatment, the mortality rate following onset of symptoms is high, approaching 50 percent. Heat stroke is caused by a dangerous build-up of heat in the body's core. The body stops sweating and attempts to conserve what is left of its fluid reserves. As a result, body temperature shoots up to fever levels. Death results if it reaches 109°F. The only treatment is rapid cooling with water, ice, or wet towels over the body. Try to have the person suffering from heat stroke drink some water if they can. Take immediate steps to counteract the effects of heat and fluid loss whenever someone begins to demonstrate confusion or indifference to their surroundings. It's a sure sign they are experiencing the advanced stages of heat disease, and may be about to lapse into unconsciousness.

Prevention is your best protection against heat disease. Your body can sweat away three to four quarts of water every hour when you exert yourself in extreme heat. Drink plenty of pure water, without ice, to replenish the fluid in your body's cooling system. Avoid salty commercial replacement fluids and heavily sugared soft drinks. When you drink something either very sweet or very salty, water is actually drawn from body cells and is dumped into the stomach in an attempt to dilute its contents. Therefore, the addition of salt or sugar in your drink only slows down its absorption into the bloodstream, defeating your purpose. And no matter how good it feels to slug down a cold beer, don't drink alcohol when you work out on a hot day. Alcohol causes your body to excrete fluid, and will actually make you thirstier in the long run.

Electrolyte replacement is very important, of course, but this is better done slowly, preferably through the food you eat. If you want a drink that contains some sugar or electrolyte, make it very dilute. Diluted fruit juice with a pinch of salt should be all you need. Another good rule of thumb is to take one 600 mg. salt tablet, a very small dose, with every two pints of fluid consumed.

When you ride on hot days, wear light-colored cotton clothing that reflects heat and wicks sweat away from your body to cool you off. Humidity compounds the problem of heat disease, since sweat does not evaporate well when humidity is high. Wear as little clothing as possible, but use a sunscreen to protect your skin from the sun's harmful rays. A fishnet shirt will allow air flow while protecting the skin, to an extent, from getting burned. Cover your head. It doesn't radiate heat well, and the more solar energy you can keep off it the better. If you are wearing a helmet, make sure it's white and has vents that provide good air flow over your head.

Finally, try to accustom yourself to the heat before taking any long rides. People who are accustomed to riding in the heat sweat more easily, with a lower level of blood flow to the skin, than cyclists who have not been acclimatized. Reduced blood flow to the extremities saves the heart from excess strain. Acclimatized riders also lose less salt through their sweat.

Be Prepared for the Cold

Riding in cold weather generates less concern, probably because riding in foul weather is not so popular as riding in the sunshine. But it deserves your attention nonetheless. Exposure to the cold can result in hypothermia, a potentially dangerous condition. Hypothermia occurs when the body's core temperature drops below 98.6°F. If your core temperature falls into the low 90s, impaired judgment and muscle function, and even death can result.

It doesn't have to be freezing outside for you to suffer from hypothermia. Long, exhausting rides in a chilling rain can end in disaster if you don't warm yourself once you stop. Hypothermia strikes when you have used up your fuel supply and have nothing left to produce heat with. Wet clothing increases heat loss. When you stop, get out of the weather as best you can and change in dry clothing. Fix yourself a hot drink, preferably something that will provide energy, like clear broth or hot cocoa.

Watch for uncontrollable shivering and difficulty in performing tasks which require some dexterity. These are the first signs of serious heat loss. They will be followed by a loss of alertness and difficulty in speaking as the body's core temperature continues to drop. The final symptom of hypothermia, like heat stroke, is a state of mental confusion and indifference to physical surroundings. People may be tempted to lie down, saying they want to rest. Don't let them. They may not be getting up again.

Watch Those Fingers and Toes! The effect of wind on the body during cold weather represents another focus of concern. The same movement of air that cools you off while riding in the heat can be dangerous in the winter. The passage of air across your body produces effective temperatures that are much lower than actual thermometer readings, a factor known as wind-chill (Table 3-1). Riding into a headwind increases the effect, and also puts you in danger by wearing down your energy reserves.

Numbness in the fingers and toes is likely to occur while riding in cold weather. You should be very concerned about

Table 3-1

WIND-CHILL INDEX

WIND SPEED	AIR TEMPERATURE (°F)														
	35	30	25	20	15	10	5	0	−5	−10	−15	−20	−25	−30	−35
4 mph	35	30	25	20	15	10	5	0	−5	−10	−15	−20	−25	−30	−35
5 mph	32	27	22	16	11	6	0	−5	−10	−15	−21	−26	−31	−36	−35
10 mph	22	16	10	3	−3	−9	−15	−22	−27	−34	−40	−46	−52	−58	−64
15 mph	16	9	2	5	11	−18	−25	−31	−38	−45	−51	−58	−65	−72	−78
20 mph	12	4	−3	−10	−17	−24	−31	−39	−46	−53	−60	−67	−74	−81	−88
25 mph	8	1	−7	−15	−22	−29	−36	−44	−51	−59	−66	−74	−81	−88	−96
30 mph	6	−2	−10	−18	−25	−33	−41	−49	−56	−64	−71	−79	−86	−93	−101
35 mph	4	−4	−12	−20	−27	−35	−43	−52	−58	−67	−74	−82	−89	−97	−105
40 mph	3	−5	−13	−21	−29	−37	−45	−53	−60	−69	−76	−84	−92	−100	−107

the possibility of frostbite to the extremities if the temperature drops very far below freezing. Cycling overshoes and gloves should be worn to protect the extremities from the cold.

Dress in layers to ward off the cold wind when you ride. Wear a light garment of a synthetic material, like polypropylene, next to your skin. Synthetic fabric will not absorb perspiration the way cotton does, which creates a cold layer right next to the skin. In case of severe cold, wear a middle layer over the first, like a very lightweight wool sweater. Over the top, wear a waterproof parka made of a laminated fabric like Gore-Tex, which will block penetration by wind and water, but allows moisture to pass away from your body. Wearing clothing in layers allows you to take them off one at a time as you begin to heat up. Heat loss from the head can be substantial, so wear a wool cap underneath your helmet.

MEETING SPECIAL NEEDS

Increasingly, medical evidence shows that exercise can have a rejuvenating effect on the human body. Science now recognizes that many of the diseases once considered the natural consequence of aging may only represent the effect of long-term inactivity. Accordingly, people who might have been written off as invalids a few years back are finding their way back to health through today's sport of cycling.

Cardiovascular Patients

People recovering from strokes and heart attacks generally experience dramatic physical improvements through exercise. Regular exercise may be necessary in order to prevent a future attack, which is more likely to be fatal than the first one. If you are a recovering heart patient who wants to start exercising, you should work closely with your doctor, who will want to prescribe an exercise routine for your recovery. Generally, your doctor will advise you to start with extremely moderate exercise and work slowly to increase your aerobic capacity and strengthen your heart. Be extra cautious about exceeding your physical limits, and learn to recognize that point when the body says it has had enough.

Through exercise, stroke victims can regain movement in areas paralyzed by the stroke. Heart patients benefit, because exercise enlarges coronary arteries and results in the development of collaterals, which are new vessels that bypass the old, obstructed ones. Exercise cannot repair tissue that has been damaged by a heart attack or stroke, and some of the effects of cardiovascular disease, like hardened arteries, are not reversible. However, while exercise may never be able to restore the cardiovascular patient to total health, it is bound to improve anyone's quality of life.

Diabetes and Cycling

If you are a diabetic who is otherwise in good health, you should be able to exercise vigorously without problems. It would probably be a good idea to start out with shorter rides and work up to longer ones, in order to assess your energy needs during a long haul. Monitor your blood sugar levels frequently as you exercise. Of course, you will need to increase your caloric intake to meet increased energy demands. Complex carbohydrates will give you greater energy reserves than refined carbohydrates and other foods will. Be sure to carry along a piece of fruit or some fruit juice for quick energy, just in case you begin to experience the effects of hypoglycemia.

Carbohydrate loading, the practice of eating a carbohydrate-rich diet in order to build up muscle glycogen stores, could be dangerous to the diabetic. If you are a diabetic, you should try at all times to maintain constancy in your diet, and the practice of carbohydrate loading calls for some drastic changes in what you eat. In particular, the phase that calls for eating a high-fat, high-protein, and low-carbohydrate diet could initiate an episode of insulin shock.

Asthma

If you are an asthmatic, your condition shouldn't keep you from cycling unless symptoms are particularly severe. Besides carrying a medication like Actifed to control asthma attacks, you should be aware of things particular to cycling that may trigger an attack. Cycling, which is a fairly continuous activity, is more likely to cause you problems than sports which require more intermittent movement. Cold and altitude also contribute to asthma attacks. If you are touring in the mountains or at high altitudes, you should be prepared to deal with respiratory problems. Automobile exhaust can also be a triggering factor. If you commute in city traffic, and smog complicates your asthma, try to find routes that are not so heavily traveled by automobiles, or else ride at times other than rush hour.

Physical Disabilities

Real technological strides have been made recently for riders who have some type of physical disability. The development of recumbent bikes has made it possible for people who do not have normal use of their legs to engage in cycling. Special recumbents are available that are driven by a hand-turned crank mounted directly in front of the rider.

A ten-speed bike can be modified for use by riders with a prosthesis on one leg. The bike is converted by removing one of the crank arms, using a toe clip on the remaining pedal to which the foot can be strapped. The main problem with one-legged pedaling is the unbalanced movement of the bike that it causes. In order to compensate for this imbalance, the rider has to keep both hands on the handlebars. That means all mechanical functions, including the shift levers, must be moved within easy reach. Using upright handlebars instead of dropped varieties will also help, allowing the rider to use his arms to "pump." I wouldn't know myself, but I can imagine that learning to ride with one leg is probably harder than it was learning to ride with two.

Pregnancy

If you are an expectant mother, you can generally keep riding up to the third trimester without problems. Avoid carrying large loads on your bike as pregnancy progresses. Morning sickness could present some problems, and the pregnant woman who exercises regularly should always be conscious of her calorie and fluid intakes. Heat will probably be less well tolerated. During the third trimester, continued cycling is not advised. Cycling at this time will become difficult because of the added weight of the baby, and may be so uncomfortable that you will want to stop riding anyway. Remember at all times that pain or bleeding would advise against continued exercise, and indicate that a visit to the doctor is necessary.

I know by now that you're well aware of all that cycling will do to improve your life. The only thing left is for you to get started. Just make sure you work into it gradually, and keep working out. There is no quick fix. We're talking long-term health and fitness here, and you don't build that overnight.

Now, let's go on to Chapter 4, where I will cover the joys of cycle touring, camping, and commuting, plus some tips on equipment.

Reference: A WAY OF FITNESS FOR EVERYBODY
Cooper, Lt. Col. Kenneth: "Guidelines in the Management of the Exercising Patient." *The Journal of the American Medical Association*, March 9, 1970.

Reference: THE IMPORTANCE OF DIET
Konopka, Dr. Peter, "Diet and the Racing Cyclist," *Bike World Magazine*, December, 1977.
Jones, Susan Smith, "It May All Be In What You Eat," *Bike World Magazine*, January, 1979.

Reference: A WORD ABOUT CHOLESTEROL
Gaston, Dr. Eugene A., "Bicycling, Cholesterol and Your Heart," *Bicycling*, March, 1980.

FOUR

GETTING THERE ON YOUR BIKE, TOURING AND COMMUTING

No matter how you try to add it up, the payback from commuting 10 miles round trip, four days a week, will pay for a good bike in a year through savings in fuel, wear and tear on the car, or in savings from not having to ride a bus or train to work. Your bike doesn't have to pass vehicle inspections (although this is not such a bad idea, given the awful condition of some bikes I've seen on the road), or suffer the slings and arrows of outrageous repair bills. Parking fees are nil, and you'll never have to circle endlessly around the block looking for a parking place. Best of all, you'll benefit *in at least eight ways*.

First, your transportation costs will be zero, or close to it. Second, you'll find yourself in radiantly good health after a few months of biking to work. Third, because your energy level is heightened and can be sustained all day, you can be more effective on the job. You'll eliminate that "wiped out" feeling that seems to creep up around three o'clock in the afternoon. Fourth, because your waistline will shrink, you can get back into your pre-bulge clothing or avoid the expense of new clothes to fit the larger (spell that "fatter") you. Fifth, if you want to move up the corporate ladder, take a look at the people on the rungs above you: today's executives are a slimmer, healthier bunch than those of a generation ago. If you're fighting for promotion—if not merely for survival in the corporate jungle—a simple bicycle can be the leverage that can get you there in more ways than one!

A sixth advantage of commuting on a bike is time. Studies have shown that while you can indeed drive a bit faster than bike to work, this time difference is misleading. You still have to get in your car, warm it up in the winter (assuming it starts and you don't have to wait for a jump start from a tow truck), and park the car in a garage. On a bike *you* provide the jump start, warming up as you exercise your body. In the winter you actually have to peel off layers of clothing as you ride, even when the temperature is in the 20s and overcoated, sedentary commuters are shivering while they wait for the bus or train. If you commute by public transportation, try going to work on your bike: you'll get there faster most of the time. I'm excluding New York suburbia here, unless you count the boroughs of Queens and Brooklyn as suburbia to those who live there and work in Manhattan. I am thinking of cities such as Philadelphia, Chicago, Boston, Seattle, and Denver. By the time you get from the house to public transportation and to the office at the other end, you have lost out to the bike. That has been my own experience. I also found that I could plan my day's activity while biking to work, whereas if I took the train I tended to doze off or read the paper on the way.

A seventh benefit of getting from home to work on a bike is sustained energy and rejuvenation of the spirit. You'll find that even though you may feel tired by the end of the day, by the time you get back home you are invigorated, more alive, hungry for good food, and capable of a great love life. You'll have energy to spare for the kids, too. Since you'll be physically healthier, you'll be healthier emotionally as well. At least that's what I found for myself. I became more stress resistant, got along much better on the job and in interpersonal relationships.

Which brings me to the eighth benefit. If you've read Chapter 3 on bicycling and health, you can understand why your bike-conditioned body will need less attention from the medical profession. When I first started biking to work, my blood pressure was 130/70. That's pretty good, actually, within the norm for my age at that time. But within six months my blood pressure had dropped to 110/60, which is the norm for persons in their twenties, if they're healthy. Twenty years later my blood pressure is still the same, 110/60. The rare times I see a doctor, the nurse has to take my blood pressure twice, once on each arm, to make sure she has read her instrument correctly. I love it! The eighth benefit, then, is reduced illness as well as the time and money saved in medical bills and time spent seeing a physician.

CYCLE COMMUTING IS COST EFFECTIVE!

If corporations would only think about this, they would realize that commuting by bike is cost effective enough to provide bike storage facilities at work (Fig. 4-1) and lockers and showers for bike commuters. The bike lockers in Fig. 4-1 are made by Bike Lockers Co., P.O. Box 445, W. Sacramento, CA 95691. An investment in these facilities pays high dividends in many ways. Healthier employees are more productive. They live longer. In the factory, they are more alert and thus less accident-prone. Insurance costs can be reduced along with time lost due to on-the-job injury. Absenteeism due to non-work related illnesses such as the common cold will be reduced and thus the cost of floating fill-in workers to take the place of workers home ill will will be cut. Finally, the expensive perks of corporate-sponsored health club memberships, along with the time wasted at them, would be eliminated if execs used their bikes to get to work. I note that some companies, and municipalities, actually pay employees a percentage of the money saved by using their bike

Fig. 4-1: Bike lockers at industrial and office locations store bicycles safely for commuting cyclists.

for short trips instead of a company car. More efficient employees give greater return on fixed labor costs, more bang for the salary buck.

How to Make Bike Commuting Even More Practical

In Chapter 2 you learned about safe cycling on city streets. I would like to add one more observation. The first time you set out for work you may be terrified. Every car may seem to be aiming at you. But within a few days, as you become more confident of your biking reflexes and street sense, you'll get used to the city traffic around you. Believe me, you will get nerves of steel. So don't give up because the first few days are highly stresed. We all go through that. There are usually safe roads for biking downtown, either through parks, off-road bike trails or safe streets. Scout out various routes to work in your car first. Your local bicycle club or bicycle shop often has bicycle routes already mapped out. The construction of freeways connecting suburbia to the high-density mess downtown is a boon to cyclists, because it takes the traffic off city streets. Just watch out for cabs and buses! In New York, avoid crosstown streets if possible, or take to the sidewalk those few short blocks across town if pedestrian traffic permits.

Here are a few tips on what to take along when you commute. First, as noted earlier, office clothing is impractical when you bike. If you do have a place to change at work, you can drive a week's supply of clothing down on Saturday, if your job demands executive duds.

You'll need a couple of spare tubes, because if you get a flat on the way to work, changing the tube is faster than finding the leak and patching it. Practice changing tubes until you can do it in minutes. Bring the tools to do it, along with a tire pump.

If you live where the weather is unpredictable, use a wetsuit, or poncho. See the list of bicycle mail order catalogs in the appendix for wetsuit and other bike equipment sources. For example, in the REI catalog you'll find an excellent two-piece rainsuit with reflective stripes and Velcro straps to keep the pants away from the chain. I've said you can bike through snow, and indeed you can because if you live in the "snow belt" the city fathers usually have the streets plowed before you set off in the morning. I find snow amazingly stable. It's only when there's ice under the snow, or the snow has turned to slush, that the going gets treacherous enough that I can't bike to work. In any case, up to two inches of newly fallen snow should not keep you from riding to work.

I would not ride if the temperature falls much below 20°F, unless you are in good shape. Three or four layers of clothes are advisable in cold weather, because you can peel off layers as you warm up. In cold weather, wear shoes a size larger so you can wear heavy wool socks. Or, keep your old shoes, and slip a neoprene bootie over them. The bootie is a wet- and cold-weather ankle-high shoe covering, available from your bike shop or from Spokes Wear, P.O. Box 71098, Seattle, WA. Spokes Wear also distributes an excellent wet/cold weather glove of leather and neoprene. MSR (Mountain Safety Research) makes a helmet liner with ear muffs for any helmet, called "Hel-muffs," that add warmth to your head and ears. Down-filled mittens keep fingers warmer than fingered gloves, but make braking more awkward. Try finger-type down-filled gloves first, along with a wool glove liner. If your fingers still get cold, then graduate to the mittens, keeping the liner if necessary. You can order these gloves from the Performance Bicycle Shop catalog (see Appendix).

If you plan to bike after dark, you *must* use a bright headlight and taillight. Some cities require bike lights. I prefer the re-chargeable battery-powered lights which use quartz halogen bulbs (Fig. 1-65). I replaced the conventional bulb in my tail-light with another quartz halogen bulb. These lights give you good visibility, and more important, tell motorists where and what you are. I keep a charger at the office and one at work. You should get at least two hours out of each charge. Carry a couple of spare bulbs with you. Remember not to touch the bulb with your fingers when you replace it. There's something on human skin these bulbs don't like, and they don't last long if they are touched. You can use a rag to install one.

Bicycle Security

Bicycles are a prime target of the rip-off artist. I remember I was having lunch once in Cambridge, Massachusetts, sitting near a window where I could watch my bike. Another bike was chained next to an adjacent parking meter from my own bike. A man walked by, carrying a large paper sack. He pointed the bag at the bike near mine and squeezed. He walked on a few feet, stopped and looked back. I saw that he had a powerful bolt cutter in the sack and that the flimsy chain which had locked the bike to the parking meter was now dangling in two pieces. Before I could get out the door the thief had mounted the bike and ridden off. I finished my lunch, went out to unlock my bike, and noticed a policeman ruefully fingering the cut chain. I said I was sorry I could not get to the bike in time to prevent its theft. The bike belonged to the police officer. The thief did not even think of trying to steal my bike, because I had one of those really tough U-shaped locks on it (Figs. 4-2 and 4-3). Of course, any lock can be defeated, but tougher locks take longer to cut, and thieves know that every extra second spent ripping off a bike adds to the risk of getting caught. A cable lock, which tucks

Fig. 4-2: U-shaped lock by Citadel can be carried on the bike frame, as shown.

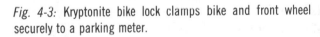

Fig. 4-3: Kryptonite bike lock clamps bike and front wheel securely to a parking meter.

Fig. 4-4: This stows cable in the hollow handlebars, fits into lock-on seat tube.

the cable away inside your handlebars (Fig. 4-4), is light and offers enough security to prevent the casual kid thief from taking your bike. The safest place to leave your bike is either in your office, or in a bike locker you can rent (Fig. 4-1).

If you have quick-releases on your wheels, I suggest you remove the wheels and lock them to the frame with your lock. Or, you could install a recently introduced substitute for the quick-release lever, a Releasy Allen cam (Fig. 4-5), which you turn with an Allen wrench. It's unlikely that a thief will carry such a wrench, although they may eventually. Because the saddles on ATBs are held with a quick-release binder bolt, they are easy to steal. Install a Releasy cam to replace the lever. Lock your helmet to the bike with a Lid-Loc helmet lock and

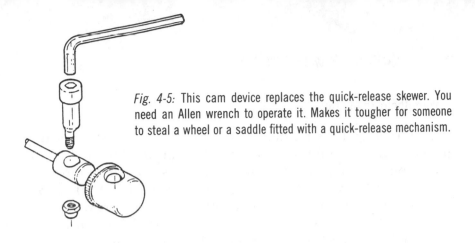

Fig. 4-5: This cam device replaces the quick-release skewer. You need an Allen wrench to operate it. Makes it tougher for someone to steal a wheel or a saddle fitted with a quick-release mechanism.

your pump with a Pump Guard lock. The Pump Guard also holds the pump in place when carrying your bike on a car.

You'll need some sort of bike pack to carry the few tools, spare tubes, patch kit, and personal stuff you need. I recommend one of the higher-quality, quickly removable handlebar bags, such as the Cannondale (Fig. 4-6) or the Eclipse (Fig. 4-7). You can mount and remove these bags in seconds, they're water resistant, and have four pockets, a main one and three smaller pockets.

Fig. 4-6: Cannondale handlebar bag can be removed from or replaced on the handlebars in seconds.

Fig. 4-7: Eclipse handlebar bag has quick-release mechanism.

A Word About the Future

I do believe that the millions of us who bike to work every day are virtually immune to rising gasoline prices and fuel short-ages. Contacts in the petroleum, natural gas, and coal industries tell me that the world has about a 30-year supply of oil, a 150-year supply of natural gas, and a 250-year supply of coal, at the present rate of consumption of these fuels. This forecast is based on consideration of present technology of resource recov-ery and exploration, and known reserves. Of course, when oil begins to be depleted, the other fuels, if converted to gasoline, will cost a bundle and be depleted much faster. If you're 30 years old now, you're going to be glad if you turn out to be a healthy 60-year-old with a good bicycle and bicycling skills—especially when we run out of non-renewable liquid fossil fuel and the cost of its replacement goes sky high.

LONG-DISTANCE TOURING

When you travel through the countryside on a bike, you move at a slow, leisurely pace. You're not stuck in a metal box with the windows shut, air conditioning on, radio blaring, oblivious to the world around you. On a bike you're keenly aware of the surrounding countryside and the people who live there. The hum of the tires, and feel of fresh air in your face, the music of songbirds in your ears, the tingle of well-being as you pedal down the road: all are your reward for touring by bike rather than by car. You can savor the countryside as you would a fine wine—tastefully and with appreciation. Wave at people work-ing in the fields or walking along the road, and they wave back. Stop when and where you will, break out a loaf of bread, some cheese, a flask of wine and lunch by the side of the road. Cool your toes in a nearby brook, watch the sky and the endless variations of clouds passing by (and hope they don't portend rain).

Whether you make camp at night or go deluxe and stay in a

motel, it's your choice. Tour alone, with a friend, or take a packaged, pre-planned bike trip with a larger group. There are advantages to each type of bike touring. Let's look at them now.

Going It Alone

When you tour alone or with just one other person (Figs. 4-8 and 4-9) you are free to plan your own route and go where you wish. You can stop and stay for a day or a week in one campsite, make exploratory trips in different directions, and return to the same camp each night. You go as fast or as slowly as you wish. Your schedule is your own.

Fig. 4-8: Touring alone is the ultimate in freedom, but it can be lonely.

Fig. 4-9: Touring with a companion gives you someone with whom to share the joys of cycling.

There are days, and I speak from experience, when you have so much energy you burst out of your sleeping bag, zip open the tent, throw on some clothes and after the morning necessary, can hardly wait to breakfast and get back on the road. Then there will be days when you just have no energy at all, when you want simply to roll over in the sack and only get up when the sun is blasting down on you. On those days its fun just to laze around the campsite, read, check over your bike, wash clothes, walk around, and talk to other campers. Bike touring alone or with one other person lets you have complete flexibility.

On the negative side, biking alone can be lonely. If you travel with one friend, compatibility is essential. For instance, you should both be content with the speed you are making, the distance you cover (Fig. 4-10), even the food you eat.

Fig. 4-10: Cycling companions should be about evenly matched physically as well as temperamentally, or the faster of the duo should have patience. This couple is on the Bikecentennial Transamerica Trail. *(Bikecentennial photo)*

You have to carry everything if you're on your own. There's no sag wagon to carry tent, sleeping bag(s), cooking gear, and spare parts. You'll have to use carriers and panniers to carry everything on your bike (Fig. 4-9), which is, to me, a great way to travel. I like the idea of total self-sufficiency.

Packaged Tours

On a packaged tour, many details and chores are taken off your backs. You don't have to plan a route (Fig. 4-11), be concerned about where you're going to sleep, or whether or not the campground will be full. Meals are planned and often cooked for you (Fig. 4-12). You can bike empty, because most planned tours

Fig. 4-11: The logistics of route planning are borne by the operators of packaged tours. You just cycle and enjoy. (Bikecentennial photo)

Fig. 4-12: Package tours usually include meals and food preparation. Here a Bikecentennial Transamerica Trail group is at breakfast in Idaho. (Bikecentennial photo)

Fig. 4-13: Large group tours usually have a skilled mechanic along to help fix flats, make minor repairs, such as the two on the left of the shoulder stripe. *(TOSRVPHOTO by Greg Siple)*

provide a sag wagon to carry your stuff. There is usually a skilled mechanic along should your bike suffer an ill (Fig. 4-13).

On a packaged tour you can relax, forget about logistics, and concentrate on the pleasures around you, not the least of which are your fellow cyclists (Fig. 4-14). At night, after a long day's ride, you will be surrounded by lots of people with whom to share adventures, conversation, companionship (Fig. 4-15).

Of course it's more expensive to take a packaged bike tour than it is to go it alone: You pay for all the advantages. But if you want a highly sociable, hassle-free trip, then a packaged tour is the way to go.

Tour providers I recommend include the American Youth Hostels, BikeCentennial, Sobek's, and the Sierra Club. See the Appendix for addresses of these and other packaged tour providers. Actually, there are so many of these providers that space forbids mentioning all of them. Tours for specific regions, such

Fig. 4-14: The people who make up a bicycle tour group are what make it so much fun. Here these exuberant cyclists are transported by joy at the 1985 Salty Dog AYH Hostel on Nantucket Island, Massachusetts. Leader is June Siple, third from left. *(AYH photo by Greg Siple)*

Fig. 4-15: Cycling group at the historic Manter Memorial Hostel in Martha's Vineyard, Massachusetts. This is the first hostel facility built as such in the U.S. *(AYH photo by Greg Siple)*

as Vermont, California, and Oregon, for example, are run by local groups in these areas. Leaf through the advertising pages of bicycle magazines to find out names of and providers of tour packages in these and other areas. New tour groups pop up almost daily, it seems, so any list I could provide would not be complete.

What to Take on a Bike Trip

I'll assume in this section that you're going on a trip you have planned, and not on a packaged trip. You can always scale back on equipment I'll cover to fit the lesser needs of a package tour. Or, if you go on your own but stay in motels and eat out, you can of course skip tent, sleeping bag, and cooking gear.

The essentials are shown in Fig. 4-16. You will see the tools

Fig. 4-16: Here's the bicycle first-aid equipment you should take on a trip: crossover cable if you have cantilever brakes; extra tube (or two); patch kit; two brake shoes; rear derailleur and rear brake cables (can be cut to fit front derailleur and front brake); tire lever; needlenose pliers; extra chain links; set of Allen wrenches; chain rivet remover; tube of grease; spoke wrench; extra spokes with nipples; spray can of chain lube; standard and Phillips head screwdrivers; 8, 9, 10, and 11mm wrenches; small adjustable Crescent wrench; pair of 13, 14, 15, and 16mm hub cone wrenches; 14 and 15mm box wrench if your bike has bolt on wheel axles.

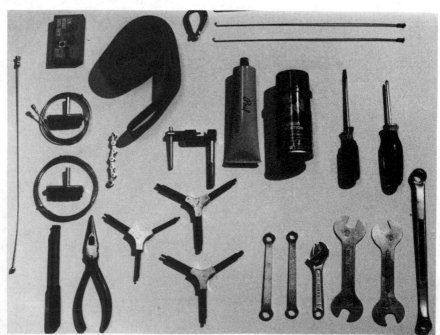

you need, and the caption tells you what they are. Note that there are extra spokes, cables, and one tube. I would carry at least three spare tubes. Not shown is another necessity, a roll of duct tape. That tape is an invaluable mender of holes in a tent and cuts in tire casings.

Other equipment I have found valuable includes:

1. Mini-binoculars.
2. 35mm camera.
3. First-aid kit with snake-bite equipment.
4. Mosquito lotion (don't leave home without it!).
5. Compass, map walker to compute miles from a map, and signaling mirror (Fig. 4-17). The compass is a *must* item. You can get lost, even at slow speed on a bike.
6. Liquid detergent concentrate (Fig. 4-18).
7. Small flashlight with rechargeable batteries and a solar-powered battery charger.
8. Extra links for bike chain.
9. Extra rim if going on a safari-type trip, along with four extra foldable tires.

Fig. 4-17: Signaling mirror if you're taking an off-road wilderness trip, mileage measure, and a good compass.

Fig. 4-18: Mosquito lotion, detergent concentrate, and fabric cleaner concentrate for Gore-Tex rainwear and tents.

10. Kerosene and candle lanterns in case flashlight is lost or breaks.
11. Multi-fuel cook stove and cook gear.
12. Waterproof matches (high-altitude matches if necessary).
13. Small radio for local weather reports.
14. Two water bottles on your bike, or one big one (Fig. 4-19).
15. Variety of plastic bottles for condiments, liquids, flour, margarine with tight lids. Plastic food containers, including egg carrier.

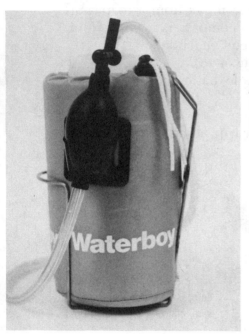

Fig. 4-19: This big water bottle holds more than two standard plastic water bottles. It's handy if you're crossing desert areas.

Fig. 4-20: I find it helpful to know how far I've gone each day, if for no other reason than to congratulate myself for having done so well, or to commiserate with my poor body for having cycled so few miles. This Union computer can clamp on your handlebars and will tell you how far, how fast, trip mileage, and pedal cadence, and keeps a record of accumulated mileage. Lets you browbeat yourself into maintaining an aerobic cadence. Available in kilometers or miles.

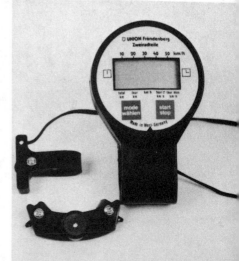

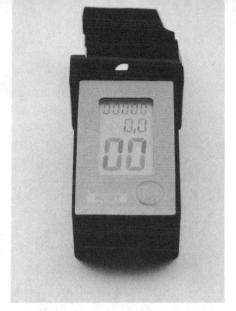
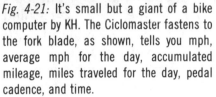

Fig. 4-21: It's small but a giant of a bike computer by KH. The Ciclomaster fastens to the fork blade, as shown, tells you mph, average mph for the day, accumulated mileage, miles traveled for the day, pedal cadence, and time.

Fig. 4-22: Another high-tech bike computer from Sachs-Huret can clip to handlebars or fork blade, reads out speed, mileage, mph, cadence, and average speed.

16. Knives, forks, a couple of sharp small hunting knives, a small hatchet.
17. Bicycle computer (Figs. 4-20, 4-21, and 4-22), which gives you daily and accumulated mileage, average and actual speed, elapsed time and pedal cadence.
18. Six medium-sized, heavy-duty plastic garbage bags to keep sleeping bags, tent, and clothing dry in the event of a heavy rainfall.
19. Small two-way radio. Radio Shack sells a pair of these little transceivers for around $65. I like them because I can chat with a cycling partner and share the interesting scenes we see as we ride along. The headset can clamp over a bike helmet, the mike is integral with the headset, and you can have a two-way conversation without removing your hands from the handlebars. Range is about ¼ mile (five blocks).
20. Maintenance kit for your stove.
21. Extra fuel bottle (can fit in a bottle cage).
22. One or two tubes of fire ribbon for starting camp fires (so you don't have to carry old newspapers).
23. A water-purifier kit is necessary equipment if you're trav

eling in Mexico, China, or anyplace where sterility of the water supply is questionable. The best models remove Giardia, pathogenic bacteria, flukes, tapeworms, cysts, larger protozoa, fallout, herbicides, pesticides and other chemicals, asbestos, and foul odors. I like the First Need Water Purifier from REI (see Appendix) for about $33.95. Weighs only 12 ounces but can save a ton of bellyaches.

24. Sunshower kit. Not every campground will have shower facilities. This kit holds 2.5 gallons of water. You hang it in direct sunlight and in three hours you'll have enough hot water for two short showers. See the REI catalog.

This seems like a lot of equipment. But each item is small and light. Add to it your personal effects, tent, sleeping bag, and foam plastic ground cloth to go under the sleeping bag, and you will still probably keep your total load under 30 pounds. If there's two of you sharing a tent, that reduces your load to one tent, and undoubtedly you will only carry one cook stove and other items that can serve you both. Two can travel a lot lighter than one.

A Word About Sleeping Bags and Tents

First, sleeping bags. Down is dandy, but man-made insulating fibers are quicker to dry, in my opinion. Goose down, when wet, is simply impossible. You can't sleep in it, it takes forever to dry, and is soggy and heavy. When it's dry, down is great, but you can't count on dryness on a bike tour. However, down bags will compress and take up less space and be lighter at any temperature rating. The bags with Dupont Quallofil insulation come close to the characteristics of down, but don't soak up moisture and are easier to dry. A good goose down-filled bag, rated at 5°F, weighs one pound, eight ounces, and costs around $189. A Quallofill bag, rated at 5°F, weighs four pounds, 14 ounces, and costs around $130. So down-filled sleeping bags do offer some very real advantages in weight and compressibility (space in your pannier) over man-made insulating fiber-filled bags. If you can be sure you'll never get a down bag wet, then that would be your best buy. There are dozens of makes, models, and a wide variation in the quality of sleeping bags on the market. I prefer a sleeping bag with a built-in pillow, and with a hood I can drawstring around my head. Your head is the one part of your body that, if exposed to cold air at night, can make you really uncomfortable. I truly hate "mummy" configuration sleeping bags. They give you very little room to twist and turn at night. You can get a "semi-mummy" sleeping bag, though, that is roomier.

You should have a Cellulite foam pad to place underneath the full length of your bag. These pads keep ground dampness and cold from the sleeping bag and are soft so they cushion you against the inevitable small stones and twigs you did not sweep away before pitching your tent.

You need a sleeping bag, first of all, that's rated to 5°F. You may never sleep in such cold weather, but I can assure you that on a cold, windy, damp night, the air can penetrate to your very bones, especially if you're at altitudes above 3,000 ft.

The sleeping bag should have plastic zippers you can operate from inside and outside. Nothing's colder against your skin than a metal zipper that conducts cold from the outside air to you. Matching bags that zip together can also be useful.

Tents for the Old Campground

On a cross-country bike camping trip you'll see as many makes, sizes, and designs of tents as there are cyclists to tote them. Good tents have common characteristics, which you should look for in the one you select. First, any cyclist's tent should have a small vestibule so you can store panniers and other gear *outside* the tent living area, but protected from the elements and light-fingered thieves. The tent should be made of fabric that breathes. I once had a tent that didn't breathe. Moisture from our bodies and breath would collect on the cold inner surfaces of this tent at night. By morning a slap on the tent sides would send drops of moisture down on us. We usually rinsed the inside of this tent in a bucket to wash out this moisture. The one time we didn't and packed it away wet from body moisture because we were in a hurry to get started, the tent became unusable the next night. What happened was that the moisture went sour, and it smelled very bad. We took the tent to a launderette and machine-washed it. No use. That odor was now a part of the tent. We wound up throwing this tent away and buying one that breathed, just so we could get a night's sleep. So get a tent made of a breathable fabric, such as Gore-Tex. The Early Winters two-person Winterlight tent (Fig. 4-23) is a good example of the kind of tent I am describing. It costs around $274. Not cheap, but one 14-day camping trip avoiding $30 a day on el cheapo motels will more than pay for this or any other good tent.

The tent you buy should also have a double-thick floor that comes up to at least six inches on the inside of the tent. In a hard rain you'll appreciate this floor, because it will keep water out. (Which reminds me to urge you *not* to dig a trench around your tent to funnel away rainwater. Camp authorities take a very dim view of this practice, which is usually forbidden, and it does not help the local ecology.) Some of the better tents also

Fig. 4-23: Two-person Winterlight tent from Early Winters is light, sets up quickly and easily.

Fig. 4-24: Moss Star Gazer is open to the sky, has adequate room for two, also sets up quickly.

come with a rain cover. The Moss Star Gazer (Fig. 4-24) comes with a tent cover (Fig. 4-25) that also provides the vestibule. Without the rain cover, the top of the Moss tent is open to the night sky, which can be pretty romantic while avoiding the crowded feeling of a small tent. This tent weighs around six pounds, but that's only three pounds apiece for two people. Try to keep the weight down to around six pounds. You can get

Fig. 4-25: Moss Star Gazer comes with a rain cover, which also provides a small vestibule, as shown.

bigger tents, but now you're talking eight to ten pounds, and after all, you're not going to spend all day in the tent, just sleep in it.

Handy additions to any tent are built-in nylon net pockets in which you can stow small items such as personal gear, a camera, playing cards, a couple of paperbacks, or a small radio. It's nice to have a place for your eyeglasses too, without having to scrounge around inside the tent to find them. It's hard to believe how messy the inside of a small tent can get in an hour or so. I blame the mess on lack of storage space, such as no dressers or closets, rather than on any natural proclivities in that direction, of course.

If you're going solo, you need the lightest, most compact tent you can find, since you'll be carrying cooking gear and other equipment, a load that could as well be shared by a companion. For a solo trip, look for a tent like the Early Winters Pocket Hotel (Fig. 4-26) made of Gore-Tex; the whole thing weighs around two pounds.

Fig. 4-26: If you're traveling solo, a small, lightweight tent such as this Early Winters Pocket Hotel weighs about two pounds.

Most modern tents feature fiberglass rods. I strongly advise that you purchase an extra set of such rods. They are tough, but sometimes they can be hard to bend into position when you're setting up the tent. If you fight the rods, you can break them. Once broken, the tent will sag and you will lose valuable living space. It's a good idea to practice setting up the tent in the back yard at least six times before taking off on a trip with it. Most tents come with extra fabrics and fabric cement so you can patch any cuts or holes you may inadvertently poke in it. Some tents require seams to be waterproofed with seam sealer. Do all your sealing when you practice setting up the tent, and re-seal every year if necessary.

About Campgrounds

Here are a few words of advice, hard-won by this writer, about campgrounds. First, try to get to one by 5:00 P.M. That gives you enough daylight hours to set up the tent, cook dinner, and relax by the campfire. Once we arrived at the campground well after dark, when the sky was moonless black. We set up the tent in the assigned site, we thought, but wondered why horses where whinnying outside the tent fly all night. Come dawn, we discovered our tent was pitched just outside the campground proper in a private pasture devoted to horses, redolent with droppings.

Second, never take a "Sorry, all full" sign as applying to you. Many rangers, at least in state and county camps, are cyclists themselves, and they can always squeeze you in somewhere. Some campgrounds have "remote sites" you can bike right up to, far from car campers (thank God). County campgrounds quite often even have better facilities and are less crowded than state or national park campgrounds. Avoid private camp-grounds like the plague. They are almost always overcrowded, jammed full of cars, trucks, campers and six-wheeled Yucka-bago monsters with all the comforts of "civilization," including bath, TV, furnace, microwave, and the like. Select a campsite that's as far away from toilet and shower facilities as possible. The loudest, most obnoxious campers tend to cluster around the toilet shacks, as though deriving some comfort from the proximity of this most basic need. Besides, if you camp near these facilities, you'll hear running water and screen doors banging all night long.

Stay as far away as possible from these self-contained hotels on wheels. I have found that the people who live in them almost always have a small terrier that yips and barks all night. The people who drive these monsters seem to love to chop wood until the wee hours of the morning, build a roaring bonfire (sometimes smokier than roarier), and leap back into the Yuckabago to watch the burning embers through a picture window. I might also caution you that quite often these umbilical cords on wheels are rented, and that the people who drive them have no concept at all of how wide they are. Cyclists have been sideswiped by them and badly hurt, even killed. Keep a weather eye out behind you, and if you see one weaving down the road while a car is occupying the lane coming at you, you can be sure that both vehicles will be alongside you when they meet. In which case, as noted earlier, hug the outermost fringe of the shoulder, or be prepared to take other evasive action. Strange, isn't it, but doesn't it often seem that when there's a vehicle a mile away, coming toward you, and one a mile away coming up from behind you, that they always seem to meet right where you are?

Lights, Cook Stoves and Other Gear

Nothing's blacker and darker than a campground on a moonless night, which can give you an idea of what it must have been like for those early pioneers who forged through the woods to homestead in the wilderness. Even when the moon is full, a safe, reliable non-electric light is a real comfort. You can read in your tent or play cards outside with a good little light such as the UltraLight kerosene lantern (Fig. 4-27). It squishes down to a small size (Fig. 4-28). With an adapter it can warm up a small bowl of soup or a cup of coffee in a metal container (Fig. 4-29). This light is available from the BikeCentennial (see Appendix) catalog. Candles are o.k., but they don't give much light and take up space in your panniers.

So you don't have to carry two fuels, kerosene for the lantern and white gas for the stove, I recommend a dual-fuel stove such

Fig. 4-27: Ultra-Light kerosene lantern uses same fuel as cookstove (multi-fuel cookstove).

Fig. 4-28: Same lantern as in Fig. 4-27, but collapsed it takes up little room.

Fig. 4-29: Ultra-Light lantern doubles as soup or coffee warmer.

as the new MSR X-GK (Fig. 4-30), or the Coleman Peak I Multi-Fuel stove (Fig. 4-31). The MSR burns white gas, leaded or unleaded automobile gas, aviation gas, deodorized or regular kerosene, Stoddard Solvent, #1 diesel fuel, and #1 stove fuel (deoderized kerosene works fine). The Coleman burns white

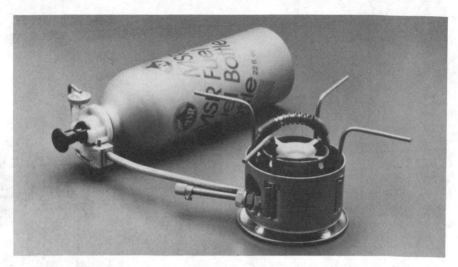

Fig. 4-30: MSR X-GK burns leaded or unleaded aviation fuel, Stoddard Solvent, or #1 diesel fuel, gasoline, kerosene, lights easily even at high altitudes, heats quickly.

Fig. 4-31: Coleman Peak-I stove uses white gas or kerosene, is compact, light, has built-in fuel tank, and comes with carrying case.

gas or kerosene. Both stoves are excellent. The MSR has a slight edge in heat output, so cooking is a bit quicker, but either stove will do just fine. I like the idea of carrying kerosene instead of gasoline, too, since it's much less volatile and thus less of a hazard. (Do not use either stove in your tent.) Butane stoves use this gas in small pressure cylinders. They put out a lot of heat, light quickly, and are quiet and clean burning. But the 12-ounce-can-sized butane containers are bulky, though light, and if you're on an off-road bike on a wilderness trail, you have to bring back the empties. You can carry more heat in less space when it's liquid kerosene than when it's gas in a can.

How to Pick a Pannier

I've used the word "pannier" five or six times in this chapter, so I hope by now you know it means a bag that attaches to a carrier on your bike that's used to carry your gear.

Panniers come in a wide variety of sizes, from around 1,200 cubic inches (Fig. 4-32) to really big ones with a capacity of around 3,000 cubic inches or more (Fig. 4-33). If you're just taking short day trips, the smaller panniers will be lighter and more convenient.

Fig. 4-32: Small panniers such as this one are ideal for short day trips.

Fig. 4-33: Larger panniers are what you'll need for extended bike tours.

The panniers on the market today are quite well made. Some do have more pockets than others, and I like lots of them. If you've ever had to rummage through a stuffed pannier to find a salt shaker, box of matches, or deck of playing cards, for example, you know how convenient it is to have panniers with many pockets, some large, some small. They are all quite water resistant, too, although some are more so than others. Some panniers, such as the Needleworks (Fig. 4-34), have a rain cover you can slip over them so that no matter how driving the deluge becomes, your goodies will remain snugly dry. The Needleworks panniers are well made but cost almost twice as much as other panniers. If you're going on a real safari and want the most reliable of panniers, though, these would be the ones to take along.

How well panniers are fastened to your carriers is very important. It's not only embarrassing to have a pannier fall off your bike into the street but it could be downright dangerous because it might cause you to make a sudden stop or abrupt turn. Once I was cycling down the cobblestone streets of a town in Belgium, going bump, bump, bump. Suddenly one of my rear panniers just bounced off the rear carrier and went tumbling off onto the street. Traffic was thin, which I was grateful for, because that was the pannier that was carrying my Hasselblad camera. I did the fastest 180-degree turn ever made on a bike, at least by me, and returned to where the pannier was resting in the middle of the street, retrieving it before the camera was run over by an oncoming truck. That was many years ago. Now most panniers have excellent retention systems

Fig. 4-34: Some makes of panniers have fitted rain covers available, such as these Needleworks (cover not shown) and Eclipse panniers.

which securely fasten them to carriers. If you use them properly, you should never lose a pannier.

For example, Needleworks makes an excellent retention system. As shown in Fig. 4-35, the system has straps which tie the panniers onto the carrier side struts and clips which fasten the panniers onto the top carrier strut so that they are held at top, bottom, and sides. It does take time to put these panniers on and to remove them, but taking the extra time is worthwhile. A quicker working locking system is made by Kirtland (Fig. 4-36); it features a one-lever lock, plus clips that hold the pannier at top and bottom on the carrier. The lever mechanism locks

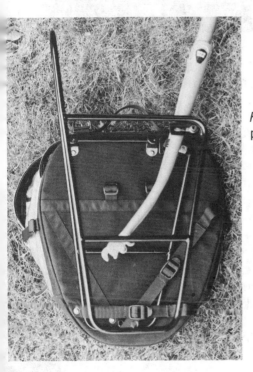

Fig. 4-35: Needleworks retention system holds panniers firmly in all directions.

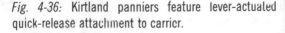

Fig. 4-36: Kirtland panniers feature lever-actuated quick-release attachment to carrier.

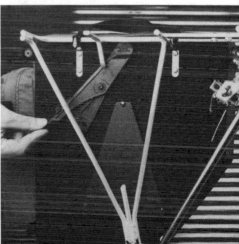

Fig. 4-37: What the well-dressed touring bike will wear on a trip. If you can't fit your equipment in these roomy Kirtland panniers, chances are good you don't need it all. Note safety reflective stripes and low-rider matching carrier and panniers on the fork.

the pannier's top clips onto the top carrier strut. A complete set of Kirtland panniers is shown in Fig. 4-37. Note the low-rider carriers attached to the fork. This keeps weight as close as possible to the ground for better balance and steering control.

All well-made panniers feature external strapping that holds the load tightly to prevent it from sagging, bouncing around, or swaying. Figs. 4-34, 4-38, and 4-39 show good examples of strapping arrangements to make loads more secure. Any load that moves of its own volition can make bike handling and steering less stable, which can contribute to loss of control and an accident. Finally, as you check out panniers, open them up

Fig. 4-38: Heavy-duty Lone Peak panniers have external straps to keep load from moving inside the panniers.

Fig. 4-39: This Kangaroo pannier has an expandable main compartment, which is partially empty in this photo. Note the external straps for keeping load from shifting in the panniers. I have covered many thousands of miles with these panniers.

and look inside for projecting seams that could catch in zippers. Few things are more frustrating than zippers that are jammed by loose threads or by excessive inside seam material. The Needleworks pannier in Fig. 4-40 is an example of a well-made pannier with smoothly sewn seams that can't catch in zippers. In Fig. 4-40 you can also see Velcro-attached compartments that can be made into various sizes, depending on your stowage plan. For extra safety, I recommend using reflective strips on panniers, as shown in Fig. 4-41. You can glue or sew them on if they don't come with them.

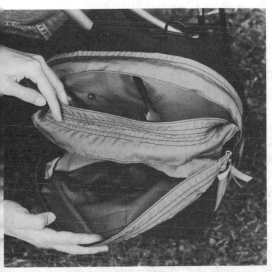

Fig. 4-40: Well-made panniers have nothing inside to catch or jam zippers, which can be a truly exasperating experience. This Needleworks unit is a good example of a very well-made pannier with nothing to get in the way of smoothly operating zippers.

Fig. 4-41: If panniers don't have reflective stripes, like this one, you can glue them on for the added safety of visibility to motorists.

More About Trailers

I discussed trailers briefly in Chapter 2 (see Figs. 2-11 and 2-38), as I reviewed how well they carried a camping-gear load safely. There are a few more features of trailers which apply specifically to their use on long-distance bike tours.

A new type of one-wheeled, slender trailer (Fig. 4-42) is narrower than your handlebar, so anywhere it's safe for you to go, this trailer can follow right behind. In Chapter 2 I discussed the technique of "drafting" (Fig. 2-52), in which a rider positions the bike behind another rider in front. The idea is to let the bike up ahead break the wind to make the going easier for the rider behind. You will recall that at least 80 percent of forward movement resistance on a bike comes from the wind, at least on the flats. If you're riding into the wind, this resistance increases. I mention this because the bike towing a trailer also breaks the wind for the trailer, so in effect, the trailer is "drafting" the bike. The drafting effect is less for wider, less streamlined trailers than it is for the trailer in Fig. 4-42. The bigger trailers have two wheels which increase rolling resistance.

The economics of trailers is interesting. For example, a set of four high-quality panniers costs around $195. A good front and rear carrier costs around $55 for both. That's a total of $250. The

Fig. 4-42: Lightweight, one-wheel streamlined bike trailer is an excellent way to carry equipment on a long trip. If your bike store does not have them, write to LifeCycle Trailer Co., Ltd., P.O. Box 12, Ste-Anne de Bellevue, Quebec, Canada H9X 3L4.

trailer in Fig. 4-42 costs around $160. The trailer in Fig. 2-11 costs about $190. So you can buy a good trailer for a lot less than the cost of high-quality panniers and their carriers, and get at least as much storage space as you get with the panniers.

The trailer has two additional advantages. One, the bike loaded down with filled panniers (Fig. 4-9) is a lot more unbalnaced and awkward to handle. Two, when you get to the campground, you can unclip the trailer from your seat post and presto, you have an unencumbered lightweight bike to ride. So much of this country is so beautiful that I like to select a scenic campsite, set up camp, and ride out in a different direction every day for a week or however long it takes to explore the area. Much scenery is missed when you barrel through the countryside, seeing only what you pass on the road, or even the trail if you're on an all-terrain bike. Not only that, when you change camps every day you waste a lot of time setting up camp, striking the tent, and packing everything away. In many camps you could leave the loaded trailer with the ranger, if you're worried about thieves. In one camp I visited in northern California, a group of thieves crept through at night stealing everything not tied down, even rubber boats and rafts. They got my fishing tackle, but fortunately the bikes were chained to a heavy picnic table.

Steering and braking techniques when cycling with a trailer:

1. You have to swing wider around corners so you don't hit the curb, as shown in Fig. 4-43. Watch a truck driver, hauling a big rig, make a right turn and you'll see what I mean.

Fig. 4-43: When towing a trailer, swing wider around corners. *(Courtesy LifeCycle Trailers)*

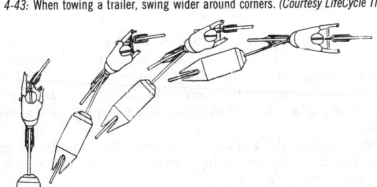

2. When you're crossing an intersection, allow for the fact that your bike with trailer is about twice as long (Fig. 4-44) as the bike alone. Make doubly sure traffic from your left or right is far enough away so you can get across the intersection. A driver may see you, but not your trailer, since it's so close to the ground.

Fig. 4-44: Your bike plus trailer is twice as long as the bike alone. Allow for this extra length when crossing an intersection. *(Courtesy LifeCycle Trailers)*

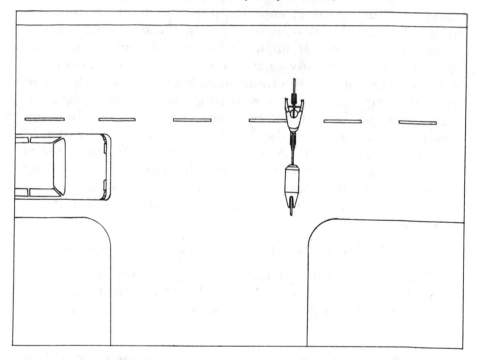

3. When passing another bicycle, remember you're towing a trailer (Fig. 4-45), so don't cut in front of that bike until you are far enough ahead of it to do so safely.
4. Don't turn so sharply that you jackknife your trailer (Fig. 4-46). Remember that 90 degrees is your maximum turning radius.
5. When loading the trailer, put heavier items, such as your tent and food staples, at the bottom and toward the rear for greater stability (Fig. 4-47).

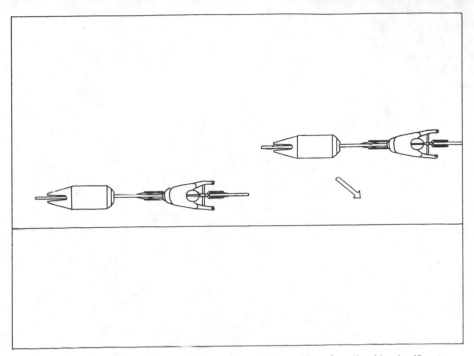

Fig. 4-45: Make allowances for the trailer when cutting in front of another bicycle. *(Courtesy LifeCycle Trailers)*

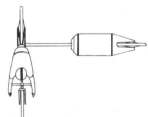

Fig. 4-46: When making sharp turns, keep them under 90 degrees to avoid jackknifing trailer. *(Courtesy LifeCycle Trailers)*

Fig. 4-47: Load a trailer with heaviest items toward the rear for greater handling stability. *(Courtesy LifeCycle Trailers)*

Fig. 4-48: Slow down over bumps to avoid stress to passengers.

6. Slow down over bumps and on rough roads to avoid damage to your trailer (Fig. 4-48).
7. If hard objects bounce around noisily inside the trailer, wrap them in your sleeping bag or cushion them with a towel.

About Food

There's a lot of good advice in Chapter 3 on diet and food for the bicyclist, as well as a list of books on this subject in the Appendix. You can of course buy a lot of excellent dried meals in camping goods stores. Unless you're going off into wilderness where you can't shop for food, you won't need dried stuff on the road.

My advice is to check out the last town you come to before the camp of your choice, and shop there for dinner and breakfast foods of your choice. In some states, notably on both coasts, you can buy delicious fresh seafood: clams, crabs, oysters, bluefish, and lobsters in the east; in the west, salmon, shark steak, albacore, squid, and crabs.

Bicycling Overseas

If you want to see the Orient, Tibet, Australia, Tasmania, or New Zealand, I recommend a package tour such as one of Sobek's (see Appendix). If you want to cycle in Europe, you have your choice of a package tour or planning one on your own. As I noted above, each type has its advantages. Here are a few tips that can make your European trip more fun, if you are making your own arrangements:

Buy your bike in the U.S.A.: If you wait till you get to Europe to buy a bike, you're never going to have the time to de-bug it. Most new bikes need minor fine-tuning of such things as cable stretch and resultant brake and derailleur adjustment—minor, yes, but a major pain if neglected. If you buy your bike from a good dealer in this country, you can be assured the bike will have been thoroughly checked out. If you ride that bike for a few months, you will know it thoroughly and be aware of what it needs. Somewhere between Paris and Moscow is no place to discover that the bike is malfunctioning.

Pre-declare anything and everything that's made outside the U.S.A.: If you don't, U.S. Customs may ask you to pay duty on these items, a cost which was included in your original purchase price. Pre-declare *everything,* even a German-made camera strap, your bike, your binoculars, clothes, camera—anything not made in this country. Then, on your return, just show that declaration to the customs agent and you're home free. To pre-declare, take your foreign-made products, including serial numbers, to the U.S. Customs office at the airport, and with the customs agent, fill in the appropriate form. Make sure a customs agent signs it. On the way back, flight attendants usually pass out customs forms so you can list items you purchased abroad. List *everything* you bought and how much you paid for it. If you show this list to an agent, you'll get faster clearance through customs.

Be certain about immunization: Check your travel agency, or a local branch of the U.S. Public Health Service, to make sure that where you're going does not require immunization shots. Most European countries don't, but if you're going to Africa, Asia, or South America, you'd better check.

About visas: If you're going to Russia, any of the Eastern-bloc countries, or China, check your travel agent to make sure you have the proper visa, if one is needed.

Never, but never, cash traveler's checks at a hotel: Always cash them at a bank when you're in a foreign country. Hotels really charge a premium for such a service. Most U.S. international airports have a foreign currency exchange, where you should get at least $100 in the currency of the first country you're visiting. That way you can eat, drink, tip porters, and hire a cab, if necessary, as soon as you arrive. My advice, though, is to have your luggage in your panniers, set up your bike on arrival, and ride away from the airport. I know that in Paris, London, Milan, and Vienna, cities I have biked to and through, you'll get to a local hotel to sleep off jet lag about as fast on your bike as you will via bus or cab.

About maps: Use Michelin maps if you're going to Europe. As you plan your route, you'll notice that the maps show roads labelled "A," "B," and "C." The "A" roads are like our inter-state highways, except that in Europe they may have no speed limit. It's not too healthy to bike on autobahns where the cars, trucks, and buses are whizzing along at 90 to 110 mph and up. "B" roads are the same as U.S. state highways, and these I would also avoid. If you want peace and quiet, use only the "C" roads, which are the equivalent of county roads in this country. European "C" roads are almost always paved and in good condition, with low traffic density. If you look closely at the map, you will also note that in some places some roads are marked by chevrons (inverted V's). Each chevron denotes a 5 percent grade. Unless you want a back-busting climb, try to avoid three-chevron roads. Finer-scale Michelin maps show bike routes, many of which are far from highways. You'll share them with mopeds, but that's no problem. Europeans are used to bikes, and you'll be treated well.

Learn about the language and currency of the countries you'll be visiting: It does little good to ask how much something is if you can't understand the answer. Learn the basics of directions, how to order food, find a hotel, a campsite, a bed-and-breakfast, or a youth hostel. Or you could use a hand-held electronic interpreter. They're available in many languages.

Remember that campgrounds abound in Europe, and once you learn how to find them, you'll always have an inexpensive place to stay. Rand-McNally publishes a source book of maps and campsites that is a handy and compact guide to American county, state, and national parks. It's available in bookstores. American Youth Hostels (AYH) publishes a compact list of hostels in this country and a list of affiliated hostel organizations in many foreign countries. The word "Youth" in AYH is a bit misleading. I've seen people of all ages staying at these hostels. Membership in the AYH is $20 for ages 18 to 59, $10 for people under 17 and seniors over 60. See the Appendix for details.

County maps are absolutely invaluable. If you're going on a long trip through several states, county maps can fill up half of one of your panniers, and that is a problem. I buy the maps locally as I go, and mail them home as I finish with them. That doesn't allow for much detailed trip planning, but I've never had problems figuring out a route with the help of friendly natives.

About airline charges for carrying a bicycle: Airlines usually charge $25 within the continental U.S. and $50 elsewhere. The best way to get your bike on a plane is to scrounge a bike box from a local bike shop. Dealers throw them away, so you should have no problem getting one.

Now here's how you pack your bike: Remove both wheels (Chapter 6). Brace the dropouts (where the wheel axle fits) with an old axle or a piece of wood, so the fork blades or rear stays can't get bent in shipment. Strap the wheels to the frame, one on each side. Remove the pedals (Chapter 14) and screw them in the cranks from the inside, or strap them to the frame. Lower the saddle (Chapter 12) as far as possible, or remove it together with the seat post if you can't close the top of the bike box. Remove the handlebars (Chapter 12) and strap them over the top tube, parallel to the bike. There should be room in the bike box to stuff at least one set of loaded panniers, which may cut down on your carry-on bags. Put your tools and spare parts in the panniers you put in the bike box. I remember having a difficult time explaining to a security person at an airport that the long tube in my hand luggage was a bike pump. I had to disassemble the pump to prove it. These security measures must be taken to keep boarding delays at a minimum. If you have to explain your bike tools to a security guard, you could miss your flight if you're running late. That also goes for return trips from overseas, particularly from England, Sweden, France, Germany, and, above all, Switzerland. Many airlines will sell you a bike box or a heavy-duty plastic bike bag at the airport, both in the U.S. and overseas, for around $5; so you can abandon your own box on arrival and pick up another one on the way back. Some airlines, such as KLM, will take your bike sans bike box if you remove the pedals and handlebars and fasten them as above. Leave both wheels on the bike, in that case. Since it's possible that the baggage compartment may not be as pressurized as the passenger compartment, it's a good idea to let some of the air out of your tires before putting it on the plane. Otherwise the reduced air pressure at high altitude may, in effect, raise the air pressure in your tires high enough to blow them out.

Watch out for poison ivy in the eastern area and midwest United States, poison oak in the western U.S., and poison sumac in the south. Look up these plants in botany books at your library, so you can recognize the leaves. Carry a tube of ½ percent hydrocortisone ointment in case you are infected. It's great for saddle sores, too, and does not require a prescription.

Do not carry Halt or Mace on your person or even in the bike box on an airplane: Save that stuff for your travels in the U.S. The electronic Dog Chaser (see Fig. 2-61 in Chapter 2) is, as far as I know, legal to carry on a plane, but I'd stuff it in the bike box and not carry it on your person.

European trains: They usually have a baggage car in which you can put your bike, although there may be a small extra fare involved. You may have to put the bike aboard the baggage car yourself. Fig. 4-49 shows a baggage car in a train in Europe, which I took because I wanted to skip some industrialized sections and get quickly into a more scenic area.

Mountains: I can't tell you how many times I've biked up a mountain, taking all day to make the crest, only to be disappointed that there was no sign to tell me how high I had gone for all my effort. A small altimeter (Fig. 4-50), while admittedly a luxury at around $150 with leather carrying case, is a compact way to record your altitude. If you're traveling by car to plot a

Fig. 4-49: Typical European baggage car. That's my bike, strapped to rail at right rear, en route from Eindhoven to Utrecht, the Netherlands.

Fig. 4-50: Small altimeter lets you know how high you are. Let me rephrase that: how high up you are. Well, the number of feet you are above sea level.

route in advance, the altimeter will help you calculate hill climbs and road grades, and prepare profile maps. If you're wilderness touring and have to read contour maps, an altimeter is helpful in checking your location, as well as in route planning.

There will come a day on a bike camping trip when your last six campsites were without showers and there were no lakes to bathe in. What I do is visit the first health club I come to in a larger city and give them a couple of bucks to use their shower. In fact, one such club was so bemused by our request that they gave us free showers and even threw in towels and soap.

Weather precautions: Earlier in the chapter I advised you to carry a small radio to pick up weather reports before you leave camp in the morning. Rainy weather does decrease visibility, so you will be less easily seen by motorists, and the water cuts down your braking capacity by at least 50 percent. You might also look up the wind-chill factor from any book in weather forecasting in your library. For example, if the air temperature is 35°F and the wind speed is 20 mph, the wind-chill factor is 12°F. On a bike the wind speed is the speed you're traveling, less the speed of the wind from your back. For example, if the wind is from the west at 20 mph and you're traveling west at 20 mph, the wind-chill index is cancelled out and the air temper-

Fig. 4-51: It's wise to make advance reservations if you're stopping at AYH youth hostels. This hostel is the Chamounix Mansion International Youth Hostel in Philadelphia, Pennsylvania. If you think it's raining, you're right. *(AYH photo)*

ature is the same as that read by the thermometer. If you're traveling east at 20 mph into a 20 mph wind (unlikely as this may be), the effective wind speed is 40 mph. At 35°F, the cooling power of the wind will be equivalent to a temperature of just 3°F.

Vineyards: If you're touring in the harvest season, in Europe especially, respect private property. Do not stop to pick grapes from a vineyard or fruit from trees, even though it's temptingly near. I have found that Europeans are pretty fussy about their property, but generous if you ask them. In Austria, for example, during the grape harvesting season, I have waved from my bike to workers in the vineyards, who would wave back with a cluster of grapes in their hands, clearly offering me some. On a warm day, they were welcome.

Wheel-rim strength: If you're riding a heavily loaded bike and you weigh over 180 pounds, consider going to 40-spoked wheels instead of the conventional 36-spoked wheel. The four additional spokes will give you a stronger rim and less chance of spoke breakage.

Fig. 4-52: In scenic Cape Cod National Seashore, this Little America Youth Hostel in Truro, Massachusetts, offers inexpensive hospitality to this lone cyclist. *(AYH photo by Greg Siple)*

Make reservations: If you're planning to stop in youth hostels, the folks at American Youth Hostels, Inc., recommend making advance reservations.

What You Should Know About Your Gears

Some new bikes come with gears that aren't suitable for bicycle touring. This is especially true of the more exotic, costly bikes, because the manufacturers assume that anybody who buys one must be as experienced and strong as Sylvester Stallone, or at least Greg LeMond, winner of the 1986 Tour de France. Look at your rear gear cluster, for instance. If it looks like either of the two at the top of Fig. 4-53, you're going to get in trouble on the first steep hill you climb, especially if your bike is loaded down with camping gear. These gears are close-ratio, with the smallest (high-speed) cog having 13 teeth and the largest (low-speed) cog having 21 teeth. Most of us ordinary tourists need "Granny" gears, such as those at the bottom of Fig. 4-53. These

Fig. 4-53: The gears (cogs) on the two top freewheels are close-ratio clusters more suited to cyclists in top physical condition. The cogs on the two bottom freewheels are wide-ratio gears for us ordinary mortals who need the low end of these clusters to climb steep hills.

Fig. 4-54: Close-ratio double chainwheel more suited to racing than to touring.

Fig. 4-55: Wide-ratio triple chainwheel, with superlow-gear 24-tooth chainring, for hill climbing.

are known also as wide-ratio gears. They come with cogs from 13 to as high as 38 teeth.

Your bike may also have a close-ratio double chainwheel, such as shown in Fig. 4-54. If you're planning to use that bike for touring, I recommend you change over to a triple-wide-ratio chainwheel, such as shown in Fig. 4-55. You can get a triple-chainwheel set with a small chainwheel of 24 teeth, which, in combination with the 38-tooth rear cog, would give you a super-low gear that lets you climb everything but a wall. Indeed, there *are* grades over 15 percent that even trained racing cyclists find it wiser to walk up, as shown in Fig. 4-56, taken during an all-terrain bicycle race in California. In Fig. 4-57, the woman shown dismounted about one second after I clicked the shutter. I didn't think she'd make it any more than I could, which was why I had my camera at the ready. You can change cogs on your freewheel and also replace a double with a triple-chainwheel set to get wider and lower gear ratios. Please refer to Chapter 9 for instructions on these changes.

Fig. 4-56: If you don't have wide-ratio gears with a superlow gear, you'll be walking up steep hills, even as these superb physical specimens must in an all-terrain bike race in central California.

Fig. 4-57: This young lady thought she could make this 15 percent grade with her low "granny" gear. I knew she couldn't do it, and in fact a second after I snapped this shot she fell over, slowly and gracefully. Some hills you just have to resign yourself to walking up.

How many gears to the inch? This is a good question, because the bicycling fraternity has lo these many years translated gear ratios to gearing in inches. The gear-inch concept is a throwback to the pre-1900 high-wheel bicycle (Figs. 4-58 and 4-59), when the gear ratio of a bicycle was simply the diameter of the big front wheel. The bigger the wheel, the faster you could go, if you had long and strong enough legs. In Fig. 4-58, for example, you can see that the bicycle in the foreground has a smaller front wheel than the high-wheeler in the background. So the bike in the foreground would be slower than the other bike because the diameter of the front wheel, or "inches," is smaller. This concept was translated to modern multi-geared bicycles by a leap of the imagination coupled with some simple math.

To arrive at the "inches" of gear for any combination of front chainwheel and rear freewheel cogs, use this simple two-step

Fig. 4-58: You can see that the Penny Farthing in the rear has a bigger-diameter front wheel than the one in the front. It can go faster than the one in the front, if the rider has long enough and strong enough legs.

Fig. 4-59: The high-wheel "Penny Farthing" or "Ordinary" of the late 1800s had a large front wheel, a small rear one, and no gears.

formula. Count the number of teeth of the freewheel cog of your choice. Do the same for the chainwheel of your choice. Find the gear ratio between these two gears by dividing the number of teeth in the chainwheel by the number of teeth in the freewheel cog. For example, say you counted 54 teeth in the chainwheel and 13 teeth in the freewheel cog: 54 ÷ 13 = 4.15, rounded off, which is the *gear ratio* of this combination. The second step in finding the *gear inches* is to multiply this *gear ratio* by the diameter of the rear wheel. For example, say your rear wheel is 27 inches, so 27 × 4.15 = 112, which is the number of inches of this gear combination. That would be, in 1900s bike parlance, equivalent to a high-wheeler with a nine-foot-diameter front wheel. Never having seen anyone who could ride such a monster, I can only conclude they were never made that big. But it does show you that technology can engineer a bike with all the speed advantages of a nine-foot direct drive wheel in a bike a five-foot-tall person could ride today. The 112-inch gear is a truly high-speed gear used by bike racing athletes.

Let's go to the other extreme and find a super-low gear, in the archaic "inch" terminology (we're stuck with it). Say you have a rear cog with 38 teeth (which is as big as they come) and a small chainwheel with 24 teeth (as small as they come). Put these two gears together and what do you have? 24 ÷ 38 = 0.6 (a negative gear ratio); 0.6 × your 27-inch wheel diameter gives you an inch-equivalent gear of 16, which is truly a wall climber.

One problem you may have in selecting your own gears is that so many combinations are either duplicates or so close as to be duplicates. I have computed a gear table (Table 4-1) for bikes with 27-inch wheels. This table also applies to bikes with 700-centimeter wheels. Table 4-2 is for all-terrain bikes with 26-inch wheels. Looking at either table, you will see many, many repetitions. For instance, in Table 4-1, a rear gear of 12 teeth and a front gear of 24 teeth produces a 54-inch gear. So do combinations of 13 and 26, 14 and 29, and many others.

Fig. 4-60: A workable gear selection for an 18-speed bicycle. Since three of the gears are duplicates, or nearly so, only 15 are usable. That's a penalty you pay for a wide range of gears, and it's worth it, believe me.

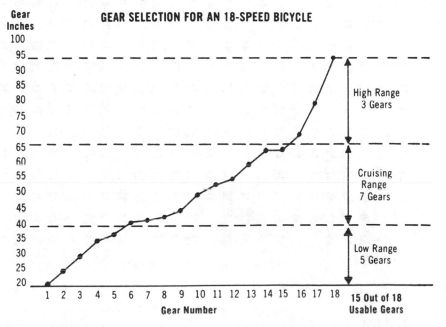

Table 4-1

NUMBER OF TEETH IN CHAINWHEEL
(For 27-inch wheels only)

	24	25	26	27	28	29	30	31	32	33	34	35	36	37	38	39	40	41	42	43	44	45	46	47	48	49	50	51	52	53	54
12	54	56	59	61	63	65	68	70	72	74	77	79	81	83	86	88	90	92	95	97	99	101	104	105	108	110	113	115	117	119	122
13	50	52	54	56	58	60	62	64	67	69	71	72	75	79	79	81	83	85	87	89	91	94	96	98	100	102	104	106	108	110	112
14	46	48	50	52	54	56	58	60	62	64	66	68	69	71	73	75	77	79	81	83	85	87	89	91	93	95	96	98	100	102	104
15	43	45	47	49	50	52	54	56	58	59	61	63	65	67	68	70	72	74	76	77	79	81	83	85	86	88	90	92	94	95	97
16	41	42	44	46	47	49	51	52	54	56	57	59	61	62	64	66	68	69	71	73	74	76	78	79	81	83	84	86	88	89	91
17	38	40	41	43	45	46	48	49	51	52	54	56	57	59	60	62	64	65	67	68	70	76	73	75	76	78	79	81	83	84	86
18	36	38	39	41	42	44	45	47	48	50	51	53	54	56	57	59	60	62	63	65	66	68	69	71	72	74	75	77	78	80	81
19	34	36	37	38	40	41	43	44	45	47	48	50	51	53	54	55	57	58	60	61	63	64	65	67	68	70	71	73	74	75	77
20	32	34	35	36	38	39	41	42	43	45	46	47	49	50	51	53	54	55	57	58	59	61	62	64	65	66	68	69	70	72	73
21	31	32	33	35	36	37	39	40	41	42	44	45	46	48	49	50	51	53	54	55	57	58	59	60	62	63	64	66	67	68	69
22	29	31	32	33	34	36	37	38	39	41	42	43	44	45	47	48	49	50	52	53	54	55	56	58	59	60	61	63	64	65	66
23	28	29	31	32	33	34	35	36	38	39	40	41	42	43	45	46	47	48	49	51	52	53	54	55	56	58	59	60	61	62	63
24	27	28	29	30	32	33	34	35	36	37	38	39	41	42	43	44	45	46	47	48	50	51	52	53	54	55	56	57	58	60	61
25	26	27	28	29	30	31	32	33	35	36	37	38	39	40	41	42	43	44	45	46	48	49	50	51	52	53	54	55	56	57	58
26	25	26	27	28	29	30	31	32	33	34	35	36	37	38	39	41	42	43	44	45	46	47	48	49	50	51	52	53	54	55	56
27	24	25	26	27	28	29	30	31	32	33	34	35	36	37	38	39	40	41	42	43	44	45	46	47	48	49	50	51	52	53	54
28	23	24	25	26	27	28	29	30	31	32	33	34	35	36	37	38	39	40	41	41	42	43	44	45	46	47	48	49	50	51	52
29	22	23	24	25	26	27	28	29	30	31	32	33	34	34	35	36	37	38	39	40	41	42	43	44	45	46	47	47	48	49	50
30	22	23	23	24	25	26	27	28	29	30	31	32	32	33	34	35	36	37	38	39	40	41	41	42	43	44	45	46	47	48	49
31	21	22	23	24	24	25	26	27	28	29	30	30	31	32	33	34	35	36	37	37	38	39	40	41	42	43	44	44	45	46	47
32	20	21	22	23	24	24	25	26	27	28	29	30	30	31	32	33	34	35	35	36	37	38	39	40	41	41	42	43	44	45	46
33	20	20	21	22	23	24	25	25	26	27	28	29	29	30	31	32	33	34	34	35	36	37	38	38	39	40	41	42	43	43	44
34	19	20	21	21	22	23	24	25	25	26	27	28	29	29	30	31	32	33	33	34	35	36	37	37	38	39	40	41	41	42	43
38	17	18	18	19	20	21	21	22	23	23	24	25	26	26	27	28	28	29	30	31	31	32	33	33	34	35	36	36	37	38	38

NUMBER OF TEETH IN REAR SPROCKET

Table 4-1: To find the gear in "inches" for any combination of freewheel sprocket teeth and front chainwheel teeth, find where both meet. For example, you have counted 14 teeth in a freewheel sprocket and 44 teeth in the chainwheel; 14 meets 44 at "85," so that's your gear in "inches."

Table 4-2, for 26-inch wheel bikes, is also rife with duplications.

This duplication of gear combinations means that you're going to find some gear combinations that are so close together as to be wasted. In an 18-speed transmission system (six cogs

Table 4-2: Some as Table 4-1, except for 26-inch wheels, such as on all-terrain and commuter bicycles.

Table 4-2

NUMBER OF TEETH IN CHAINWHEEL
(For 26-inch wheels only)

	24	26	28	30	34	36	38	40	42	44	46	48	50	52
12	52	56	61	65	74	78	82	87	91	95·	100	104	108	113
13	48	52	56	60	68	72	76	80	84	88	92	96	100	104
14	45	48	52	56	63	67	71	74	78	82	85	89	93	97
15	42	45	49	52	59	62	66	69	73	76	80	83	87	90
16	39	42	46	49	55	59	62	65	68	72	75	78	81	85
17	37	40	43	46	52	55	58	61	64	67	70	73	76	80
18	35	38	40	43	49	52	55	58	61	64	66	69	72	75
19	33	36	38	41	47	49	52	55	57	60	63	66	68	71
20	31	34	36	39	44	47	49	52	55	57	60	62	65	68
21	30	32	35	37	42	45	47	50	52	54	57	59	62	64
22	28	31	33	35	40	43	45	47	50	52	54	57	59	61
23	27	30	32	34	38	41	43	45	47	50	52	54	57	59
24	26	28	30	33	37	39	41	43	46	48	50	52	54	56
25	25	27	29	31	35	37	40	42	44	46	48	50	52	54
26	24	26	28	30	34	36	38	40	42	44	46	48	50	52
27	23	25	27	29	33	35	37	39	40	42	44	46	48	50
28	22	24	26	28	32	33	35	37	39	41	43	45	46	48
29	22	23	25	27	30	32	34	36	38	39	41	43	45	47
30	21	23	24	26	29	31	33	35	36	38	40	42	43	45
32	20	21	23	24	28	29	31	33	34	36	37	39	41	42
34	18	20	21	23	26	28	29	31	32	34	35	37	38	40
36	17	19	20	22	25	26	27	29	30	32	33	35	36	38
38	16	18	19	21	23	25	26	27	29	30	31	33	34	36

NUMBER OF TEETH IN REAR SPROCKET

rear, three chainwheels front) you will find only 15 of the 18 speeds really usable. You pay a penalty in unusable gears (duplicates) to get super-low gearing plus a wide enough range of other gears to let you handle just about any grade road under 15 percent. Fig. 4-60 shows a reasonably good gear selection for an 18-speed bike, as does Table 4-3.

How fast you'll be pedaling is a function of your cadence, the gear (inches) you're in, and "pi." Cadence is simply how many times you spin the cranks each minute. If you spin the cranks (or turn a pedal through 360 degrees, which is your cadence) at the rate of one crank revolution per second (60 crank rpm per minute), and you're in a 26-inch gear, you'll be traveling at the fantastic speed of 4.64 miles per hour. Table 4-4 tells you how

Table 4-3

GEAR COMBINATIONS FOR AN 18-SPEED TOURING BICYCLE

GEAR NO.	NUMBER OF TEETH IN FREEWHEEL	NUMBER OF TEETH IN CHAINWHEEL	GEAR, INCHES
1	32	24	20.3
2	26	24	24.9
3	22	24	29.5
4	32	40	33.8
5	19	24	34.1
6	16	24	40.5
7	26	40	41.5
8	32	50	42.2
9	14	24	46.3
10	22	40	49.1
11	26	50	51.9
12	19	40	56.8
13	22	50	58.7
14	16	40	67.5
15	19	50	67.5
16	14	40	77.1
17	16	50	84.4
18	14	50	96.4

Table 4-3: This is a tabular version of Fig. 4-60. These gear combinations will give you a wide gear selection for almost any terrain you will encounter. You may have to walk up grades much greater than six degrees (10.5 percent).

Table 4-4

THE SPEED IN MPH EQUALS PI TIMES THE GEAR   TIMES THE CRANK RPM TIMES 60 DIVIDED BY 63,360

REVOLUTIONS PER MINUTE OF THE CRANK ARM

GEAR	60	70	80	90	100	110	120	130	140	150	160	
26	4.64	5.41	6.19	6.96	7.73	8.51	9.28	10.06	10.83	11.60	12.38	MPH
27	4.82	5.62	6.43	7.23	8.03	8.84	9.64	10.44	11.25	12.05	12.85	MPH
28	5.00	5.83	6.66	7.50	8.33	9.16	10.00	10.83	11.66	12.49	13.33	MPH
29	5.18	6.04	6.90	7.76	8.63	9.49	10.35	11.22	12.08	12.94	13.80	MPH
30	5.35	6.25	7.14	8.03	8.92	9.82	10.71	11.60	12.49	13.39	14.28	MPH
31	5.53	6.46	7.38	8.30	9.22	10.14	11.07	11.99	12.91	13.83	14.76	MPH
32	5.71	6.66	7.62	8.57	9.52	10.47	11.42	12.38	13.33	14.28	15.23	MPH
33	5.89	6.87	7.85	8.84	9.82	10.80	11.78	12.76	13.74	14.73	15.71	MPH
34	6.07	7.08	8.09	9.10	10.11	11.13	12.14	13.15	14.16	15.17	16.18	MPH
35	6.25	7.29	8.33	9.37	10.41	11.45	12.49	13.54	14.58	15.62	16.66	MPH
36	6.43	7.50	8.57	9.64	10.71	11.78	12.85	13.92	14.99	16.06	17.14	MPH
37	6.60	7.71	8.81	9.91	11.01	12.11	13.21	14.31	15.41	16.51	17.61	MPH
38	6.78	7.91	9.04	10.17	11.30	12.44	13.57	14.70	15.83	16.96	18.09	MPH
39	6.96	8.12	9.28	10.44	11.60	12.76	13.92	15.08	16.24	17.40	18.56	MPH
40	7.14	8.33	9.52	10.71	11.90	13.09	14.28	15.47	16.66	17.85	19.04	MPH
41	7.32	8.54	9.76	10.98	12.20	13.42	14.64	15.86	17.08	18.30	19.52	MPH
42	7.50	8.75	10.00	11.25	12.49	13.74	14.99	16.24	17.49	18.74	19.99	MPH
43	7.68	8.95	10.23	11.51	12.79	14.07	15.35	16.63	17.91	19.19	20.47	MPH
44	7.85	9.16	10.47	11.78	13.09	14.40	15.71	17.02	18.33	19.63	20.94	MPH
45	8.03	9.37	10.71	12.05	13.39	14.73	16.06	17.40	18.74	20.08	21.42	MPH
46	8.21	9.58	10.95	12.32	13.68	15.05	16.42	17.79	19.16	20.53	21.90	MPH
47	8.39	9.79	11.19	12.58	13.98	15.38	16.78	18.18	19.58	20.97	22.37	MPH
48	8.57	10.00	11.42	12.85	14.28	15.71	17.14	18.56	19.99	21.42	22.85	MPH
49	8.75	10.20	11.66	13.12	14.58	16.04	17.49	18.95	20.41	21.87	23.32	MPH
50	8.92	10.41	11.90	13.39	14.87	16.36	17.85	19.34	20.82	22.31	23.80	MPH
51	9.10	10.62	12.14	13.66	15.17	16.69	18.21	19.72	21.24	22.76	24.28	MPH
52	9.28	10.83	12.38	13.92	15.47	17.02	18.56	20.11	21.66	23.20	24.75	MPH
53	9.46	11.04	12.61	14.19	15.77	17.34	18.92	20.50	22.07	23.65	25.23	MPH
54	9.64	11.25	12.85	14.46	16.06	17.67	19.28	20.88	22.49	24.10	25.70	MPH
55	9.82	11.45	13.09	14.73	16.36	18.00	19.63	21.27	22.91	24.54	26.18	MPH
56	10.00	11.66	13.33	14.99	16.66	18.33	19.99	21.66	23.32	24.99	26.66	MPH
57	10.17	11.87	13.57	15.26	16.96	18.65	20.35	22.04	23.74	25.44	27.13	MPH
58	10.35	12.08	13.80	15.53	17.25	18.98	20.71	22.43	24.16	25.88	27.61	MPH
59	10.53	12.29	14.04	15.80	17.55	19.31	21.06	22.82	24.57	26.33	28.08	MPH
60	10.71	12.49	14.28	16.06	17.85	19.63	21.42	23.20	24.99	26.77	28.56	MPH
61	10.89	12.70	14.52	16.33	18.15	19.96	21.78	23.59	25.41	27.22	29.04	MPH
62	11.07	12.91	14.76	16.60	18.44	20.29	22.13	23.98	25.82	27.67	29.51	MPH
63	11.25	13.12	14.99	16.87	18.74	20.62	22.49	24.37	26.24	28.11	29.99	MPH
64	11.42	13.33	15.23	17.14	19.04	20.94	22.85	24.75	26.66	28.56	30.46	MPH
65	11.60	13.54	15.47	17.40	19.34	21.27	23.20	25.14	27.07	29.01	30.94	MPH
66	11.78	13.74	15.71	17.67	19.63	21.60	23.56	25.53	27.49	29.45	31.42	MPH
67	11.96	13.95	15.95	17.94	19.93	21.93	23.92	25.91	27.91	29.90	31.89	MPH
68	12.14	14.16	16.18	18.21	20.23	22.25	24.28	26.30	28.32	30.34	32.37	MPH
69	12.32	14.37	16.42	18.47	20.53	22.58	24.63	26.69	28.74	30.79	32.84	MPH
70	12.49	14.58	16.66	18.74	20.82	22.91	24.99	27.07	29.15	31.24	33.32	MPH
71	12.67	14.79	16.90	19.01	21.12	23.23	25.35	27.46	29.57	31.68	33.80	MPH
72	12.85	14.99	17.14	19.28	21.42	23.56	25.70	27.85	29.99	32.13	34.27	MPH
73	13.03	15.20	17.37	19.55	21.72	23.89	26.06	28.23	30.40	32.58	34.75	MPH
74	13.21	15.41	17.61	19.81	22.01	24.22	26.42	28.62	30.82	33.02	35.22	MPH
75	13.39	15.62	17.85	20.08	22.31	24.54	26.77	29.01	31.24	33.47	35.70	MPH
76	13.57	15.83	18.09	20.35	22.61	24.87	27.13	29.39	31.65	33.91	36.18	MPH
77	13.74	16.04	18.33	20.62	22.91	25.20	27.49	29.78	32.07	34.36	36.65	MPH
78	13.92	16.24	18.56	20.88	23.20	25.53	27.85	30.17	32.49	34.81	37.13	MPH
79	14.10	16.45	18.80	21.15	23.50	25.85	28.20	30.55	32.90	35.25	37.60	MPH
80	14.28	16.66	19.04	21.42	23.80	26.18	28.56	30.94	33.32	35.70	38.08	MPH
81	14.46	16.87	19.28	21.69	24.10	26.51	28.92	31.33	33.74	36.15	38.56	MPH
82	14.64	17.08	19.52	21.96	24.39	26.83	29.27	31.71	34.15	36.59	39.03	MPH
83	14.82	17.28	19.75	22.22	24.69	27.16	29.63	32.10	34.57	37.04	39.51	MPH
84	14.99	17.49	19.99	22.49	24.99	27.49	29.99	32.49	34.99	37.48	39.98	MPH
85	15.17	17.70	20.23	22.76	25.29	27.82	30.34	32.87	35.40	37.93	40.46	MPH
86	15.35	17.91	20.47	23.03	25.58	28.14	30.70	33.26	35.82	38.38	40.94	MPH
87	15.53	18.12	20.71	23.29	25.88	28.47	31.06	33.65	36.24	38.82	41.41	MPH
88	15.71	18.33	20.94	23.56	26.18	28.80	31.42	34.03	36.65	39.27	41.89	MPH
89	15.89	18.53	21.18	23.83	26.48	29.13	31.77	34.42	37.07	39.72	42.36	MPH
90	16.06	18.74	21.42	24.10	26.77	29.45	32.13	34.81	37.48	40.16	42.84	MPH
91	16.24	18.95	21.66	24.37	27.07	29.78	32.49	35.19	37.90	40.61	43.32	MPH
92	16.42	19.16	21.90	24.63	27.37	30.11	32.84	35.58	38.32	41.05	43.79	MPH
93	16.60	19.37	22.13	24.90	27.67	30.43	33.20	35.97	38.73	41.50	44.27	MPH
94	16.78	19.58	22.37	25.17	27.96	30.76	33.56	36.35	39.15	41.95	44.74	MPH
95	16.96	19.78	22.61	25.44	28.26	31.09	33.91	36.74	39.57	42.39	45.22	MPH
96	17.14	19.99	22.85	25.70	28.56	31.42	34.27	37.13	39.98	42.84	45.70	MPH
97	17.31	20.20	23.09	25.97	28.86	31.74	34.63	37.51	40.40	43.29	46.17	MPH
98	17.49	20.41	23.32	26.24	29.15	32.07	34.99	37.90	40.82	43.73	46.65	MPH
99	17.67	20.62	23.56	26.51	29.45	32.40	35.34	38.29	41.23	44.18	47.12	MPH
100	17.85	20.82	23.80	26.77	29.75	32.72	35.70	38.67	41.65	44.62	47.60	MPH
101	18.03	21.03	24.04	27.04	30.05	33.05	36.06	39.06	42.07	45.07	48.08	MPH
102	18.21	21.24	24.28	27.31	30.34	33.38	36.41	39.45	42.48	45.52	48.55	MPH
103	18.39	21.45	24.51	27.58	30.64	33.71	36.77	39.84	42.90	45.96	49.03	MPH
104	18.56	21.66	24.75	27.85	30.94	34.03	37.13	40.22	43.32	46.41	49.50	MPH
105	18.74	21.87	24.99	28.11	31.24	34.36	37.48	40.61	43.73	46.86	49.98	MPH
106	18.92	22.07	25.23	28.38	31.53	34.69	37.84	41.00	44.15	47.30	50.46	MPH
107	19.10	22.28	25.47	28.65	31.83	35.02	38.20	41.38	44.57	47.75	50.93	MPH
108	19.28	22.49	25.70	28.92	32.13	35.34	38.56	41.77	44.98	48.19	51.41	MPH
109	19.46	22.70	25.94	29.18	32.43	35.67	38.91	42.16	45.40	48.64	51.88	MPH
110	19.63	22.91	26.18	29.45	32.72	36.00	39.27	42.54	45.81	49.09	52.36	MPH
111	19.81	23.12	26.42	29.72	33.02	36.32	39.63	42.93	46.23	49.53	52.84	MPH
112	19.99	23.32	26.66	29.99	33.32	36.65	39.98	43.32	46.65	49.98	53.31	MPH
113	20.17	23.53	26.89	30.26	33.62	36.98	40.34	43.70	47.06	50.43	53.79	MPH
114	20.35	23.74	27.13	30.52	33.91	37.31	40.70	44.09	47.48	50.87	54.26	MPH
115	20.53	23.95	27.37	30.79	34.21	37.63	41.05	44.48	47.90	51.32	54.74	MPH
116	20.71	24.16	27.61	31.06	34.51	37.96	41.41	44.86	48.31	51.76	55.22	MPH

CALIBRATED BY AN IBM 360 AND PROGRAMMED BY SAM RHOADS

Table 4-4: Once you know your gear in inches and your cadence, you can calculate how fast you're going from this table. For example, if your chain is on sprockets that give you a gear of 40 inches and you're pedaling at a rate of 70 crank revolutions per minute, you're traveling at 8.33 miles per hour. I was going to eliminate this table from this fourth edition of my book, because bicycle computers make it obsolete. However, not everyone has such a computer, so here's the table again.

fast you are going for a broad selection of gear inches and crank rpm. To use the table, simply find your gear inches in column one, and your cadence in the rpm line at the top of the table. Where the two numbers meet, read your speed in miles per hour. I've given you one example from this table in this paragraph. For another, say you're in a 70-inch gear and spinning your cranks at 80 rpm. From Table 4-4, you can see you'd be traveling at 19.04 mph, a respectable speed by anyone's book.

"How can I tell when I'm in the right gear?" This is a question I'm often asked. My stock reply is: "When it feels comfortable." It's best to spin the cranks as fast as it feels comfortable. I can spin the cranks at around 70 rpm all day, so I choose a gear that lets me do that. The gear I use depends on the grade of the road. As the grade increases, I shift to a lower gear. You may be able to spin faster than 70 rpm, and that's fine. On hills you'll probably have to spin more slowly even in a super-low gear. The best combination of front and rear gears, however, is whichever one is not causing you strain or pain, yet asks that

Table 4-5

CONVERSION FROM DEGREES OF GRADE TO PERCENT OF GRADE

DEGREES	PERCENT
1	1.7
2	3.5
3	5.2
4	7.0
5	8.8
6	10.5
7	12.3
8	14.1
9	15.8
10	17.6

Table 4-5: This table converts a road grade in degrees into percent grade. Percent grade is defined as the number of feet (altitude) you climb up or down per 100 feet of forward travel. For instance, if you have an inclinometer and you measure a hill as six degrees, that would be a grade of 10.5 percent. So on a six-degree hill you would change 10.5 feet in altitude for every 100 feet of that hill.

you put some effort into pedaling. You could shift to too low a gear for the grade you're on, and just sit there and twiddle the pedals with hardly any strain at all. It would be far better for you, aerobically, to shift to a higher gear so you can convert that energy of yours into more go power.

As noted above, there are some hills you just have to get off your bike and walk up. Because some hills are graded in degrees and others in percent grade, Table 4-5 converts from one to the other. For me, even in my lowest 24-inch gear, any hill over 15 percent grade is one I walk up.

More Tips About Comfort

You can alleviate pressure on your hands and upper torso by shifting hands from one to the other of the four different positions on downturned handlebars, as shown in Figs. 4-61 though 4-64. You only have one position for your hands on ATB handlebars (Fig. 4-65), but they permit a more upright position that eases hand pressure. If you want to cut wind resistance by bending farther forward, you could add a pair of Moots bar extenders (Fig. 4-66).

As I noted in Chapter 1, if your arms are shorter or longer for your height, you could change stem lengths so you can reach the handlebars more comfortably. Downturned handlebar

Fig. 4-61: One of the four basic positions for your hands on downturned handlebars is on the top flat section, which is where I have my hands most of the time.

Fig. 4-62: When my hands begin to pain from pressure on the nerve in the palm of my hand, I shift to this position for a while.

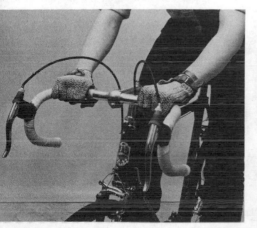

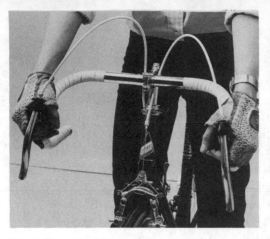 

Fig. 4-63: Another thing you can do to shift pressure on your hands is to rest them on top of the brake lever covers.

Fig. 4-64: Still another position is on the drops of the handlebars. This is the position I use when "honking" up hills, or when I want to tuck down into a more streamlined position to go faster.

Fig. 4-65: Flat handlebars, such as on commuter and all-terrain bicycles, offer you only one position for your hands. However, they also give you a more upright stance, so there's less weight on your hands and thus less pain on a prolonged trip. I find the more upright stance a lot more comfortable than the bent-over position required by downturned handlebars. The stem shown is available in two lengths, 75 and 110 mm (3 and 4 inches), from SunTour through your bike shop. The hole you see in this stem, for the front brake cable, was drilled by your author. The flat bars and stem are on an Alex Singer touring bike, and replaced downturned handlebars.

Fig. 4-66: Moots (see your bike shop) makes extenders for flat handlebars for those cyclists who want to assume a bent-over stance.

stems are available from 60 to 120mm (2.4 inches to 4.8 inches), in 10mm (⅜-inch) increments. You can also change ATB stems, unless your stem and handlebars are one piece (Figs. 4-66 and 4-67), in which case you'd have to switch to a two-piece stem and handlebar (Fig. 4-65). You could install a 75mm or 110mm (3- or 4-inch) SunTour stem (Fig. 4-65), or keep your old stem and install a handlebar that curves closer or farther away, Fig. 4-68. See Chapter 9 for details.

In the next chapter you'll learn how to adjust your brakes for maximum safe stopping power.

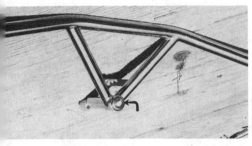

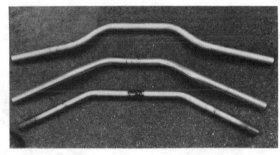

Fig. 4-67: This one-piece handlebar and stem comes in a fixed-stem length. The stem in Fig. 4-66 also comes in just the one length.

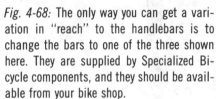

Fig. 4-68: The only way you can get a variation in "reach" to the handlebars is to change the bars to one of the three shown here. They are supplied by Specialized Bicycle components, and they should be available from your bike shop.

Fig. 4-69: Top and crotch-lined shorts from Emily Kay are very comfortable.

Fig. 4-70: AC Targa helmet, Emily Kay jersey and tights, and Nike Velo sports cycling shoes.

Fig. 4-71: MSR helmet, Emily Kay outfit, Nike Velo shoes with KHS Triathlete bicycle.

Fig. 4-72: Triathlete shirt with padded shoulder, MSR helmet.

Fig. 4-73: Close-up of padded-shoulder triathlete shirt, which eases strain of running with bike in these races.

Fig. 4-74: Vigorelli shorts are breathable, have lined crotch for comfort. Jersey is by Nike, helmet by MSR.

Fig. 4-75: Jersey, arm and leg warmers, and shorts by Vigorelli. Warmers are a good idea when starting off on a chilly morning, can be easily removed as you warm up.

Fig. 4-76: Another Vigorelli top is truly comfortable. Gloves are from Spenco, with soft, padded palm lining to ease pressure on hands.

Fig. 4-77: For colder weather, jersey at left and wind jacket at right, by Vigorelli, are designed for comfort and durability.

Fig. 4-78: Wet-weather jacket and pants from Bike-A-Lite are highly water resistant, have elastic water stops on ends of sleeves and legs, and a hood that can be closed and fit under a helmet. The bicycle cover by Cycle Stash keeps your bike protected from the elements on car carrier, at the campground, and when shipping by airplane. It can also double as a rainy-day poncho or as a small tent.

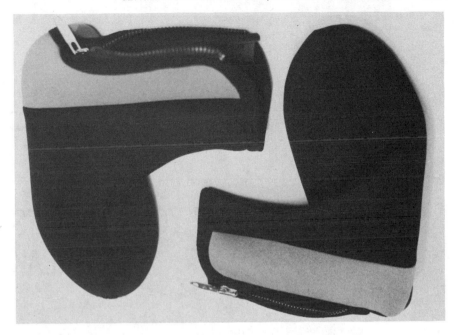

Fig. 4-79: Extremities can get coldest in wet and frigid weather. These booties, from Spokes Wear, slip on over bike shoes, are of insulating neoprene and water-resisting nylon, and are made in France.

Fig. 4-80: When the going gets cold, the cold don gloves to keep fingers warm. These gloves, from Spokes Wear, are made of Nylon 2 neoprene for superior insulation and flexibility. These gloves are also excellent for wet-weather cycling.

FIVE

HOW TO GIVE YOUR BRAKES A BREAK

A child runs out into the street in front of your bike. A truck runs a red light while you're in the intersection. You're building up dangerous speed going down a steep hill. These are just a few of the dozens of braking situations you may encounter every time you go out for a bike ride. And if your brakes won't stop you in time, you could be injured. Your brakes may work very well when you know in advance that you will have to stop, but will your brakes work in an emergency? Will they *always* stop you? Are they near failure right now? This chapter is about helping you know when your brakes need attention, and showing you how to keep them in safe operating condition.

Since this chapter is the first of seven on maintenance, I'd like to start by making sure we both speak the bicycle language. If I name a part of a bike, it's important that you know where on the bike that part is located. So take five minutes and study Fig. 5-1, the anatomy of a bicycle. The caption is numerically keyed to the names and locations of all bike parts.

After you've become familiar with the basic parts of a bike, turn your attention to the subject of this chapter—your brakes. I will specify how tight a particular part should be in terms of

Fig. 5-1: Anatomy of a bicycle. Key to bicycle parts:

 1. Chainwheel
 2. Pedal
 3. Chain
 4. Rear derailleur
 5. Front derailleur
 6. Caliper brake
 7. Brake lever
 8. Brake cable
 9. Handlebars.
10. Handlebar stem
11. Saddle
12. Seat post.
13. Quick release for hub
14. Bottom bracket
15. Shift lever, front derailleur
16. Freewheel
17. Rim
18. Spoke
19. Valve stem
20. Tire
21. Hub (high-flange type)
22. Chain stay
23. Lug
24. Fender
25. Fork crown
26. Fork
27. Front-wheel dropout
28. Seat cluster lug
29. Seat stay
30. Seat tube
31. Head tube
32. Tension roller, rear derailleur
33. Top tube
34. Fender stay
35. Down tube
36. Cotterless crank
37. Rear-wheel dropout
38. Headset (bearings inside head tube)

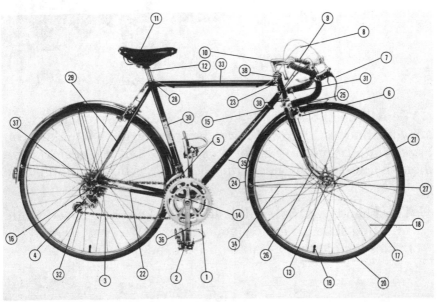

"inch/pounds of torque." Torque is the force of a rotating movement, as when you use a wrench to tighten a nut or a bolt. The
torque specifications throughout this book ensure that each part
is turned to the safest possible maximum tightness. If a part

gets loose, vibration from road shock could loosen it further until suddenly it falls off your bike, possibly tangling in the spokes and causing an accident in more ways than I care to think about. As we go through the subsequent chapters on maintenance I will point out the consequences of not tightening a specific part.

The only way you can be really sure a nut or bolt is safety tightened is to use a torque wrench. Sears Roebuck sells a torque wrench (Fig. 5-2) for around $16 or $20. Use it on every nut and bolt on your bike. Some torque wrenches are calibrated in foot-pounds, but the torque wrench you buy should be calibrated in inch-pounds (Fig. 5-2). Let's leave the foot-pounder to truck mechanics.

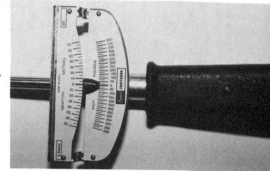

Fig. 5-2: Torque wrench.

You will need other tools besides the torque wrench to work on your brakes. They will vary according to the brakes you have. You may not use all of those listed, but it's best to have them because you'll need them for other bike maintenance problems.

1. Third hand (Fig. 5-3) will hold the brake shoes closed while adjusting shoe clearance (you could wrap a strap around the brakes to hold them, but the third hand is easier).

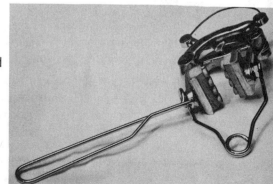

Fig. 5-3: Third hand, to hold brakes closed while you make adjustments.

Table 5-1

TIGHTENING TORQUE VALUES FOR BRAKES
(In inch/pounds)

PART	SIDEPULL	CENTERPULL	U-BRAKE	CAM	CANTILEVER
Brake shoe binder bolt	43–60	43–60	50–75	53–80	53–80
Cable binder nut	57–70	57–70	50–75	70–90	57–85
Brake mounting bolt or nut	70–88	70–88	50–70	70–90	45–60
Brake lever clamp bolt/nut	50–70	50–70	55–80	55–80	55–80
Brake lever shaft bolt*	13–22	13–22	NA	NA	NA

* Where applicable, not all caliper brake levers have tightenable shafts.

2. Fourth hand will hold cable tension while tightening the cable binder bolt (Fig. 5-4). You could use a pair of pliers, if you have three hands.
3. A 15mm cone (thin) wrench is necessary if you have cam brakes (Fig. 5-5).

Fig. 5-4: Fourth hand, to keep tension on brake cable while you use two wrenches and two hands to tighten brake cable binder bolt.

Fig. 5-5: This wrench normally used on wheel hubs but in this chapter used to adjust cam-action brake arm spring tension.

4. A set of 4, 5, or 6mm Allen wrenches in sockets that fit the torque wrench. (You're going to need bigger sizes for other bike parts, so get a set from 4 to 12mm.)

5. A set of 6, 8, 9, 10, and 12mm metric sockets to fit the torque wrench. (Buy a complete metric socket set, because you'll need sizes from 4 to 17mm. You'll be able to use them for other bicycle parts, and for your foreign car, too.)

6. Wire cutters to clip off ends.

7. Lubriplate grease will help cables run smoothly and can also be used for derailleur cables (see Chapter 6).

The Hazard of Extension Levers

Extension brake levers (Fig. 5-6) lull you into a false sense of braking security. They are easier to reach than the main brake levers, particularly if, like most of us, you ride with your hands on top of downturned handlebars. In a panic stop you may reach for the extension levers automatically, and this is why they are so dangerous.

If your bike has extension brake levers, go out, squeeze them hard, and take a look. Unless your brakes are perfectly adjusted, you will very likely find that these levers can be squeezed all the way, or very close to the handlebars. Still holding them closed, now look at the main brake levers. You will see that they still have more room to travel. In fact, you can probably hold one extension lever closed and still be able to push the bike so that the wheel turns. Yet the *main* brake lever will lock up that wheel so it will skid along the floor if you push the bike. There are two reasons why extension levers are much less ef-

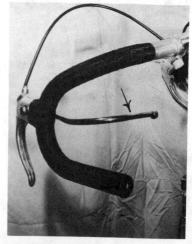

Fig. 5-6: Extension levers (arrow) are dangerous and should be removed. See text for details.

fective than main brake levers. First, extension levers inherently have a shorter distance of travel than the main levers, so they are very likely not going to stop you in an emergency, even though you can squeeze them all the way down to the handlebars. Second, brake-cable stretch and brake-shoe wear allow brake shoes to rest farther from the rim, so that extension levers become even less effective. In fact, I have checked dozens of brand-new bikes, right on the sales floor (mostly in discount stores, to be sure), and found extension levers squeezable down to the handlebars with at least an inch of travel left in the main brake levers. These bikes are an accident waiting to happen. Even if your brakes are perfectly adjusted so that the extension levers will stop you safely, they won't always do so. As I noted, brake cables stretch, brake shoes wear, and so your brakes slowly get out of adjustment until the extension levers are virtually useless.

When I mentioned the dangers of extension levers to the bicycle buyer of a major multi-store sporting goods firm, he sent a memo to the bicycle section manager in each store to remove these levers from every bike in stock. He then went to his bicycle suppliers and ordered them removed from bikes on order.

Removing Extension Levers

Follow these steps to remove extension levers:

1. With a screwdriver, turn the extension lever clamp bolt counterclockwise all the way (Fig. 5-7). Remove the extension lever and *throw it away*.

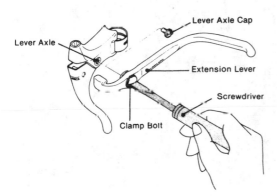

Fig. 5-7: Remove extension levers by removing brake lever binder bolt. See text for full instructions.

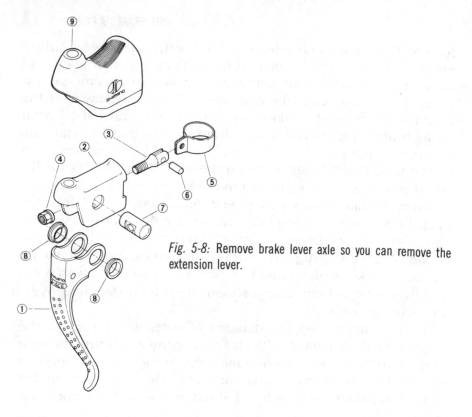

Fig. 5-8: Remove brake lever axle so you can remove the extension lever.

2. Remove the lever axle ("7" in Fig. 5-8), the washers ("8" in Fig. 508), and replace the axle with a shorter one you can buy from your bike store. Take the old one in for a replacement that fits. You need the shorter axle because the old one will stick out like a nail (Fig. 5-9) and cause pain if you wrap your hands around the brake body as you strain uphill.

Fig. 5-9: Replace old brake lever axle with a new shorter axle.

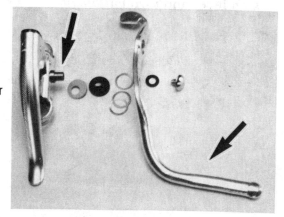

3. Replace the axle clamp nut and tighten it clockwise with the screwdriver (see Table 4-1 for correct tightening torque). The whole job should take about ten minutes.

Brake Shoe Clearance Adjustment

Centerpull brakes (Fig. 5-10), sidepull brakes (Fig. 5-11), cantilever brakes (Fig. 5-12), cam action brakes (Fig. 5-13), the new Shimano U-brake (Fig. 5-14), and the new Mathauser hydraulic brake (Fig. 5-15), have *four* common, basic adjustment requirements.

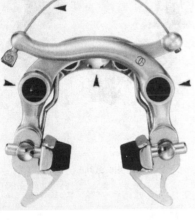

Fig. 5-10: Centerpull brake.

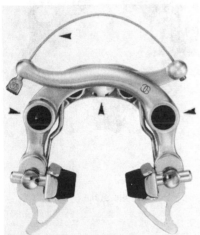

Fig. 5-11: Sidepull brake.

Fig. 5-12: Cantilever brake.

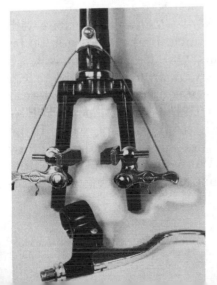

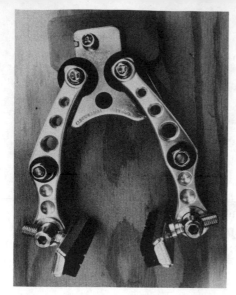

Fig. 5-13: Cam-action brake.

Fig. 5-14: U-brake.

Fig. 5-15: Hydraulic brake.

Safety Requirement One: Brake Shoe Clearance: We start with adjustment No. 1, brake shoe clearance. Brake shoes get too far away from the rim for two reasons. One is cable stretch. On a new bike especially, brake cables will stretch within 50 to 100 miles of riding to a point at which brake shoes are dangerously far from the rim, leading to decreased brake response and effectiveness. The second reason is due to brake-shoe wear. If the brake shoes are worn or have become age-hardened, they should be replaced (see below). Worn shoes cut response time and hardened shoes greatly reduce braking effectiveness. Together, worn and age-hardened shoes can cut braking ability to a very dangerous level.

Before you can adjust the brake shoe clearance, the wheels must be true. If wheels are wobbly or show side-to-side (lateral) unevenness, see Chapter 10 for instructions on wheel truing. When wheels are not accurately aligned, brake shoes cannot grip rims evenly, and shoes may then be the correct ⅟₁₆th to ⅛th of an inch from the rim in one position, and twice or half that amount on another spot on the rim.

Here's how to adjust brake shoe clearance:

1. Hold the brake shoes onto the rim flats with the third hand tool (Fig. 5-3) or with your own hand.
2. Make sure any brake-release devices are *closed*. These devices permit you to spread the brake shoes apart, so you can remove the wheel easier if the tire is wider than the brake-shoe setting. You will find these levers in three places, depending on the make and the type of brake and age of the bicycle:
   a. On the cable guide, for both front and rear brakes. Fig. 5-16 shows the release lever, arrow "C."

Fig. 5-16: Brake-release lever on cable guide (arrow c) spreads brakes apart for tire clearance when removing wheel.

    b. On the brake lever (Fig. 5-17).

    c. On the brake itself (Fig. 5-18).

3. Brake shoes should be no more than ⅟₁₆th to ⅛th inch away from the rim, as shown in Fig. 5-19.

4. Remove minor cable stretch at the adjusting barrel. These barrels may be on the cable guide (Fig. 5-16), on the brake lever (Fig. 5-20), or on the brake (Fig. 5-21). To adjust the

Fig. 5-17: Brake release on the brake lever.

Fig. 5-18: Brake release on the brake itself.

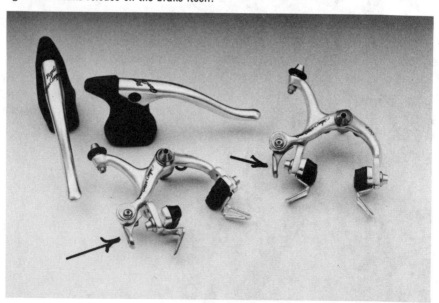

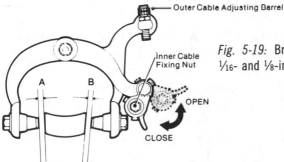
Outer Cable Adjusting Barrel

Inner Cable Fixing Nut

A   B

OPEN

CLOSE

Fig. 5-19: Brake shoes should be between ¹⁄₁₆- and ⅛-inch from the wheel rim flat.

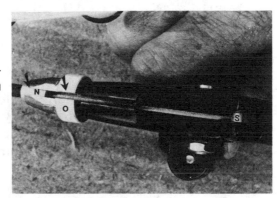

Fig. 5-20: Adjusting barrel to re-move cable stretch, located on the brake lever.

Fig 5-21: Adjusting barrel on the brake itself (arrows).

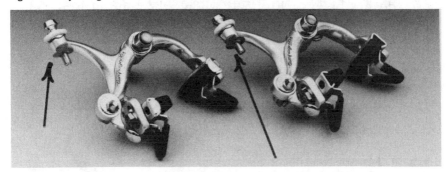

barrel, turn the barrel locknut ("B" in Fig. 5-16) counter-clockwise until it is loose. Turn the adjusting barrel ("A" in Fig. 5-16) counterclockwise until the brake shoes are the correct distance from the rim. Turn the barrel locknut clock-wise until it is tight.

5. If the cables have stretched so far that you can't adjust the brakes to the correct distance from the rim with the adjusting barrel, follow the steps below:

a. Reverse step 4 at the adjusting barrel. That is, loosen the adjusting barrel locknut a half-turn counterclockwise, then screw the adjusting barrel clockwise all the way down (closed), then tighten the locknut clockwise.

b. Loosen the cable binder nut on the cable carrier ("A" in Fig. 5-4). You will need two wrenches, usually 8 and 9mm. Hold the binder bolt ("B" in Fig. 5-4) with one wrench, and loosen the binder bolt nut with the other. Either pull the excess cable slack through the binder bolt ("H" in Fig. 5-4) with a pair of pliers or use the fourth hand tool ("M" in Fig. 5-4) to hold the cable taut, as you hold the binder bolt with one wrench, and tighten the binder bolt nut with the other wrench to the correct torque (see Table 5-1). *Caution!* If the binder bolt nut is not tight enough, the cable could slip out of the hole in the binder bolt. If this happens you have no brakes! This is especially important on cantilever, cam action, and Shimano U-brakes, because their motorcycle-style brake levers (Fig. 5-22) can exert more pulling force on cables than brake levers on downturned handlebars!

c. You can also correct shoe-to-rim distance by moving the brake shoe in and out (only on cantilever or cam-action-design brakes). Fig. 5-12 shows the type of brake shoe you can move closer to or farther away from the rim. This type of shoe has a round spindle or shaft that is held in a hole in the brake arm. To move the brake in or out, hold the spindle with an Allen wrench (usually 8mm), loosen

Fig. 5-22: Motorcycle-type brake levers, on the flat handlebars of all-terrain bicycles, can exert more pulling torque on brake cables than the brake levers on dropped handlebars.

the spindle nut with a 10mm wrench, adjust lateral position of the brake shoe, and tighten the spindle nut to the torque for your type of brake in Table 5-1. This nut is also called a brake-shoe fixing bolt on other types of brakes. If you have cam-action brakes, see special instructions for their adjustment, below.

Safety Requirement Two: Brake Shoe Alignment

Brake shoes must be parallel to the rim surface, as shown in Fig. 5-23, and about ¹⁄₃₂-inch below the top of the rim. No part of the brake shoe must touch the tire!

1. Loosen the brake binder bolt and move the brake shoe up or down as necessary.
2. While you have the brake shoe movable, also move it so it is parallel to the rim (Fig. 5-23).

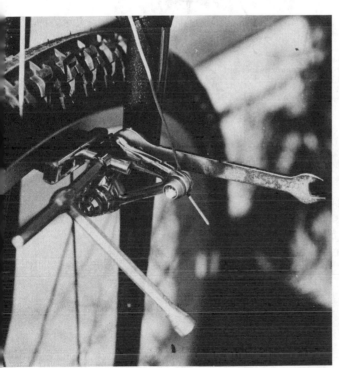

Fig. 5-23: Brake shoes must be aligned parallel to the wheel rim flat and be about ¹⁄₃₂-inch below the top of the rim. Brake shoes must not touch the tire!

3. Brake shoes should also be toed-in, as shown in Fig. 5-24. Some brake shoe binder bolts have offset washers, as shown in Fig. 5-25. If your brake shoes do not have these washers, you can toe in the brake shoe by gently twisting the brake arm with an adjustable Crescent wrench. This toe-in provides more even application of the brake pad to the rim and also helps prevent or reduce squealing as brakes are applied. Tighten brake shoe binder nut. On cantilever and cam brakes, tighten, as shown in Fig. 5-23, to values in Table 5-1.

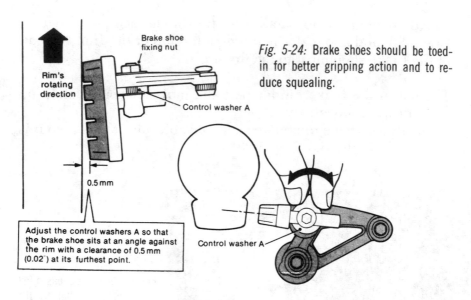

Fig. 5-24: Brake shoes should be toed-in for better gripping action and to reduce squealing.

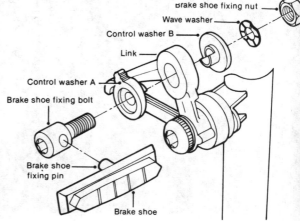

Fig. 5-25: If your brake-shoe binder bolts are fitted with offset washers, as shown here, toe-in of brake shoes is by rotating these washers for correct angle.

Centering Sidepull and Centerpull Brake Shoes

Brake shoes should be the same distance from the rim, on each side of the rim. I am going to assume that the rim is true and that the wheel has been correctly inserted in the drop-outs so it is centered between the fork blades and/or the seatstays and chainstays (see Fig. 5-1 for location of stays). If one brake shoe is closer to the rim than the other one, loosen the brake mounting bolt (Fig. 5-26), center the brake shoes, and retighten (Table 5-1).

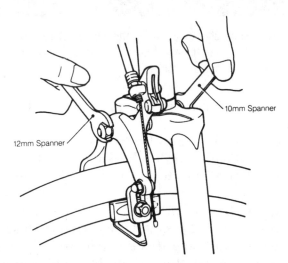

Fig. 5-26: Brakes should be adjusted so both brake shoes are the same distance from the rim. If not, loosen brake binder bolt, center brakes, and retighten this bolt.

Centering Cantilever Brake Shoes

Cantilever brakes are essentially self-centering. However, if one shoe is a bit farther away from the rim than the other one, you can move the brake in or out slightly by loosening the brake fixing bolt, moving the brake shoe, and retightening this bolt (Table 5-1). *Caution!* If the brake shoe mounting nut is not sufficiently tightened, the brake shoe could become loose enough to dive under the rim (Fig. 5-27) when you squeeze the brake lever. In this case, the brake shoe could get caught in the

Fig. 5-27: If cantilever brake-shoe binder bolts and nuts are not tight enough (see Table 5-1), brake shoes can dive under the wheel rim as shown here, possibly jam in spokes as well as cause loss of braking and an accident.

spokes, and/or you could lose braking capacity. In either case, an accident could occur.

Something else to be careful of: If you raise the handlebars of a bike equipped with cantilever, cam action, or U-brakes you will, in effect, shorten the front brake cable. This causes the front brake shoes to be positioned closer to the rim. You can possibly raise the handlebars so far that the brake shoes will rub on the rim. That makes pedaling a great deal harder, of course, and wears out brake shoes much faster. To readjust the brake if you do raise handlebars, simply hold the brake shoes against the rim, loosen the cable binder nut ("A" in Fig. 5-4) while holding the binder bolt, use the fourth hand tool as shown or let a little of the cable out ("H" in Fig. 5-4), and retighten the cable binder nut. Make fine brake-shoe clearance adjustments at the brake-lever adjusting barrel (Fig. 5-20). Tighten cable binder bolt to the torque specified in Table 5-1.

If you lower the handlebars of a bike with cantilever, cam action, or U-brakes, you in effect lengthen the brake cable. In this case the front brake shoes will be farther away from the rim, reducing braking response time and efficiency. If you lower the handlebars, follow the steps above, pull excess cable slack through, retighten the cable binder nut, and make final brake-shoe clearance adjustments, if needed, at the brake-lever adjusting barrel (Fig. 5-20).

Cam Action Brake Adjustments

Brake-shoe clearance and adjustments are the same on cam brakes as they are on other brakes. However, making these adjustments is a bit different on these brakes.

1. You can make gross adjustments at the brake cable binder bolt on the cam plate (Fig. 5-28). Hold the brake shoes on the rim, loosen the cable-binder bolt and nut and pull cable slack through the cable binder bolt. Tighten this bolt (Table 5-1).
2. Make fine adjustments at the brake lever, as shown in Fig. 5-20, and at the brake shoe. The brake shoes have threaded bolts which screw into the brake-shoe fixing bolt, as shown in Fig. 5-29. To adjust, loosen the brake-shoe fixing nut and bolt, turn shoe clockwise or counterclockwise to the correct clearance ($\frac{1}{16}$th to $\frac{1}{8}$th of an inch from rim) and tighten cable fixing bolt and nut (Table 5-1).

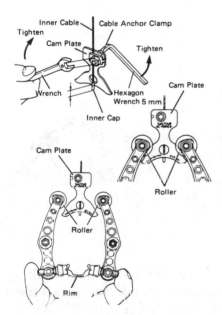

Fig. 5-28: On cam-action brakes, make gross brake-shoe clearance adjustment at the cam plate by loosening cable binder bolt and nut, pulling excess cable through, and retightening this nut and bolt.

Fig. 5-29: Cam-action brake shoe binder bolts are threaded.

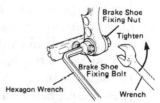

3. If the brake shoes are not centered because one brake arm is too far away or too close to the rim, make these adjustments: With a 10mm wrench, loosen the brake-arm fixing nut (Fig. 5-30). Then turn the adjusting bushing (Fig. 5-30) in one direction or the other with a thin hub cone wrench (Fig. 5-5) to move each brake arm as necessary so they are both the same distance from the rim, as shown at the bottom of Fig. 5-30.

4. To remove a wheel, move one brake arm, as shown in Fig. 5-31, so brake shoes are spread wide enough to permit tire clearance.

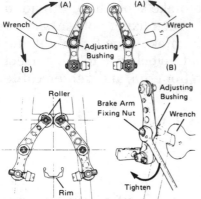

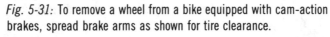

Fig. 5-30: Adjust cam-action brake tension as shown. Please see text for details.

Fig. 5-31: To remove a wheel from a bike equipped with cam-action brakes, spread brake arms as shown for tire clearance.

Adjusting U-Brakes

1. Shimano U-brakes, Fig. 5-14, have the same basic brake-shoe rim clearance and alignment specifications as the brakes above. The brake shoe is threaded (Fig. 5-32) so you can make some adjustments at the shoe, as you could with cam-action brakes.

2. If you move the handlebars up or down, you will also have to readjust brake-shoe clearance as I noted above in the cantilever and cam-brake sections.

Fig. 5-32: These U-brake-shoe binder bolts are threaded.

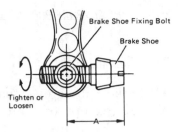

Fig. 5-33: The center wire on U-brakes should be long enough to maintain brake shoes at the correct distance from the rim.

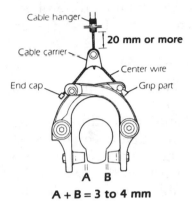

A + B = 3 to 4 mm

Fig. 5-34: Make fine adjustments on the U-brake-shoe clearance by tightening or loosening the brake-shoe force screw with a 2mm Allen wrench as shown.

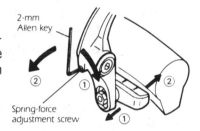

3. The center wire (Fig. 5-33) should be just long enough so that both brake shoes are at or close to the same distance from the rim. Make this adjustment at the center wire binder bolt, if necessary installing a new center wire if the old one is too short. Tighten the center wire binder bolt when the brake shoes are equidistant from the rim.

4. There should be at least 20mm of cable between the cable hangar and the cable carrier, as shown in Fig. 5-33. Adjust this cable distance at the cable fixing bolt on the cable carrier.

5. You can make finer brake-shoe clearance adjustments at the handlebar adjusting barrel (Fig. 5-20) and at the brake-shoe spring force adjustment screw (Fig. 5-34) using a 2mm Allen wrench. Make the shoe centering adjustment, so shoes are equidistant from the rim.

Cable Replacement

All brake cables eventually fray and wear and need to be re-placed (except of course for the new Mathauser hydraulic brakes). No matter what type of brake you have, the replacement procedure is essentially the same, with minor differences between downturned handlebar brake levers and cantilever, cam, and U-brake levers.

Follow these steps for cable replacement:

1. Before replacing any cable, add a light layer of grease, such as Lubriplate, on the new cable.
2. For brake levers on downturned handlebars, thread a new cable, bell end last, into the slot in the brake lever. On most bikes the cable exits at the top of the brake lever. A more recent design allows the cable to exit from the base of the brake lever body (Fig. 5-35). The cable is routed under the handlebar tape for a clean, uncluttered look. Another nice feature of this design is that you can reach in and unscrew the brake-lever mounting bolt, as shown, without having to remove the cable or depress the brake lever (which other-

Fig. 5-35: The brake cable on this dropped-handlebar brake lever leaves the brake body from underneath, and is routed underneath the handlebar tape.

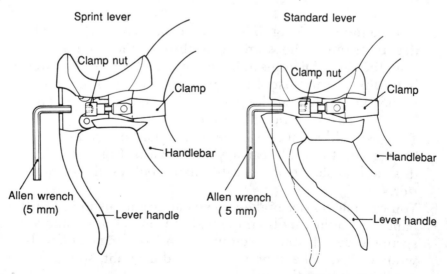

wise would be in the way), should you wish to move the brake levers to a more convenient position.

3. The motorcycle-type brake levers used on all-terrain bicycles (Fig. 5-22) require a different type of cable end than the bell-shaped lead end used on downturned handlebar brake levers. To change the cable in these levers, follow these steps:

   a. Loosen the cable binder bolt in the cable carrier (Fig. 5-33 or the cam plate for cam-action brakes, Fig. 5-28), pull the old cable out of the binder bolt.

   b. Align the slots in the adjusting barrel "N" and "O" with the slot in the cable body in Fig. 5-20. Lift the cable up out of the cable body and pull the inner cable end out of the brake lever (Fig. 5-36). Replace with a new cable, reversing the above steps. Be sure to tighten the cable binder bolt and nut to the value specified in Table 5-1.

Fig. 5-36: Remove the cable from motorcycle-style ATB brake levers by pulling the leaded end up and away from slotted hole in brake lever.

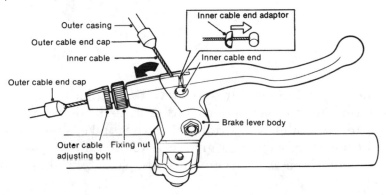

Replacing Brake Shoes

As noted earlier, when brake shoes become worn down or age-hardened, they should be replaced with new ones. Never replace only one, but all four at once so you have the best possible stopping power. To replace any brake shoe, simply loosen the brake-shoe binder bolt, remove the shoe, and replace it with a new one. By this time I am sure you know where

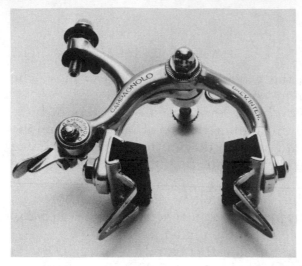

Fig. 5-37: Some brakes have brake-shoe holders that are open at one end, so the shoe can be replaced. This open end *must* face toward *rear* of bicycle.

Fig. 5-38: Closed end of the brake shoe *must* face toward *front* of bicycle.

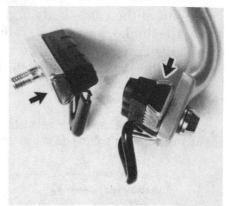

the brake-shoe binder bolt is located. If not, please refer to the material above for instructions and refer to Table 5-1 for tightening torque value when replacing the brake shoes. I have found Kool-Stop brake pads give me excellent braking, so I can recommend them as replacement pads. Your bike shop should have them.

Caution! Some brake shoes have open end as shown in Fig. 5-37. This end must always face toward the *rear* of your bicycle! Otherwise, the first time you brake, the brake shoe will slide right out of its retainer and you will have no brakes. Fig. 5-38 shows open and closed ends of this type of brake shoe. Unfortunately, manufacturers do not have an arrow showing which way this type of shoe should face; if they did, it would reduce the possibility of an accident caused by the brake shoe facing the wrong direction.

Caution! Some brake shoes have a uni-directional tread. For best braking, these brakes *must* face the right direction. They

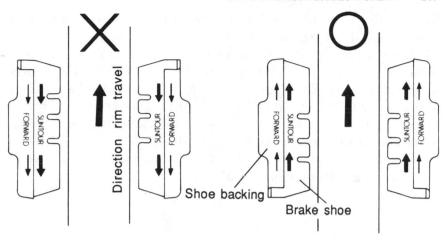

Fig. 5-39: Brake shoes with directional tread are marked so you can tell which end faces toward the front of the bike. The arrow on this brake shoe should be pointing toward the front of the bike.

usually have an arrow and/or the word "Forward" to tell you that the brake shoe should face with the arrow facing toward the front of the bike, as shown in Fig. 5-39.

Hydraulic Brakes

The bike brake wizard of Anacortes, Washington, Bill Mathauser, has come up with yet another brake innovation. His hydraulic braking system (Fig. 5-15) holds great promise, in my opinion. The samples I've seen and tried work very well indeed. They do not require brake cables. Hydraulic brakes eliminate the major hazard of brake failure due to cable stretch.

At 118 grams (4.2 ounces), the Pro Model of these hydraulic brakes is lighter than leading mechanical brakes. Mathauser's hydraulic brakes require only two basic adjustments. We have already discussed these adjustments above, but I'll repeat them just to make sure. The brake shoe should be about 1/32-inch below the top of the wheel rim, and parallel to it. These adjustments, once made, need never be redone except when you change brake blocks.

Years ago, Shimano sent me a set of their hydraulic brakes. They did work well, but they were very heavy. They aren't made anymore. Some time later, a Chicago company introduced yet another hydraulic system, which used a corrosive fluid as the hydraulic medium. The brakes worked until they succumbed to corrosion, and now *they* are no longer made. Mathauser's brakes do not use a corrosive liquid. They will stay with us, I believe. The price is right, at $165.95 for the sports model and $184.95 for the Pro model. These prices are about $40 more than the top-line non-hydraulic brakes. However, you won't need brake cables and you won't have to make brake adjustments to compensate for cable stretch.

In the next chapter I will discuss the care and feeding of your gear-shifting system, your derailleurs.

HOW TO KEEP YOUR DERAILLEURS DERAILING

The word "derailleur" was originally French. Like so many words from that charming language, it is now part of the English language, along with words such as café, champagne, and petite. The word "derailleur" means a device that derails or moves something from one position to another. In this case the moving action is on the chain.

As you know, your bicycle has two derailleurs. One derailleur moves the chain from one to another of the freewheel gears. A second derailleur moves the chain from one to another of the chainwheels up front.

Usually, within a few months after you ride away from the store on your new bike, you will experience difficulty in shifting. This difficulty occurs because the cable that goes from the shift lever to the derailleur has stretched. When the cable stretches, you may not be able to shift up to the large rear cog (low gear) or to the large chainwheel (high gear). You will have to make adjustments to both of these derailleurs.

There are two types of derailleur systems now on the market. One type is the conventional manual shift system that has been the mainstay of gear selectors at least for the past 50 years. The newest technical advance in bicycle gear shifting is known, generically at least, as *index shifting*. This system moves the chain very precisely from one gear to the next. It eliminates the need for feeling your way with the shift levers to move the chain to the gear you have selected. Index shifting lets you concentrate on where you are going, eliminates the need for looking back and down to check the gear you're in, and thus should be a positive contribution to safe cycling.

I'll get into adjustments of index shifters later in this chapter. Since there are more bikes with conventional derailleurs, I would like to start with them.

First, though, here are the tools you will need to adjust derailleurs:

1. Torque wrench (inch/pound model) (Fig. 5-2)
2. Small Phillips head screwdriver
3. 4, 6, and 8mm Allen sockets for torque wrench
4. Park fourth hand tool (Fig. 5-4)
5. Cable cutter (Fig. 6-1)
6. Workstand (optional). You could also hang your bike from ceiling hooks. I like the Minoura collapsible work stand (Fig. 6-2). It's available from The Third Hand for $45.95,

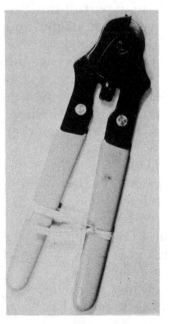

Fig. 6-1: This cable cutter, from SunTour, does a neat, clean job of snipping off outer and inner cables.

Fig. 6-2: This workstand, from Minoura, is collapsible and so takes up little room when not in use.

and folds up out of the way when you're not using it. I carry it around the country when I work as an expert witness on bike accidents for attorneys, because folded, it fits in my suitcase. The Third Hand has a well-stocked catalog of nothing but tools. They can be reached at Box 212, Mount Shasta, CA 96067, phone 916-926-2600.

Table 6-1

TORQUE TABLE FOR DERAILLEURS*
(Values in inch-pounds)

Front and rear derailleur cable fixing bolts	35–53
Front derailleur clamp fixing bolt	53–65
Rear derailleur mounting bolt	70–85
Shift lever fixing (clamp) bolt	35–53
Shift lever fixing bolt (holds shift lever onto shift lever boss)	18–23
Jockey and idler wheel axle nuts	50–60

* See data on torque in Chapter 5 for use of torque wrench, and torque values as they relate to safety.

Conventional Rear Derailleur Adjustment

I want to make it clear that when I say "conventional" I mean a non-index shifting system (which I will review later in this chapter). Figs. 6-3, 6-4, 6-5, and 6-6 are examples of racing or close-ratio gearing systems derailleurs. These are derailleurs

Fig. 6-3: This Sachs-Huret close-ratio derailleur is rated at 30 teeth total capacity, is made of forged light-alloy aluminum, and weighs 7.86 ounces.

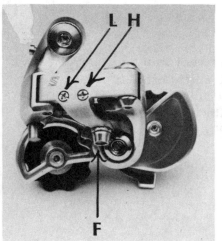

Fig. 6-4: SunTour Superbe derailleur is rated at 26 teeth total, weighs 6 ounces, and features slant parallelogram movement, double spoke guard, and non-bending cable feed.

Fig. 6-5: Campagnolo Record derailleur is rated at 28 teeth, is made for racing or fast touring, and features an articulated parallelogram movement with perpendicular movement to the chain. Wheels run on ⅛-inch roller ball bearings on a heat-treated nickel chrome steel track. Movement is controlled by three springs, two main ones and one secondary. Cage plate is of heat-forged aluminum alloy.

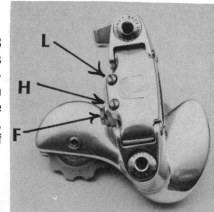

Fig. 6-6: Mavic S.S.C. derailleur features an adjustable chain guide to keep chain at a minimum for a wide variety of gears. Chain guide can be adjusted for a freewheel with cogs from 12 to 18 teeth, a racing setup. Or it can be adjusted for a freewheel with cogs from 13 to 32 teeth for wider-range gearing for touring. Weight is 6.4 ounces.

Fig. 6-7: SunTour Alpina wide-ratio rear derailleur has a capacity of 34 teeth. It's a sturdy derailleur at the budget end of the price scale.

Fig. 6-8: Campagnolo's answer to the need for a high-capacity rear derailleur for all-terrain and general touring bicycles, this GT model has a capacity of 34 teeth.

that give fast, snappy, and accurate shifting when you have, say, freewheel cogs from 13 to 24 or 28 teeth. Figs. 6-7, 6-8, 6-9, and 6-10 are examples of wide-ratio touring and all-terrain bicycle derailleurs that can give excellent shifting on freewheels with as wide a range as 13 all the way up to 38 teeth. Some of these wide-range derailleurs have a capacity of 40 teeth (there's data on derailleur capacity later in this chapter). Fig. 6-11 shows one of these monster 38-tooth cogs, which I happen to have on my all-terrain bike so I can climb everything but walls.

Fig. 6-9: SunTour XC derailleur has a capacity of 38 teeth, a parallelogram movement, heavy-duty construction for rugged, all-terrain bicycling. In addition to the long cage for wide-ratio gearing, derailleur wheel sizes can be changed to accommodate different gear ratios.

Fig. 6-10: Sachs-Huret wide-range derailleur has a capacity of 42 teeth, which makes it the widest-capacity derailleur on the market. It's well made of highly polished, heat-treated aluminum-alloy, and has a parallelogram movement.

Fig. 6-11: This superlow-gear rear cog, left, has 38 teeth for easier hill climbing.

As you look at the derailleurs in Figs. 6-3 through 6-10, you will notice that the low gear adjuster "L" is always closer to the top of the derailleur, under the mounting bolt. The high gear adjuster "H" is always lower on the derailleur. These adjusters, shown more clearly in Fig. 6-12, limit derailleur travel to the left and to the right.

It's important, for safety reasons, that your rear derailleur be adjusted so that the chain cannot be overshifted so far to the right that it falls off the low gear cog and jams between that cog and the spokes. Fig. 6-13 shows just such a situation. Here the chain has overshifted to the left, has fallen off the low gear cog, and has now caused the rear wheel to be jammed. Sometimes, if the rear wheel does not lock up due to this chain jam, the chain can suddenly skip as you pedal, and as your foot slips you could lose balance and control. I have also seen the chain cut off four or five spokes in a row as it rotated smack up against

Fig. 6-12: High-gear adjuster "H" and low-gear adjuster "L" limit derailleur travel to the right and to the left, respectively.

Fig. 6-13: When low gear adjustment permits overshifting, chain can fall off large cog and get jammed between that cog and the spokes, as shown here.

them when lodged between the spokes and the base of the freewheel. Either situation has caused accidents and injury in the past.

If the rear derailleur high gear adjuster lets the chain move too far to the right, the chain can fall off the small cog and wedge between it and the chainstay, as shown in Fig. 6-14. In this case you would experience pedal lockup, as though a strong arm suddenly grabbed the chain and kept you from pedaling. You may then lose control and balance, which could lead to an accident. Now let's learn how to adjust your rear derailleur so you can shift with ease, accuracy, and above all, safety.

Here are a few of the newer derailleurs in exploded view, in

Fig. 6-14: If chain overshifts to the right, it can jam between the small cog and the chain stay, in the position shown by arrow "A."

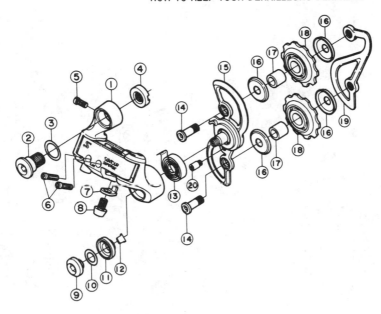

Fig. 6-15: Exploded view of derailleur in Fig. 6-4, the SunTour Superbe close-ratio derailleur. Parts are: 1) body assembly; 2) mounting bolt; 3) washer; 4) mounting nut; 5) cable anchor clamp; 6) cable anchor bolt; 7) adjusting screw; 8) outer cage; 9) pulley cover; 10) pulley bushing; 11) pulley; 12) inner cage; 13) pulley axle bolt; 14) cage tension nut; 15) shim; 16) bushing; 17) spring retainer; 18) spring; 19) cage stop pin.

case you have to replace any of the moving parts such as springs and sideplates. Fig. 6-15 is an exploded view of the derailleur in Fig. 6-4, the SunTour Superbe. Fig. 6-16 shows an exploded view of the Shimano XC derailleur shown in Fig. 6-9, with a super-long cage that has a 38-tooth capacity. Please refer to picture captions for parts location and description.

1. *Check for cable slack:* With the rear wheel off the ground (ideally, the bike should be on a bike stand or suspended from the ceiling), shift the chain to the small cog. With your finger halfway down the downtube, lift the rear derailleur cable. If there is any slack, the cable has stretched. The slack must be removed before making any other adjustments.
2. *Remove cable slack:* Shift the chain to the small rear cog. To remove the slack, loosen the cable fixing bolt (see Figs.

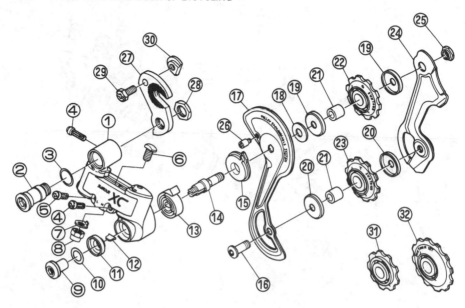

Fig. 6-16: Exploded view of SunTour XC derailleur shown in Fig. 6-9. Parts are: 1) body assembly; 2) mounting bolt; 3) adjusting shim; 4) 12mm adjusting screw; 5) 10mm adjusting screw; 6) cable anchor bolt; 7) cable anchor clamp; 8) cable anchor nut; 9) tension nut; 10) adjusting shim; 11) bushing; 12) spring retainer; 13) tension spring; 14) cage axle; 15) spring bushing; 16) pulley bolt; 17) outer cage plate; 18) spacer; 19) guide pulley dust shield; 20) tension pulley dust shield; 21) pulley bushing; 22) guide pulley with ten teeth; 23) tension pulley with ten teeth; 24) inner cage plate; 25) cage axle nut; 26) cage stop pin; 27) mounting bracket; 28) mounting lock nut; 29) mounting bracket fixing bolt; 30) mounting bracket fixing nut; 31) pulley with nine teeth; 32) pulley with 12 teeth. Pulleys No. 31 and 32 are interchangeable with pulleys No. 22 and 23.

6-3 through 6-10 for location of cable fixing bolt) and pull the excess cable through with a pair of pliers as shown in Fig. 6-17, or with the Park fourth hand tool. Some derailleurs, as in Fig. 6-7, have a cable slack adjustment barrel which you can use to remove cable slack as the cable stretches over time. Turn the barrel counterclockwise to remove slack, clockwise to add slack.

3. *Check high-speed adjuster:* With the shift lever and while you rotate the pedals, shift the derailleur all the way to the right, so the chain is on the high gear (small) cog. If the chain won't shift to the small cog, you will need to let out

a bit of cable through the cable fixing bolt. Try letting out about ⅛-inch at a time until you can get the chain to shift over to the small cog. Retighten the cable fixing bolt to 35 to 53 inch/pounds. If the top small wheel on the derailleur (the jockey wheel) is not now directly under the small cog, as shown in Fig. 6-18, make these adjustments:

a. If the jockey wheel is to the left of the small cog, turn the high-speed adjuster counterclockwise until it is aligned as in Fig. 6-18.

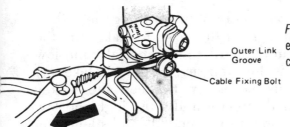

Outer Link
Groove

Cable Fixing Bolt

Fig. 6-17: Remove cable slack by loosening cable fixing bolt, pulling excess cable through, retightening this bolt.

Fig. 6-18: Align small rear cog (high-speed cog) with derailleur wheel as shown.

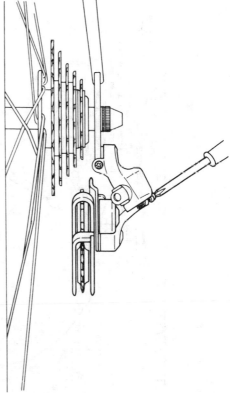

b. If the jockey wheel is too far to the right, turn the high-speed adjuster clockwise until this alignment is obtained.

4. *Check low-speed adjuster:* Shift whiie pedaling until the jockey wheel is directly under and vertically aligned with the large (low gear) cog, as in Fig. 6-19. Turn the low-speed adjuster one way or the other until the jockey wheel is aligned as shown in Fig. 6-19. If the chain won't move up to the low gear cog, there is too much slack in the cable. Shift back to the small rear cog and remove this slack as shown above.

5. *Check shifting on all rear gears:* While turning the pedals, shift up and down through all the gears to make sure the chain will seat accurately on all cogs, especially the low and high gears. Repeat this step several times. Make any fine-tuning adjustments necessary to keep the jockey wheel vertically aligned directly under the high and low gear cogs. The chain should run smoothly and silently on

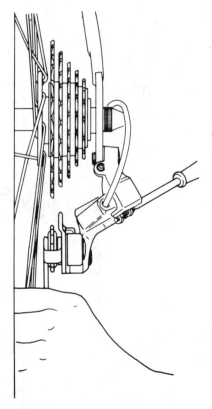

Fig. 6-19: Align large rear cog (low-speed cog) with derailleur wheel as shown.

both high and low gears. If you hear any rubbing or grinding noises on either of these gears, the probability is very high that the derailleur jockey wheel is not directly aligned under each gear, causing the chain to be inaccurately seated. This is a good way to shorten the life of both chain and freewheel cog.

6. *Check derailleur mounting bolt:* The derailleur mounting (a.k.a. fixing bolt) should be torqued to 70 to 80 inch/pounds.

7. *Lubricate rear derailleur pivot points* with light oil every month, more often if you ride a lot.

8. *Rear Derailleur trouble-shooting:*

    a. Chain skip: If the chain skips as the pedals are turned, one or more of the freewheel cogs may be worn to the point where they get little lips or overhangs, such as shown in Fig. 6-20 (arrows) that catch the chain. In this case the only cure is to install new cogs. Fig. 6-21 shows a new set of freewheel cogs, untouched by bicycle chain. You can see the difference between work and

Fig. 6-20: Arrows point to worn teeth on this cog, which could cause chain to skip or jump. Such a cog should be replaced.

Fig. 6-21: New freewheel, showing unworn cogs (this is a Campagnolo aluminum and titanium cog freewheel that costs around $200).

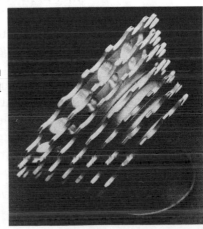

272 THE COMPLETE BOOK OF BICYCLING

new freewheel cogs by comparing these two photos. Please see Chapter 8 for cog change instructions.

b. Chain skip: A worn chain will also cause chain skip. Please see Chapter 8 for data on checking chain wear and installing a new chain.

c. Chain skip: Worn chainwheel teeth may also cause chain skip. Fig. 6-22 compares a worn chainwheel with a new one. You can see that the lower (low-speed) chainwheel is worn down (and that the rider, your author, preferred this lower gear). See Chapter 8 for more information on replacing worn chainrings with new ones.

d. Chain noise: If the chain seems to have trouble settling down on the cog you have selected, but instead makes a grinding noise, it's telling you that you probably have not shifted accurately. Any time you hear a grinding noise from the freewheel (or the chainwheel), remember that, 99 percent of the time, you can quiet things down with a tiny adjustment of the shift lever one way or the other. One of the blessings of the index shifting system is that you don't have to worry about where the chain lands as you shift. The system does this automatically, and does it very well when properly adjusted. You can concentrate on where you're going and not have to be concerned about accurate shifting, so the index system should prove to be a safety feature. I'll discuss index shifting systems later in this chapter.

e. Can't shift to low rear gear: If you have installed a new chain and it's too short, you may not be able to shift to the large cog. See Chapter 7 for data on correct chain length.

f. Chain falls off gears: If the chain is too long, it can flop around and fall off the rear cog or off the chainwheel, especially on a bumpy road going downhill when you are in the high-speed gear. This is especially true of all-terrain bicycles, even when the chain is the correct length. On an ATB, when you're embarking on a rough downhill trail run, keep the chain as taut as possible by shifting to the low gear combination front and rear, or at least put the chain on the largest rear cog and the second largest chainwheel (most ATBs have triple chain-

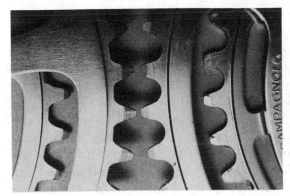

Fig. 6-22: The chainwheel at the top is new, does not have worn teeth. Chainwheel at bottom has worn teeth on the smaller of the two rings, and is reaching a point at which replacement should be considered.

Fig. 6-23: Peg on chainwheel keeps chain from tangling in your feet if it slips to the right off the big chain-wheel. This is a good safety measure.

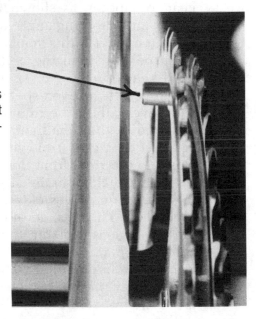

wheels). You can always reshift after you finish the downhill run. Some makes of chainwheels have a small protuberance on the outside of the high-speed (large) chainwheel, next to the crankarm. The arrow "B" in Fig. 6-23 shows such a fitting. It's designed to keep the chain from sliding down the crank and off onto the pedal where it can wrap itself around your ankle or drag on the street and cause an accident. All such chainwheels should have this type of safety fitting.

g. Chain falls off or jams on idler wheel (lower derailleur wheel): The SunTour AG rear derailleur has a movable outer cage so you can remove the derailleur without having to remove the chain, as shown in Fig. 6-24. If the derailleur idler-wheel axle nut is not tight, this movable outer plate may slip down and permit the chain to slip off the idler (bottom) wheel. Derailleur wheel axle nuts should be tightened to 50 to 60 inch/pounds.

h. Grinding noise or chain-rubbing sound from front derailleur: Sometimes you will hear a grinding noise coming from the front derailleur cage, after you have shifted to a higher or lower rear gear but have not shifted the front gear. This is because as you shift from one rear gear to another, as shown in Fig. 6-25, the chain assumes an increasing angle with respect to the front derailleur cage. Try this yourself. With the bike on a stand or suspended from the ceiling, shift the chain to the third gear of a five- or six-speed freewheel, or to the fourth gear of a seven-speed freewheel. With the front shift lever, adjust the front derailleur until the chain is centered in the derailleur cage. Shift the chain to the smallest rear cog. You will see that the chain moves closer to the right front derailleur cage plate as you do so. Shift the chain to the largest rear cog. You will note that the chain moves closer to the left front derailleur cage plate. This change of chain angle in the front derailleur cage as you shift the chain from one rear cog to another explains why you can have chain rub and noise from the front derailleur. The solution to this chain rub and noise is simple. Just be aware that you may have to move the front shift lever slightly to move the front derailleur cage enough to keep the chain from rubbing on it, as you shift to another rear cog. This is especially true when you have shifted two or three cogs away from the original position. This problem of chain rub is particularly acute if you have a seven-speed freewheel and a three-speed chainwheel, as you can see in Fig. 6-25.

i. Chain jumps off chainwheel: Another cause of chain jump is a bent chainwheel. Chainwheels are made of aluminum and can easily be bent out of shape. If you suspect a chainwheel is bent, remove the chain from it, spin the cranks, and eyeball the chainwheel from the rear. Mark any bent place with chalk. With a Crescent

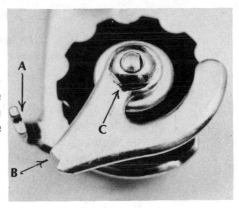

Fig. 6-24: Some SunTour rear derailleurs have an openable cage on the lower wheel for easy chain removal. "A" is the section where lip "B" fits when the cage is closed. "C" points to the axle nut, which should be loosened to move the lower cage to be opened, but tight when the cage is closed.

Fig. 6-25: Sometimes, as you shift rear gears, you may hear a rubbing sound from the front derailleur. This is because as the chain is shifted, it assumes an increasing angle where it can rub on the front derailleur cage plate. At left is shown angles of a five-speed freewheel, at right are more acute angles for a seven-speed freewheel. Solution is to move front derailleur shift lever a bit to keep the chain centered in the cage after each shift of the rear derailleur.

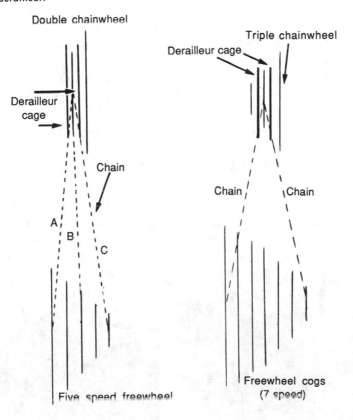

wrench, *gently* force the chainwheel back to true. When you do this, remember that aluminum has a very limited modulus of elasticity, and it won't take many bends back and forth to break it. One such bend, back to true, is what you should try to aim for.

9. *Changing the rear derailleur cable:* Eventually the rear derailleur cable (as with all bike cables) will wear out. If you see a frayed strand, it's time to change to a new cable. Cables come in two parts, the casing (spaghetti-like tubing) and the stranded steel cable that runs inside the casing. I like the Shimano SIS cable with casing liner. It's flexible, without the undue compression that tends to create resistance to cable movement inside the casing. The SIS cable is the type Shimano recommends for their index shifting system, and any bike shop should have it in stock. One more point about cables and casings. Do avoid those "flexible" steel casings, such as shown in Fig. 6-26, because they are stiff and add back pressure to the cable.

    a. Release the cable fixing bolt at the derailleur (Fig. 6-15). Push on the casing near the shift lever until the leaded end of the cable comes out of the shifter (Fig. 6-27).

    b. Remove both casing and cable and replace with the new cable and casing. If you have cut the casing to trim off unneeded length, be sure to file off any burrs or rough edges on the cut end. I use a bench grinder for this purpose.

    c. Put a light coat of a water-resistant grease, such as Lu-

Fig. 6-26: Stainless-steel outer-cable casings such as shown here (arrow) are stiff, should be avoided for smoother shifting.

Fig. 6-27: To remove cable from handlebar-mounted shift levers (the kind on ATBs), pull the cable out by the leaded end (arrow).

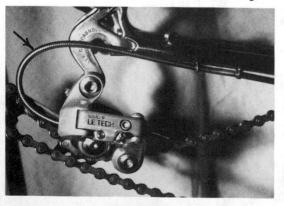

briplate, on the cable before inserting it into the casing. Insert the free end of the cable into the shifter, so the leaded end fits into a recessing opening in the shift lever, as shown in Fig. 6-27 for all-terrain shifters and handlebar-end shifters on downturned handlebars, and Fig. 6-28 for downtube-mounted shifters.

    d. Take up cable slack as discussed in step 2. Recheck rear derailleur adjustments as noted above.

    c. Leave from 1 to 1½ inches of cable beyond the cable fixing bolt. Snip off excess cable. I like the cable cutter in Fig. 6-1. It's from SunTour and it does a neat job of cutting without letting cable strands unravel. To keep ends from fraying after you cut off excess cable, slip a lead cap (available from bike shops) on the cut end and melt the cap with a match or soldering iron.

10. *Check derailleur wheels:* Remove, clean, and replace the derailleur wheels. The jockey and idler wheels on a rear derailleur take a lot of punishment from dust and dirt, and so are subject to a lot of abrasion and wear. One way to get smoother derailleur adjustment is to replace these little wheels with sealed-bearing jockey and idler wheels (Fig. 6-29). They are made by SunTour and should be available

Fig. 6-28: To remove cable from downtube-mounted shift levers, pull cable out (or push it out) by the leaded end (arrow).

Fig. 6-29: Sealed-bearing derailleur wheels run more smoothly, last longer, require less maintenance.

from your bike shop. To clean and relubricate them, just remove them, pry out the thin dirt seal with a thin-bladed knife, wash out old grease and dirt in kerosene with a small brush, and relube with Lubriplate or Phil Wood grease. Then reinsert the seals and put the wheels back in the deraillcur. Fig. 6-30 shows these wheels disassembled. The wheels labeled "A" and "B" are sealed-bearing; the other wheel is a plain bearing with no seal and, in fact, no bearings other than the plain hole into which is fitted the axle insert "G." "C" shows a sealed-bearing seal removed. These seals are thin and easily bent, so go easy when prying them out and when reinserting them.

11. *Check and adjust chain wraparound:* The jockey wheel should be as close as possible to all freewheel cogs, without touching them. I like about a ⅛-inch clearance on all gears. Check wraparound on all gears by shifting through them and watching how close the jockey wheel is from each cog. There are three simple ways to get the jockey wheel closer to the cogs. One is to adjust the derailleur angle with its chain tensioner bolt (if your derailleur has one). This bolt is shown by arrow "T" in Fig. 6-7. The second way is to move the wheel back farther in the dropouts, if your bike has horizontal dropouts. You won't be able to do this with vertical dropouts. The third way is to remove a link or two from the chain for the same result. See Chapter 7 for data on chain length change.

Fig. 6-31 is an excellent illustration of good and bad chain wraparound. Chain "1" shows good wraparound with the chain on seven teeth of this 14-tooth cog. Chain "2" shows the chain on only four teeth. Obviously this chain is far more likely to skip. Again, when the chain skips or jumps, your foot will slip if you've been pedaling hard, and you could lose balance and control.

As a general rule, as you shift through all the rear gears, the chain should fall on nearly half the teeth of each cog. For example, on a 24-tooth cog, the chain should be wrapped around at least ten teeth; on a 34-tooth cog, around at least 15. I would not quibble about a tooth more or less, though, just so the chain is hanging on approximately half or a few teeth less than half. Anything less and you're risking chain skip and an accident. However, you

Fig. 6-30: Sealed-bearing wheels (top) have ball bearings. Conventional wheels (bottom) simply run on bushing "G." Complete sealed-bearing wheel "A" with seals in place. "B" has one seal pried out. "C" is the pried-out seal. "D" is conventional wheel cover, "F" is its axle, "E" is plastic wheel.

Fig. 6-31: An example of chain wraparound. Chain on cog No. 1 is on almost half its teeth, which is good. Chain on cog No. 2 is on fewer teeth, which is bad and can cause chain skip.

can get the derailleur too close to the freewheel cogs. Fig. 6-32 shows what can happen when the derailleur jockey wheel gets too close to the cog; the chain is jammed between the jockey wheel and the right side of the derailleur cage plate. This situation can lock up the pedal motion unexpectedly and contribute to loss of control and an accident.

12. *Chain position on derailleur wheels:* Fig. 6-33 shows you how the chain should fit on the derailleur wheels. If you have changed the derailleur or removed the chain for cleaning, you may puzzle for a while about which wheel and in which direction on each wheel the chain should fit. Fig. 6-33 shows that the chain should be in front of the top (jockey) wheel and behind the lower (idler) wheel. This is

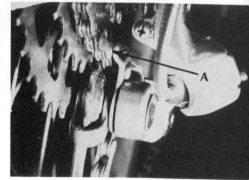

Fig. 6-32: Chain skip can cause chain to wedge between upper derailleur wheel cage and cog, as shown by arrow "A."

Fig. 6-33: This is how the chain should fit. Chain at top goes around front of jockey wheel. Chain at bottom goes around rear of tension wheel.

also a good photo to remind you that when you are removing the rear wheel, you will need to grasp the derailleur and pull it back to let the freewheel clear the derailleur as the wheel comes out. Before removing the rear wheel, always shift to the small (high gear) freewheel cog to make it easier to move the chain out of the way as you pull the wheel out of the dropouts.

A Word About Derailleur Capacity

It's important to know how derailleur capacity is arrived at and what it means to you. For example, you may be unhappy with the gear ratios you now have. You want a lower gear, let's say, to ease your way when your bike is gear-laden and the hills are steep. To change gears you will of course have to change your low freewheel gear to one with more teeth, or change the small chainwheel to one with fewer teeth. Or, change the chainwheel setup from a double to a triple chainset with a smaller chainwheel at the low end. (See Chapter 7 for gear change instructions.)

So you want to select front and rear derailleurs that have the capacity to handle the larger gears you plan to install on your bike. Here's how to determine what derailleur capacity you need.

To compute derailleur capacity, you simply subtract the number of teeth in the smallest rear cog from the number of teeth in the largest rear cog. Then you subtract the number of teeth in the smallest chainwheel up front from the number of teeth in the largest chainwheel. Then you add these two numbers for the total capacity of the derailleur.

For example, my ATB has a super granny rear gear of 13 teeth on the small cog and 38 on the rear cog: $38 - 13 = 25$. The small chainwheel has 28 teeth and the big one has 48 teeth: $48 - 28 = 20$. Now add these together: $25 + 20 = 45$. That's the rear derailleur I am supposed to be using. I say "supposed" because there is not a derailleur on the market rated at 45 teeth. Not, at least, the last time I looked. The penalty I pay for this wall-climbing set of gears is that I can't use the biggest (low gear) freewheel cog and the biggest (high-speed) chainwheel at the same time. To me this is no penalty at all. So far as I am concerned, to put the chain on the two largest gears is insane anyhow. And I positively, absolutely love the hill-climbing low gear I get with this combination. Sometimes I believe I could walk up hills faster than when my chain is on the 38-tooth freewheel and on the 28-tooth chainwheel, but when I try I soon discover that, slow as it seems, riding uphill is a whole lot easier and a lot more comfortable than walking and shoving the bike along.

If you want bigger (granny) gears than your bike now has, I can recommend either the SunTour AG Tech or the SunTour MounTech. When fitted with a super long cage, the capacity of these derailleurs is 40 teeth. The part number for the AG Tech is 24149008, for other SunTour models it's 27909007. I recommend you bring your old SunTour derailleur to the dealer and have him fit the longer cage on it. He'll probably have to order the cage from his wholesaler, so allow a couple of weeks for the longer cage to arrive at the shop. Another excellent derailleur, also rated at 40 teeth, is Shimano's Model RD-525-SGS. The SGS means "super long cage" and it too works very well indeed.

Modern top-of-the-line rear derailleur design has solved most of the shifting problems that have plagued cyclists for years. The better derailleurs, the more expensive ones made by Shimano, SunTour, Campagnolo, Mavic and Sachs-Huret, for example, have sealed mechanisms, sturdy single and in many cases double spring mechanisms, and a parallelogram movement which keeps the jockey wheel a uniform distance from the freewheel cogs.

FRONT DERAILLEUR ADJUSTMENT

Like the rear derailleur, it is very important that the front derailleur be correctly adjusted for safety and ease of shifting, for five reasons:

1. If the derailleur is adjusted so the chain moves too far to the left, and it falls off the small chainwheel and onto the bottom bracket shell, the chain may get jammed between the fixed cup of the bottom bracket and the base of the chainwheel. Such sudden jamming can lock up or create considerable resistance to pedaling and cause you to lose balance and

control. Or, the chain may simply rotate on the bracket shell so that you experience sudden zero resistance to pedaling. If you were pedaling hard when this happened going uphill, you could lose control of the bike and have an accident.

2. If the derailleur is adjusted so the chain moves too far to the right, it may fall off the large chainwheel and down onto the crank or the pedal or your foot and, again, cause loss of control and an accident. The fitting shown in Fig. 6-23 will help prevent chain slippage down onto the pedal, but it won't prevent sudden loss of pedal resistance, which can cause your foot to slip suddenly forward, resulting in loss of balance and an accident.

3. If the derailleur is positioned at an angle relative to the chainwheels, the chain can get jammed between the large chainwheel and the derailleur cage while shifting from the small to the large rear cog or vice versa. Such a jam may lock up the pedals and cause loss of control and an accident.

4. If the derailleur is positioned too high, you will be able to shift the chain to the large chainwheel but not off it.

5. If the derailleur is positioned too low, you won't be able to shift up to the large chainwheel. The derailleur cage will rub on the large chainwheel.

So much for all the reasons why you need to properly adjust the front derailleur. Now here's how to do it:

1. *Shift the front derailleur to the low gear position* (small chainwheel).

2. *Check parallel position:* The derailleur cage should be positioned parallel to and from ⅟₃₂-inch to ⅛-inch above the large chainwheel, as shown in Fig. 6-34.

Fig. 6-34: Vertical and parallel adjustments for front derailleur.

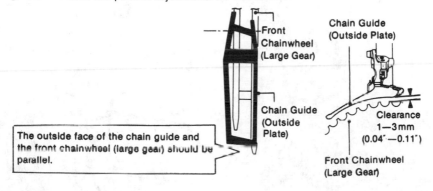

3. *To reposition the derailleur:* Loosen the derailleur clamp fixing bolt, Fig. 6-35, move the derailleur up or down and to the right or left as necessary, and tighten the clamp fixing bolt to 53 to 64 inch/pounds.

4. *Remove cable slack:* While turning the cranks, shift the front derailleur to the small chainwheel. With a finger, lift the cable about halfway down the downtube. If there is any slack, remove it by loosening the cable fixing bolt as shown in Fig. 6-36. Pull excess cable through the fixing bolt and tighten this bolt to 35 to 53 inch/pounds. The fourth hand tool (Fig. 5-4) makes holding the cable taut while tightening the cable fixing bolt a lot easier. Leave about 1 to 1½ inches of cable beyond the cable fixing bolt. To keep ends from fraying after you cut off excess cable, slip on a lead cap that you can buy from the bike shop and melt it with a match or soldering iron. Grind off any jagged edges of the cable tubing if you installed a new cable. Grease the inner cable before sliding it through the outer cable tubing.

5. *Adjust left and right derailleur travel:* Like a rear derailleur, a front derailleur has two adjusters, a high-speed adjuster, which limits its travel to the right, and a low-speed adjuster, which limits its travel to the left. Fig. 6-37 is a close-up of these two adjusters. You can see that the low-

Fig. 6-35: To make vertical adjustment of front derailleur, loosen clamp bolt as shown, slide derailleur up or down on seat tube as necessary.

Fig. 6-36: To remove cable slack from front derailleur, loosen cable fixing nut, as shown, pull excess cable through cable fixing bolt, tighten nut.

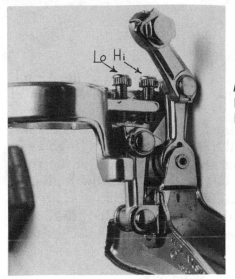

Fig. 6-37: Super close-up of low ("L") and high ("H") gear adjusters on front derailleur.

Fig. 6-38: Arrows point to location of low and high gear adjusters on front derailleurs.

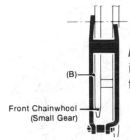

Fig. 6-39: For low-speed adjustment, turn adjuster to bring the inner face of the derailleur cage plate close to but not touching the small chainwheel.

speed adjuster is always the one closest to the clamp that holds the derailleur on the bike frame (the seat tube). You can also see that as you screw the adjuster one way or the other it gets closer to or farther away from the stops on the derailleur. The location of these adjusters is also shown in Fig. 6-38.

6. *Adjust low gear (left) travel:* While turning the cranks, shift the front derailleur so the small chainwheel (low gear) is close to, but not touching, the inner surface of the left chainguide plate, as shown in Fig. 6-39. Turn the low gear adjus-

ter (Fig. 6-40) clockwise or counterclockwise, as necessary, to limit left movement of the derailleur to this location of the small chainwheel.

7. *Adjust high gear (right) travel:* While turning the cranks, shift the front derailleur so the large chainwheel (high gear) is close to, but not touching, the inner surface of the right chainguide plate, as shown in Fig. 6-41. Turn the high gear adjuster, Fig. 6-42, clockwise or counterclockwise, as necessary, to limit right movement of the derailleur to this location of the large chainwheel.

Fig. 6-40: Make low-speed front derailleur adjustments by turning the low-speed adjuster one way or the other as shown, to bring the left cage plate closer to but not touching the small chainwheel.

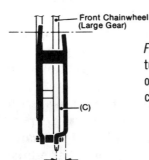

Front Chainwheel
(Large Gear)

(C)

Fig. 6-41: Make high-speed front derailleur adjustments by turning the high-speed adjuster to bring the inner right side of the derailleur cage plate close to but not touching the large chainwheel.

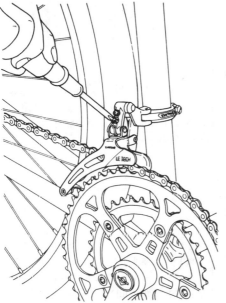

Fig. 6-42: Turn the high-speed adjuster with a small Phillips screwdriver to make this adjustment.

About Shift Levers

Shift levers may be located in four places. They can be on the handlebars, as on all-terrain bicycles (Fig. 6-43), on the down-tube, on the end of downturned handlebars, and at the stem. The stem location is, in my opinion, the worst possible place for shift levers, because if you have an accident that propels you over the handlebars, and you're male, you could injure or leave behind a crucial part of your reproductive system—not a possibility to consider lightly. Shift levers in the stem position stick up like little blunt surgical tools that I would not care to make contact with in a headlong propulsion over the bars.

Fig. 6-43 also shows what to me is the best location of the shift levers on the flat handlebar of an ATB. Here the levers are located near your hand, close enough so that a slight movement of the wrist brings your fingers in contact with the shift lever. You also have three selections of shift lever placement with

Fig. 6-43: Shift levers can be located as shown here on all-terrain bicycle handlebars.

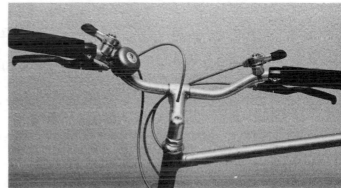

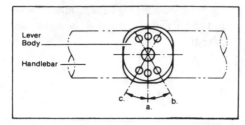

Fig. 6-44: There are six holes in the base of all-terrain handlebar-mounted shift levers, into which fit small pins in the shift-lever body.

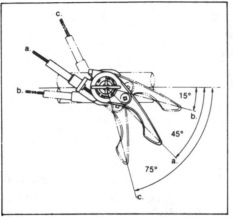

Fig. 6-45: Depending on where you fit the small pins, you can obtain three locations of the shift-lever handle on ATB handlebars, to fit your finger length.

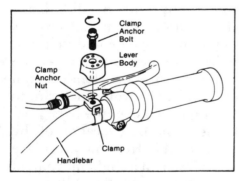

Fig. 6-46: Shift-lever base is bolted to shift-lever clamp, as shown.

respect to the handlebars, as shown in Fig. 6-44. In that drawing you will see three holes in the base of the shift lever body, or rather three holes at the top and three at the bottom. The shift lever arm has matching pins which fit into one of the top and one of the bottom holes. You can select which combination of these holes will position the shift lever to fit your finger length. Fig. 6-45 shows these three locations and how they affect shift lever placement and cable angle. Since ATB handlebars come in a wide range of angles, you should select the shift lever angle that gives the least cable angle, for smoother shifting. Figs. 6-46 and 6-47 show exploded views of the shift lever. Fig. 6-48 is an exploded view of a downtube or stem-mounted shift lever. Fig. 6-49 is a handlebar-end shift lever (for downturned handlebars). To install a bar-end shift lever, remove the handlebar plugs, fit the lever body into the handlebar ends and tighten the lever fixing bolt ("18" in Fig. 6-49) with a 6mm Allen wrench.

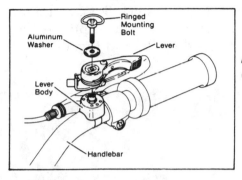

Fig. 6-47: Shift-lever assembly fits down over base and is held by wing nut.

LD-3200

Fig. 6-48: Downtube shift lever, exploded view. This is SunTour's LD-3200 clamp-on model that goes on the downtube. Parts are: 1) frame; 2) inner washer; 3) right lever; 4) left lever; 5) outer washer; 6) pressure disc; 7) cover; 8) star washer; 9) friction adjuster screw; 10) clamp bolt; 11) clamp nut.

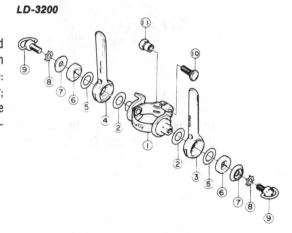

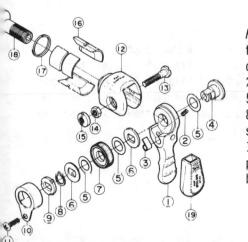

Fig 6-49: Bar-end shifters. The expanding section No. 16 fits into the end of the handlebars, on downturned bars. Parts are: 1) lever; 2) ratchet spring; 3) ratchet pawl; 4) washer; 5) spring washer; 6) ratchet ring; 7) circlip; 8) pressure disc; 9) ratchet cover; 10) cover screw; 11) body; 12) axle/friction screw; 13) axle nut; 14) axle locknut; 15) clamp expansion shoe; 16) expander ring; 17) expansion bolt; 18) hood.

If the front or rear derailleurs seem to shift by themselves so that you find the chain on a gear combination you don't want, the shift-lever wing nut is the most likely culprit. All shift levers have such a wing nut, as shown at the top of Fig. 6-48. Some use a bolt that can be tightened with a dime. In any case, these bolts work loose after a time, and need to be retightened.

Excellent front derailleurs for close-range gearing are shown in Figs. 6-50, 6-51, 6-52, and 6-53. For wide-range gearing I can recommend the front derailleurs in Figs. 6-54, 6-55, and 6-56. Descriptions of these derailleurs are given in the captions. Fig. 6-57 shows an exploded view of the derailleur in Fig. 6-55, the SunTour XC.

Fig. 6-50: Campagnolo front derailleur has a double hinge between the bolt and the arm which moves on heat-treated nickel-chrome-steel pivot pins. Cage is of carbonitrated steel for maximum wear resistance.

Fig. 6-51: Mavic S.S.C. front derailleur has a housing and link rods of polished and anodized dural. The cage is hardened, tempered, and chromed steel. Link rods are hardened and precision-made. Shifting is fast and precise.

Fig. 6-52: SunTour's Superbe front derailleur is their top-line model designed for racing and close-ratio touring gearing. Features parallelogram movement, has cage of heat-treated and chromed steel with an aluminum body.

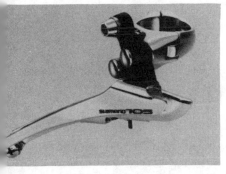

Fig. 6-53: Shimano's latest front derailleur, the 105, has a streamlined body, sealed movement designed for close-ratio gearing.

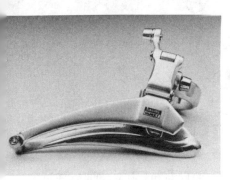

Fig. 6-54: Sachs-Huret front derailleur for wide-ratio gearing has a 26-tooth capacity, weighs but 4.2 ounces, suitable for triple chainwheel.

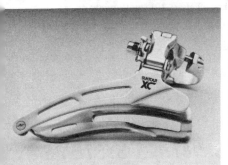

Fig. 6-55: SunTour XC front derailleur for wide-range gearing has a 22-tooth capacity, accommodates a triple chainwheel, is designed for all-terrain bicycles. The cable anchor clamp has a heli-coil built into the clamp bolt hole for more secure cable anchoring, which is a good idea, considering the strain ATB shift cables are given. The cage design is such that it does not interfere with the rear derailleur cable.

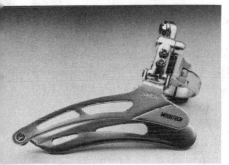

Fig. 6-56: SunTour Mountech front derailleur can handle from 26 teeth down to six teeth, has a super wide-range parallelogram movement for triple chainwheels.

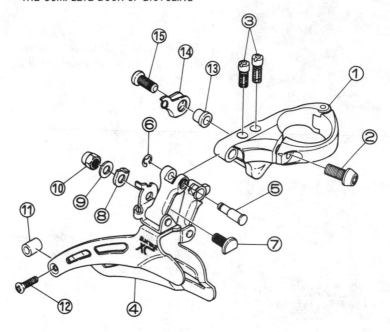

Fig. 6-57: Exploded view of SunTour XC front derailleur. Parts are: 1) mounting clamp; 2) mounting bolt; 3) adjuster screw; 4) derailleur body; 5) pivot pin; 6) circlip; 7) cable anchor bolt; 8) cable anchor clamp; 9) cable anchor washer; 10) cable anchor nut; 11) chain roller; 12) roller screw; 13) cable guide bushing; 14) cable guide; 15) cable guide bolt.

INDEX SHIFTING SYSTEMS

Index shifting systems take the guesswork out of accurate shifting from one gear to another. Originally developed for racing cyclists to permit them to shift quickly and accurately to a specific gear without distraction from the race, these systems are now on the market as original equipment on most makes of bicycles.

I see properly adjusted index shift systems as a safety device as well as a way of fast and precise shifting. For example, as I noted above, shifting with a conventional derailleur system takes practice to move the chain to the gear you wish. Inaccurate manual shifting can put the chain partway on and partway off a cog, for instance. Such shifting not only wears out the cog and the chain faster, it can contribute to chain skip, possible loss of control, and an accident. This type of accident is one of rider error, to be sure, and can be avoided by learning how to shift smoothly and accurately. A better way to smooth, accurate, and safe shifting to the gear you want is with an index shifting system. The index system moves the chain precisely on the cogs of the freewheel and chainwheel. There's no guessing or fiddling with shift levers to get the chain to ride on the gear without noise or rubbing. You always know which gear you're in. You won't ever have to look down and back at the rear cogs to see which gear the chain is on, or down at the chainwheel for the same reason. All of which means *safety*, because you can concentrate on traffic, road, or trail conditions (yes, all-terrain bikes are starting to come with index systems too) without concern about where you have shifted the chain.

Index shifting systems operate with a definite "click," which you hear each time you shift the chain on the freewheel cogs or on the chainwheels. Even uphill shifting is easier, because you can get the chain to a lower gear quicker than with a conventional system, although I don't really buy claims of some riders that these systems let you shift to a lower gear even as you strain hard on the pedals uphill. It's definitely unhealthy, or at least inconvenient, to wait until you are grunting and groaning up a steep hill to admit that you need a lower gear and then try to shift to it. One way to shift under power like that is to zig-zag across the road to reduce the angle of climb. I *strongly* advise against that technique, because it brings you into the line of both lanes of traffic, which is very dangerous. Another way is to dismount and walk up. Still a third way is to ride into a driveway or side road long enough to shift down before continuing up the hill. You could, and should, relax pedal pressure as you try to shift. Index systems are a big help there. Trouble with conventional systems is that if you slack off on pedal pressure going up a steep hill, the bike stops before you can complete the shift. With index shifting, the chain moves fast, precisely, and without any further need to fine-tune where you have placed the chain. The system is self-tuning, if it's adjusted correctly in the first place. I'll get into such adjustments now.

How to Adjust Index Shifting Systems

The first commercially available index shifting system was introduced to the U.S. market by Shimano in 1984. Since that time Shimano and SunTour have refined their index systems to the point where they are pretty foolproof. Campagnolo has recently introduced their system, but it is so new at this writing that I have not seen it as original equipment on new bicycles.

If you have purchased a bike recently that costs much over $300, it very likely is equipped with one of the three makes of index shifters on the market at this writing. Fortunately, they all work pretty much on the same principle, so the adjustment instructions I will give you should apply to all of them. Remember, as we go through these steps, that index systems have two modes. One is the conventional shifting mode, called the friction mode. The other is the index mode. The friction mode is there in case the index system gets out of adjustment when you're on the road. If the index system does not work, you can always get home using the friction mode. Here are the steps in adjusting index shifting systems:

1. *High-speed adjustment:* Loosen the cable fixing bolt at the derailleur and pull about a half inch of cable free. Shift to the small freewheel cog. Eyeball the derailleur jockey wheel and this cog to make sure the cog is lined up parallel with it. If not, turn the high-speed adjuster (Fig. 6-58) clockwise or counterclockwise until it is lined up.
2. *Low-speed adjustment:* Shift the chain to the big freewheel cog (low gear). The derailleur jockey wheel should line up with that cog. If not, adjust the low-speed adjuster clockwise or counterclockwise until the jockey wheel is lined up with

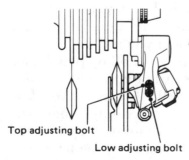

Fig. 6-58: High- and low-speed adjustments on an index shifting system require that the rear derailleur jockey wheel be aligned just under the high and low gear cogs. Alignment is made with adjuster screws.

Top adjusting bolt

Low adjusting bolt

the cog, as shown in Fig. 6-58. Remember, the low-speed adjuster is always the one at the top of the derailleur, closest to the derailleur mounting bolt.

3. *Remove excess cable slack:* The critical part of any index system is maintaining the correct cable tension. If the cable is too slack, the chain won't shift from the high (small cog) to the next cog. If it's too tight (too much cable tension), the chain may skip a gear as you shift to a lower gear. Move the rear derailleur shift-lever wing bolt to the friction mode, as shown in Fig. 6-59. Be sure to turn the little ring back down flat again after you switch from one mode to the other. If the ring is not flat, the derailleur system can switch from one mode to the other, which may be a bit disconcerting.

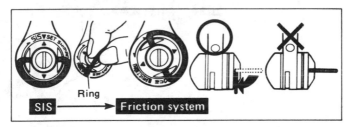

Fig. 6-59: Index shift systems have two modes, the index and the friction (conventional) mode. If something happens to the index mode, you can always shift to the friction mode by turning the wing nut, as shown here. But always turn the wing nut flat after moving to another mode, as shown in the drawing at the right, so the system won't shift between modes by itself.

Shift to the high (small rear cog) gear. Pull excess cable through the derailleur cable fixing bolt and tighten it to 35 to 53 inch/pounds. You can fine-tune cable tension at the inner cable tension barrel on the derailleur, as you make the following adjustments.

Adjust Inner Cable Tension

1. Turn the shift lever wing bolt so the system is in the index mode as shown in Fig. 6-60.
2. Now shift from the small freewheel cog to the next biggest cog. If the chain won't move to this gear, turn the cable

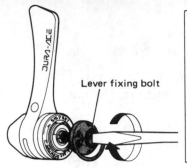

Lever fixing bolt

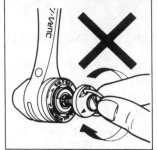

Fig. 6-60: To prevent unwanted shifts, tighten the shift lever axle bolt with a screwdriver.

Fig. 6-61: Fine-tune cable tension by using the inner cable tensioner, as shown.

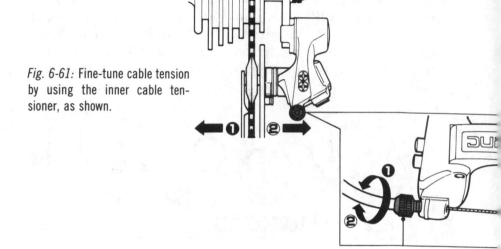

tension adjuster (Fig. 6-61) counterclockwise one or two turns. Try shifting again. If the chain overshifts and moves to the third gear, turn the cable slack adjuster clockwise a half to one turn and continue this cable slack fine-tuning until the chain falls exactly on the second gear.

3. With the chain on the second gear, turn the inner cable tension adjuster counterclockwise while you turn the pedal forward, as if you were cycling. As you turn the adjuster, watch the rear third cog and the chain. As the chain just begins to approach the third cog, stop twisting the adjuster.

4. Shift back to the small rear cog. Repeat step 6 on each of the freewheel cogs, fine tuning with the inner cable tension adjuster on the derailleur (Fig. 6-61), as necessary.

5. Put the chain on the smallest chainwheel and the largest freewheel. Turn the derailleur angle adjustment screw (arrow in Fig. 6-62) to bring the derailleur jockey wheel as close to the big rear cog as possible, but without touching it as shown in Fig. 6-63.

Fig. 6-62: The derailleur angle can be adjusted to help bring the jockey wheel as close as possible to the rear cogs in all gears without actually touching the cogs. Screw the angle adjuster (arrow) in or out as necessary.

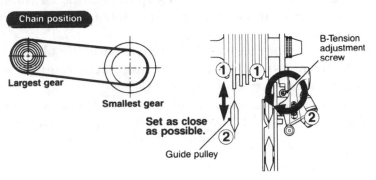

Fig. 6-63: Derailleur angle adjuster (also called the tension adjustment screw) is shown here. The adjuster moves the entire derailleur body closer to or farther away from the cogs. Clockwise moves the derailleur away from the cogs, counterclockwise moves it closer to the cogs.

6. For the final adjustment step, turn the cranks in reverse, i.e., backpedal. If the chain rubs when you're backpedaling, the jockey wheel is too close to the large rear cog. Turn the tension adjustment screw clockwise until you can backpedal without having the derailleur jockey wheel rub on the big (low gear) rear cog.

7. Adjust the front derailleur as noted in the section above, headed "Front Derailleur Adjustment." Front derailleur adjustments for index shifters are the same as for conventional shift systems.

Retrofitting Index Shift Systems

You can install an index shift system on your current bicycle, but there are a lot of ifs, ands, and maybes associated with retrofitting an index system. Here are the major problems:

- For starters, it's 90 percent certain that you won't be able to use your existing freewheel, rear derailleur, shift levers (for sure), chain, and cable. For example, Shimano systems require their index-related shift levers, rear derailleur, freewheel, and the Shimano UG chain, Sedis chain, or Regina CX chain. SunTour also requires special matching components. I suggest you check with your bike dealer to make sure all the components for a given make of index system will work together if you want to go the index route. At this writing, only Shimano, SunTour, and Campagnolo have index systems on the market.
- If the rear dropout on your bike is not perfectly aligned, you have to have it straightened. This alignment requires a special dropout correction tool (Fig. 6-64).
- If your bike has brazed-on shift levers on the downtube, the width of the brazed-on boss has to be no more than 5.75mm (7/32-inch) wide, exclusive of paint. The flat sides of the shift-

Fig. 6-64: If you plan on installing an index system on your present bike, be sure to check frame alignment, or have it done in a bike shop. If the frame is even slightly out of line, the index system most likely will not work. This illustration shows where and how to check frame alignment.

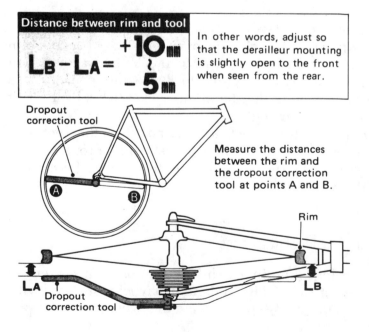

Distance between rim and tool

$$L_B - L_A = \begin{array}{c} +10\text{mm} \\ \wr \\ -5\text{mm} \end{array}$$

In other words, adjust so that the derailleur mounting is slightly open to the front when seen from the rear.

Dropout correction tool

Measure the distances between the rim and the dropout correction tool at points A and B.

A   B

Rim

L_A L_B

Dropout correction tool

lever boss must be parallel to the down tube. If these two criteria are not met, the bike is not suited for index shifting without major surgery for installing new bosses. Such brazing will also require a major repaint job. Shimano says, however, that this is not necessary on their latest index system. If you buy such a system, make sure it's the version that will fit any boss, because the older Shimano index systems still require the dimensional limitations noted above.

- If your bike has cable routing through the frame, cable movement resistance very likely will be too great for index shifters, unless the routing has no sharp turns and you use lined outer cables and keep the inner cable well greased. I would say that retrofitting index systems on a bike with internal cable routing is marginal, however. You may be lucky. I'd make an arrangement with the dealer that you can return the system if it won't work on your bike with internal cable routing. Save the boxes.
- You will have to change the rear derailleur cable and cable tubing (the spaghetti tubing through which the cable runs) to a lined tubing and a stainless steel *inner* cable. You can't use a stainless steel *outer* cable tubing such as that shown in Fig. 6-26. If you replace any cables on your bike with index shifting, be sure to use the same cables, both inner and outer, that were original equipment.
- At this writing, none of the index shift systems have bar-end shifters, and I think it's unlikely they will be made unless some way is found to overcome the added cable friction involved. So if you want index shifting, you'll have to give up bar-end shifters. It's a good swap, in my opinion, to get the advantages of indexing.
- While the Campagnolo system has all of the requirements just listed, their Synchro index shift system is claimed to be adaptable in terms of required matching components. For example, the Synchro system can be used with current (1987 on) Campagnolo derailleurs, including Victory, Triomph, Record, Super Record, and Nuova Record. Campagnolo says it will work with most freewheels, but preferred freewheels are made by Campagnolo, Regina, GTM, Maillard, the new SunTour, and the Shimano models. Preferred chains are Regina CS, Sedis Sport Silver, SunTour 6000, and Shimano UniGlide. If shift-lever bosses are brazed on, they must be

made by Campagnolo or made to their specifications and tolerances. If the shift lever is clamped onto the downtube or top tube, a Campagnolo clamp must be used.

In the next chapter I will cover the care and feeding of the rest of the bicycle's transmission system, the chain, freewheel, chainwheels, and the bottom bracket.

SEVEN

THE TRANSMISSION SYSTEM— CHAINS, CHAINWHEELS, BOTTOM BRACKETS, FREEWHEELS

The transmission system of a bicycle includes the chain, chain-wheels, freewheel, and the bottom bracket. Let's start with the chain. First, though, I urge you to buy a bike stand (Fig. 7-1), so you can reach every part of your bike quickly and easily. If your bike shop doesn't have one, check one of the bicycle mail order catalogs in the Appendix.

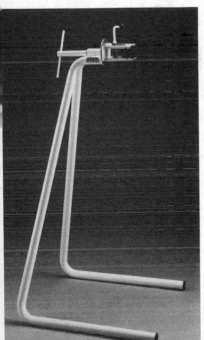

Fig. 7-1: Use a bike stand to make your bike maintenance easier.

CHAIN CARE

More than any other part of your bike, the chain is not only exposed to abrasives such as dirt, sand, and mud, but to water as well, which washes away protective lubricants. It's the one part of your bike that wears out fastest and needs the most maintenance. All-terrain bicycle chains need more frequent maintenance if ridden on sandy trails or through water. A new chain should last 2,000 to 3,000 miles; if neglected, it can wear out in only 1,000 miles. It takes only one one-thousandth of an inch of wear on each of the 116 chain pins (Fig. 7-2) for the chain to stretch ⅛-inch. That much play in the chain can cause it to skip off front or rear sprockets, causing loss of control and an accident.

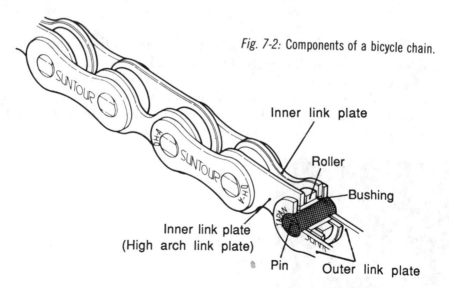

Fig. 7-2: Components of a bicycle chain.

Inner link plate

Roller

Bushing

Inner link plate
(High arch link plate)

Pin

Outer link plate

Follow these steps to keep your chain healthy.

1. *Clean the chain:* Clean your chain any time it looks dirty and before every long trip. A dirty chain not only wears out faster, it also wears down the teeth of your freewheel and chainwheels, and their replacement costs a bundle. Clean your chain while it's on the bike, or remove it for a more

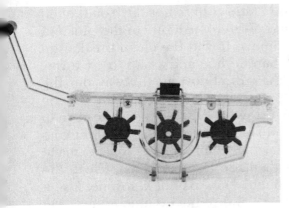

Fig. 7-3: The messy job of chain cleaning is easier with this Vetta chain cleaner.

thorough cleaning. If it's on the bike, clean it with a Vetta chain cleaner (Fig. 7-3), which clips over the rear derailleur cage. The chain passes over brushes in the unit as you turn the crank counterclockwise. You'll need about a half pint of kerosene to put in the Vetta. It's small and light enough to carry along on your trip, and if your cookstove uses kerosene you can use the same fluid in the Vetta chain cleaner. Or you could spray the chain with a degreaser such as Link Clean (Fig. 7-4), which flushes out dirt and cleans the chain. This is also a good way to clean the chain when you're on a bike trip; do it every few days if you're covering 50 to 80 miles daily.

Fig. 7-4: You can spray the chain with a solvent such as Link Clean to clean the chain while it's on the bike.

2. *The best way to clean your chain is to remove it:* You'll need a chain "breaker" tool (Fig. 7-5) to push one of the pins out of the chain so you can remove it. Put the chain breaker on a chain pin and turn the handle five and a half to six turns, just far enough to push the pin almost all the way out the other side of the chain. Leave about 1/32-inch of the pin inside the outer cage plate (arrow in Fig. 7-6) so you can snap the chain back together. SunTour Superbe Pro and Shimano chains require their own special chain breaker tool, so make sure you buy the one that's made for your chain. Clean the chain by agitating it thoroughly in a pan of kerosene. Use a brush to clean out old grease and remove sand and grit. Do not use highly flammable solvents such as gasoline or naphtha to clean your chain!

Fig. 7-5: A "chain breaker" tool is used to push a chain pin out far enough so you can remove the chain.

Fig. 7-6: When using the chain breaker, leave about 1/32-inch of the pin inside the outer cage plate.

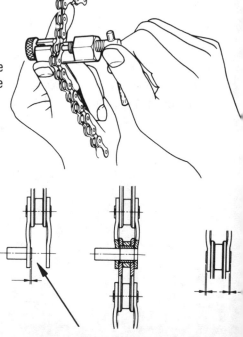

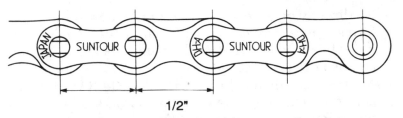

1/2"

Fig. 7-7: Check chain stretch by counting off 24 links. If the distance between the first and the 24th link is 12¹⁄₁₆ of an inch or more, the chain should be replaced.

Fig. 7-8: Another check for chain wear is to bend a new chain and an old chain and compare them. The old chain at bottom bends farther than the new one at top and should be replaced.

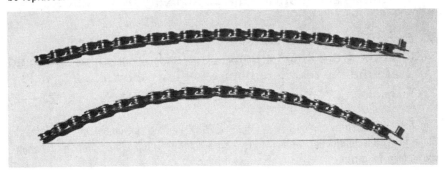

3. *Check chain wear:* As I noted above, worn chain pins cause chain stretch. Check chain wear this way. Remove the chain, lay it flat and count off 24 links. Since link pins are a half-inch apart (Fig. 7-7), 24 links should measure 12 inches. If they measure much more, say 12¹⁄₁₆ inches, replace the chain. Another way to check chain wear is to bend the chain and compare it with a new chain, as shown in Fig. 7-8. The chain at the bottom is worn and should be replaced.

4. *Lubricate the chain:* If you've cleaned the chain, checked it for wear, and believe it to be sound, apply one of these lubricants before re-installing it.
   a. Soak the chain overnight in melted paraffin. Melt the paraffin over warm water on low heat. Never melt the paraf-

fin directly over heat! Paraffin penetrates to the pins and forms a protective coat to which abrasives won't adhere. I have been using paraffin for years and have found my chains last at least 3,000 miles.

b. Another excellent lubricant is 80 or 90 SAE automotive gear oil. Heat the oil over warm water, soak the chain in the oil overnight. Never heat the oil over direct heat!

c. You could also soak the chain overnight in 50 SAE motor oil. You won't need to heat this oil.

d. When you're biking on the road, use spray cans of lubricant containing molybdenum in a petroleum base, such as Dri-Slide or DuPont Teflon in a petroleum base such as Tufoil (Figs. 7-9 and 7-10). Carry a spray can in your pannier and lubricate the chain every two to three days.

5. *To replace the chain:*

a. Thread the chain through the front derailleur cage and around the rear derailleur wheels as shown in Fig. 6-33.

Fig. 7-9: Carry a spray can of Dri-Slide for chain lubrication while you're on a long trip.

Fig. 7-10: Another convenient chain lubricant is a spray can of Tufoil, which contains Teflon in an oil base.

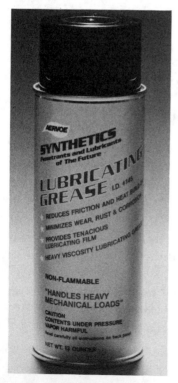

b. Push the two ends of the chain together. The ⅟₃₂-inch of the pin you left inside the outer plate (Fig. 7-6) should hold the chain together while you push the pin back with the chain breaker. Leave about ⅟₆₄-inch of the pin outside the chainplate (Fig. 7-11).

c. Remove the chain breaker. Twist the link from side to side to free it up. Otherwise the link might be stiff and cause chain skip.

d. *Caution!* SunTour Superbe Pro chains have "high arch" inner links (Fig. 7-12). A conventional chain design is shown in Fig. 7-13. When you replace the SunTour chain, be sure the arched part of the outer link goes over the gear teeth as shown in Figs. 7-12 and 7-14.

e. *Caution!* If you replace or add links to your chain, be sure to use the same make and model links. Never mix different makes of chain links.

Fig. 7-11: Leave about ⅟₆₄-inch of the chain pin showing when you reassemble the chain.

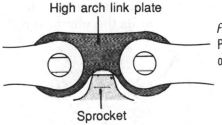

High arch link plate

Sprocket

Fig. 7-12: When replacing a SunTour Superbe Pro chain, be sure the arched outer link goes over the gear teeth.

Fig. 7-13: A conventional chain design does not have a high-arch link plate.

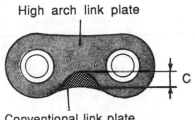

High arch link plate

C

Conventional link plate

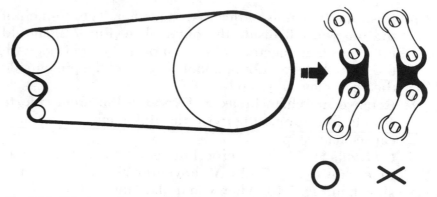

Fig. 7-14: "O" shows the correct location of the SunTour chain arch on the chainwheel; "X" shows the wrong location.

6. *Installing a new chain:*
   a. Use the same make and model of your original chain. Other chains may not be compatible with your freewheel and derailleurs, particularly with index shifting systems. If in doubt, take your old chain to the bike shop for an exact replacement. Make sure the new chain has the same number of links as the old one. Chains come in 112-, 116-, or 120-link sizes.
   b. Make sure the chain is long enough so you can shift to the large freewheel cog and short enough so the chain won't skip or jump off a gear. Shift the chain so it's on the largest freewheel sprocket and the largest chainwheel. The rear derailleur should now be almost parallel to the chainstay (Fig. 7-15). If you can't shift the chain to a 36-

Fig. 7-15: The derailleur should be in this position when the chain is on the largest freewheel cog and the largest chainwheel.

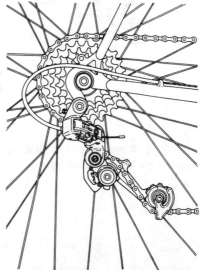

or 38-tooth freewheel sprocket and to the largest freewheel, the chain is too short. In this case don't add links
to the chain because if you do, the chain will be dangerously loose when you shift to the smallest freewheel
sprocket. Console yourself that you have a super-low
granny gear for steep hills. If, on the other hand, your
biggest sprocket has 34 teeth or less, you should be able
to shift so the chain is on that sprocket and on the large
chainwheel. If not, add one or two links.

c. Shift the chain to the smallest freewheel sprocket and the
smallest chainwheel. The rear derailleur should be about
vertical to the ground, Fig. 7-16. If not, remove one or two
links.

d. Check and adjust chain wraparound (Figs. 6-7 and 6-31),
as described in Chapter 6.

e. As I noted in Chapter 4, always carry the chain breaker
and three or four extra links in your tool kit. The day I left
my chain breaker home was of course the day the chain
broke on a rural road in Wisconsin. I pounded the broken
link pin out with an old nail and a rock I found nearby. I
removed the broken link and pounded the pin back into
the now shorter chain. What a pain!

f. I recommend installing a chain guard (Fig. 7-17) on your
chainstay, to prevent occasional chainrub from damaging
its finish. The guard self-adheres to the stay, but clean the
stay before installing it.

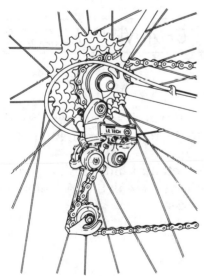

Fig. 7-16: The derailleur should be in this position when the chain is on the smallest freewheel
cog and the smallest chainwheel.

Fig. 7-17: Protect the finish of your chainstay
with a chainguard.

7. *Chains for coaster brake bikes:* You don't need a chain breaker tool to remove or install a chain on a bike with coaster brakes. All you do is press off the master link (Fig. 7-18) with a screwdriver and pull the chain apart at that link.

Caution! Coaster brakes are actuated by back pedaling. If the chain breaks, you have no brakes! Accidents have happened this way. When replacing the master link, be sure it's tight. Some master links are split (open) at one end. The open end of this master link must face toward the rear of the bike (Fig. 7-19), otherwise it can pop off and the chain will fall apart and off the bike.

Fig. 7-18: Remove the master link to remove a coaster bike chain.

Fig. 7-19: The open end of a coaster brake chain master link *must* face toward the rear of the bike.

CHAINWHEEL CARE

Tools you will need:

- 5mm Allen wrench to remove the dust cap (or a screwdriver for some types of dust caps) and to remove or tighten the chainwheel binder bolts (Fig. 7-20).
- 6mm Allen wrench for Allen-type crank binder bolts, and a 14 or 15mm socket wrench for bolt-type crank binder bolts.
- Inch-pound torque wrench (Fig. 5-2).
- Slot wrench for chainwheel binder bolts (Fig. 7-20).
- Crank puller (Fig. 7-20).

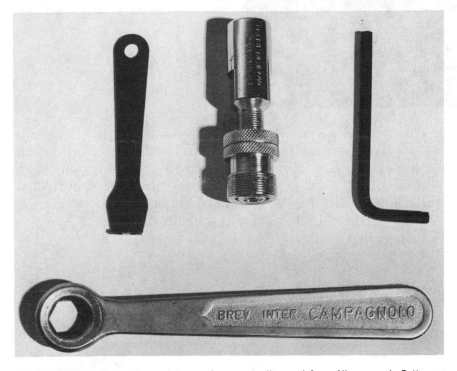

Fig. 7-20: Top, left to right: a slot wrench, crane puller, and 6mm Allen wrench. Bottom: a crank binder bolt wrench.

Table 7-1

CHAINWHEEL TORQUE SPECIFICATIONS*

(Torque is in inch/pounds)

Crank binder bolts	300–325
Chainwheel binder bolts	70–100

* Please refer to Chapter 5 for a discussion of torque and how to use a torque wrench.

1. *Clean the chainwheel often:* Abrasives such as sand and road dirt can wear out the aluminum-alloy teeth of a chainwheel. Use a small brush and kerosene to remove gunk from the chainwheel every time you clean the chain. I know it's not easy to reach behind the chainwheels, especially the middle of a triple chainset (Fig. 7-21), but it's important you get both sides of all the teeth clean to prevent premature wear and costly replacement.

Fig. 7-21: A triple chainwheel set. Be sure to clean both sides of all wheels every few months.

2. *Check teeth wear:* The teeth of your chainwheels should look like those in Fig. 7-22. Worn chainwheel teeth often cause chain skip. If the teeth are worn more to a point than those in Fig. 7-22, it's time to replace the chainwheel. Most touring cyclists use the smaller of a double chainwheel (Fig. 7-23) or the middle of a triple chainwheel (Fig. 7-24), so inspect that chainwheel closely for wear.

Fig. 7-22: This is how the teeth of your chainwheel should look.

Fig. 7-23: A high-quality Campagnolo double chainwheel with cranks and pedals. You'd probably use the small chainwheel more often, so inspect it for wear at least once a year.

Fig. 7-24: The center (second) chainwheel of a triple chainset is most likely the one you'd use the most, so check it for wear at least once a year.

3. *Inspect chainwheel alignment:* Bent chainwheels can cause chain skip, so check them for alignment after you clean them. Remove the chain and spin the cranks while you hold a pencil next to each chainwheel. If the chainwheel moves closer to or farther away from the pencil, mark that spot with chalk. With an adjustable Crescent wrench or tool, such as shown in Fig. 7-25, gently straighten the chainwheel.

Fig. 7-25: Straighten a bent chainwheel *gently* with a tool such as this, or with a crescent wrench.

4. *Tighten chainwheel binder bolts:* I was ride-testing a new bike for a magazine article a few years ago. When I shifted the chain from the small to the large chainwheel, the pedals suddenly locked and I almost lost control. I discovered that the chainwheel binder bolts either had not been sufficiently tightened or had worked loose, which allowed the two chainwheels to be spread so far apart that when I shifted, the chain fell down between them. These bolts can work loose, so check them after every long trip, or every few months. You'll need a 5mm Allen wrench and a slot wrench (Fig. 7-20). A double chainwheel set (Fig. 7-26) has five binder bolts, and a triple chainwheel set (Fig. 7-27) has 10 binder bolts. To tighten these bolts, use the slot wrench to hold a side and the 5mm Allen wrench to do the tightening. Tighten each bolt to a torque of 70 to 100 inch/pounds. Fig.

Fig. 7-26: Tighten the five binder bolts on a double chainwheel twice a year.

7-27 shows the binder bolts, "A," on a triple chainset that hold the two larger chainwheels. The binder bolts on the small chainwheel are on its left side, as shown in Fig. 7-28.

Fig. 7-27: The ten binder bolts of a triple chainwheel should be tightened twice a year. The arrow points to one of them.

Fig. 7-28: The chainwheel binder bolts for the smallest chainwheel are on the inside of the chainset. The arrow points to one of them.

5. *Remove the chainwheels:* Cranks are fastened to the bottom bracket spindle three ways: with a bolt (Fig. 7-29); with an Allen bolt (Fig. 7-30); or with a cotter key (Fig. 7-31). The bolt-on crank type is by far the most widely used. Next:

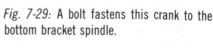

Fig. 7-29: A bolt fastens this crank to the bottom bracket spindle.

Fig. 7-30: An Allen bolt fastens this crank to the spindle. Use a 6mm Allen wrench to remove it.

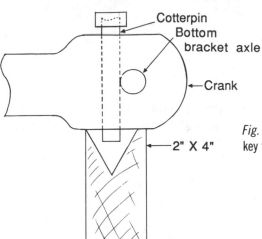

Cotterpin

Bottom
bracket axle

←Crank

←—2" X 4"

Fig. 7-31: Cottered cranks use a tapered key to hold the crank on the spindle.

a. Remove the dust cap with a 5mm Allen wrench (Fig. 7-32) or with a screwdriver if the dust cap is the slotted type.
b. Remove the crank binder bolt with a 14 or 15mm wrench (Fig. 7-33).
c. Remove the crank with the crank puller. This tool has two parts ("A" and "B," Fig. 7-34). Hold part "A" and turn part "B" counterclockwise as far as it will go, until the spindle end of part "B" is flush with the threaded end of part "A," as shown in Fig. 7-34.

Fig. 7-32: Remove the dust cap with a 5mm Allen wrench, or if it's slotted, use a screwdriver.

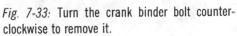

Fig. 7-33: Turn the crank binder bolt counterclockwise to remove it.

Fig. 7-34: Use this tool to remove your cranks. Part "A" threads into the dust cap opening. Then turn part "B" to force the crank off the bottom bracket spindle.

    d. Thread part "A" clockwise into the dust cap opening (Fig. 7-35). You can see a few threads showing on part "A," but the puller is threaded in as far as it will go on this particular crank. Some cranks have deeper dust cap threaded sections, so you may be able to thread the crank puller farther into the crank than as shown in Fig. 7-35. The crank puller must be threaded all the way into the dust cap threads to avoid stripping them as you force the crank off the spindle (Fig. 7-36).

Fig. 7-35: Part "A" of the crank puller is threaded into the dust cap opening (see Fig. 7-34).

Fig. 7-36: To remove the crank, turn the crank puller clockwise until the crank is loose.

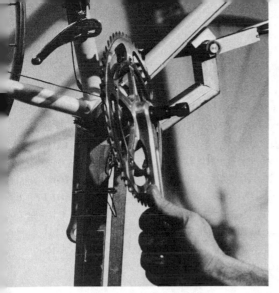

Fig. 7-37: Once the crank is loose it can be easily removed from the tapered spindle.

   e. Turn part "B" of the crank puller clockwise with a 14 or 15mm wrench until the crank is pulled off the bottom bracket spindle (Fig. 7-37). If the crank won't come off after you have turned the crank puller to 325 inch-pounds, tap the end of the puller with a hammer and continue turning the crank puller. Repeat as necessary until the crank works loose. Remove the crank puller.

Allen bolt cranks: The Allen bolt cranks (Fig. 7-30) do not require a crank puller. Turn the Allen bolt counterclockwise with a 6mm Allen wrench (Fig. 7-38) until the crank is loose enough to pull off the spindle. The Allen bolt is integral to the crank and remains in it when the crank is removed from the spindle. The Allen bolt crank was a great idea because it was so easy to remove. Thieves agreed, because soon after they were introduced as original equipment, a lot of $115 cranksets disappeared.

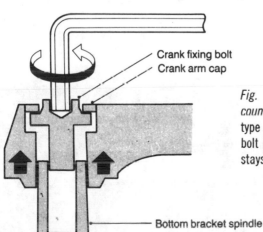

Crank fixing bolt
Crank arm cap

Fig. 7-38: Turn a 6mm Allen wrench counterclockwise to remove an Allen bolt type crank from the spindle. The crank bolt is an integral part of the crank and stays in it when you remove the crank.

Bottom bracket spindle

Allen bolt cranks have two other drawbacks. Like all cranks, they must be tightened to a torque of 300 to 325 inch/pounds. That's hard to do with an itty-bitty skinny Allen wrench, so a lot of folks were not getting the cranks tightened down enough. When cranks aren't tightened enough they eventually work loose and start to slip on the tapered shank of the steel bottom bracket spindle (Fig. 7-39). When that happens, the aluminum crank square mounting hole (Fig. 7-40) becomes rounded off, which ruins the crank. Allen bolt cranks also require a pedal with a large-diameter spindle to fit them (Fig. 7-41). Only the crank manufacturer makes such a pedal.

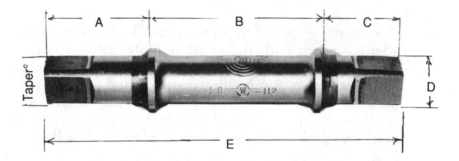

Fig. 7-39: Bottom bracket spindle. Section "A" is longer than Section "C," so it can accommodate the chainwheels. "D" shows the taper, which is usually 2 degrees. Section "B" is the distance between the bearing lands and "E" is the spindle length. If you're changing spindles, take your old one to the bike shop for a replacement that fits.

Fig. 7-40: The square hole in an aluminum crank can become rounded unless you tighten the crank binder bolt to the correct torque (see text).

Fig. 7-41: The threaded hole for a pedal is larger on the Allen bolt–type crank than it is on the conventional bolted crank (right).

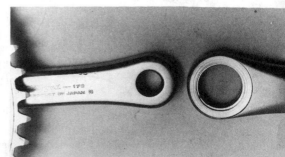

d. To install the cranks, place the crank on the bottom bracket spindle and tighten the binder bolt to a torque of 300 to 325 inch/pounds. Do not grease the bottom bracket spindle! That would make it easier for the crank to slip and would reduce the tight drive fit of the crank.

Cottered cranks: These are held on the bottom bracket spindle by a tapered cotter key that matches the taper of the spindle (Fig. 7-31). To remove them, cut a V-notch in a two-by-four and brace the crank against it (Fig. 7-42). Turn the cotter key nut "A" in Fig. 7-42 counterclockwise two or three turns, but not all the way off. With the cranks braced as shown, hammer the cotter key down until it pops out. The two-by-four absorbs hammer shock that would otherwise damage the bottom bracket bearings. Cottered cranks were very popular 10 or 15 years ago, even on some fairly expensive touring bikes. Today you'll only find them on inexpensive bicycles. To install them, reverse the above steps.

Fig. 7-42: To remove the cotter key from a cottered crank, brace the crank over a notched two-by-four and hammer the key out.

One-piece "Ashtabula" cranks: Remove these cranks (Fig. 7-43) by first removing the pedal on the left side of the bike. Then remove the bottom bracket lock nut and adjustable cup (see instructions on bottom bracket maintenance in this chapter) and pull the crank out through the bottom bracket shell along with the bearings. Replace it the same way.

Fig. 7-43: One-piece "Ashtabula" crankset is found today only on very inexpensive bicycles.

The Chainwheel Approach to Lower Gears

If you need a lower gear so you can climb hills with less strain, you can do the following. If you have a double chainwheel, say with 42- and 52-tooth chainwheels, you could replace the 42-tooth chainwheel with a 28- or even a 24-tooth chainwheel. That way you'd have a "granny" low gear up front. (Later in this chapter we'll discuss changing the freewheel cogs.) But now

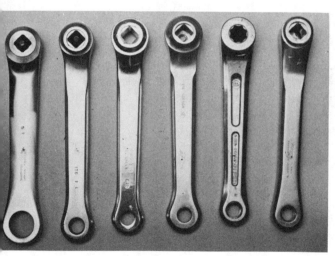

Fig. 7-44: Cranks come in five different lengths. See Table 7-2 for a match between bicycle frame size and appropriate crank length.

Fig. 7-45: Crank lengths are stamped on the inside of the crank, along with the pedal diameter and thread specification.

you'd also experience a drastic gear drop as you shift from the 52-tooth chainwheel to the low gear 28- or 24-tooth chain- wheel. You'd also lose some of the intermediate gears that help you up moderate hills (see discussion on gears and Tables 4-1 and 4-2 in Chapter 4). Spend a bit more money and convert your double chainset to a triple by adding a 24- or 28-tooth chainwheel and a longer bottom bracket spindle, and keep the 42- and 52-tooth chainwheels.

To remove and install chainwheels, see the instructions above on tightening them. Use the same tools to remove the binder bolts (Fig. 7-46), install the new chainwheel(s) and tighten the binder bolts to 70 to 100 inch/pounds. Replace the

Fig. 7-46: You can change chainwheels to different sizes by removing binder bolts "B" and spacers "C" from the chainwheel crank "A." Be sure any new chainwheel fits your old chainwheel crank.

chainwheel on the bottom bracket spindle and tighten the crank binder bolt to 300 to 320 inch/pounds as noted above. Note: If you're converting to a triple chainset, you'll have to install a bottom bracket spindle that's longer on the chainwheel side so the small chainwheel won't rub on the chainstay. Fig. 7-47 shows such a longer spindle—you can see that the chainwheel side "AA" is longer than side "A." Instructions on changing spindles are given later in this chapter. Whether you use a smaller chainwheel on your double chainset or install a new triple chainset, you still have to be concerned about chainwheel compatibility.

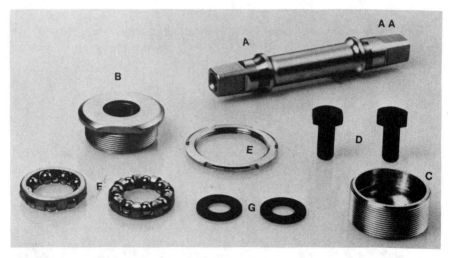

Fig. 7-47: Bottom bracket components. Note that the spindle (upper right) has two tapered shank lengths. Shank "AA" is longer than shank "A" to accommodate a triple chainwheel set. "B" is the fixed cup, "C" the adjustable cup, "D" the crank binder bolts, "E" the adjustable cup lockring, "F" the bearings, and "G" the binder bolt washers.

Not All Chainwheels Are Interchangeable

Not all chainwheels are created equal. For example, you may buy a new chainwheel and discover, when you try to install it on your chainset, that it won't fit. I could give you a long list of chainwheel compatibilities between makes, but manufacturers change their specifications frequently and what I give you might not work on chainsets that are still on the drawing board at this writing. Better to take your old chainset and bottom bracket spindle to the bike shop and make sure you buy the new chainwheel(s) that fit your old parts. Here's what to look for.

There are two areas of compatibility between chainset makes. One is whether or not the chainwheel you want will fit on the chainset you have. For example, Fig. 7-48 shows a combination that does fit. As you can see, I have installed a triple Shimano Biopace chainset on a Sugino AT crank. This was a compatible match. But until you actually put the new part on your old one, you can never be sure of a fit.

The second area of compatibility is how the chainwheel fits on the bottom bracket spindle. For example, if the taper of the chainwheel spindle (usually 2 degrees) is not the same as the taper of the chainwheel crank hole (Fig. 7-48), the fit won't work. If the square hole in the chainwheel crank (Fig. 7-48) is not the same dimension as well as the same taper as the spindle, you also have a bad fit. How cranks fit on the spindle's tapered shank is what machinists call a "press fit," which is why the chainwheel binder bolt tightening torque of 300 to 320 inch/pounds is so great. If the fit is not accurate, the chainwheel can work loose under the strain of pedal pressure and eventually the square holes will round off and the crank will be ruined, as noted above.

Fig. 7-48: Some combinations of chainwheels and crank are compatible, like these Shimano Biopace chainwheels and the Sugino crank.

Fig. 7-49 shows a misfit, where the crank is forced all the way against the spindle so it is impossible to tighten the crank sufficiently. You could add washers behind the binder bolt. But then you could not thread all of the binder bolt into the bottom bracket spindle, so it would be easy to strip the bolt when you torque it to 300 to 325 inch/pounds. Fig. 7-50 shows another mis-fit, where the crank hole is smaller than the spindle shank. Since the spindle is almost flush with the outside of the crank, you could not use the crank puller to remove the crank when you want to disassemble the bottom bracket for maintenance, because the binder bolt head is almost flush with the outside of the crank—there would be no room to thread the crank puller into the crank and so there would be no way to remove the crank. Fig. 7-51 shows another misfit, where the crank is too far back on the spindle shank because the crank hole is larger than the spindle.

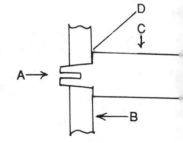

Fig. 7-49: A bad fit between the crank and the spindle. Here the crank is butted up against the spindle shoulder and could work loose.

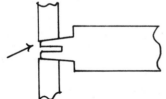

Fig. 7-50: Another bad fit of crank and spindle. Here the crank is too far to the left so the spindle end is near the edge of the dust cap threads. A crank puller could not be used to remove this crank.

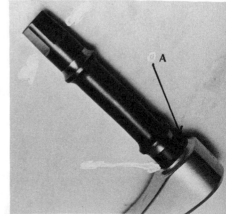

Fig. 7-51: This crank is a poor fit on the spindle. You can see that the crank does not go far enough up on the tapered spindled shank ("A").

This all means that you can't buy any old chainwheel and count on it fitting on your crank, or a new crankset and count on it fitting your bottom bracket spindle. Fig. 7-52 shows a good fit of the crank on the bottom bracket spindle shank. Here the crank is properly positioned on the shank, not so far that it butts up against the spindle shoulder, yet far enough that there is room to insert a crank puller and thread the binder bolt fully into the spindle. Again, my advice is to take your old parts to the bike shop so that the dealer can make sure the parts he sells you fit your equipment. Note: After cranks have been replaced, you should tighten them again every 50 miles for the first 200 miles. Check crank binder bolt tightness at least yearly.

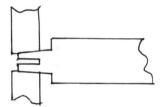

Fig. 7-52: This is a good crank-to-spindle fit. There is room for the crank puller in the dust cap threads, and there is a good match between the dimensions and the tapers of the crank hold and spindle shank.

Elliptical Chainwheels

About 50 years ago bicycle engineers decided to try and do something about the "dead" points of pedal rotation—what happens when your foot reaches the six and 12 o'clock points as in Fig. 7-53. This "dead" point won't respond to pedal pres-

Fig. 7-53: When the cranks are at the 12 o'clock and six o'clock positions, it's difficult to apply much energy to the cranks.

Fig. 7-54: Even past the dead spots noted in Fig. 7-53, it's still impossible to apply your full energy to the pedals.

Fig. 7-55: This elliptical chainwheel is an attempt to eliminate dead spots of pedal rotation.

sure until your foot passes a few degrees over either point (Fig. 7-54). Engineers thought making chainrings elliptical instead of round would help even out pedal pressure throughout the 360 degrees of crank rotation. One of the more extreme attempts at building an elliptical chainwheel is shown in Fig. 7-55. I found this chainwheel usable on slow climbs up steep hills, but when riding on the flats the faster I spun the cranks the more my stroke became uneven—slow when the high spots were flat and lurching as the chainwheel high point passed the two o'clock position (Fig. 7-55).

The computer-assisted design of the Shimano Biopace chainwheel (Fig. 7-56) does provide pedal power around the entire turn of the chainwheel. Unlike the chainwheel in Fig. 7-55, the Biopace high points are where they should be, at or near the "dead" spots of six and 12 o'clock. I have a set on both

Fig. 7-56: Shimano's Biopace is a computer-designed chainwheel that does a good job of letting you apply full energy through all 360 degrees of pedal rotation.

my road and all-terrain bike and can report a marked improvement in smoothness of pedaling on the flats as well as uphill. The drawback of the Biopace is that the smallest chainring available has 28 teeth. That's not much of a drawback, though, since you can still get a low, low gear with a combination of a 28-tooth chainwheel and a 34-tooth freewheel. I like an even lower gear, though, so I substituted a non-Biopace 24-tooth chainwheel for the 28-tooth Biopace. Shimano advises against this, but it works fine for me. The Biopace is available with double or triple chainwheels.

About Crank Lengths

Cranks come in five different lengths (Fig. 7-44). As you might guess, longer cranks give you more leverage and power on the pedals. If they're too long they can be hazardous because they can hit the ground as you lean into a turn, or hit the front wheel as you turn the handlebars. Longer cranks give more power on slow climbs up steep hills, but can be awkward on hills and on the flats if your legs aren't long enough to reach the pedals comfortably. Table 7-2 matches crank length to frame size. Use longer cranks, for example, if you have long legs and ride a bigger frame bike. Your legs will reach the pedals, but you still have to be sure that the longer cranks will clear the ground and the front wheel on a turn.

Table 7-2

CRANK LENGTH TO FRAME SIZE

CRANK LENGTH		FRAME SIZE	
(mm*)	(inches)	(cm)	(inches)
165	6.55	48.3–53.3	19.5–21
170	6.75	57.2	22.5
172.5	6.85	5.84	23
175	6.95	59.7	23.5
180	7.15	>59.7	>23.5

* Crank lengths are given in millimeters and are so marked on the backside of the crank (Fig. 4-45). I converted millimeters to inches for your convenience.

Bottom Bracket Maintenance

The bottom bracket assembly consists of two sets of cups, bearings, crank binder bolts, and a spindle. The cranks and chainwheels are bolted to the spindle (Fig. 7-57). There are two types of bottom brackets—a cup-and-bearing assembly (Fig. 7-58), and a sealed bearing assembly (Fig. 7-59). Each has different maintenance requirements and advantages. For example, you can completely disassemble the ball-and-cup type, replace any worn part, and presto, have a new bottom bracket. You can't disassemble most sealed-type bearings. That's a shop job requiring an arbor press and special tools. You can perform minor maintenance on sealed bearing units, though, as you shall see below. If the bearings wear out, as they will eventually (though it may take years), it will be a toss-up as to whether it's less expensive for you to buy and install a new sealed-bearing bottom bracket than for the shop to replace the bearings. I'd opt for a new bottom bracket.

Fig. 7-57: The cranks on this bike are bolted to the bottom bracket spindle.

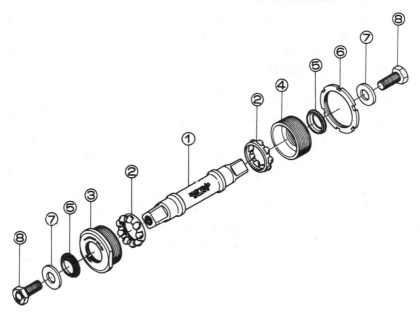

Fig. 7-58: A conventional cup-and-bearing bottom bracket assembly. Parts are: 1) spindle; 2) ball bearings in retainers; 3) fixed cup; 4) adjustable cup; 5) dust shield; 6) lockring; 7) washer; 8) spindle binder bolt.

Fig. 7-59: Sealed bearing bottom bracket. Parts are: 1) sealed bearing; 2) "O" ring seal on bearing; 3) left-hand cup; 4) right-hand cup; 5) lip seal; 6) left-hand lockring; 7) right-hand lockring; 8) spindle washer; 9) crank binder bolt.

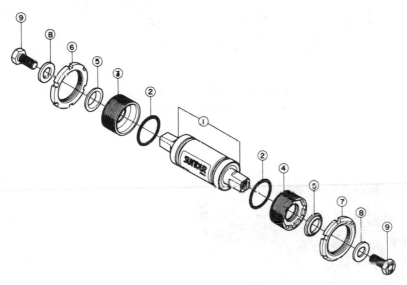

The sealed bearing cartridge type (Figs. 7-59, 7-60, 7-61, 7-62, and 7-63) hold a unique advantage over the cup-and-bearing unit in that you can adjust the chainline (see below) by moving the cartridge left or right. The sealed bearing units are better protected against abrasives and water than the more open cup-and-bearing unit, though they still require routine lubrication. In fact, I'll state categorically that there's no such animal as a "sealed" bearing, only bearings that are better sealed than others. All bearings require maintenance. The danger with the sealed types is that you can be lulled into thinking they never need maintenance, until one day you find the cranks resist turning, at which point you'll have to replace the entire unit. Since more bikes are produced with adjustable cup-and-bearing bottom brackets, I'll start with them.

Follow these steps for cup-and-bearing bottom bracket maintenance:

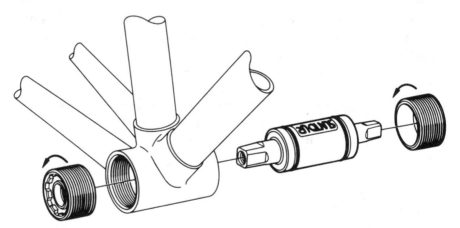

Fig. 7-60: This sealed-bearing bottom bracket can replace a conventional bottom bracket. It lasts for about 8,000 miles before requiring replacement.

Fig. 7-61: Sealed-bearing bottom bracket cartridge for a triple chainwheel.

Fig. 7-62: Avocet sealed-bearing bottom bracket.

Fig. 7-63: Durham sealed-bearing bottom bracket.

Tools you will need:

- Lockring wrench: Be sure to buy one that fits your bottom bracket lockring slots ("D" in Fig. 7-64). Each manufacturer seems to have slots spaced so that only their own lockring wrench will fit. For example, Fig. 7-65 shows a Campagnolo lockring wrench on a Campagnolo bottom bracket and Fig. 7-66 shows a Shimano lockring wrench on a Shimano bottom bracket.

Fig. 7-64: Bottom bracket lockring has slots cut to fit the manufacturer's lockring wrench. Lockrings vary in width and spacing of slots, so buy the one that fits your bike.

Fig. 7-65: This Campagnolo lockright wrench fits the Campagnolo lockring and few others.

Fig. 7-66: Shimano lockring wrench fits their lockrings, not many others.

- Pin wrench for the adjustable cup: The adjustable cup has holes for a pin wrench (Fig. 7-67), as shown in "A" in Fig. 7-68 and in Fig. 7-69. Although a pin wrench will fit any hole spacing, not every manufacturer's holes are the same diameter. Make sure the pin wrench you buy will fit the holes in your adjustable cup.

Fig. 7-67: Use this pin wrench to re-move and adjust the setting of the bottom bracket adjustable cup.

Fig. 7-68: Campagnolo bottom bracket adjustable cup has holes so you can adjust it with the pin wrench.

Fig. 7-69: Not every adjustable cup has holes that will fit every pin wrench. This Shimano cup uses its own pin wrench, which won't fit other manufacturers' adjustable cups.

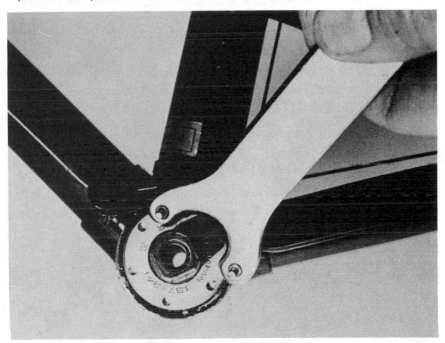

• Fixed cup wrench: The fixed cup has flats for a special wrench (Fig. 7-70). You'd only need this wrench, though, to change to a completely new bottom bracket assembly—for example, to a cartridge-type sealed bearing. I recommend that you not invest in this tool for only this one-shot purpose. You can remove the fixed cup in a vise. Better, have the fixed cup removed by a bike shop which has special tools for this operation. It's a tough job and you can damage the frame if you're not careful. If you do buy this wrench, make sure it fits your fixed cup. See instructions below for fixed cup removal.

Fig. 7-70: Shimano fixed cup wrench. The other end is for pedals.

Disassembly: The only way you can do a good job of cleaning hardened grease and accumulated abrasives from your non-sealed bottom bracket is to take it apart, as follows:

a. Remove both cranks as shown in the chainwheel instructions above.
b. Remove the lockring counterclockwise (Fig. 7-71).

Fig. 7-71: Remove the lockring counterclockwise.

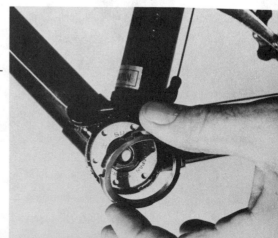

c. Remove the adjustable cup counterclockwise (Fig. 7-72).

d. Remove the outer set of bearings, the axle, and the inner set of bearings (Fig. 7-73). The bearings in older bikes may be loose instead of in a retainer, so be ready to catch them.

e. Clean dirt and old grease from cups and bearings with kerosene.

f. Inspect the bearings for wear. If your bike is relatively new or hasn't had much use, chances are that all you need to do, after cleaning the bearings, cups, and spindle, is to repack the bearings with grease and replace them. If your bike is

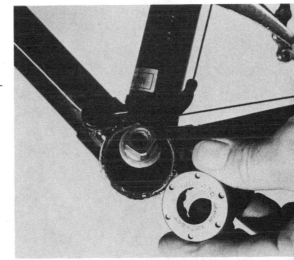

Fig. 7-72: Remove the adjustable cup counterclockwise.

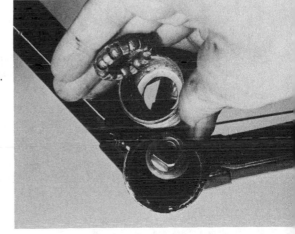

Fig. 7-73: Remove the bearings and axle.

over three years old or has had a lot of use, I recommend scrapping the old balls along with their retainer (Fig. 7-73) and replacing them with loose balls. This will give you 11 instead of nine balls per bearing set, so the bottom bracket spindle will run more smoothly and the additional balls will add to both bearing and cup life. Most modern bottom brackets use ¼-inch balls, but take your old ones to the bike shop to make sure you get the same size replacements.

g. Inspect the cups (Fig. 7-74) for signs of galling or brinelling, indicated by pitting or grooves worn in the racetrack, and replace them if necessary.

Fig. 7-74: Check the fixed and adjustable cup bearing races for rust, pits, and scoring, but don't remove the fixed cup.

Assembly: Now that you have cleaned your ball-and-cup type bottom bracket and replaced any worn parts, you are ready to put it back together. Depending on how you ride, you have three choices of bottom bracket grease. For example, if you're going into the wilderness on your all-terrain bike, I recommend boat-trailer wheel-bearing grease. It adds a bit more pedaling drag but won't wash out as fast as ordinary grease when you run through water or mud. For road bikes I recommend a lighter grease such as Phil Wood or Lubriplate, available at your bike shop or hardware store. Here are the steps for assembly:

a. Roll the loose balls in grease until they are thoroughly covered.

b. Put a layer of grease on both cups.

c. Put the loose balls in the cups. The grease will hold them in place.

d. Insert the spindle into the bottom bracket. Make sure the longer spindle end goes in first, because that's the spindle side for the chainwheels. If your bottom bracket did not come with a plastic protective cover, it's a good idea to install one (Fig. 7-75) to keep away abrasives and water that get into frame tubes and work down into the bottom bracket shell.

e. Thread the adjustable cup clockwise into the bottom bracket shell and turn it by hand as far as possible. Use the pin wrench to continue turning it until it's snug. Back the cup off a half turn.

f. Thread the lockring onto the adjustable cup by hand. Hold the adjustable cup with the pin wrench so it can't turn, and tighten the lockring firmly with the lockring wrench.

g. Check bearing adjustment for tightness. With your thumb and forefinger twirl the spindle. It should rotate smoothly. If it feels rough or is hard to turn, loosen the lockring and turn the adjustable cup counterclockwise about a quarter turn, and tighten the lockring. Check the adjustment and repeat this step as necessary.

h. Check the bearing adjustment for looseness. Install the left crank, per instructions in the chainwheel maintenance section above. Place the crank at the 12 o'clock position and move it sharply from side to side, toward and away from you. If you feel looseness, turn the lockring counterclock-

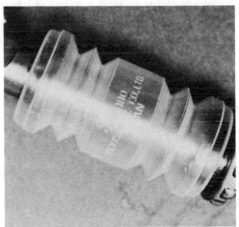

Fig. 7-75: If your bottom bracket doesn't have a plastic shield like this one, it's a good idea to install one when reassembling the bottom bracket.

wise until it's loose and turn the adjustable cup clockwise about a quarter turn. Hold the adjustable cup with the pin wrench and tighten the lockring. Check this adjustment and repeat this step as necessary. Install the other crank with its chainwheels. Grasp both cranks, one in each hand, and again move them from side to side as a final check for looseness. Adjust bearings as necessary. Spin the cranks. They should rotate smoothly and stop gradually.

Fixed Cup Removal

Fig. 7-70 shows a Shimano fixed cup removal tool. If you're lucky, you could use this tool to thread off the fixed cup. However, most fixed cups, particularly on older bikes, are on so tight it takes a lot more torque (turning energy) than you can apply with this tool. As I noted, the only reason to remove the fixed cup is to change to another make or model bottom bracket assembly. You could remove the fixed cup by holding the cup flats in a machinist's vise and turning the entire bike. Your vise must have undamaged jaws for this operation, otherwise the fixed cup flats will slip out of the vise. If the bike was made in the U.S.A., France, or Italy, turn the bike clockwise. If it's made anyplace else, chances are the cup is right-hand threaded, so turn the bike counterclockwise.

Triple Chainwheel Conversion

You can convert your dual chainwheel to a triple chainset by replacing your old spindle with a longer one that allows clearance for the small chainring. Otherwise the small chainring will scrape on the chainstay. You must install a spindle that will fit your bottom bracket shell. Take your old spindle to the bike shop so they can measure it for a longer spindle that will fit your bike.

Sealed Bottom Bracket Maintenance

Tools you will need:

• Combination adjustable cup and lockring wrench for SunTour units (Fig. 7-76), or cup wrench for Phil Wood units (Figs. 7-77 and 7-78).

Fig. 7-76: Use this combination pin and lockring wrench to remove or install a SunTour sealed-bearing bottom bracket cartridge.

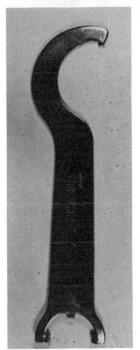

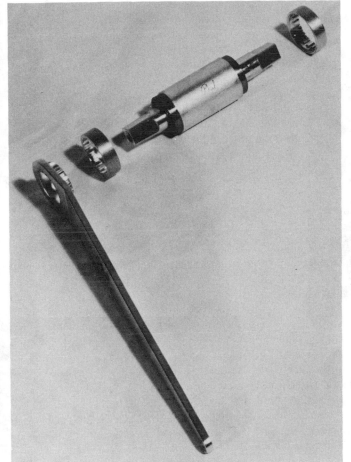

Fig. 7-77: Shop version of the Phil Wood bottom bracket tool is easier to use if you have several bikes with these bottom bracket cartridges.

Fig. 7-78: Use this inexpensive tool to remove and adjust Phil Wood bottom brackets.

Portable
ringwrench

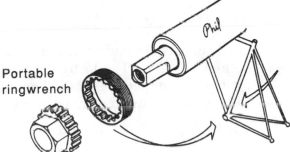

- Snap-ring pliers, from any hardware store, to remove the snap ring from the sealed-bearing bottom bracket on some all-terrain bikes, such as the Fisher (Fig. 7-79).
- Thin-bladed knife, such as an X-acto knife, to pry off bearing seals.
- Small grease injector (Fig. 7-80, optional).

Fig. 7-79: If your bike has a bottom bracket that looks like this, you can't remove it with home tools. Remove the snap ring and the bearing "O" ring seals, stuff in grease, and re-install these parts.

Fig. 7-80: Use this small grease injector when adding grease to sealed bearings.

SunTour Cartridges

SunTour recommends that you not service their sealed-bearing bottom brackets. The bearings are double-sealed, and according to the manufacturer should not require replacing for around 8,000 miles. However, if you've pedaled through water a lot, I recommend that you remove the cartridge seals and stuff in some grease, as shown below. Or, you could remove the cartridge and replace it with a new one every four or five years. It will cost around $45, not much for all those miles. If you decide to remove the cartridge, the seals, and stuff in the grease, here are the steps to follow. Reverse these instructions to replace the cartridge.

a. Remove the cranks as shown in the section on chainwheels.
b. Remove the lockrings ("6" and "7," Fig. 7-59).
c. Remove the cups ("3" and "4," Fig. 7-59). If your bike was made in the U.S.A., England, or Japan, the right-hand cup threads off clockwise (left-hand threads). If your bike was made in France, Belgium, or Italy, in most cases the right-hand cup threads off counterclockwise, unless the manufacturer decided to join the 20th century and use left-hand threads like every other manufacturer. If the cup won't come off one way, try turning it in the other direction. The left cup threads off counterclockwise on all bikes.
d. Remove the cartridge ("1," Fig. 7-59).
e. Pry out the O-rings ("2," Fig. 7-59).
f. Wipe off any accumulated debris and old grease from the bearing face with a cloth. Use a small grease injector (Fig. 80) or your finger to force grease into the bearings. You probably won't be able to force grease the whole way to the inside of the bearing, but as you ride, it should coat the whole bearing.
g. Replace the O-rings and the other parts. Tighten the cups.
h. Twist the spindle between thumb and forefinger. If after greasing as above the bearings still feel rough, you should replace the entire cartridge.

Phil Wood Cartridges

a. Remove the cranks.
b. With the Phil Wood cup tool, remove the cups. Remember threading direction on the right-hand cup, as noted above.
c. These hubs don't have double seals, so you should add grease to them every year, or more often if you ride a lot.

Remove both O-ring seals (Figs. 7-81 and 7-82) with a thin-bladed knife.

d. Use a small grease injector (Fig. 7-80) or your finger to push grease into the bearings. Replace the seals and replace the cartridge in the bike's bottom bracket shell.

e. Replace and tighten the cups, and spin the spindle to make sure you haven't over-tightened the cups. Readjust cups if necessary.

Forget about replacing the bearings yourself. Phil Wood declares that's a job for his shop, and I agree. If the bearings are shot, have your bike shop return them to Phil for replacement.

Fig. 7-81: This is what the bearings look like when the "O" ring seal is removed. The "O" ring is at the left. This is a Phil Wood sealed-bearing hub, but the bottom bracket is similar in appearance.

Fig. 7-82: Another view of a sealed bearing with the "O" ring seal removed.

Other Sealed Bearings

Some all-terrain bikes have pressed-in sealed-bearing bottom bracket bearings (Fig. 7-79) that require special tools to remove. *Do not attempt to remove them yourself, unless you have a machine shop!* Fortunately, these bearings are easily regreased, as noted below:

a. Remove the snap rings on both sides of the bottom bracket.

b. Carefully pry out the O-ring seals on both sides of the bottom bracket.

c. Remove any old grease and dirt with a rag, and stuff fresh grease into the bearing with a grease injector (Fig. 81) or by hand.

d. Re-install the O-rings and snap rings.

One-Piece Cranks

You can disassemble one-piece "Ashtabula" cranks on American bikes as noted above in the chainwheel maintenance section. Once the cranks have been removed, the bearings can be removed, cleaned, regreased, and the unit reassembled.

How to Convert One-Piece to Three-Piece Bottom Brackets

Some older American bikes that feature light, well-made frames have heavy, one-piece Ashtabula cranks. If you have one of these bikes, upgrade it by removing the entire crankset, bearings, and cups, and replacing it with a SunTour sealed-bearing bottom bracket (Figs. 7-83 and 7-84) or a Durham unit, (Fig. 7-85), either of which should be available from your bike shop. To install the conversion unit, fit one adapter ring on the chainwheel side, install the cartridge, and put the other adapter ring on the left side of the bottom bracket. With the 4mm Allen wrench that comes with the SunTour unit, tighten the adapter rings. Thread on the cups and tighten them as noted above. Install the Durham adapter unit the same way. Install new aluminum alloy cranks and chainwheels as described above.

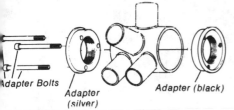

Adapter Bolts

Adapter (silver)

Adapter (black)

Fig. 7-83: You can update an old bicycle by removing the heavy one-piece crank and chainwheels and installing this sealed-bearing bottom bracket adapter kit from SunTour, along with aluminum-alloy cranks and chainwheels.

Fig. 7-84: Finish the conversion illustrated in Fig. 7-83 by tightening the left and right cups with a 4mm Allen wrench.

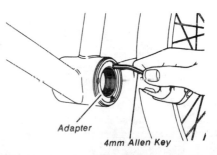

Adapter

4mm Allen Key

Fig. 7-85: You can also update your bike by replacing a one-piece crankset with this Durham sealed-bearing conversion kit. Parts are: mounting bolts ("A"), left and right hand cups ("B"), spindle length adjusters ("C").

Tandem Adapter

If you have a tandem bicycle and would like to have your child ride with you but find that his feet won't reach the pedals, Phil Wood has a solution. A bottom bracket adapter (Fig. 7-86) will bolt onto the seat tube at a height that allows a child's feet to reach the pedals. It fits a 1⅛-inch diameter seat tube. *Do not use this adapter on a single-rider bike. The bike will be too big for anyone with short legs, and dangerous to ride!*

Fig. 7-86: Want your child to pedal with you on a tandem? Then install this Phil Wood sealed-bearing bottom bracket conversion kit on the downtube so your child's feet can reach the pedals.

Chainline Adjustment

As noted earlier, you can move a sealed-bearing bottom bracket left or right so the chain will be at a minimum angle through all gear combinations. For example, with your bike mounted on a work stand, shift through all your gear combinations and watch what happens to the chain angle. You'll notice that the chain is at an extreme angle when it's on two combinations—the small freewheel cog and the small chainwheel, and on the large free-wheel cog and the large chainwheel. If the chainline is not correct, the angles and the wear and tear on all components of the transmission system will be greater. The optimum chain-line for any combination of freewheel cogs and chainwheels is when the chain is centered between the freewheel gears and the chainwheels, as shown in Figs. 7-87 through 7-93. In Fig. F-87, for example, the chain is on a single chainwheel and the third gear of a five-speed freewheel. In Fig. 7-88, you will see

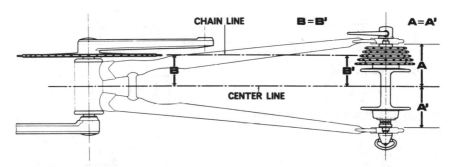

Fig. 7-87: Chainline for a five-speed bicycle.

Fig. 7-88: Chainline for a ten-speed bicycle.

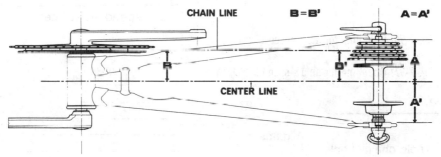

that the chain is centered between the double chainwheels and on the third cog of a five-speed freewheel. In Fig. 7-89, the chain is centered on the second of a triple chainwheel and the third cog of a five-speed chainwheel. In Fig. 7-90, the chain is centered between a double chainwheel and the third and fourth cogs of a six-speed freewheel; in Fig. 7-91, it's centered on the center chainwheel of a triple chainset and between the third and fourth cogs of a six-speed freewheel; in Fig. 7-92, between a double chainwheel and on the fourth gear of a seven-speed freewheel; and in Fig. 7-93, on the center of a triple chainwheel and the fourth gear of a seven-speed freewheel.

To adjust the chainline when you have a sealed-bearing bottom bracket, simply loosen the left lockring and tighten the right lockring to move the chainline to the left, and vice versa to move it to the right. Note: You can't adjust the chainline on sealed-bearing bottom brackets without a lockring, like the one in Fig. 7-79.

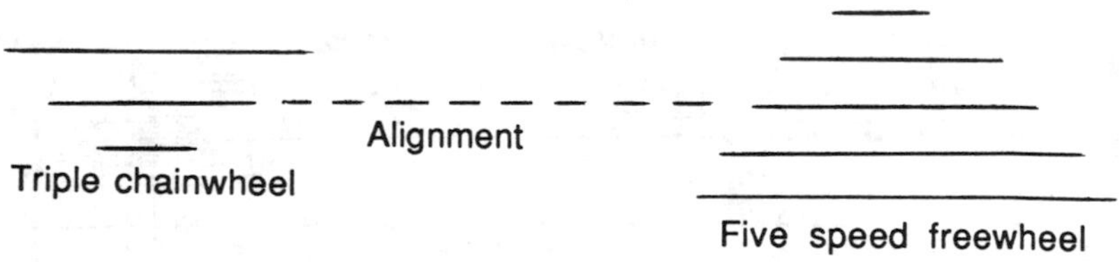

Alignment

Triple chainwheel

Five speed freewheel

Fig. 7-89: Chainline for a 15-speed bicycle.

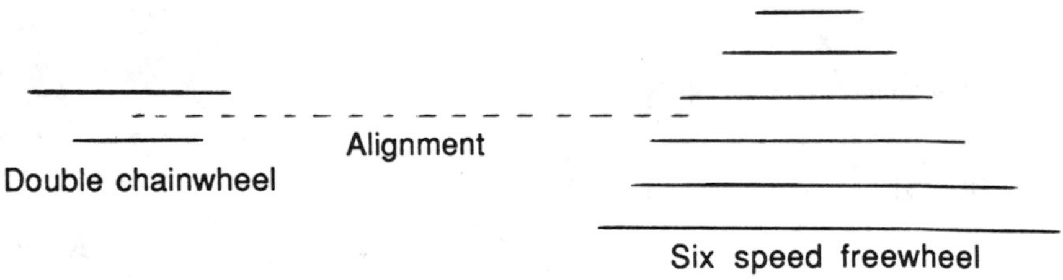

Alignment

Double chainwheel

Six speed freewheel

Fig. 7-90: Chainline for a 12-speed bicycle.

Fig. 7-91: Chainline for an 18-speed bicycle.

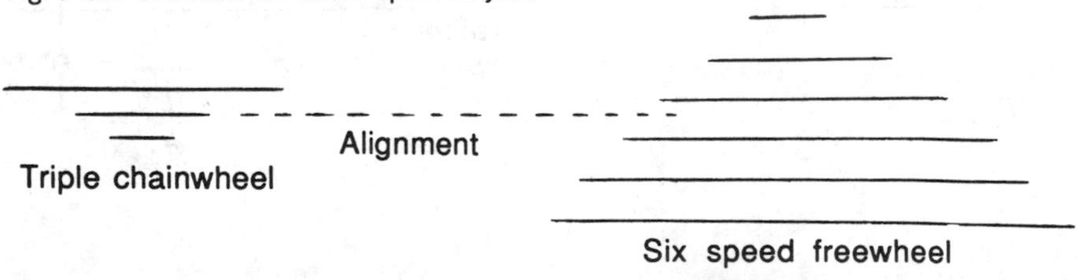

Alignment

Triple chainwheel

Six speed freewheel

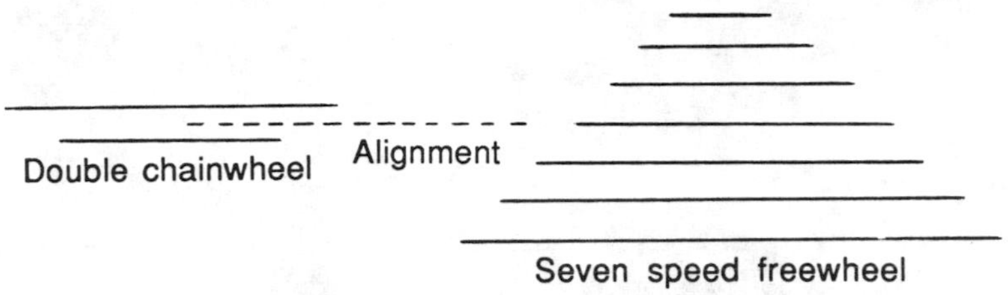

Double chainwheel   Alignment

Seven speed freewheel

Fig. 7-92: Chainline for a 14-speed bicycle.

Fig. 7-93: Chainline for a 21-speed bicycle.

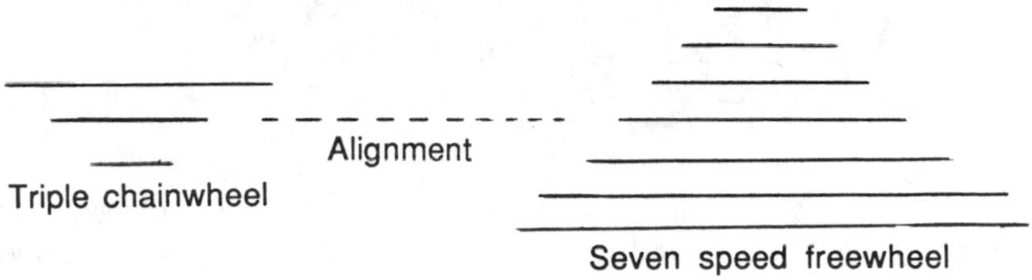

Alignment

Triple chainwheel

Seven speed freewheel

Freewheel Maintenance

The freewheel (Fig. 7-94), like the chain, is exposed to abrasives and water and should be cleaned every time you clean the chain. Follow these steps to maintain the freewheel:

Tools you will need:

- Freewheel remover (Fig. 7-95). Buy one that fits your freewheel.
- Cog remover if you change cogs (Fig. 7-96).
- Freewheel vise (Fig. 7-97, optional).
- Freewheel grease injector (Fig. 7-98, optional).

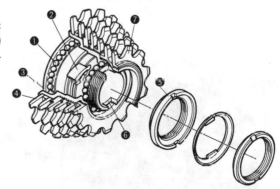

Fig. 7-94: Anatomy of a freewheel. Parts are: 1) bearings; 2) pawl; 3) left-hand seal; 4) low-gear cog; 5) lockring; 6) body; 7) low-gear cog.

Fig. 7-95: As you can see, virtually every make of freewheel, and in some cases every model of the same make, use a different remover tool. Be sure to buy the one that fits your freewheel.

Fig. 7-96: Turn this freewheel cog remover counterclockwise to remove a cog, clockwise to tighten it. You can use two of these tools to remove cogs from a freewheel that's on the hub—one to hold the large cog, the other to turn the small cog.

Fig. 7-97: You can hold a freewheel in this freewheel vise when you change cogs.

Fig. 7-98: For a virtually noiseless freewheel, fill it with grease with this injector. The grease also helps keep out dirt and water.

1. For routine cleaning, leave the wheel on the bike and clean the cogs with kerosene, a rag, and a brush. Keep kerosene away from the tire to prevent tire damage. Apply *light* oil to the bearings on both sides of the freewheel, Fig. 7-94. Note: Never take the freewheel body apart. You can clean the freewheel innards easily and effectively without dismantling the body by following these steps:

   At least once a year, remove the freewheel for more serious cleaning, as follows:

   a. Remove the wheel from the bicycle.
   b. Remove the quick release unit or, if your bike has a solid axle, the axle bolt on the freewheel side.
   c. Insert the freewheel remover (Fig. 7-95) in the freewheel (Fig. 7-99). If the hub locknut on the freewheel side won't permit you to insert the freewheel tool, remove the locknut with a cone wrench (Fig. 7-100). Hold the locknut on the left side of the hub in a vise or with another cone wrench.
   d. Hold the freewheel tool with the quick-release or an axle bolt, Fig. 7-101. The quick release or bolt should be loose enough so you can turn the freewheel tool counterclockwise a half to one turn with a wrench. You could also hold the freewheel tool in a vise and turn the wheel counterclockwise. When the freewheel breaks loose, remove the quick-release or the axle bolt and finish removing the freewheel by turning the freewheel tool by hand. As the freewheel approaches the last few threads, hold it firmly so it comes off the hub without harming the softer aluminum hub threads.
   e. Agitate the freewheel in kerosene and with a brush and rag clean each cog.
   f. Dry the freewheel with an airhose to remove kerosene.

Fig. 7-99: Freewheel removers like this fit into grooves in the freewheel body.

Fig. 7-100: Remove the hub locknut with a cone wrench if freewheel remover won't fit over it. Hold the left-side locknut in a vise or with another hub wrench.

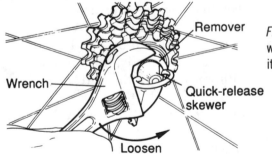

Fig. 7-101: Hold the freewheel remover in place with the quick-release or axle bolt while you turn it with a wrench.

g. Use light oil to lubricate the bearings on *both* sides of the freewheel (Fig. 7-94). Or, use a grease injector (Fig. 7-98). Thread the injector into the back (hub side) of the freewheel and inject grease with a grease gun or a tube of light grease until grease comes out the other side. The grease eliminates the clicking sound that comes from the freewheel pawls as you pedal along. It also helps keep out dirt and water.

h. Check the spokes on the freewheel side for signs of

breakage. Look for cracks that foretell metal fatigue. Replace any suspect spokes and re-true the wheel as discussed in Chapter 10.

i. Thread the freewheel back on the hub, *carefully!* Remember, the hub threads are aluminum and the freewheel threads are steel. Unless you get the first threads started accurately, it's easy to strip them. A bike shop may be able to re-thread the hub with a thread cutter. If not, you'll need a new hub and a wheel relacing job—so be careful. Note: A particle of dirt can lodge behind a freewheel pawl ("2" in Fig. 7-94). When that happens you have freewheeling no matter which way you turn the pedals. You can turn the cranks, but the bike will stay put. The solution is to squirt kerosene into the freewheel while you turn the cranks by hand (the bike should be on a stand or upside down) to loosen the offending particle(s). You could use cookstove fuel in an emergency, but if it's gasoline, be careful!

Removing Cogs from the Freewheel

If you want to replace a worn freewheel cog, or change to a bigger Alpine hill-climbing cog, follow these steps:

a. If the freewheel is on the hub you can use two cog removers (Fig. 7-96). One will hold the big cog to keep the freewheel from turning, the other will remove the small cog.

b. If the freewheel is off the hub, put it in a freewheel vise (Fig. 7-97) and put *that* vise in a bench vise. Or do what I do, and drill two holes in your wood workbench to hold two bolts, spaced to fit the holes in the large freewheel cog (Fig. 7-102), that will hold it while you remove the small cog.

Fig. 7-102: Another way to hold the freewheel while you remove cogs is to slip the big cog over two bolts in your workbench as shown here.

c. Use the cog remover to turn the small freewheel cog counterclockwise. Remove it. On most freewheels only the small
cog is threaded on. If the second cog is also threaded on,
remove it the same way. Now you can slide off the remaining cogs and their spacers. As you remove these parts, make
a note of which spacers go where, because some may be
thinner than others (Fig. 7-103). If the space between *any*
two cogs is too narrow, the chain may slip when you shift
and cause an accident.

Fig. 7-103: As you remove cogs, keep track of which spacers fit between them. Cogs must
be far enough apart for chain clearance.

d. You may find that some cogs, once the small one is removed,
come off the freewheel as a unit because they are bolted
together (Fig. 7-104). In this case remove the three bolts to
replace a cog.

e. Cogs of one make won't fit other makes, and even cogs of
the same make won't always fit another model of the same
make freewheel. So for an exact fit, take your freewheel to
the bike shop when you buy another cog.

Fig. 7-104: Four of the five cogs on this freewheel are held by three bolts, one of which is shown by the arrow. Turn the nuts on these bolts counter-clockwise so cogs can be removed.

Freehub Maintenance

Freehubs combine the hub and the freewheel in one piece. As you can see in Fig. 7-105, the cogs are mounted on splines and held in place by the small freewheel cog which is threaded on. It's claimed that the freehub permits a stronger wheel because it doesn't have to be "dished" (see Chapter 10), and that the axle is stronger because it extends all the way out to the end of the freewheel. I tend to believe both of these claims. In fact, many makes of top-line all-terrain bikes now come with the Shimano Dura-Ace EX freehub. Racing cyclists also prefer them.

To maintain the Dura-Ace EX freewheel:

a. Remove the cogs (if you wish to change them or replace worn ones) by removing the small freewheel with the cog tool (Fig. 7-96).

Fig. 7-105: Freehubs combine the freewheel as part of the hub. Note that the axle extends through the freewheel body—the four largest cogs fit over splines on the freewheel body —and the smallest cog threads on and holds the other cogs on the splines.

b. Remove the freewheel assembly with a special Shimano freewheel assembly tool (Shimano part TL-FH10). Insert this tool into the freehub body (Fig. 7-106). Hold the other end of this tool in a vise (Fig. 7-106) and twist the wheel counterclockwise to remove the freehub assembly.

c. With the freewheel assembly removed you can get at the bearings, which should be cleaned and repacked with grease (see Chapter 8).

d. Replace the freewheel assembly on the hub and tighten it to 110 foot/pounds—and be prepared to use a lot of muscle on the freewheel tool.

The maintenance instructions above also apply to Shimano's 600 EX freewheel, except that you use a 10mm Allen wrench to remove the freewheel assembly from the hub (Fig. 7-107). When you re-install the assembly, tighten it to 307 to 440 inch/pounds. Be careful not to overtighten so you don't damage the bolt collar. But if you do, the bolt is easily replaced.

In the next chapter I'll show you how to keep your hubs running smoothly, fix punctures when your tire goes flat, and how to keep your pedals in top working order.

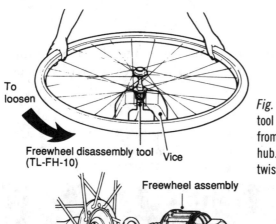

To loosen

Freewheel disassembly tool (TL-FH-10)

Vice

Freewheel assembly

Stopper   Freehub removal tool

Area A (must be free from oil)

Fig. 7-106: Use the special removal tool to remove the freewheel body from a Shimano Dura-Ace EX freehub. Hold the tool in a vise, top, and twist the wheel counterclockwise.

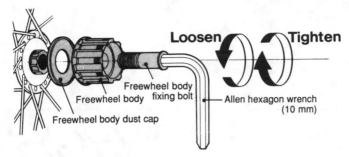

Fig. 7-107: Use a 10mm Allen wrench to remove the freewheel body from a Shimano 600 EX freehub.

EIGHT

ALL ABOUT TIRES, HUBS, AND PEDALS

Until recently, most bikes came fitted with non-sealed hubs (Figs. 8-1 and 8-2). Less expensive bikes are still equipped with cheaper versions of these hubs. Today, many bikes have sealed bearing hubs (Figs. 8-3 and 8-4). Both types of hubs have advantages and drawbacks.

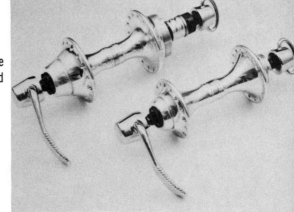

Fig. 8-1: These Campangolo hubs are typical of high-quality non-sealed hubs.

Fig. 8-2: These Shimano non-sealed hubs give years of service when properly maintained.

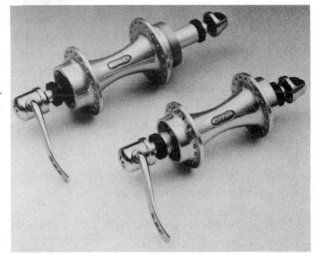

Fig. 8-3: Mavic sealed bearing hubs.

Fig. 8-4: SunTour XC sealed bearing hubs.

Pros and Cons of Non-Sealed Hubs

Non-sealed hubs are easier to maintain. You can find replacement parts in most bike shops. If a bent axle binds up the hub bearings and makes pedaling impossible, a simple adjustment of the hub cone will usually free the axle enough so you can limp home, and when you get there you can easily replace the bent axle. Conversely, these hubs are vulnerable to abrasives and water and require more frequent maintenance. For example, on a trip through the hills of Vermont, I heard grating sounds coming from my rear wheel. I stopped, turned the bike over, spun that wheel, heard the same sounds, and felt grinding when I placed my finger on the axle end. I dismantled the hub, cleaned out the sand that had worked its way into the bearings, stuffed fresh grease around the bearings, put everything back together and was on my way in 30 minutes with a now silent, freely spinning hub. Had I not been able to remove the sand, my bearings could have been ruined by the time I arrived at camp 80 miles away, which would have meant a costly replacement of the entire hub if the bearing races were badly scored.

Sealed Bearing Hubs

Sealed bearing hubs are shielded against abrasives and, to some extent, water. Requiring less maintenance than non-sealed hubs, they are ideal for extended trips on the road or trail. However, abrasives and water will *eventually* work their way into these hubs. Don't think that simply because they're sealed they will require no maintenance. Even sealed bearing hubs will wear and on occasion bind up and stop turning if not periodically lubricated. If you bend the sealed bearing hub axle badly enough to lock up the wheel, you won't be able to adjust the bearings to get the wheel turning so that you can ride home at all. You usually can fix up a non-sealed bearing hub so you can limp home. There is no side-play adjustment on sealed bearing hubs.

Here's how to keep non-sealed and sealed bearing hubs turning smoothly, starting with the former:

Non-Sealed Bearing Hub Maintenance

Tools and supplies you will need:

1. Thin hub cone wrenches, 13, 14, 15, 16, and 17mm (Fig. 8-5).
2. 13, 14, or 15mm sockets for an inch/pound torque wrench (see Fig. 5-2) if hubs have axle bolts instead of a quick-release.
3. Axle vise to protect axle threads (Fig. 8-6; optional).
4. Water-resistant grease, such as Phil Wood.

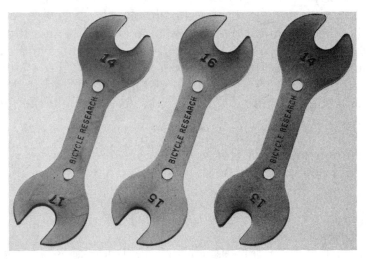

Fig. 8-5: Thin hub cone wrenches.

Fig. 8-6: This hub vise protects pedal spindle threads when holding them in a bench vise.

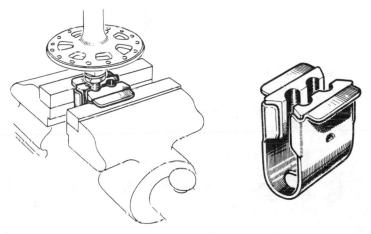

Follow these steps to maintain your non-sealed bearing hubs:

1. Remove the wheel from the bicycle.
2. If you're working on the rear wheel, remove the freewheel as shown in Chapter 7.
3. If the wheel is held by axle bolts, remove them. Or remove the quick-release mechanism. Hold the quick-release adjusting nut (1 in Fig. 8-7) while you turn the quick-release lever (4) counterclockwise until the adjusting nut comes all the way off the skewer threads (3). Remove the spring (2) from the skewer. Grasp the quick-release lever and pull the skewer out of the hollow axle (14) and catch the other spring (2) so you don't lose it. Put the springs and the adjusting nut back on the skewer so you don't lose them.
4. Put the axle vise in a bench vise as shown in Fig. 8-6 and hold the axle threads in the axle vise. Or hold the locknut in a bench vise.
5. Hold the adjustable cone (13 in Fig. 8-7) with one cone wrench and turn the locknut counterclockwise with the other cone wrench, as shown in Fig. 8-8. Remove the locknut and the spacing washer (12 in Fig. 8-7).

Fig. 8-7: Exploded view of non-sealed hub. Parts are: 1) quick-release adjusting nut; 2) springs; 3) skewer shaft; 4) quick-release lever; 5) lever body; 6) lever bearing; 7) washer; 8) locknut; 9) dust cap; 10) bearings; 11) locknut; 12) washer; 13) adjustable cone; 14) spindle.

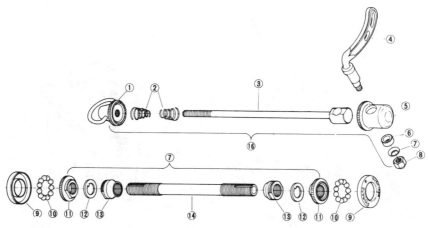

Fig. 8-8: Disassemble a non-sealed bearing while holding the adjustable cone with one wrench and removing the locknut with the other wrench.

6. With the cone wrench, turn the adjustable cone a few turns counterclockwise. You should now be able to unscrew it by hand. Remove it from the axle.
7. With a screwdriver, carefully pry off the dust cap (9).
8. Lay a rag out on the workbench next to the wheel. Hold the axle end facing you with one hand and loosen the vise just enough to remove the wheel. Still holding the axle securely in the hub, carefully lay the wheel on the rag.
9. Lift the wheel off the rag enough so you can pull the axle out. As you do so, be ready to catch loose ball bearings (10) as they fall out of the hub. Remove the other dust cap as above, and the bearings from both sides of the hub.
10. Roll the loose balls around in a cup of kerosene to remove old grease and dirt. Carefully spread them on the rag and dry off the kerosene.
11. Clean both hub cups (Fig. 8-9) and the adjustable cones, the dust caps, and the axle with a rag dipped in kerosene.

Fig. 8-9: Remove old grease and foreign particles from the hub cups (arrow).

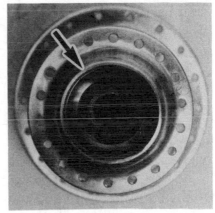

12. Examine the hub cups (Fig. 8-9) and the adjustable cones (Fig. 8-10) for signs of galling and brinelling, such as the grooves worn in the adjustable cone in Fig. 8-10.

13. Examine the loose ball bearings for wear. If you've had the bike for three or four years, I recommend you replace them. Take a sample ball bearing to your bike shop to make sure you get the right size. Buy a couple of extra balls in case you drop one on the floor and lose it forever.

14. Hold the axle in the axle vise (this is where the axle vise helps). Hold the other adjustable cone with the cone wrench and remove the locknut, washer, and adjustable cone.

15. Check the axle alignment. Roll it on a smooth, flat surface, such as an old piece of plate glass. Replace it if it's bent. Take the axle to your bike shop for an exact replacement.

16. Cover the loose balls in grease. Layer in grease in both hub cups and on the adjustable cones.

17. Thread the adjustable cone, washer, and locknut on one end of the axle to about where they were before you removed them. Hold the adjustable cone with a hub wrench and tighten the locknut with another hub wrench. Then look at both ends of the axle. If you are working on the rear wheel, more threads should be showing on the freewheel side than the other. If you are working on the front wheel, both ends of the axle should show the same number of threads when you replace the other adjustable cone.

18. Replace the loose balls in one side of the hub and put a generous layer of grease on top of them. The side of the tire you marked in Step 2 should be facing toward you.

Fig. 8-10: Check both adjustable cones for signs of wear, such as shown here, and replace them if necessary.

There should be enough grease on the balls and in the hub cup to hold the bearings in place.

19. Replace the dust cap in the hub.
20. Put the axle into the hub. The adjustable cone, washer, and locknut should face toward you.
21. Hold the other side of the axle while you turn the wheel over and put it, axle side down, on the workbench.
22. Put the remaining balls in the hub cup, cover them with grease, and thread on the adjustable cone by hand as far as possible (Fig. 8-11). Replace the remaining dust cap.
23. Hold one adjustable cone with the cone wrench and tighten the locknut down with another cone wrench.
24. Check the bearing adjustment for tightness. Spin the axle between your thumb and forefinger. It should spin without binding. If it binds, use the cone wrenches to loosen the locknut and the adjustable cone about ¼ turn, tighten the locknut as above, and check tightness again. Repeat this adjustment until the hub spins smoothly.
25. Check the bearing adjustment for looseness. Push the axle in and out and up and down. If you feel sideplay, readjust as in Step 24, except tighten the adjustable cone ¼ turn, and make further adjustments until all sideplay is removed and the axle spins smoothly.
26. Replace the freewheel on the rear wheel and put both wheels back in the dropouts. Tighten the front-wheel axle

Fig. 8-11: Thread the adjustable cone on the spindle by hand as far as possible, as shown here, as the first step in hub reassembly.

bolts to 250–260 in./lbs. and the rear-wheel axle bolts to 300–350 in./lbs. Or tighten the quick-release mechanism as described in Chapter 2, Figs. 2-41 to 2-51.

Sealed Bearing Hub Maintenance

Tools you will need:

1. Special locknut wrench for SunTour hubs (Fig. 8-12).
2. Thin-bladed knife to pry off seals.
3. Hub cone wrenches (Fig. 8-5) for Avocet and Mavic hubs.
4. Circlip pliers and a pin wrench for Mavic hubs.

Follow these steps for sealed bearing hub maintenance:

1. Remove the wheels from the bicycle.
2. Remove the freewheel (see Chapter 7) so you can remove the rear-wheel bearing seals.
3. *Carefully* pry off the outer seal with a thin-bladed knife. The arrow in Fig. 8-13 shows this seal removed from a Durham sealed bearing. On Mavic hubs (Fig. 8-14), remove the circlip (1) with circlip pliers, the spacer (4), washer (5), and the bushing nut (3) before removing the seal with a pin wrench (Fig. 8-15). Fig. 8-16 is a close-up of a sealed-bearing hub with the outer seal removed. The arrow points to the seal. On Avocet hubs (Fig. 8-17), remove the locknut with a cone wrench. Fig. 8-18 shows pry points (arrows) where a thin-bladed knife should be able to pry out the seal of all but Mavic hubs. *Caution:* these seals are thin and easily bent and distorted, and replacement seals are *not* available.
4. With the seals removed, clean off old grease with a rag, and stuff in fresh grease with a small grease injector or by hand. Replace the seals and any other parts you have removed, reversing the steps above.

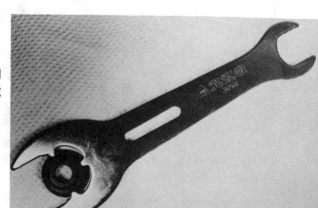

Fig. 8-12: Use this special wrench when disassembling SunTour hubs.

Fig. 8-13: Parts on this Durham sealed-bearing hub are: 1) Bearing seal removed from bearing; 2) bearing; 3) spindle binder bolt; 4) spacer; 5) bearing with seals in place; 6) hub body; 7) spindle.

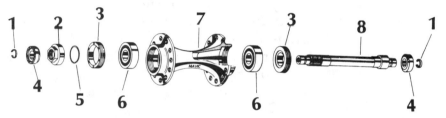

Fig. 8-14: Mavic sealed-bearing hub. Parts are: 1) circlip; 2) locknut; 3) seal; 4) spacer; 5) O-ring; 6) bearing; 7) hub body; 8) spindle.

Fig. 8-15: Remove the seal on Mavic hubs with a pin wrench in seal holes "A" and "B."

Fig. 8-16: This typical sealed bearing hub has its seal (arrow) removed.

Fig. 8-17: Avocet sealed-bearing hubs have replaceable bearings.

Fig. 8-18: Remove bearing seals with a thin-bladed knife at the pry points indicated by arrows.

5. You can replace the sealed bearings of Durham and Mavic hubs. The Durham hub (Fig. 8-13) is easily disassembled by removing the axle spacers with an Allen wrench. Take the axle and punch out the sealed bearing. Replacement bearings are available from Durham through your bike shop or from a specialty bearing store. Take the old bearing to the store for an exact replacement. Mavic hub sealed bearings (Fig. 8-14) can be removed by removing the circlip (1), spacer (4), locknut (2), washer (5), bushing (3), and punching the bearings out carefully with a blunt tool so you don't dent the seal. SunTour bearings are removable, as noted above, but I recommend getting this done in a bike shop with the proper tools to avoid damage to the hub. Phil Wood hub bearings (Fig. 8-19), as noted above, can only be removed by a machine shop. If these bearings wear out, have your bike shop return the hubs to Phil Wood for bearing replacement.

Fig. 8-19: Phil Wood sealed-bearing hub bearings can only be removed and replaced by the manufacturer. At the top is a complete hub, at the bottom are the spindle and bearings.

Coaster Brake and Three-Speed Internal Gear Hubs

Bikes with coaster brakes and three-speed hubs are generally inexpensive and ridden around town or on the flats by children, casual riders, or by delivery people on industrial-type bikes or tricycles. Hubs on these bikes tend to be neglected, yet they will run for years if you use an occasional squirt of SAE-30 oil into the hub body through a capped hole (K.645 in Fig. 8-20).

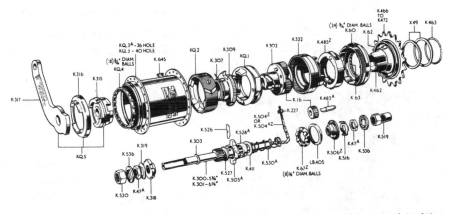

Fig. 8-20: This exploded view of a coaster brake three-speed hub should be enough to deter you from taking it apart. Leave maintenance on this hub to your bike shop.

Don't take these hubs apart! If nothing else, its myriad tiny parts as shown in Fig. 8-20 will make reassembly a nightmare! Let your bike shop replace any worn parts. Once they are replaced, your hub should run for another five or six years. Squirt oil in the hub every three months.

However, shift cables on three- or five-speed internal hubs will stretch in time. When this happens you will need to readjust the cable adjuster (Fig. 8-21) as follows:

1. On a five-speed hub, shift to the third gear. On a three-speed hub, shift to the second gear.
2. Turn the cable-adjust locknut (2 in Fig. 8-21) one turn to loosen it, then turn the adjuster barrel (1) clockwise or counterclockwise until the end of the indicator rod is level with the ends of the axle. The rod locations can be seen in the window in each axle nut (3 in Figs. 8-21, 8-22, and 8-23).

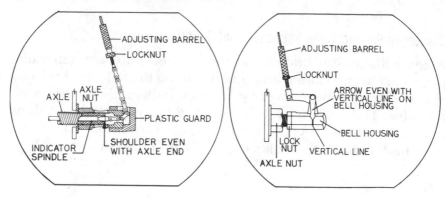

Fig. 8-21: Make shift adjustments on three- and five-speed coaster brake hubs at the indicator spindle (left) and the bell housing (right). See text for instructions.

Fig. 8-22: Another view of the bell housing on a three-speed coaster brake hub, showing correct location of the shift rod end (arrow).

Fig. 8-23: The indicator rod (B) on this three-speed hub is shown correctly adjusted at the end of the spindle.

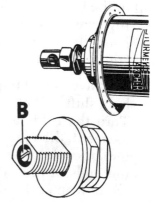

3. Tighten the cable-adjust locknut.
4. If you can't adjust the hub as above, you may have to move the clips (Fig. 8-24) that hold the shift cable on the frame tubes to add or remove a small amount of cable play.

Fig. 8-24: Remove cable slack on a three-speed hub by moving these cable carriers.

Now you know how to get your hubs in shape! The next section discusses how to reduce the incidence of flat tires, fix them when they go flat, and select the tire tread that's best for the biking you do.

ALL ABOUT TIRES

There are two types of tires in wide use today—tubular tires (Fig. 8-25), and wired-on tires (Fig. 8-26). Wired-on tires have a wire bead (Fig. 8-26) that fits inside a ledge in the rim. They are the most popular bike tire today for touring, trail riding on ATBs, race training, and for road, triathlon, and cyclo-cross racing. Tubular tires have the tube sewn up inside the tire casing (which is why they are also called "sew-ups") and are glued onto the rim. Tubular tires are much lighter than wired-ons and can be inflated to 140 pounds per square inch of pressure, thus offering less rolling resistance; this is why they are so widely used for racing. But they are also more flat-prone than wired-on tires and harder to repair once punctured, as you will discover later in this chapter.

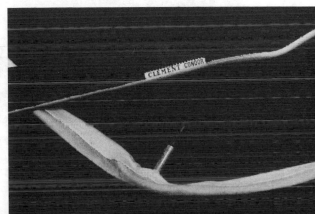

Fig. 8-25: Here's a typical tubular tire, otherwise known as a "sew-up," because the tube is sewn up inside the tire.

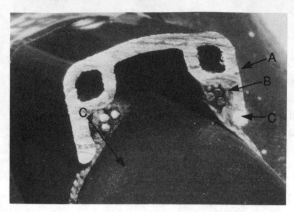

How to Fix a Flat

Since wired-on tires are the most widely used, I'll start with how to fix them when they are punctured, then do the same for tubular tires.

Tools and equipment you will need:

1. A tire lever. I like the Quick Stik lever in Fig. 8-31. One lever should do for all but the most stubborn tire.
2. Patch kit (Fig. 8-27).
3. A small roll of duct tape from any hardware store.

Follow these steps to repair your wired-on tires:

1. Release remaining air from the tube by holding down or unscrewing the valve core (Figs. 8-28 and 8-29).
2. Remove the wheel from the bicycle.
3. Squeeze both sides of the tire all the way around to free it from the rim (Fig. 8-30).

Fig. 8-27: This patch kit will repair both wired-on and tubular tires. Components are: A) tubular tire; B) roll of duct tape; C) rim strip for wired-on tire rims; D) patch kit and patches; E) rim cement for mounting the tubular tire on the rim; F) tube for a wired-on tire.

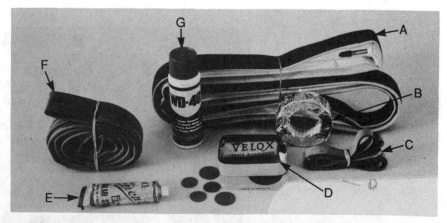

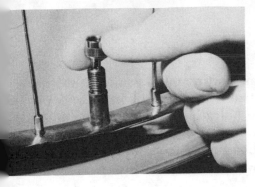

Fig. 8-28: Let air out of a Schraeder valve tube by turning the valve core with the valve cap.

Fig. 8-29: Let air out of a Presta valve by turning the valve core counterclockwise by hand. The valve core is shown in the open position. Press valve core down to remove air.

Fig. 8-30: Break tire-to-rim adhesion by peeling back the tire casing to ease tire removal.

Fig. 8-31: Remove a tire with a tire lever or, if the tire is stubborn, with two tire levers as shown.

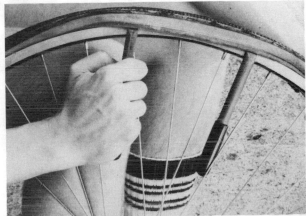

4. Remove the tire from the rim, starting on the side opposite the valve (Fig. 8-31). If the tire is really stubborn, use two tire levers as shown—one to hold the tire off the rim, and the other to separate the tire bead from the rim. Once you get about ten inches of the bead off, you should be able to remove the rest of the bead with one lever. You can remove fat ATB tires with one lever.
5. Remove the tube, starting at the side opposite the valve (Fig. 8-32).
6. Remove the tire from the rim by hand.
7. Pump air into the tube so you can check for the leak (Fig. 8-33).
8. There are three ways to find a leak:
    a. The best way is to dunk the tube in water and watch for the source of air bubbles (Fig. 8-34).
    b. If water isn't available, try listening for the hiss of escaping air (Fig. 8-35).
    c. Or put the tube next to your cheek to feel escaping air (Fig. 8-36).

Fig. 8-32: Remove the tube when one side of a wired-on tire is free from the rim.

Fig. 8-33: Pump air into the tube so you can check for the location of a puncture.

Fig. 8-34: Check for location of the puncture by immersing the tube in water. The arrow points to bubbles which come from a puncture.

Fig. 8-35: Find a puncture by listening for the hiss of escaping air.

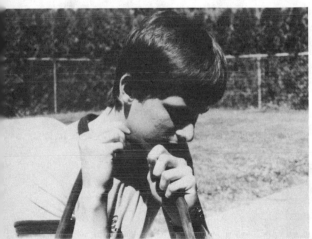

Fig. 8-36: Find a puncture by feeling the jet of air as it escapes through a leak.

9. Circle leak(s) with chalk, a pen, or anything that will leave a mark on the tube (Fig. 8-37).
10. Roughen the area around the puncture with the sandpaper that came with your patch kit (Fig. 8-37). *Don't use a metal scraper*—it can weaken the tube. Replace the metal scraper in your patch kit, if you have one, with a few small squares of medium-rough sandpaper.
11. Put a few drops of patch glue around the puncture area (Fig. 8-38), spread it out with the nozzle of the glue tube, and wait a minute until it gets dry.
12. Peel the backing paper off a patch (Fig. 8-39), put it on the puncture, and press it down firmly with your fingers.
13. Pump up the tube and check it again for punctures and leaks as above. Moisten the top of the valve to make sure the valve core is seated. If you see bubbles, tighten the valve core (Figs. 8-28 and 8-29). If the valve still leaks on a Schraeder valve (Fig. 8-28), you can buy a new one from your bike shop or a service station. Presta valve cores aren't replaceable.
14. Carry at least one spare tube on a long trip so you can repair the punctured tube later. If you don't have a spare tube, the steps above will get you home. You can even make temporary repairs to badly punctured or blown-out tubes (See Figs. 8-40, 41, and 43) with large or multiple-overlaid

Fig. 8-37: Abrade the area around a leak with sandpaper from the patch kit. *Never* use a metal scraper.

Fig. 8-38: Apply a few drops of patch glue on the tube. Let it get tacky.

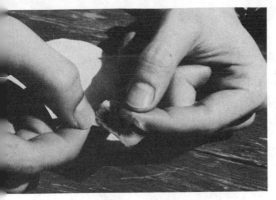

Fig. 8-39: Peel off a patch cover and apply it to the tacky glue.

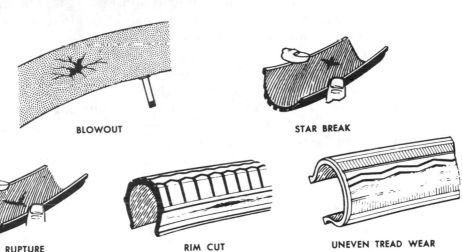

BLOWOUT

STAR BREAK

RUPTURE

RIM CUT

UNEVEN TREAD WEAR

Fig. 8-40: Here are common types of tube and tire damage. *Courtesy Schwinn Bicycle Company.*

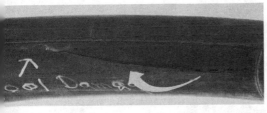

Fig. 8-41: This is the type of tube rip that starts with a pinch of the tube between the rim and a tire lever. The pinch area is shown by an arrow on the tube. *Courtesy Schwinn Bicycle Company.*

Fig. 8-42: Here's evidence of a blowout. This tube can't be repaired. *Courtesy Schwinn Bicycle Company.*

Fig. 8-43: The arrow points to a typical puncture caused by a spoke projecting too far from the nipple. It could also have been caused by a missing rim strip.

patches. Reinforce these patches by wrapping the tube with several layers of duct tape. You may have to add air to the tube every few miles until you can replace it with another tube. Spare tubes aside, my advice is to carry several patch kits. Check your tube(s) of patch glue and replace any that have dried out.

15. Inspect the tire tread for embedded nails, pieces of glass, thorns, or whatever caused the flat and remove them. Inspect the inside of the tire (Fig. 8-40 and 8-44) for cuts and bruises that can pinch and puncture the tube.

16. If the tire is badly cut and you don't have a spare, here's what to do: Roughen the cut area on the *inside* of the tire with sandpaper, cover it with patch glue, and when it dries cover the cut with a canvas patch from your patch kit or with a piece of duct tape. This will keep the tire from pinching the tube and causing another flat.

17. Remove the rim strip (Fig. 8-45) and snip off any spokes that protrude from the nipples and could puncture the tube. Install a new rim strip if necessary.

18. Lay the tire on a flat surface and put the tube in it (Fig. 8-46).

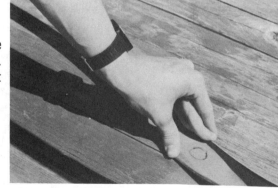

Fig. 8-44: Check the inside of the tire casing for cuts or other tire damage. Cover cuts with a canvas patch or duct tape.

Fig. 8-45: Check condition of the rim strip before replacing the tire.

19. Some tire treads are directional, so make sure the tread faces in the direction marked on the tire when replacing it.
20. Place the tire and tube over the rim and push the valve stem through the rim hole (Fig. 8-47).
21. Place one side of the tire on the rim, fitting the tire in both directions from the valve (Fig. 8-48). Continue until one side is fitted completely in the rim (Fig. 8-49).

Fig. 8-46: Insert the tube in the tire before putting the tire on the rim.

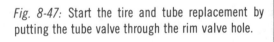

Fig. 8-47: Start the tire and tube replacement by putting the tube valve through the rim valve hole.

Fig. 8-48: Place one side of the tire all the way on the rim, working in alternate directions from the valve.

Fig. 8-49: Start placing the other side of the tire on the rim, working alternate sides from the valve.

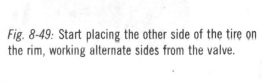

22. Turn the wheel over and finish fitting the tire into the rim, again working evenly from both sides of the valve. You should be able to work by hand (Fig. 8-50). If you have trouble, use the tire lever but be *very* careful because it's easy to squeeze and puncture the tube between the tire lever and the rim.

23. Make sure the tire is seated *evenly* in the rim, especially at the valve area. Push the valve up into the tire about an inch, then squeeze the tire walls until the tire is seated in the rim. Otherwise the tire wall will protrude (Fig. 8-51) and the tube will blow out, possibly causing an accident.

Fig. 8-50: Finish tire replacement on the rim by gripping the tire as shown and pushing the casing over the rim by hand. Try to avoid using the tire lever so you don't squeeze the tube between the rim and the lever and cause another puncture.

Fig. 8-51: If the tire is not seated correctly in the rim, it can protrude as shown to cause a blowout. See text for correct seating method.

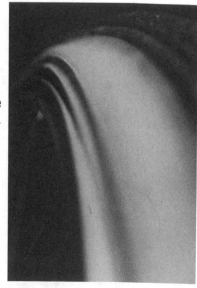

How to Avoid Flats

Most flat tires are avoidable. When scanning the road ahead for traffic, watch for anything on the road immediately in front of your bike that could cause a puncture and be ready to take evasive action.

Keep your tires inflated to the maximum pressure noted on the sidewalls. Road tires can be inflated to at least 90 pounds per square inch (p.s.i.). Fat all-terrain bike tires should be inflated to at least 30 p.s.i., although for road use you can go as high as 50 p.s.i. Some racing wired-on tires and tubular tires should be inflated from 100 to 140 p.s.i. Underinflated tires are more flat-prone because an impact can pinch the tube against the rim.

When you pump up a tube with a hand pump, hold the pump steady so it doesn't move from side to side (Fig. 8-52). When removing the pump, punch it downward so you don't bend the valve (Fig. 8-53). Presta valves (Fig. 8-54) break easily (Fig. 8-55), and once the valve is broken the tube must be replaced. If a tubular tire valve is broken, it will have to be replaced at a cost of from $13 to $45, depending on the tire.

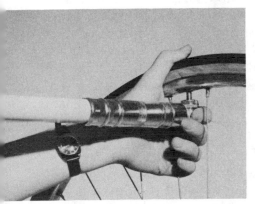

Fig. 8-52:

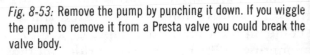

Fig. 8-53: Remove the pump by punching it down. If you wiggle the pump to remove it from a Presta valve you could break the valve body.

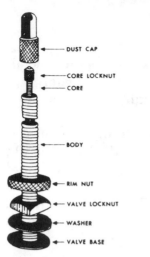

Fig. 8-54: Exploded view of a Presta valve.

Fig. 8-55: Here's what can happen to a Presta valve when you wiggle the pump to remove it, instead of punching it down as in Fig. 8-53. Compare this valve to the one in Fig. 8-29.

Learn to reduce impact on your tires if you *must* run over a pothole by pulling back on the handlebars as the front wheel hits the pothole, then moving forward on the saddle as the rear wheel does the same. If you want protection against the debris on city streets, install a heavy-duty plastic tire liner—such as Mr. Tuffy—between the tire and the tube. This liner comes in sizes to fit most tires. In areas such as the Southwest, where barbed thorns can cause many flats, use thicker thorn-resistant tubes (Fig. 8-56).

Before *every* ride remove anything stuck in your tires—glass shards, nails, thorns, and small stones in the tread. Replace worn tires and those with weather-cracked sidewalls. The cost of new tires is a small price to pay to avoid accident-causing tire failure. On long downhill runs, alternate braking from front to rear wheels to avoid heat build-up that could cause a blow-out, or cause the glue that holds tubular tires on the rim to soften and let a tire come off the rim. A tire scraper (Fig. 8-57), fitted on the brake mounting bolt so its wire loop rides on the tire, helps scrape off particles before they can penetrate to the tube.

When you change tires be sure to match the rim width to the tire width. The width of the rim, as measured between the bead ridges ("B" in Fig. 8-58), should be close to half the width of the tire ("A" in Fig. 8-58). For example, if the tire is 2.125 inches wide—a popular width for ATB tires—the rim should be 1⅛ inches wide. Fitting a tire that's too wide or too narrow for the rim is dangerous because the tire can pop off the rim and cause an accident.

Fig. 8-56: A thornproof tube, left, is much thicker and heavier than a conventional tire tube, right.

Fig. 8-57: These tire savers help scrape particles off tires before they cause a flat. Mount the scrapers on brake mounting bolts.

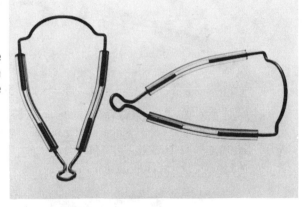

Fig. 8-58: Mount a tire that's sized for the rim width. A tire that's too wide or too narrow can come off the rim and cause an accident. The rim width ("A") should be about half that of the tire width ("B").

Always carry a tire pump. They come in different lengths to fit specific frame sizes, so when you buy one take your bike to the shop to make sure the pump fits your bike frame. A new pump—the Puffup, from Italy (Figs. 8-59 and 8-60)—collapses to only five inches so you can carry it in a handlebar bag. It has a Presta valve head and comes with a Schraeder valve adapter. The Puffup is especially useful for ATB biking, because a branch on a narrow trail or hard impact on a fast downhill run could dislodge a frame-mounted pump and cause an accident. If your bike shop doesn't stock it they can buy it from the manufacturer, Pubblitre srl, 40060 Osteria Grande, Bologna, Italy, Via Lombardi, 13. You could also carry a CO_2 cartridge kit (Fig. 8-61). One cartridge will fill a spare tube in seconds, but it's a costly way to pump up a tube to check for leaks.

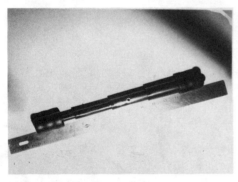

Fig. 8-59: This tire pump collapses to less than half the length shown so it can be carried in a bike bag.

Fig. 8-60: The tire pump in Fig. 8-59 collapses to only five inches in length.

Fig. 8-61: This CO_2 cartridge unit can fill any bike tube quickly.

A Word About Tire Treads

Most tire tread patterns, with the possible exception of the slick tires I mentioned in Chapter 2, adhere well to road surfaces. Racing tires offer less rolling resistance but also less road adhesion. I like the tread on the Michelin Hi-Lite tire (Fig. 8-62) for touring on road bikes. When you're going in a straight line this tire rolls smoothly on its central ridge. When you lean into a turn, the side tread grips the road and helps keep you upright. For touring with an ATB on the road, the Specialized "Streetstomper" (Fig. 8-63) also rolls smoothly on the center ridge and grips well when you leave the road for the trail. If you know you're going to ride on both road and trail, use the Specialized "Crossroads" tire on your ATB (Fig. 8-64), or one like it. This tire has a center ridge for the road and a more aggressive knobby tread on its sides for trail riding on a variety of surfaces such as sand, grass, or mud. If most of your ATB riding will be on the trail, use Cycle Pro's "Snakebelly" (Fig. 8-65), or the Specialized "Tri-Cross" (Fig. 8-66). Its tread is designed to throw off dried mud that could otherwise coat the tire and reduce its adhesion to the road.

Fig. 8-62: Use a tire like this for stability, road adhesion, and low rolling resistance on a road bike.

Fig. 8-63: Use this type of tread when you use your ATB for both road and trail riding. The center ridge rides on the street and the knobby bumps on the side give stability when you go off the road.

Fig. 8-64: Use this tread when most of your ATB riding will be off-road, on the trail. The center ridge cuts rolling resistance on pavement, the side knobbies give excellent traction on the trail.

Fig. 8-65: Use this tire when you'll be riding only on the trail or on sandy roads. It also gives good traction on slippery surfaces such as snow.

Fig. 8-66: Use this tread when you'll be riding through mud and dirt. The tread is designed to throw off mud which would clog the tire so it loses traction.

How to Fix Tubular Tire Flats

1. Remove the wheel from the bicycle.
2. Remove the tire from the rim. If the tire has been applied with a heavy coating of tubular tire glue, it may take some muscle to pry off the tire.
3. Finding a tubular tire puncture can be difficult (Fig. 8-67) because the tire is sewn and, in effect, sealed, so air can escape *anywhere* there's a puncture in the tire casing, including around the base of the valve. Pump air into the tire. If you hear or feel escaping air, or see air bubbles when you dunk the tire in water (Figs. 8-34, 35, and 36), the tube puncture will *probably* be under or near that spot. Circle the leak(s) with chalk.
4. Pull away the casing strip in the area you marked with chalk, to uncover the stitches (Fig. 8-68).
5. Cut one stitch and knot the cut end.
6. Pull out about eight inches of thread (Fig. 8-69) and cut it off. Knot the end still in the tire.
7. Pull out the tube and inspect it for a puncture. If necessary, dunk the tube in water to search for air bubbles from the puncture. Circle the puncture with chalk.
8. Roughen the puncture area with fine sandpaper. Tubular tire tubes are much thinner than wired-on tire tubes, so go easy when you apply the sandpaper.

Fig. 8-67: Before repairing a tubular tire examine the exterior for signs of a puncture to help locate the leak in the tube.

Fig. 8-68: Next, remove the tire liner from over the stitches.

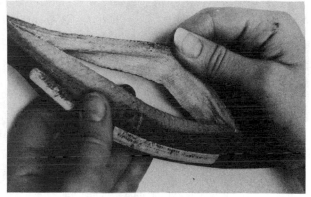

Fig. 8-69: Then remove the stitches from the puncture area.

9. Apply a few drops of patch glue to the puncture area (Fig. 8-70) and let it dry until tacky.
10. Peel off patch cover(s) and apply the patch over the puncture. Fig. 8-71 shows *two* patches because the puncture went through both sides of the tube.
11. Inspect the tire for puncture damage, such as a rip in the casing (Fig. 8-72). Abrade the tear area with sandpaper, apply the patch glue, and when it's tacky, cover the tear with a canvas patch from your patch kit.
12. Stitch the tire back together, using the old stitch holes (Fig. 8-73). Use the waxed linen thread that comes with the tubular tire patch kit. Other thread will cut the tire as it flexes while you ride and cause a blowout. In an emergency you could use waxed dental floss.
13. Knot each end of the re-sewn area, as shown in Fig. 8-74.
14. Apply patch glue over the stitched area (Fig. 8-75), and when it's tacky, press the casing cover back down.
15. Inspect the rim for spokes that protrude through the nipples and snip them off. Fig. 8-76 shows spokes that have been snipped on a wired-on rim.

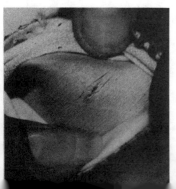

Fig. 8-70: Apply patch glue to the roughened puncture area on the tube.

Fig. 8-71: When the glue is dry, apply the patch. Two may be needed if the puncture is on both sides of the tube.

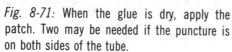

Fig. 8-72: Check the inside of the tire for cuts and cover then with a canvas patch.

Fig. 8-73: Sew the tire with special thread from the tubular-tire patch kit.

Fig. 8-74: Knot the new thread at both ends.

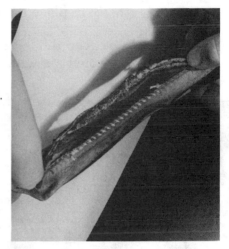

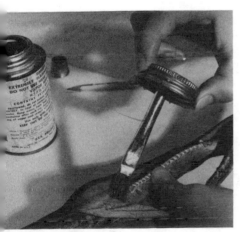

Fig. 8-75: Apply glue over the threads and re-place the tire strip.

Fig. 8-76: Check the rim and cut off any spokes that protrude above the nipples. This is a wired-on tire rim, but this applies to tubular rims as well.

16. True the rim if it's misaligned, as detailed in Chapter 10.
17. Layer tubular tire glue—Tubasti, for example—on the rim.
18. Fit the tire on the rim, valve first. Screw the valve rim nut (Fig. 8-54) almost but not all the way down.
19. Working from one side of the valve and then to the other side, put the tire on the rim as shown in Figs. 8-77 and 8-78. Replace the wheel on the bike and inflate the tire.

I've covered hubs and tires so far in this chapter, and now I'd like to conclude with data on pedals.

Fig. 8-77: Replace the tire on the rim, using your hands to force it on.

Fig. 8-78: Finish the tire replacement by forcing the tire on the rim with your thumbs.

WHAT YOU SHOULD KNOW ABOUT PEDALS

The pedals on your bike sit closer to the ground than any other part except tires, so they take heavy wear from dust, dirt, and water. Their tiny ball bearings are subjected to pressure of 50 pounds in moderate pedaling, 170 pounds when racing, and 350 pounds by strong riders straining uphill. So pedals require periodic cleaning and lubrication, especially after hard riding over trails and through water.

Here's how to maintain your pedals:

Steps in Pedal Maintenance

Tools you will need:

1. 8, 10, 11, and 15mm wrenches
2. Special wrench for Shimano PD-7400 platform pedals—Shimano part No. TL-PD30, available from your bike shop.

The steps below apply to most pedals, but not sealed-bearing pedals. I'll cover these later in this chapter. Study Fig. 8-79 to become familiar with the parts I'll mention below.

Fig. 8-79: Study this view of the parts of a non-sealed pedal so you can take yours apart for maintenance. Parts are: A) cup; B) spindle; C) bearings; D) adjustable cone; E) washer; F) locknut; G) dust cap; H) cone; I) rattrap body.

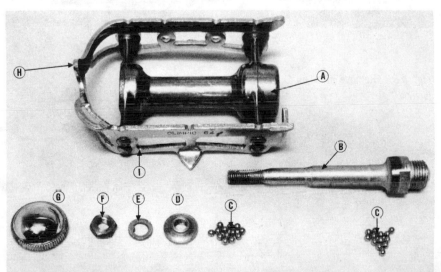

1. Hold the pedal body between two blocks of wood in a vise. Remove the dust cap. The cap shown in Fig. 8-80 can be pried counterclockwise with a screwdriver. Other dust caps may require a 15mm wrench (arrow, Fig. 8-81).
2. Hold the pedal spindle shank—not the threads—in a vise and remove the locknut (Fig. 8-82). The locknut takes a 9, 10, or 11mm wrench, depending on the make of pedal. *Note:* The locknut on Mavic 640 and 645 LS pedals (Fig. 8-83) threads off clockwise, all others thread off counterclockwise. See Step 15 below for special instructions on Mavic 640 and 645 LS pedals. See Step 16 for special instructions on Shimano PD-7400 pedals and similar Shimano pedals.
3. Remove the tongued washer under the locknut, if there is one (Fig. 8-84).
4. Remove the adjustable cone with a small screwdriver (Fig. 8-85).

Fig. 8-80: Remove the dust cap with a small screwdriver.

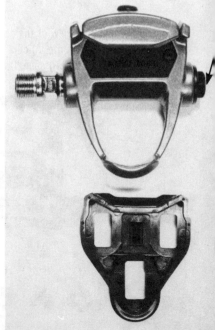

Fig. 8-81: Remove this dust cap with a 15mm wrench.

Fig. 8-82: Remove the locknut with a 9, 10, or 11mm wrench (depending on make of pedal).

Fig. 8-83: The locknut on this Mavic pedal threads off clockwise.

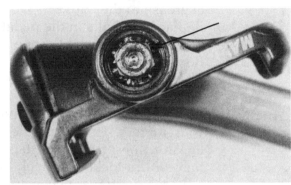

Fig. 8-84: Remove the tongued washer.

Fig. 8-85. Remove the adjustable cone with a small screw-driver.

5. Hold the pedal spindle as you remove the pedal from the vise and lay it flat on a rag to catch loose balls (Fig. 8-86).
6. Pull the spindle out of the pedal body.
7. Remove the balls, clean old grease off them and off the pedal cups in both sides of the pedal body.
8. Roll the balls around in grease to coat them. Apply a layer of grease to the cups.
9. Replace the balls in the pedal body. Replace the spindle.
10. Tighten the adjustable cone by hand as far as possible.
11. Replace the washer.
12. Place the pedal in the vise, hold it as in step 2 above. Tighten the locknut.
13. Remove the pedal from the vise and twirl the spindle with your fingers. If the spindle is tight or binds, loosen the locknut, loosen the adjustable cone about ¼ turn, and re-tighten the locknut. Check for binding or tightness again. Repeat this step as necessary.
14. Check for spindle sideplay by moving it from side to side in the pedal. If you feel looseness, place the pedal in the vise as above, loosen the locknut, and tighten the adjustable cone about ¼ turn. Tighten the locknut and check again for sideplay. Repeat this step as necessary.
15. On Mavic 640 and 645 LS pedals, when the locknut is removed, place a block of wood on the locknut side of the spindle and use a hammer to gently tap the spindle out of the body. Remove the ball and needle bearings, clean off old grease from them and from the pedal cup. Regrease the

Fig. 8-86: Remove the ball bearings, clean all parts, reassemble, and adjust the bearings as noted in the text.

bearings and replace them and the spindle in the pedal, reversing the above steps. The locknut threads on counter-clockwise.

16. On Shimano PD-7400 Dura Ace and Shimano Dura-Ace 600 EX and 600 AX pedals, remove the spindle as follows:

    a. Please refer to Fig. 8-87 as you disassemble these pedals. With the special wrench (12) remove the lockring (3).

    b. Place the pedal on a rag on your workbench and with the 15mm end of the special wrench, remove the adjustable cone (5).

    c. Pull the spindle (1) out of the pedal body.

    d. Remove the needle bearings (2) and the ball bearings (6).

    e. Clean old grease off the bearings and from the spindle and adjustable cone.

    f. Grease all bearings and place a layer of grease on both spindle races and on the adjustable cone.

    g. Reassemble the pedal by reversing the above steps.

Fig. 8-87: The Shimano PD-7400 adjustable-foot-position pedal. Parts are: 1) spindle; 2) needle bearings; 3) locknut; 4) washer; 5) cup; 6) bearings; 7) cone; 8) binder nuts for pedal rattrap; 9) toe-clip holder; 10) toe clip; 11) cone; 12) special wrench to remove locknut (3) and cup (5).

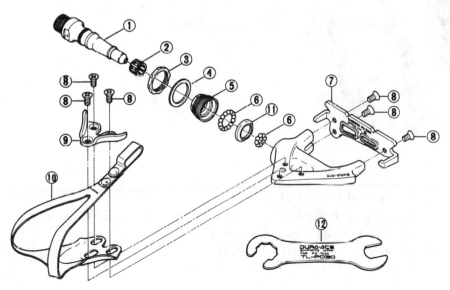

h. Check the spindle for tightness and binding by twirling the spindle with your fingers. If it's tight, loosen the locknut and loosen the adjustable cone about ¼ turn. Tighten the locknut and check again. Repeat as necessary.

i. Check the spindle for looseness by moving it from side to side. If it's loose, loosen the locknut, tighten the adjustable cone ¼ turn, tighten the locknut, and check again. Repeat as necessary.

Sealed-Bearing Pedals

Durham sealed-bearing pedals (Fig. 8-88) are maintainable like all the pedals above, and their bearings are replaceable. Remember to follow these steps:

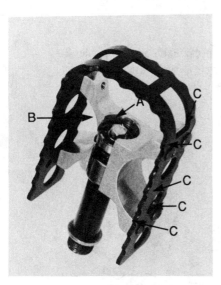

Fig. 8-88: Remove the bearings on a Durham pedal by removing the lockbolt ("A") and the circlip ("B"). Replace the rattrap cage by removing the Allen bolts ("C") on both sides of the pedal.

1. Remove the locknut.
2. With circlip pliers or a small screwdriver, remove the circlip (also known as a "split washer").
3. Remove the bearings, then clean, regrease, and replace them by reversing the above steps.

Phil Wood Pedals

Phil Wood pedals (Fig.8-89) are *not* maintainable. If the bearings wear out, they can be replaced, but the pedals must be returned to the factory by your dealer for this operation. However, the Phil Wood pedals on my road bike (Fig. 8-90) are fine after six years of touring in Europe and up and down both U.S. coasts.

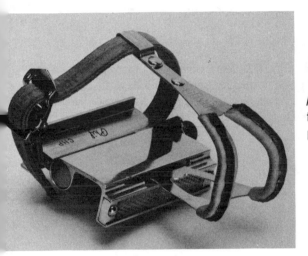

Fig. 8-89: Return Phil Wood pedals to the manufacturer for bearing replacement. You can't do it yourself.

Fig. 8-90: After six years and around 5,000 miles, this Phil Wood pedal is still working well on the author's road bike.

Pedal Body Replacement

The aluminum alloy rattrap section of ATB pedals will eventually wear out and need to be replaced. The outer section on SunTour XC-II pedals (Fig. 8-91) can be removed with a 2mm Allen wrench. The alloy rattrap section of Durham road pedals (Fig. 8-88) can also be removed and replaced.

Fig. 8-91: Replace the rattrap cage on ATB pedals by removing the eight binder bolts with a 2mm Allen wrench. Remove the cage to disassemble the pedal bearing system on these SunTour X.C.-II pedals.

Foot "Twist"

Most of us have some degree of what I call "foot twist," which is the angle your feet assume on the pedals. This angle differs for each foot, and it's related to the twist of the shin bone. For example, the heel of my left foot points outward—away from the bike—as I pedal. But the rattrap pedal frame (Figs. 8-92 and 8-93) forces my foot to align with the pedal frame, so I can't pedal with my foot at its preferred natural angle or twist. As a

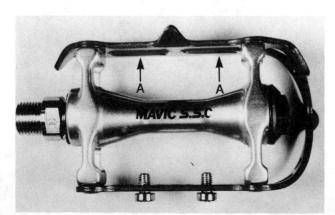

Fig. 8-92: The shoe cleat tunnel fits onto the pedal frame ("A") so your foot is aligned with the frame. See text for explanation.

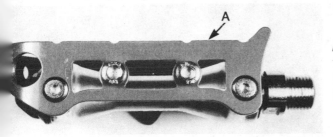

Fig. 8-93: This second view of the pedal frame ("A") shows how it aligns with the rider's foot. See text for explanation.

result of this forced realignment, I often feel pain in my left knee. The same thing happened to a lesser extent with my right foot and knee. Most bike riders share this problem.

Shoe cleats (Figs. 8-94 and 8-95), along with toe clips and straps (Figs. 8-96), clamp your feet to the pedal frame so you can pull up with one foot while you push down with the other for greater pedaling efficiency. The problem, as noted above, is that the rider's foot twist angle is almost always different from the angle of the pedal frame. Toe clips and straps, by locking your foot into this unnatural angle, exacerbate this problem.

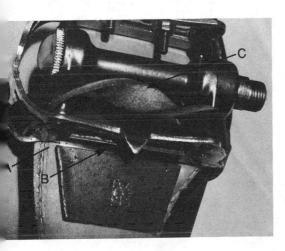

Fig. 8-94: The shoe cleat tunnel ("A") fits on the pedal frame ("B") so the rider can pull the pedal up with one foot and push it down with the other foot. The twist in the toe strap ("C") helps keep it from slipping on the pedal.

Fig. 8-95: This shoe cleat is adjustable in directions "A" and "B". The threaded hollow bolts ("C") are for mounting the three-way adjustable cleat and pedal shown in Fig. 8-97. A third hollow bolt is under the cleat ("A").

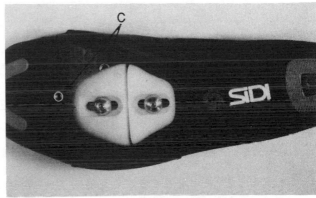

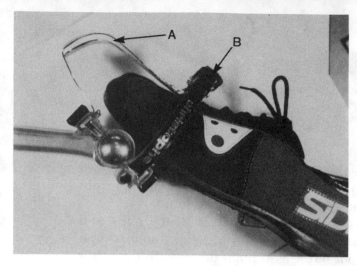

Fig. 8-96: Toe clip ("A") and strap ("B") can cause pain on a long bike ride.

Before the new generation of twist-adjustable pedals, the only way you could position cleats on your bike shoes was to pedal for at least 50 miles *without* the cleats. Pedal pressure would then leave a mark, which was almost never straight across, on the bike shoe's leather sole. The cleat would be attached to the shoe so its tunnel was aligned with the mark made by the pedal on the sole. The problem here is that the cleat alignment never agreed with the alignment forced on you by the fixed angle of the pedal frame, as noted above.

Adjustable Angle Pedals

Adjustable angle pedals (Fig. 8-97) have solved almost all foot twist problems. These pedals permit a left or right swing angle of around 28 degrees as well as fore and aft adjustment. They also eliminate the need for pain-causing toe clips and straps.

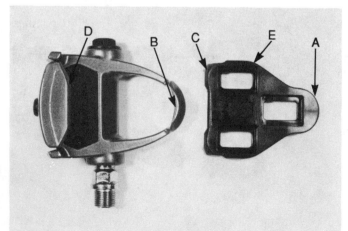

Fig. 8-97: Install the cleat "E" on bike shoes. To use on a three-way adjustable pedal, insert the heel section ("A") into the pedal heel retainer ("B"), then push your foot down so the cleat section ("C") snaps into the pedal cleat retainer ("D").

Fig. 8-98: Remove your foot from this three-way adjustable pedal by swiveling your heel ("A") left on the left pedal or right on the right pedal so it moves out of the pedal retainer, and pull your foot up and out of the forward pedal retainer ("B").

Fig. 8-99: This shoe is made for a three-way adjustable cleat pedal. The cleat ("A") is bolted to the shoe bolts (arrows).

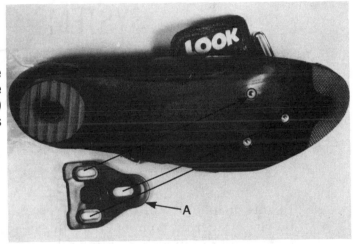

To use the strapless, adjustable pedals, insert the rear part of the shoe cleat ("A" in Fig. 8-97) into the cleat holder on the rear of the pedal ("B"). Then push your toe down until you feel the front of the cleat ("C"), snap into the front pedal cleat holder ("D"). Remove your foot by swiveling your heel to the left on a left pedal, or to the right on the right pedal, from the cleat holder ("A" in Fig. 8-98), lift your heel up, and pull the shoe away from the front cleat holder ("B"). Fig. 8-99 shows a French shoe designed for adjustable pedals, the Look, which is popular for road and triathlon racing as well as for touring on road bikes.

In the next chapter I'll cover the maintenance of steering and seating systems and the safe use of carriers and installation of fenders.

NINE

THE STEERING AND SEATING SYSTEMS—HEADSETS, HANDLEBARS, STEMS, SADDLES, AND SEATPOSTS

In this chapter I will discuss the care and adjustment of the bicycle's steering components—the headset, handlebars, and stem—and the bicycle saddle and seatpost. I'll also cover the pros and cons of fenders and how to install them.

HEADSETS, YOUR LIFELINE TO THE ROAD

The headset (Fig. 9-1) takes a terrific beating, especially on rough roads. The lower set of balls is under thrust stress (Fig. 9-2), the upper set is under radial stress. Thrust stress is force applied toward or away from an object, like the reactive force on the springs of a car on a rough road or when you strike a nail with a hammer. Radial stress is force spread outward, like the ripples a pebble makes when it's dropped in a pond. Road shock tends to flatten bearings, but mostly the bottom set as seen in Fig. 9-2. Road shock will also wear grooves in the headset races (Fig. 9-3). And as the headset wears, it becomes looser.

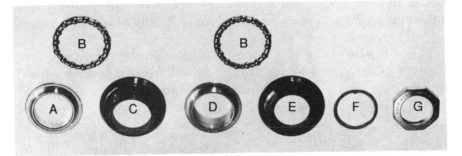

Fig. 9-1: The headset parts are: A) bottom cone; B) bearings in retainers; C) bottom cup; D) top cone; E) adjustable cup; F) washer; G) locknut.

Fig. 9-2: Shimano headset on a high-quality Ibis all-terrain bicycle. Parts are: A) locknut; B) washer; C) adjustable cup (bearings are inside the cup); D) bottom cup (bearings are inside the cup). *Maury Cohen photo.*

Fig. 9-3: Along with the bottom cup, the bottom headset cone, ("A") is the point of greatest bearing wear. Check all cones and cups for grooves and dents. "B" points to the sidepull brake mounting bolt.

Loose headsets will cause wheel shimmy, loss of control, and an accident. Please see Chapter 2 for a review of the hazards of wheel shimmy.

Make these two checks for headset adjustment every few months if you ride a lot. 1. Straddle the bike, squeeze the front brake lever hard, rock the bike back and forth (Fig. 9-4), and watch the headset locknut (Fig. 9-1) as you do so. If you feel looseness, if the locknut moves in any direction, or if it's so loose you can turn it by hand, readjust the headset bearings to prevent hazardous wheel shimmy, as shown below. 2. Raise the front brake lever, lift the front wheel off the floor and turn the handlebars from side to side. The handlebars should turn smoothly without binding or locking. If they don't, the headset is too tight, bearings will wear prematurely, and wheel shimmy will eventually occur. See Steps 16 through 20 below for headset adjustment instructions.

Fig. 9-4: Check for headset looseness by squeezing the front brake lever and rocking the bike back and forth.

Disassemble, clean, and readjust the headset every four to six months and install new bearings every year. Here's how to do it:

Tools you will need:

1. A pair of 32mm wrenches (Fig. 9-5) that fit Campagnolo (Fig. 9-6), SunTour (Fig. 9-7), and older Shimano headset locknuts and adjustable cups.
2. A pair of special wrenches for newer Shimano headsets (Fig. 9-8).
3. A pair of special wrenches for Mavic headsets (Figs. 9-9 and 9-10).
4. 6mm Allen wrench or 12mm wrench for stem binder bolt (Fig. 9-11).
5. 10mm wrench to remove a sidepull brake.

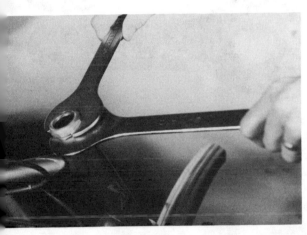

Fig. 9-5: Hold the adjustable cup with one 32mm wrench and loosen the locknut with another 32mm wrench as shown. Reverse this procedure when reassembling the headset.

Fig. 9-6: Campagnolo makes this high-quality headset.

Fig. 9-7: SunTour Superbe is an example of a high-quality headset.

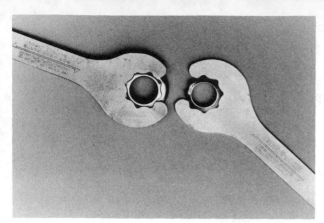

Fig. 9-8: Use these special wrenches on newer-model Shimano headsets.

Fig. 9-9: Use these special wrenches to work on Mavic headsets.

Fig. 9-10: Mavic headset designed for more expensive road and racing bicycles.

Fig. 9-11: Use a 6mm Allen wrench to loosen the stem binder bolt Mark the stem height adjustment with a piece of chalk, so you retain the original handlebar height.

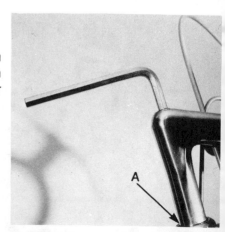

Steps in Headset Maintenance:

1. Remove the front wheel.
2. Squeeze and hold cantilever or centerpull brake shoes (Fig. 9-12).
3. Pull the crossover cable ("A" in Fig. 9-13) out of the carrier ("B"), or from the brake arm ("A" in Fig. 9-14).

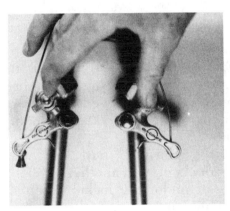

Fig. 9-12: Squeeze cantilever, centerpull, or cam brake shoes so you can remove the crossover cable for handlebar removal.

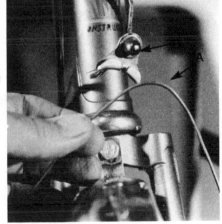

Fig. 9-13: Remove the crossover cable ("A") from the carrier ("B").

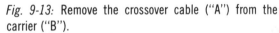

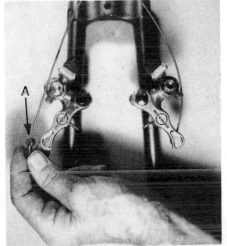

Fig. 9-14: Or remove the crossover cable from the brake arm slot ("A").

4. Remove a front sidepull brake by unscrewing the brake mounting nut (Fig. 9-2).
5. Remove the cam ("A" in Fig. 9-15) from a front cam brake by squeezing the brake shoes.
6. With chalk, mark the stem where it comes out of the locknut ("A" in Fig. 9-11), so you can replace it at the original height. Unscrew the stem binder bolt with a 6mm Allen wrench or 10, 11, or 12mm wrench (Fig. 9-11), but do not remove it all the way.
7. With a hammer and piece of wood, tap the stem binder bolt down until it's loose (Fig. 9-16). One tap should do it. The expansion bolt (Fig. 9-16) has a nut that expands against an angle cut in the stem (Fig. 9-17). As it's tightened, it wedges the stem tightly inside the fork steering tube. The stem bolt must be *tapped* open to break the wedge lock.
8. Remove the stem and handlebars (Fig. 9-18), and set them out of the way, on the top tube.
9. Remove the locknut. Hold the adjustable cup with one wrench while you loosen the locknut with another wrench (Fig. 9-5). Remove the washer under the locknut, or remove the centerpull brake cable guide (Fig. 9-19).

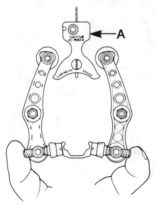

Fig. 9-15: Squeeze the brake shoes to remove the cam ("A") from a front cam brake.

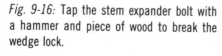

Fig. 9-16: Tap the stem expander bolt with a hammer and piece of wood to break the wedge lock.

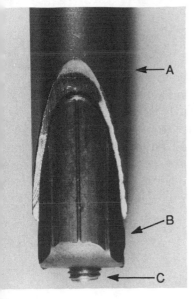

Fig. 9-17: The expander bolt holds the stem in the fork steering tube. "A" is the fork steering tube, "B" is the expander nut, "C" is the stem bolt.

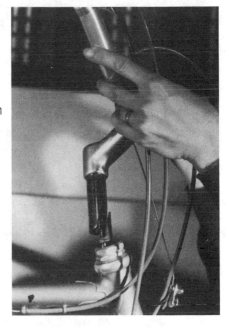

Fig. 9-18: Remove the stem and handlebars and set them on the top tube so you can work on the headset.

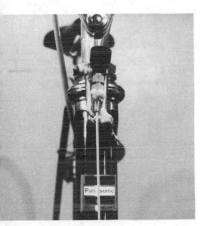

Fig. 9-19: If your bike has centerpull brakes, remove the centerpull front brake cable guide (arrow) after removing the headset locknut.

10. Loosen the adjustable cup until you can turn it by hand. Hold the fork in the bike with one hand while you remove the adjustable cup (Fig. 9-20). Carefully remove the fork. Catch loose bearings if they're not in a retainer (Fig. 9-21). Or put a rag on the workbench, put the bike on it, and catch loose balls as you withdraw the fork.

11. If the headset has dust shields like the SunTour headset in Fig. 9-22, remove them so you can remove the ball bearings.

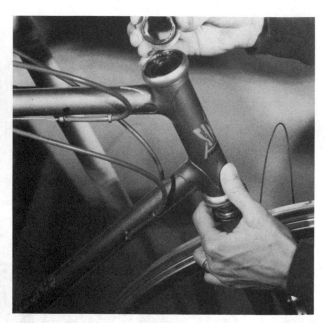

Fig. 9-20: Unscrew the adjustable cup with one hand as you hold the fork up with the other hand.

Fig. 9-21: Remove the ball bearings from the retainer shown at the left, and add two more balls for improved road shock absorption and longer bearing life. The retainer at the left holds 20 ball bearings, as does the adjustable cup at the right. As you can see there's room for two more.

Fig. 9-22: Remove the dust shield (arrow) from a SunTour headset so you can remove the bearings.

12. Remove the bearings. Clean off old grease. If the bearings fall out or are easily plucked out of a retainer, install new balls *without* the retainer as noted in Step 16 below.
13. Clean old grease out of the adjustable cup and the top and bottom cones and cup (Fig. 9-1).
14. Examine cups and cones for grooves, rust, or wear (Fig. 9-2). If they're worn, take your bike to the bike shop and have them replaced. Don't do this yourself. This job requires special tools and skills (see Fig. 9-23). Have your bike shop check the seats where the cones and cups fit (Figs. 9-23, 24, and 25) to make sure the factory has accurately machined them. If not, have them remachined so that cups and cones seat accurately and the bearings absorb road shock evenly and wear uniformly. Uneven bearing wear can loosen the headset and cause wheel shimmy.

Fig. 9-23. Avoid damage to precision headset cups and cones by having the bike shop install a new set if needed. You need special tools for this operation, such as the bottom cone installing tool shown here.

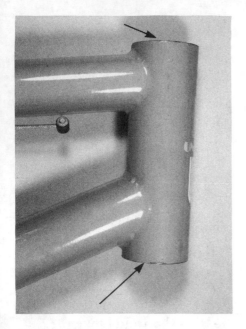

Fig. 9-24: Make sure the steering tube ends (arrows) are accurately machined before installing a new headset, so that the new cups and cones seat accurately.

Fig. 9-25: Inspect the steering head (arrow) for accurate machining before installing a new bottom cup (left). Here's a close-up of the same steering head bottom cone seat. It's poorly machined, so the cone will be misaligned and the headset will wear faster (right).

Fig. 9-26: Inspect the races—the ball-bearing contact area—for signs of galling, pitting, and roughness. Replace your headset if the races (arrow) are as rough as this one.

15. Headset cups and cones that look like Fig. 9-26 are made of poor-quality steel that will wear out in a year or so of hard riding. Spend $50 on a higher-quality headset, as in Fig. 9-27—it's a good investment in safe, shimmy-free cycling.

16. Remove the bearings from the retainer if they're in one. Discard the retainer and add two more ball bearings so you'll have a stronger bearing set, with more bearings to absorb road shock (Fig. 9-20). Take an old ball to your bike shop for a replacement of the exact size. Depending on make, headset balls may be $\frac{3}{16}''$ or $\frac{5}{32}''$.

Fig. 9-27: Install a new high-quality headset if necessary, such as this Mavic set with precision ground races.

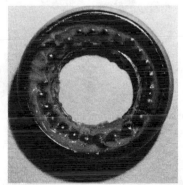

Fig. 9-28: Grease the ball bearings to hold them in the races as you reassemble the headset.

17. Reassemble the headset. Grease the bearings, cups, and cones (Fig. 9-28.) If balls are in a retainer, install the retainer so its contour is the same as the cup (Figs. 9-29 and 9-30). Replace any seals. Replace the bottom set of bearings on the bottom cone with enough grease to hold them in place (Fig. 9-28).

18. Replace the fork and hold it in place while you replace the top bearings on the top cone. Thread on the adjustable cup by hand as far as possible.

19. Turn the adjustable cup with a wrench *carefully* until it's snug against the bearings. Back it off a half turn.

20. Install the washer or the centerpull brake cable guide over the adjustable cup.

21. Thread on the locknut. Hold the adjustable cup with one wrench and tighten the locknut with the other wrench.

22. Replace the handlebars. The stem should be at the height marked in Step 5 (Fig. 9-14). *At least 2½ inches of the stem must be inside the fork steering tube. See Fig. 1-44 in Chapter 1.* Tighten the expander bolt to 180 inch/pounds. *Note:* Readjust cantilever or cam front brake shoe clearance if you installed the stem at a different height than that originally marked. See Chapter 5 for instructions.

23. Replace the crossover cable or the sidepull brake. Tighten the sidepull brake mounting nut to 70–88 inch/pounds.

24. Replace the front wheel.

25. Check the headset for looseness. Mount the bike, squeeze the front brake, and rock the bike back and forth (Fig. 9-4). If the fork feels loose, hold the adjustable cup with one wrench and turn the locknut counterclockwise one turn. Turn the adjustable cup clockwise ¼ turn, hold it with the

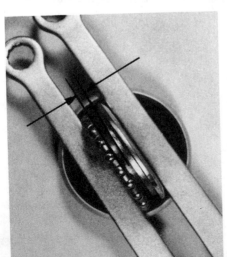

Fig. 9-29: Install retainer bearing sets so the retainer curve matches the race contour. This photo shows the retainer upside down, with a large gap (arrows) between the bearings and the race.

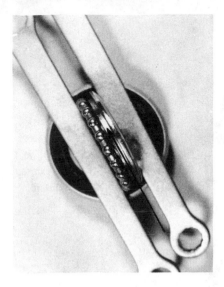

Fig. 9-30: Mate the contours of the ball-bearing retainer and the cone race so that there is no gap (arrow) between them when reassembling the headset.

wrench, and tighten the locknut. Repeat until the fork has no free play.

26. Check the headset for tightness. Lift the front wheel off the ground and turn the handlebars in both directions. Tilt the bike so the handlebars move freely by gravity, without binding or tightness. If the handlebars stick or bind, hold the adjustable cup with a wrench, loosen the locknut, then loosen the adjustable cup ¼ turn and hold it with a wrench while you tighten the locknut. Repeat until the fork turns freely.

A Word About Wheel Shimmy

I've mentioned the dangers of wheel shimmy several times so far in this book. Once started, shimmy is difficult or impossible to stop. You can easily lose control and go for a spill. Loose headsets are the cause of most wheel-shimmy accidents. Headsets work loose more often in all-terrain bicycles than in other bike types because trail shock flattens the headset bearings, which loosens the adjustable cup and the locknut. About one quarter of the dozens of ATBs I've checked while investigating bike accidents had dangerously loose headsets. Replace the stock locknut with a SunTour double-locking binder nut (Fig. 9-31) that clamps to the steering tube so it won't work loose under road shock.

Now that you know how to fix what you steer with, I'll go on to what you sit on—the saddle and its support, the seatpost.

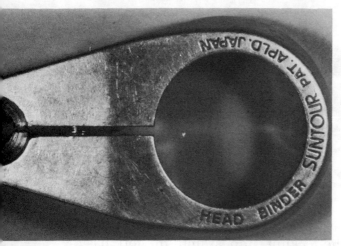

Fig. 9-31: Replace the locknut on your ATB with this SunTour binder locknut, so your headset won't loosen and cause wheel shimmy.

THE SADDLE, SEATPOST, AND FENDERS

I covered adjustment of the saddle pitch and height in Chapter 1. Here are a few more tips about saddles and their care, and about seatposts and fenders.

Leather Saddle Selection and Care

The saddle in Fig. 9-32 is a good example of how not to take care of a leather saddle. Whoever owns it must have a low threshold of pain. Keep *your* fine leather saddle (I'll cover other saddle materials below) in shape for years of riding comfort. Here's how:

Fig. 9-32: It hurts just to look at this badly neglected, swaybacked leather saddle. Don't let yours get that way.

1. Time and miles are the only way to break in a new leather saddle. It takes at least 500 miles of riding to make a new saddle pliable enough to fit your anatomy. I've worn the Brooks Professional saddle in Fig. 9-33, for example, on four of my bicycles for thousands of miles and it fits me like a glove. Look at Fig. 9-33 carefully. You'll see that there's more of the saddle on the right side than on the left, just as there is more of me on the right side than on the left. The Brooks B66 leather saddle (Fig. 9-34) is newer and still in the breaking-in process on my indoor exerciser, and its shape is still the way it came when new.
2. Don't try to break in a new leather saddle by soaking it in neat's-foot oil. This will over-soften the leather so that it will be nearly as swaybacked as the saddle in Fig. 9-32.
3. Apply a light coat of a good leather preservative such as Brooks Proofhide (Fig. 9-35) or neat's-foot oil every few months. Apply it on both sides, let it soak in overnight, then rub off any excess before riding again.

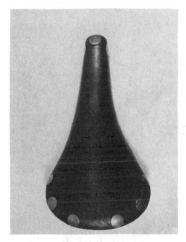

Fig. 9-33: This Brooks Professional leather saddle has been ridden thousands of miles by the author on four of his bikes. You can see that there's more of the saddle on the right side than on the left, which conforms to the rider's body.

Fig. 9 34. This Brooks B66 saddle is wider than the saddle in Fig. 9-33 and has more support for the casual rider or the commuting cyclist than narrow racing saddles such as the Brooks Professional.

Fig. 9-35: Treat leather saddles with a preservative such as this Brooks Proofide leather dressing two or three times a year and after the saddle has dried out after soaking.

4. Dry the saddle at room temperature—not under a lamp or in the sun! Apply Proofhide as above after every ride through rain. This is especially important if your bike doesn't have fenders to keep water and mud off your saddle.
5. Check your leather saddle for stretch every four months, more often the more you ride. If you can depress the saddle by hand more than ⅛th of an inch, the leather has stretched. Remove the stretch by turning the stretch adjuster nut clockwise (arrow in Fig. 9-36).

Fig. 9-36: Remove stretch from a leather saddle by turning the ter nut (arrow) counterclockwise unti saddle is firm.

Excellent Brooks leather saddles include the Professional for about $33, the Team Pro Special for $40, and the Colt for about $30. The Professional and Team pro models also come designed for women and in pre-softened versions for about $3 more. San Marco also makes fine leather saddles such as the Selle San Marco Regal line for about $46. For something completely different, check out the high-style lizard-skin model for $136.

Saddles with Springs

If jarring and pounding on the trail or rough roads is leaving you sore or chafed or bruised, try a spring-loaded leather saddle. I use a Brooks B66 (Figs. 9-34 and 9-37) on my all-terrain bike. The B66 costs around $16 and comes in both men's and women's models (Fig. 9-38). The Selle Italia Lady Turbo leather saddle for women costs $23.

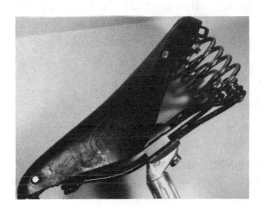

Fig. 9-37: The resilient leather plus the springs of this Brooks B66 soak up road shock.

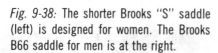

Fig. 9-38: The shorter Brooks "S" saddle (left) is designed for women. The Brooks B66 saddle for men is at the right.

Four-Wire Adapter

The popular Brooks B66, B72, and similar spring saddles have four saddle wires (Fig. 9-39). You can install this saddle on a standard seatpost, but the seatpost clamp will hold the saddle by only two of its four wires (Fig. 9-40). If you install a four-wire saddle on a seatpost built for two wires, a saddle wire may bend, especially for heavy or strong riders. When the saddle wire bends, the saddle will tilt off-center. If you decide to use a four-wire saddle, install a Breeze four-wire adapter (Fig. 9-41). Insert the adapter between the wires (Fig. 9-41), so that the two-wire seatpost clamp grips all four saddle wires. You'll need a longer seatpost clamp bolt because the four-wires are higher; the bolt should come with the adapter. If not, ask your bike shop for one. The adapter fits Campagnolo Gran Sport and Nuevo Record, Sugino and S.R. twin bolt (Fig. 9-42), LaPrade, and many other makes of seatposts, and costs about $15. If your bike shop doesn't have one, write to the manufacturer: Breeze and Angell, P.O. Box 5401, Mill Valley, CA 94942; (415) 388-1217.

Fig. 9-39: Spring-loaded saddles like this have four wires that require an adapter for secure mounting on most seatposts.

Fig. 9-40: This seatpost clamp (arrow) holds only two of the four wires of this saddle, which could be bent by a strong cyclist.

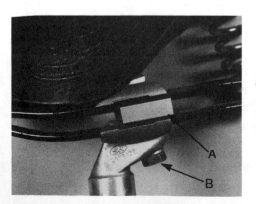

Fig. 9-41: Use an adapter, ("A") and a longer seat-post clamp bolt ("B") for a safe, secure four-wire saddle mount. This way the seatpost clamp holds four instead of two saddle wires.

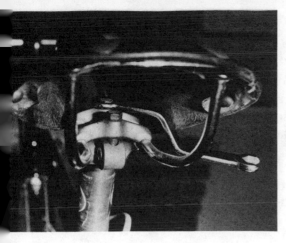

Fig. 9-42: The Breeze four-wire adapter also fits on two-bolt seatposts like this one. Adjust saddle tilt downward by tightening the forward bolt and loosening the rear one and vice-versa for upward tilt.

Non-Leather Saddles

Plastic saddles, even foam-filled models, will never shape to your anatomy. On the other hand, they don't need breaking in, won't stretch, are immune to water, dust, and dirt, and require little or no maintenance. Because they're lighter—as low as 253 grams for the Selle San Marco Condor ($25) in contrast to 453 grams for the Brooks Team Pro special—racing cyclists like them. Plastic saddles for women, such as the Avocet GelFlex ($30) are wider to accommodate the female pelvic area.

If you like your saddle but it's a pain on long rides, you could cover it with a Spenco elastic polymer pad that more evenly distributes pressure and absorbs road shocks. It costs around $23.

Automatic Saddle Height Adjuster for All-Terrain Bikes

As I noted in Chapter 2, the safest way to ride an all-terrain bicycle downhill is to lower the saddle and put as much of your weight as far back over the rear wheel as possible. Then, when you reach the flats or start the next hill, raise the saddle to your normal riding position.

Raising the saddle up and down a lot is a bother. You nearly always have to stop, dismount, open the seatpost quick-release binder bolt (Fig. 9-43), adjust the saddle height, tighten the quick-release bolt, mount the bike, and pedal off.

The best solution is to install a Breeze Hite-Rite adapter. It comes with all the necessary washers, nuts, and bolts to install on your quick release binder bolt and seatpost. Install it with your saddle at your normal riding height (Fig. 9-44). When you want to lower the saddle, reach down while you ride (carefully), open the quick release, push down the saddle, and close the quick release with the saddle in the lowered position (Fig. 9-45). To raise the saddle, open the quick release, lift your weight off the saddle so the Hite-Rite spring can lift it up, close the quick release, sit back down, and continue pedaling. The saddle will be back to your normal riding height. The Hite-Rite is available from your bike shop. If not, write to Breeze and Angell (address is on p. 418).

Fig. 9-43: Adjust an ATB saddle height by opening the quick-release binder bolt lever, moving the saddle, and closing the lever as shown.

Fig. 9-44: Hite-Rite adjuster (arrow) moves the saddle up to normal riding height when the quick-release is opened.

Fig. 9-45: The Hite-Rite adjuster (arrow) in the closed position with the saddle lowered for a downhill run.

The Seatpost Quick Release

Most all-terrain bikes come with a seatpost quick-release binder bolt. If not, you can install one. Remove the old binder bolt and install the quick release. Make sure the quick release you buy fits in the binder bolt hole on your bike. If it doesn't, you can't install it. Don't drill the bolt hole to a larger diameter because that would weaken the seat tube binder bolt fitting (Fig. 9-46), which can break when you tighten the quick release. If that happens you're in for a costly repair job. The seat tube fitting on some inexpensive bikes (Fig. 9-46) is weak to begin with and could break with repeated quick-release bolt opening and closing. Have your bike dealer check this fitting before installing a quick-release mechanism. Fig. 9-47 shows a strong quick-release binder bolt fitting on a high-quality ATB.

A quick-release seatpost binder bolt is handy even on a road bike, because changing saddle height slightly during the ride helps avoid fatigue. The quick release makes it easy to take your saddle with you if you lock your bike up. Thieves know this too.

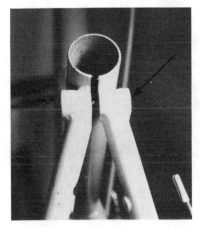

Fig. 9-46: This seattube fitting (arrow) is too weak to be used with a quick-release binder bolt. It's designed for a standard nut and bolt.

Fig. 9-47: A high-quality, strong seatpost clamp fitting designed for use with a quick-release seatpost binder bolt.

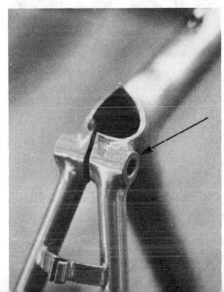

About Seatposts

High-quality all-terrain bikes have precision seat tubes that allow the seatpost to slide up and down easily. Grease the seatpost so you can make saddle height adjustments even easier, with or without the Hite-Rite. Have your bike shop ream out your seat tube if the seatpost won't slide easily inside it.

Install a longer seatpost if the one that came with your ATB won't get you up high enough. Seatposts come in 200mm and 280 mm lengths (Fig. 9-48). Make sure the new seatpost is the same diameter as your old one. Never force a seatpost into a seat tube. If it won't fit easily you have the wrong diameter seatpost. Seatpost diameters are 26.4mm, 26.67mm, 26.8mm, 27mm, and 27.2mm.

Fig. 9-48: Seatposts come in two lengths, 200mm (top) and 280mm (bottom). Use the longer seatpost if you need more saddle height on an ATB.

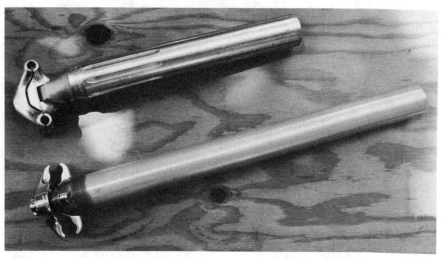

The Hazard of Banana Saddles

Some children's bikes are fitted with a banana saddle (Fig. 9-49). These saddles invite passengers who dangle their feet, which can in turn catch in spokes; their added weight causes inaccurate steering and poor braking. Banana saddles are dangerous! You can replace them with an inexpensive conventional saddle that costs around $15, and I urge you to do so. Replace high-rise handlebars (Fig. 9-49) with conventional flat handlebars. High-rise handlebars force the child to steer with his arms at an unnatural height so that accurate steering is difficult. If he falls, a handlebar can jab into the child's stomach and cause an injury. It's happened.

Make sure that at least 2½ inches of the seatpost are *inside* the seat tube (Fig. 1-39), so that the seatpost won't snap off and cause an accident.

Fig. 9-49: Kids should not ride piggyback on bikes, which is what this banana saddle invites. Accidents are likely. The highrise handlebars place the child's arms at an awkward height, which makes accurate steering difficult.

About Fenders

Install fenders on your bike (Fig. 9-50) if you live where it rains a lot, or if you bike on mud-spattered roads or through snow. Without fenders, bike wheels scoop up dirty, oily water and road debris and deposit it in a streak up your back, on your bike, under the saddle, on the chain, and on the hub and bottom bracket bearings. After moving to southwest Washington from Chicago a few summers ago I noticed most bikes here have fenders, which seemed odd to my midwestern eyes. By fall I found that fenders were a must because it rains a lot here, which is why the natives call themselves "webfoots."

Check fender-to-pedal clearance before installing fenders. Sit on the bike, rotate the pedal so it's as close as possible to the front tire, turn the handlebars, and make sure your toe won't contact the tire when you make a turn. The bike in Fig. 9-51, for example, has a short wheelbase that brings the front wheel close to the fork. If a fender is installed on that bike, the rider's foot *could* hit the fender and cause loss of control and an injury.

Look at Fig. 9-52. The rider's foot is touching the fender. Unfortunately, this bike came factory-equipped with fenders. This bike is dangerous because when the rider makes a left or right turn, the fender will interfere with the rider's pedaling. I know of at least one accident where the fender knocked the rider's foot off the pedal. His leg fell down and wedged between the crank and the downtube, which caused a spill and an injury.

Fig. 9-50: Fenders will keep water, debris, and mud off your clothing and bike bearings.

Fig. 9-51: This bike does not have safe clearance for fenders. The rider's foot passes too close to the fenderless wheel—which means that his foot *could* tangle in fenders if they were installed.

Fig. 9-52: This bike does not offer adequate fender-to-toe clearance. The rider's foot could touch the fender on a turn, which could throw it off the pedal and cause an accident.

Adjust fender stays so fenders clear ATB tires by at least 1½ inches (Fig. 9-50), so that mud, snow, or ice under the fenders won't rub on the tires.

In the next chapter I'll tell you how to keep your wheels true to you, how to replace spokes, and how to lace up a new wheel from scratch.

TEN

HOW TO KEEP YOUR WHEELS AND FRAMES TRUE TO YOU

As wheels go bump on the street they can gradually get out of alignment, especially if the spokes are not accurately tensioned. Road shock stretches and loosens spokes, so the wheel wobbles from one side to the other. When the rim is out of line, brakes become less effective, steering becomes less accurate, and wheel shimmy can occur. For safety's sake, it's important to keep your wheels accurately aligned. Check your wheels this way:

Set your bike on a bike stand, hang it from the ceiling or lift it up, then spin the front wheel. Do the same with the rear wheel. If the wheel passes closer to the brake shoe and then farther away from it, it is misaligned and should be trued for five reasons. One, an untrue rim, as noted, cuts braking ability (see Chapter 5 for details); two, a wobbly rim means one or more spokes are loose; three, when a rear wheel spoke loosens it can break, tangle in the chain or the freewheel gears, and cause an accident; four, out-of-line wheels make accurate steering difficult; and five, wobbly wheels can cause front wheel shimmy and loss of control.

Hitting potholes will dent a rim, but if the wheel has been properly trued it should stay aligned unless the rim is warped by the impact. Correctly trued wheels can take an incredible beating. For example, I once slammed into the rear bumper of a large car that stopped in front of me without warning. I hit it so hard I bent my fork backward and destroyed the frame. But the wheel stayed true. Another time I bounced all day over bumpy cobblestone roads as I biked around Brussels, Belgium. I checked both wheels that night and they were as true as the day they left my truing fixture back home.

There are two degrees of wheel truing. The first is simple maintenance truing you must do two or three times a year until you have removed spoke stretch and fitted each spoke for the same or nearly the same tension. The second more difficult and time-consuming type of wheel truing is necessary after you have built a completely new wheel from scratch, with new spokes in a new rim. In this chapter I will first demonstrate maintenance wheel truing, because that's the kind you'll do most often. Then I'll discuss wheel building and show you how to true a newly built wheel that will stay true unless it's run over by a truck.

Simple Wheel Truing Is Easy

Tools you will need:

1. A spoke wrench (Fig. 10-1).

Fig. 10-1: Use a spoke wrench to adjust spoke tension and true wheels. On the left, a Spokee; center, a standard spoke wrench; right, a Park Tool spoke wrench.

2. A simple truing fixture (Fig. 10-2), or use your bike as shown below.
3. A bike work stand (Fig. 10-3), optional.
4. If you use your bike as a truing fixture, get four $\frac{3}{16}$" x 1½" bolts, eight nuts, and eight washers to fit the bolts.

Fig. 10-2: Accurate wheel alignment is fast with an accurate truing fixture like this.

Fig. 10-3: Use a good workstand to hold your bike steady if you are going to true the wheels using the bike as a fixture. This Park Tool stand has a heavy steel base, tool shelf, and accepts thick- and average-diameter tubing.

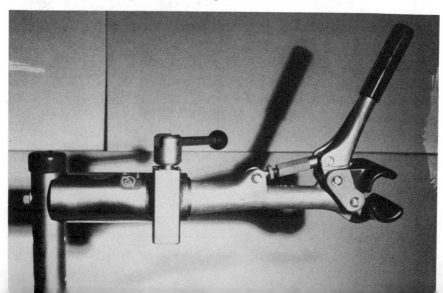

If you don't have a truing fixture:

1. Put your bike in a work stand (Fig. 10-3) or hang it from the ceiling or turn it upside down.
2. Remove both wheels. Remove the tires, tubes, and rim strips.
3. Remove all four brake shoes (see Chapter 5).
4. Replace both wheels. Make sure the rear wheel is as far back in the dropouts as possible and that the front wheel is as far up in the fork dropouts as possible.
5. Spin the rear wheel slowly. Find a place where each side of the rim is the same distance from the seat stays (Fig. 10-4), and mark that spot with crayon on each side of the rim. Do the same with the front wheel, using the fork blades as a reference.
6. Put one bolt, two washers, and two nuts in each brake arm (Fig. 10-5), or a bolt or Allen wrench in a cantilever brake arm (Fig. 10-6).
7. Find the spot you marked in Step 5. Adjust the bolts so they touch each side of the rim on that spot.

Fig. 10-4: Center the rim between the chainstays or fork blades if you use your bike as a truing fixture.

Fig. 10-5: Use bolts and nuts (arrows) in brake arms as truing indicators if you don't have a truing fixture.

Fig. 10-6: Or a pair of Allen wrenches in cantilever arms can replace a truing fixture. Allen wrench "A" is adjusted to check concentric trueness, while Allen wrench "B" is adjusted to check lateral trueness.

If you use a truing fixture:

1. Remove both wheels, tires, tubes, rim strips and the freewheel (see Chapter 7).
2. Set a wheel in the truing fixture.
3. Adjust the truing fixture indicators as you spin the wheel slowly until the indicators are the same distance from each side of the rim. Mark this spot on both sides of the rim with crayon.

Follow this truing procedure whether you use your bike or a truing fixture:

1. Squeeze a drop of light oil, such as WD-40, on the top of spoke nipples in the rim. Wipe off excess oil so it won't damage the rim strip or tube when you replace them.
2. Check the spokes, especially on the freewheel side, where they curve up from the hub, and replace any that are bent, twisted, or cut (Fig. 10-7).
3. Pluck each spoke, starting at the tire valve. Tighten loose spokes by turning the nipple clockwise until each spoke is at about the same tension as the others. If the nipple keeps

Fig. 10-7: Remove the freewheel to check the condition of the spokes on that side. Replace damaged spokes, such as those shown (arrows) gouged by the chain. Readjust the rear derailleur so that it won't shift the chain off the freewheel where it can jam between it and the spokes (see Chapter 6).

turning but the spoke won't tighten, the nipple is stripped. Replace that spoke and nipple and tighten it until it's at an equivalent tension.

4. Study Fig. 10-8. Note that tightening a left spoke nipple (clockwise) pulls the rim to the left, and tightening a right spoke nipple pulls the rim to the right. Similarly, loosening the left-side spoke moves the rim to the right while loosening a right-side spoke nipple moves the rim to the left. The "right and left" sides of a rim are arbitrary. If you're working on the side of the wheel that's on the left side for you, then that's the left side.

5. Make sure the truing indicators (on the bike or in the truing fixture) touch the side of the rim marked with crayon. That mark is where the rim is true laterally from side to side and that's your starting point.

6. Rotate the rim until one side moves as far away as possible from the truing indicator. Mark that spot with crayon.

7. Make a ¼ turn of a spoke nipple that will pull the rim toward the indicator. If the rim is too far to the left, tighten a right side nipple. The wheel should be positioned as in step 6.

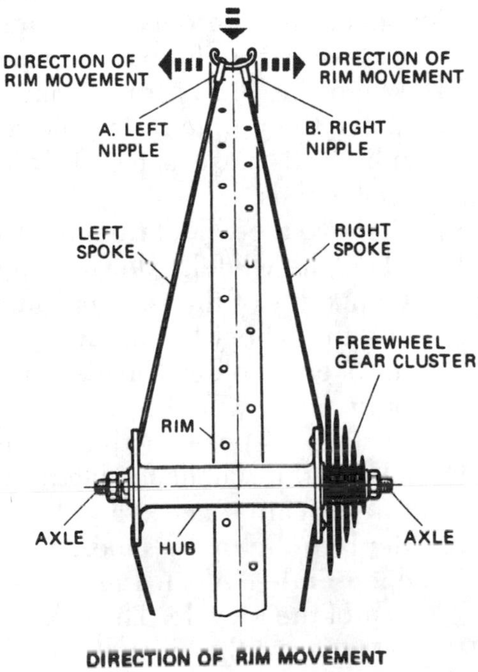

Fig. 10-8: Tighten a left nipple to pull the rim to the left or a right nipple to pull it to the right, as shown.

DIRECTION OF RIM MOVEMENT

DIRECTION OF RIM MOVEMENT

A. LEFT NIPPLE

B. RIGHT NIPPLE

LEFT SPOKE

RIGHT SPOKE

FREEWHEEL GEAR CLUSTER

RIM

AXLE

HUB

AXLE

DIRECTION OF RIM MOVEMENT

8. Make rough truing adjustments, taking a ¼ nipple turn at a time until the rim is almost true.

9. Make final touch-up truing adjustments, taking a ⅛ nipple turn at a time until the rim is true from side to side.

10. If you can't true the rim by tightening a spoke, loosen a spoke on the opposite side ¼ turn. For example, if the rim is too far to the right and you can't tighten a left-side spoke to pull it back, loosen a right-side spoke ¼ to ⅛ turn.

11. When you have set the wheel laterally true, check for concentric (roundness) trueness. With the truing indicator on top of the rim ("B" in Fig. 10-6, for example), spin the wheel. Note the average concentric trueness and make a mark anywhere the rim moves up or down from that average.

12. Correct concentric untrueness by tightening a spoke nipple on the left side and the right side ⅛ turn at the high spot on the wheel, loosening one right- and left-side nipple ⅛ turn at the low place. *Use two adjacent spokes to pull the rim up or move it down. That way you keep the wheel laterally true while you correct concentric untrueness.* Repeat this step until you have removed all high and low spots and the rim is concentric.

13. Check the rim once more for side-to-side trueness and if necessary true it up as shown above.

14. When the rim is true, make sure spokes do not protrude above the nipple inside the rim, where they can pierce the tube and cause a flat. File down or snip off protruding spoke ends.

15. Remove the wheel from the truing fixture or bicycle.

16. Place the wheel, axle side down, on the workbench. Grasp both sides of the rim and push down hard (Fig. 10-9). Rotate the wheel ¼ turn and push down again. You can skip this step on older wheels, but it's important when you have built a new wheel and have trued it for the first time.

17. Turn each spoke another ⅛ turn to remove spoke stretch.

18. Check the wheel for lateral and concentric trueness and true it again if necessary.

19. Replace the brake shoes. Note: Some brake shoes have an open end—"A" in Fig. 10-10. This must face toward the rear of the bicycle. The closed end, "B" in Fig. 10-10, must face toward the front of the bicycle. If the open end of the

brake shoe faces forward it will slide out of the shoe holder the first time you apply the brakes, and possibly cause an accident.

20. Replace the rim strip, tube, and tire. See Chapter 8.
21. Replace the wheels on the bike.

Fig. 10-9: Remove any "spoke stretch" from a newly trued wheel by pushing it down in at least four places as shown.

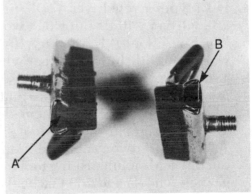

Fig. 10-10: Replace brake shoes with the closed end ("A") toward the front of the bike. The open end ("B") should face toward the rear of the bike. Not all brake shoes have an open end, so check yours to make sure. These are Campagnolo brake shoes.

HOW TO BUILD A WHEEL

If you have dented a rim beyond repair, want to upgrade your hubs, bought a new frame and want to add your own components, or want an extra set of wheels for your ATB—one set for the trail, one for the road—you have a choice of having a professional wheel builder lace (spoke) the wheels or of doing it yourself. You save about $22 when you build and true one wheel, but it takes three hours if you're not used to it. Spokes for one wheel cost about $4.50. Bike shops charge about $30, including the spokes, to build and true a wheel.

Every bicycle enthusiast should build his or her own wheels at least once to understand what it takes to create wheels that will see you through hell and high water. You'll appreciate this new-found skill if you ever get stuck in the boonies and have to replace a busted spoke or if you live where bike shops are scarce. If you ever plan a bike tour in a Third World country, wheel-building ability is a must.

Steps in Wheel Building

Tools you will need:

1. Wheel truing fixture ("A" in Fig. 10-11), or you could use your bicycle as above.
2. Caliper ruler ("B" in Fig. 10-11) or accurate straight ruler.
3. Spoke wrench ("C" in Fig. 10-11).
4. Push-type screwdriver ("D" in Fig. 10-11); an ordinary screwdriver will do but won't work as fast.
5. "Dishing" tool ("E" in Fig. 10-11) for centering the front wheel and "dishing" the rear wheel. Make your own out of a straight piece of 2 x 4 with offset blocks at each end. Then use a 10-inch bolt with two nuts and lockwasher for the center indicator. The homemade version is cumbersome. The Campagnolo dishing tool ("E") fits only 27-inch and 700-C rims, so you can't use it on 26-inch ATB wheels. You can buy a Minoura dishing tool for about $10 that fits 26- and 27-inch wheels and 700-C wheels.

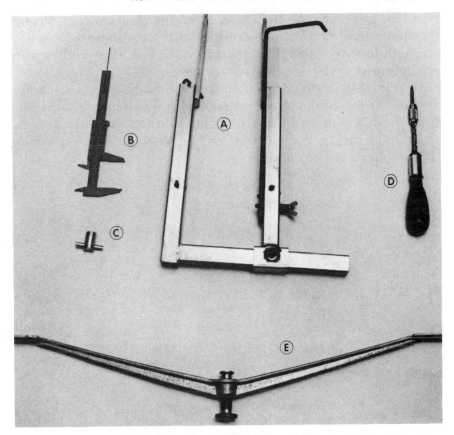

Fig. 10-11: Use these tools to build new wheels: ("A") wheel truing fixture; ("B") caliper ruler; ("C") spoke wrench; ("D") push-type screwdriver; ("E") wheel-centering and "dishing" tool.

ABOUT SPOKES

Spokes come in eight different lengths as shown in Table 10-1.

Spokes come in three gauges: 14, 15, and 15 double-butted. The lower the gauge, the thicker and stronger the spoke. For example—a 14-gauge spoke is 2mm thick and a 15-gauge spoke is 1.56mm thick, so the 14-gauge spoke is about 22 percent thicker. Fifteen-gauge double-butted spokes are 14-gauge thickness for about 50mm (2 inches) at the spoke head end, the part that goes into the hub. Use 14-gauge if you want a strong, durable wheel or 15-gauge double-butted for some sacrifice in strength to save a few ounces in weight. Use 15 straight gauge for lightness at the expense of strength.

I prefer Swiss precision-made D.T. stainless-steel 14-gauge spokes. They are the strongest spokes you can buy, in my opinion. The few ounces 14-gauge spokes add to your wheels might concern a racing cyclist, but for the average touring cyclist these ounces are unimportant.

Table 10-1

AVAILABLE SPOKE LENGTHS*

INCHES	MILLIMETERS
11¹³⁄₃₂	290
11½	292
11²¹⁄₃₂	295
11²³⁄₃₂	298
11¹³⁄₁₆	300
12	305
12⅛	308

* Have your bike shop make up spokes to fit your combination of hub, spoke crossing, and rim diameter, if the stock spokes in this table won't fit. Many bike shops have a spoke cutter/threader machine.

Use oval or bladed spokes, available in 15-gauge thickness, for maximum aerodynamic benefits on light 18 lb. track or 22 lb. road-racing bicycles. Bladed spokes offer the least wind resistance as the wheels turn. Oval spokes cost about $8 a wheel, and bladed about $15 a wheel. Don't use them for anything but racing. Both types are more susceptible to sidewinds than the conventional round spoke.

Four-Cross vs. Three-Cross Lacing

You can lace your wheels with spokes crossed every third spoke (Fig. 10-12), or every fourth spoke (Fig. 10-13). Three-cross spoking gives you a stiffer wheel, which more efficiently translates muscle power to go-power. But the stiffer wheel also sends road shock back into the frame that can be fatiguing on a long ride.

Four-cross spoking requires longer spokes, which soak up road shock better than the stiff three-cross pattern. Use the three-cross pattern for racing and the four-cross for casual riding and long-distance touring and for all-terrain bicycling.

Cut a few ounces off a track-bike time trial (see Chapter 12) by radially lacing the *front* wheel, which makes the spokes shorter, since they are fitted straight up and down, like the spokes of a wagon wheel—not crossed. Radially laced spokes are too weak for street riding or touring. Some racing cyclists use radial lacing on the left side of the rear wheel and three-

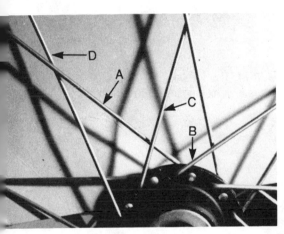

Fig. 10-12: For a three-cross spoking pattern, cross spoke "A" over spokes "B" and "C" and under spoke "D."

Fig. 10-13. For a four-cross spoking pattern, cross spoke "A" over spokes "B," "C," "D," and under "E."

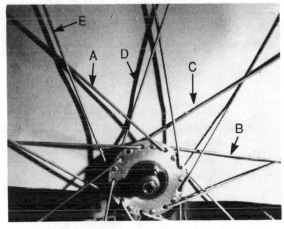

cross on the driving (chain) side. Never radially lace both sides of a rear wheel—it will collapse at the first powerful thrust of your leg muscles or on the first hard bump.

Low-Flange vs. High-Flange Hubs

You get a softer ride with low-flange hubs (Fig. 10-14) than with high-flange hubs (Fig. 10-15) because the low-flange hubs require longer spokes. Use high-flange hubs and a three-cross spoke pattern for the stiffest wheels and low-flange hubs with a four-cross spoke pattern for the softest ride.

Fig. 10-14: Use low-flange hubs like these for a softer ride on touring and all-terrain bicycles.

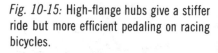

Fig. 10-15: High-flange hubs give a stiffer ride but more efficient pedaling on racing bicycles.

About the Number of Spokes

Hubs and rims come drilled for 28, 32, 36, and 40 spokes. Use 28- or 32-spoke hubs and rims for racing, 36 spokes for touring and ATB trail riding, and 40 spokes on tandems or on the rear wheel of a touring bike if you're a heavyweight spoke buster.

Steps in Building Four-Cross Wheels

1. Select the correct spoke length. There are far too many combinations of spoke crossings, rim diameters, rim widths, hub flange diameters, and spoke hole drillings in hubs and rims to generate one table that gives the correct spoke length for all of them. New hub and rim designs hit the market so frequently that even if one could come up with a comprehensive spoke length table, it would be obsolete in short order. Have your bicycle dealer select the correct length of spokes for you when you buy a new hub and rim, or take an old spoke to the bike shop for a replacement.
2. Note that rim holes are staggered so that every other hole is closer to one side of the rim than the one preceding it or the one following it (Figs. 10-16, 17, and 18).

Fig. 10-16: Look closely and you'll see that the rim holes are offset from the center of the rim.

Fig. 10-17: Another view of a laced wheel showing the offset in rim hole drilling.

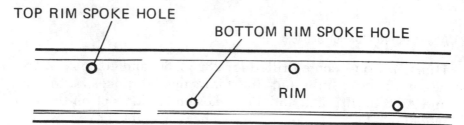

Fig. 10-18: This is an exaggerated view of how rim spoke holes are drilled offset.

3. Some hubs have one side of every other hole chamfered so the spoke bends gradually instead of at a sharp angle (Fig. 10-19). Insert spokes in the hub as noted in Step 7 below, so that the spoke bend follows the curve of the chamfer. If you don't, the spoke bends sharply and can break where it angles up out of the hub. Most modern hubs have a slight chamfer on both sides of all holes.

4. Poke the spoke through the rim hole to make sure it's big enough to accept the spoke, but not so big that the spoke could move around in the hole under the stress of road shock and break off. For example, some hubs are drilled for

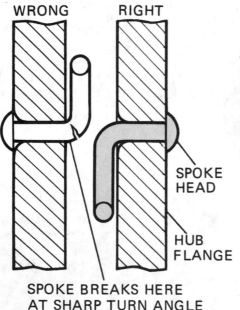

Fig. 10-19: Install spokes so they bend over the chamfered (rounded off) side of the hub spoke hole. This relieves the stress of a sharp bend, which can break off spokes. Modern hubs usually have a slight chamfer on both sides of rim spoke holes.

15-gauge spokes but are too small for 14-gauge spokes, and vice versa. If the holes are too big, exchange hubs or use a 14-gauge instead of 15-gauge spokes.

5. Note that the hubs in one flange are offset to the holes in the facing flange (Fig. 10-20).
6. Drill a half-inch hole in your workbench, or in a 12-inch square of 2-inch thick planking to hold the hub while you lace up the wheel. Remove the quick-release skewer or the axle nuts.
7. Insert a spoke down every other hole in *both* flanges, so the spoke heads face upward (as in Fig. 10-21).

Fig. 10-20: Hub spoke holes offset from the opposite side flange spoke holes. For example, spokes "A" and "D" fall midway between spoke holes "B," "C," "E," and "F" in the opposite flange.

Fig. 10-21: Step 1: Place spoke heads up in alternate hub flange spoke holes.

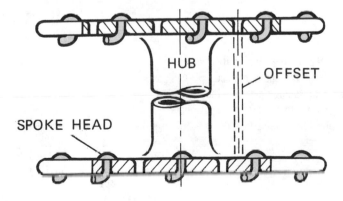

HUB

OFFSET

SPOKE HEAD

8. Sweep the spokes up, turn the hub over, and insert spokes as in Step 7. The hub should look like Fig. 10-22, so that every other spoke hole has a spoke head facing up.

9. Sweep both sets of spokes up and put the hub in the hole in your workbench or block of wood (see Step 6).

10. Lay the rim over the hub on the workbench.

11. Locate the valve hole in the rim. Look at the first hole to the *right* of the valve hole. If it's a *top* rim hole, take any spoke in the *top* flange of the hub that has its spoke head facing *up*, and insert it in this rim hole and thread on a nipple four turns. If the first hole to the *right* of the valve hole is a *bottom* hole, insert this spoke into the first hole to the *left* of the valve hole (Fig. 10-23).

12. Count off four empty rim spoke holes to the *right* (not counting the valve hole). This should be a top rim hole.

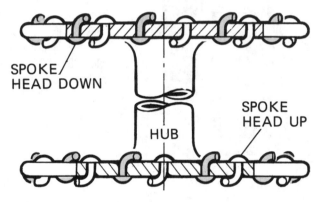

SPOKE HEAD DOWN

SPOKE HEAD UP

HUB

Fig. 10-22: Step 2: Place spoke heads down in alternate hub flange spoke holes as shown.

Fig. 10-23: Step 3. Look closely at the photo. You will see that the spoke marked "S" has its rounded head facing upward in the flange. Insert this spoke into the first rim spoke hole (T) to the right of the valve hole (V).

Take the next spoke with its spoke head facing up in the top hub flange and insert it into this fourth rim hole.

13. Insert every spoke with a face-up head in the top hub flange, into every fourth top rim hole, working to your right. You should now have nine spokes in the rim, each with a nipple threaded on four turns. There should be three empty rim holes between each spoke.

14. Hold the hub so it can't turn. Twist the rim to the right so the spokes are at an acute angle, just grazing the outside of their adjacent empty *hub* spoke holes. If a spoke crosses over the *rim valve hole*, twist the rim to the *left* instead of to the right.

15. Take any *head-down* spoke (a spoke with its head *under* the hub flange) in the top hub flange (Fig. 10-22) and, going in the *opposite* direction from the first nine spokes, cross it *over* three spokes and *under* the fourth (as in Figs. 10-13 and 10-24). For example, in Fig. 10-24, spoke "A" goes to the left and crosses *over* spokes "B," "C," "D," and *under* spoke "E." Continue this spoke lacing pattern until the wheel looks like Fig. 10-24, with one empty spoke hole between each pair of spokes and each spoke going in an alternate left-right direction, nipples threaded on four turns.

16. This is the most critical step in wheel lacing. Turn the wheel and hub over. Sweep all but one of the unlaced spokes out of the way. Refer to Fig. 10-20 and note that the

Fig. 10-24: Step 4: The wheel should now have spokes in sets of two, as shown. Spoke "A" goes to the left over spokes "B," "C," "D," and under "E." See text.

top and bottom hub flange spoke holes are offset, so that if you poke a spoke straight down in a top flange hole it stops midway between two of the bottom flange spoke holes. Now look closely at Fig. 10-25. Find spoke "A" and note that its spoke head, facing up in the top hub flange, is just to the right of spoke head "B" and is centered midway between spokes "B" and "C" in the bottom hub flange.

17. Place any head-up spoke on the top hub flange into the position shown by spoke "A" in Fig. 10-25, starting in a top rim hole. Note that this spoke goes to the right.

18. Put all the remaining head-up hub flange spokes in the rest of the top rim holes (every other empty spoke hole), working to the right. Spokes should now be in groups of three (Fig. 10-26).

19. Pull any hub top flange head-down spoke to as sharp an angle to the *left* as possible, so that it's almost touching a head-up spoke in the top hub flange, and put it in the only bottom rim hole it will reach. If it sticks out more than half an inch from the rim spoke hole, move the spoke to the next left bottom rim hole. If it won't go that far, go back one bottom rim hole to the right.

20. Continue lacing the remaining head-down spokes to the left, crossing *over* three spokes and *under the fourth spoke.* When you are finished, the spokes should be in groups of four and look like Fig. 10-27.

21. Tighten each spoke two turns at a time, then one turn at a time, then a half turn, until the spokes are about evenly tensioned and the wheel looks almost straight. It won't be, but you will correct and true up the wheel as noted earlier in this chapter, except for the rear wheel, which will need to be "dished."

Fig. 10-25: Step 5: Turn the wheel over and insert spokes from what is now the top flange, starting to the left. For example, spoke "A" starts midway between spokes "B" and "C."

Fig. 10-26: Step 5 is completed: spokes are in groups of three.

Fig. 10-27: Step 6 is completed: spokes are in groups of four. The wheel building job is finished.

How to True a Newly Built Front Wheel

It's easier to true a freshly laced front wheel because it doesn't have to be "dished" like a rear wheel. I'll explain the "dishing" process in the section below on truing a rear wheel. Follow these steps in truing a front wheel:

1. Assemble the tools shown in Fig. 10-11, with this exception: use a Minoura or home-made centering and dishing tool for 26-inch ATB wheels because the centering tool

shown here only works on 27-inch and 700C wheels. You can use your bike as a truing fixture, as described earlier in this chapter, but a wheel truing fixture is more accurate, easier, and quicker to use.

2. The hub and rim measurements that follow apply to one hub, the SunTour XC. Use these measurements as an example, but make your own on the hubs and rims you are using. Measure the space between locknuts (Fig. 10-28). In Fig. 10-29 it's 10 millimeters, or about 4 inches.

3. Measure the width of the rim. In Fig. 10-30 it's 2.3mm or ³⁄₁₆th of an inch.

4. Subtract the rim width—2.3mm—from the width between the axle locknuts—10mm—which equals 7.7mm.

5. Divide the figure obtained in step 4—7.7mm, or 3 inches —by 2, which equals 3.85mm or 1½ inches. (To convert millimeters to inches multiply by .03937.) This is the correct distance from each side of the rim to each hub axle locknut in this example (Fig. 10-29) when the rim is trued. Again, these measurements apply to one make of hub. Make your own measurements on the hub/rim combination you are using.

6. Lay the centering tool on a flat surface. Turn the measuring bolt until the bottom is 1½ inches from the flat surface (Fig. 10-31).

Fig. 10-28: Step 1: Measure distance between locknuts.

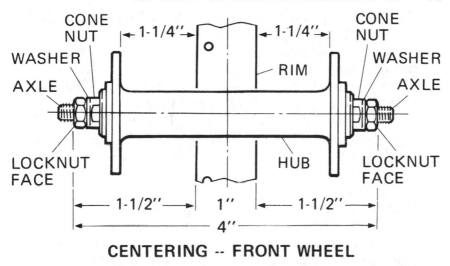

CENTERING -- FRONT WHEEL

Fig. 10-29: Step 2: Center the front rim between the hub flanges and hub locknuts.

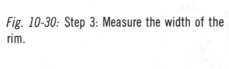

Fig. 10-30: Step 3: Measure the width of the rim.

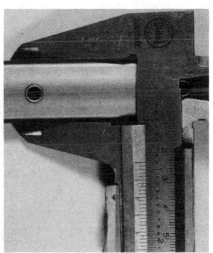

7. Lay the wheel on the workbench and put the rim centering tool on it (Fig. 10-32).

8. Study Fig. 10-8 and review the truing instructions given earlier in this chapter.

9. Adjust the group of four spokes nearest the rim valve hole and the four spokes across from the valve hole—on the opposite side of the rim—until the rim-centering tool flat ends (arrows, Fig. 10-32) touch each side of the rim. Wiggle

the centering tool to make sure both flats lay evenly on each rim. If not, adjust the spokes until they do.

10. Turn the wheel over and repeat Step 9. Mark both sides of the rim where the centering gauge shows the rim is centered. Review Fig. 10-29, which shows how the rim is centered between the hub flanges and the axle locknuts.

11. Put the wheel in the truing fixture (Fig. 10-33).

12. Adjust the side-to-side (lateral) truing fixture indicators until they touch both sides of the rim where you marked it in Step 10. This is your beginning guide to truing the newly laced wheel.

13. Finish truing the wheel as shown earlier in this chapter. Remove the wheel from the truing fixture and check side-to-side adjustment with the centering gauge a few times to make sure the rim is centered between the hub flanges and axle locknut (Fig. 10-34).

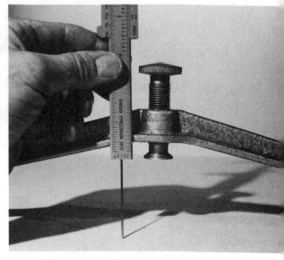

Fig. 10-31: Step 4: Subtract the Step 2 measurement from the Step 1 measurement, divide that by 2, and set the wheel-centering tool to that dimension as shown.

Fig. 10-32: Step 5: Use the wheel-centering tool to establish the setting from Step 4 as a guide in truing the wheel. See text.

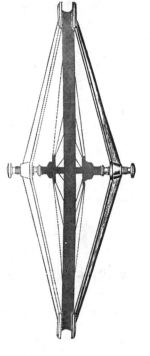

Fig. 10-33: Step 6: Put the wheel in the truing fixture and true the wheel laterally, as explained in the text.

Fig. 10-34: Use the centering tool when "dishing" a rear wheel, as explained in the text.

Truing the Rear Wheel

You trued the front wheel and centered the rim between the axle locknuts. Do the same with the rear wheel, except "dish" it so that the rim is centered between the locknuts so the chain won't rub on the spokes when running on the large rear freewheel cog. The rear wheel will automatically "dish" as you follow Steps 1 through 13 above. Dishing moves the rim closer to the right hub flange than to the left hub flange (as shown in Figs. 10-35 and 10-36), centers it between the axle locknuts, and keeps the spokes safely far from the chain.

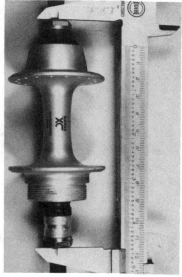

Fig. 10-35: Start truing the rear wheel by measuring the distance between locknuts.

Fig. 10-36: Center the rear rim between the axle locknuts, but *not* between the hub flanges. See text.

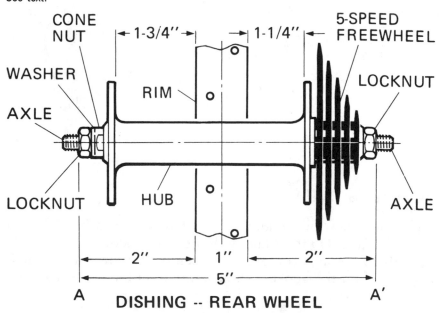

DISHING -- REAR WHEEL

HOW TO CHECK FRAME ALIGNMENT

If you must constantly balance and correct the steering on your bike as you pedal, you may have a bent frame or fork that can cause wheel shimmy and an accident. Always check your frame and fork alignment after any hard collision with a deep pothole, curb, or any other obstruction. Check the frame of a second-hand bike before you buy it.

Start with the simple checks I'll give you first, which you can make without disassembling the bike, then progress to the more involved inspections to be sure your bike frame is safely aligned.

Do not attempt to straighten or align a bent frame. It's a job that requires special tools and alignment jigs, plus experience. An improperly aligned frame is unsafe. If it can't be re-aligned accurately, remove the parts and install them on a new frame.

Use the alignment tests and checks below as a guide in deciding whether to have the bike frame cold-straightened by your bike shop, taken to a frame builder for hot straightening (and a new paint job), or scrapped. Minor frame bends can be cold-straightened, but more serious bends require careful heating before straightening and badly bent tubes or a fork may be replaced. Don't buy a used bike with frame damage—that's why it's for sale. Repairs would probably not be worth the cost.

Simple Frame Alignment Checks

Study Fig. 10-37 until you are familiar with the names of the frame tubes.

Inspect the Fork

1. Inspect the front dropouts, where the wheel axle fits into the fork. Rotate the wheel with a pencil or ruler next to the rim (Fig. 10-38). If the rim wobbles toward and then away from the ruler, the wheel is out of line. Before going any further, true the wheel as shown above. Replace the trued wheel in a fork and repeat the check in Fig. 10-38. Use the ruler to

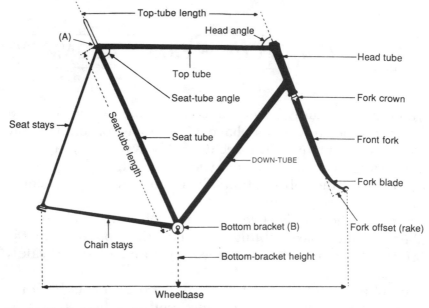

Fig. 10-37: The tubes of a bicycle frame.

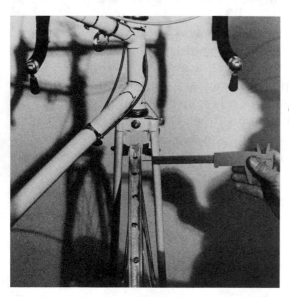

Fig. 10-38: Check wheel alignment in the front fork.

make sure the rim is centered between the fork blades. If the rim stays to one side or the other, the fork may be bent. Made additional fork alignment checks shown below.

2. Remove the front wheel. If you have trouble fitting it back, the fork blades may be bent or the dropouts misaligned.

3. Remove the front brake. Attach a plumb line to the brake mounting hole in the fork crown. Measure the distance between the plumb line and the sides of both fork blades as shown in Fig. 10-39—they should be the same. Have a minor misalignment cold-straightened by a bike shop. Replace the fork if one fork blade is closer to the plumb line than the other fork blade.

4. Insert an old axle or a quick-release unit into the fork dropouts. Place a carpenter's square under the fork crown (Fig. 10-40). The quick-release skewer or axle should be the same distance from the fork crown at all points on the axle. If not, the fork steering tube, the head tube, or a fork blade is bent.

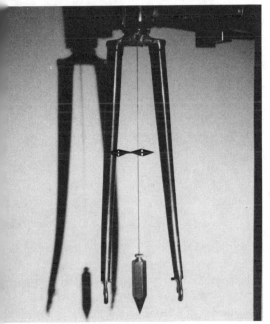

Fig. 10-39: Make this plumb line test to check for a bent fork blade.

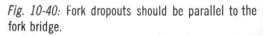

Fig. 10-40: Fork dropouts should be parallel to the fork bridge.

5. Place a straight-edge (any straight piece of bar stock will do) alongside the head tube and the front wheel rim. The straight-edge should be aligned with the wheel rim (Fig. 10-41). If not, the fork is bent, most likely at the steering tube.
6. Make this test if you've made all the above fork alignment checks and still have wheel shimmy or other steering problems that seem to come from the fork. Remove the fork (see Chapter 9) and lay it on a flat surface with the dropouts facing up (Fig. 10-42). Grasp the steering tube and wiggle the fork from side to side. The dropouts should not wiggle. Have the fork blades cold-straightened if you detect any wiggle. A very slight misalignment of the fork blades can cause a wheel shimmy and an accident.

Fig. 10-41: Use a straight-edge to check fork blades.

Fig. 10-42: Place the fork on a flat surface and move it from side to side. If it wobbles, the fork blades are bent.

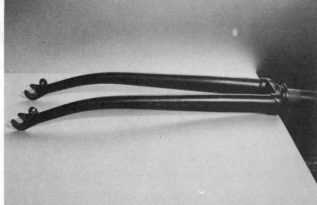

Check the Frame Tubes

1. Look for wrinkled paint where tubes join other tubes. For example, Fig. 10-43 shows a frame that sustained a hard front impact. I know because I was on it when it happened. The arrows in Fig. 10-43 point to wrinkled paint and buckled tubing where the top and downtubes join the head tube. If your bike has such damage, a custom bike builder or bike shop with frame-straightening tools may be able to straighten it.
2. Remove the rear wheel and check the dropouts for alignment. Measure them in two places (Fig. 10-44). Make sure the measurements are identical. Have them cold-straightened if they are bent.

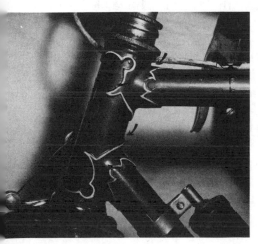

Fig. 10-43: The arrows point to places where a hard frontal impact bent the bike tubing. The wrinkled paint betrays the wrinkled tubing underneath it.

Fig. 10-44: Measure the rear dropouts in two places. If the measurements differ, the dropouts are not parallel to each other and should be straightened.

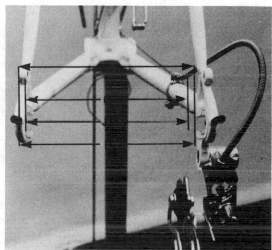

3. Replace the rear wheel. Make sure the inner face of each dropout is parallel to the hub locknuts (see the data above on wheel truing for the location of the locknuts). If either dropout is slanted away from the locknuts or if you have trouble fitting the axle into the dropouts, have the dropouts cold-straightened.

4. True the rear wheel for this dropout check. Place the rear wheel in the dropouts and adjust it so that each side of the rim is the same distance from both chainstays (Fig. 10-45) and both seatstays (Fig. 10-46). If you can't fit the wheel to the same distance from the stays, proceed to Step 5 below.

5. Check the rear wheel "dish" (see wheel truing instructions earlier in this chapter). The wheel rim should be centered between the axle locknuts. Fig. 10-47 shows a correctly "dished" rear wheel, with the spokes flatter on the right side of the wheel and the rim centered between the locknuts. If you still can't adjust the rim as above, have the dropouts cold-straightened.

6. Remove the rear brake and repeat Step 3 from the fork test above. Measure the distance from the plumb line to each dropout. If one dropout is closer to the plumb line than the other one, a dropout or a chainstay or seatstay may be bent.

7. Repeat Step 5 from the fork test above on the inside flats of each rear-wheel dropout. The dropouts should be parallel to the brake bridge. If not, have them cold-straightened.

8. Hold two straight-edges next to the rear dropout flats as shown in Fig. 10-48 and have someone measure the distance between them in two places, as shown. The measurements at "A" and "B" in Fig. 10-48 should be the same. If not, the dropouts are not parallel to each other. Have them straightened.

Fig. 10-45: Align a trued wheel in the dropouts so that the rim is the same distance from the chainstays. If you can't do it, the wheel is not accurately "dished" or the chainstays are bent.

Fig. 10-46: Align a trued wheel with the seatstays. If you can't do it, the wheel is not accurately "dished" or the seatstay is bent.

Fig. 10-47: This wheel is accurately "dished." Each side of the rim is the same distance from each locknut, yet the rim is closer to the right hub flange than it is to the left hub flange. The spokes on the right side are "flatter" than they are on the left.

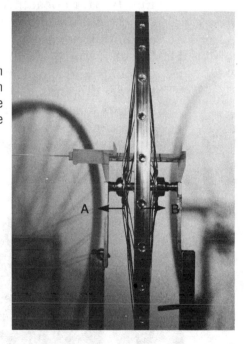

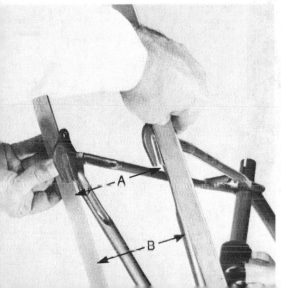

Fig. 10-48: Use two straight-edges to check alignment of the dropouts.

9. Make this check *only* if the seat tube and the downtube are the same diameter (some all-terrain bikes use tubes of different diameters). Check the alignment of the downtube and the seat tube with the bottom bracket shell. Remove a pedal and measure the distance from the crank arm to the downtube (Fig. 10-49). Move the crank arm to the downtube and repeat this measurement (Fig. 10-50). Both measurements should be the same.

10. Check alignment of the headtube with the bottom bracket shell. Place a straight-edge on the bottom bracket shell and measure the distance from it to the headtube as shown in Fig. 10-51. Repeat this check on the other side of the headtube. Cold-straighten the headtube if both measurements are not the same.

11. Check vertical alignment of the headtube with the rear dropouts and the seat tube. Tie a piece of string to one of the rear dropouts, pass the string around the headtube, and back to the other rear dropout, as shown in Fig. 10-52. Measure the distance from the seat tube to the string on both sides of the seat tube. The measurements should be identical—if they aren't, have the headtube cold-straightened.

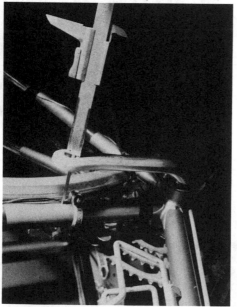

Fig. 10-49: Measure the distance from the crank to the downtube. It should be the same as the measurement in Fig. 10-50.

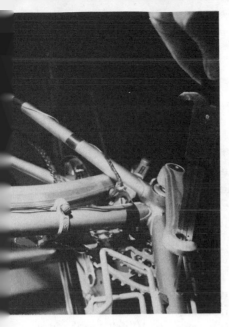

Fig. 10-50: Measure the distance of the same crank in Fig. 10-49 to the downtube. Both measurements should be the same.

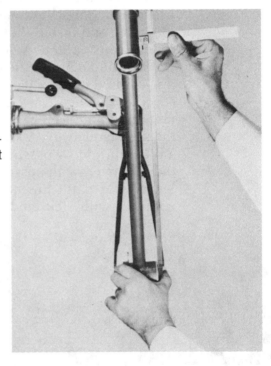

Fig. 10-51: Use a straight edge to check alignment of the headtube with the bottom bracket shell.

Fig. 10-52: Wrap string from one rear dropout around the headtube and back to the other rear dropout. Measurements on both sides or the seattube should be the same.

12. Check the headtube for twist. Tie one end of a piece of string to a rear dropout, pass it around the *bottom* of the headtube and back to the other dropout, then from around the *top* of the headtube and back to both dropouts, as shown in Fig. 10-53. Measure the distance from the seat tube to both strings on both sides of the seat tube. All four measurements should be identical. If these measurements are not the same, the headtube is twisted. Have it cold-straightened if possible. If you see wrinkled paint or metal as in Fig. 10-43, the headtube may have been shoved back into the top and downtubes. A bike shop with the right frame-straightening equipment may be able to realign the frame. If it can't be done, remove the bike parts from the old frame and install them on a new one.

13. When you tighten a loose kickstand bolt it's easy to squeeze and damage the chainstays. Remove the kickstand if it's bolted on the chainstays (Fig. 10-54) and check these stays for damage caused by over-tightening the kickstand mounting bolt. You can't do much about this except throw the kickstand away. A kickstand is an unstable way to keep a bike upright. A passing child, even the wind, can knock the bike over, with possible damage to the derailleur, brake levers, and paint finish. This is why expensive bikes are not fitted with kickstands.

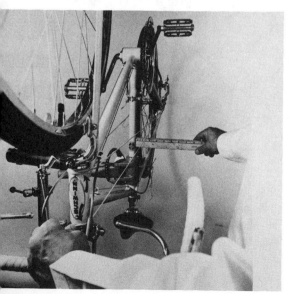

Fig. 10-53: Pass string from a rear dropout, around the *bottom* of the steering head to the other rear dropout, then back around the *top* of the headtube to the rear dropout. Measurements from both strings on both sides of the seattube should be the same.

Fig. 10-54: Remove the kickstand to check for damage to the chainstays caused by overtightening the kickstand mounting bolt.

Nicks and Scratches

Repair minor nicks and scratches with matching paint you can buy from the bike shop. Feather the edges of the area to be retouched with fine sandpaper, as shown in Fig. 10-55. Follow directions on the pressurized spray can. Make a quick circular spray in the air and then quickly spray the feathered area. Apply at least three coats, letting each coat dry before spraying the next and sanding with fine sandpaper between coats.

In the next chapter I'll take you into the bicycle racing scene, describe the various kinds of races, and tell you how to watch each type so you can enjoy the sport. If you want to race, you'll also find out how to get started.

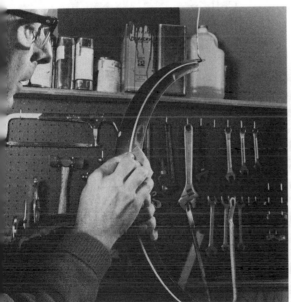

Fig. 10-55: Use sandpaper to feather nicks and gouges in the paint finish.

ELEVEN

THE RACING SCENE— INTO THE '90s

Not too long ago, all the big names in bicycle racing were European. North America had no figures to even remotely compare with racers such as Eddy Merckx or Jacques Anquetil, both five-time winners of the Tour de France, the premier event of the bicycle racing world.

It hadn't always been that way. Following the original bicycle boom of the 1890s, American racers rivaled the achievements of their European counterparts. In those days, professional American cyclists competed both at home and abroad. North American tracks were packed with enthusiastic fans. They went to see events such as the grueling six-day-long races that came to be called madisons, after the famous New York City arena where these races got their start.

America's fascination with speed and gadgetry eventually turned our attention to cars and airplanes. With the beginning of the communications age, sports fans tuned in to team events such as baseball, which could easily be broadcast over radio and TV. These media were considered ill-suited for the enjoyment of a long bicycle race. As a result, American racing went into decline. For a long time, the U.S. had no professional racers. There was always a large amateur circuit, but the amateurs just didn't match up to the European national teams. Until 1984, the United States had not won an Olympic medal in cycling for 72 years.

Now, the pendulum may be swinging back our way. Bicycle racing is on the rise in North America. The United States now boasts an international event to compare with the great European tours, called the Coors Classic. A growing league of U.S. pros are competing for prize money internationally. Some of them, such as racers Andy Hampsten and Greg LeMond, are ranked with the best racing cyclists in the world.

And they are winning big. As a case in point, consider the history of the Tour de France. This isn't a race for just anybody. Only 150 of the best cyclists in the world can participate, and only by invitation. Since the Tour was first held in 1903, no cyclist from the United States was invited to race until Jacques Boyer competed in 1981 (Fig. 11-1). Americans have been there ever since, and in 1986, Greg LeMond became the first American in history to win the Tour de France.

Fig. 11-1: For several decades, bicycle racing was the exclusive domain of European cyclists. Today, many of the ascending stars are North Americans. Up front is Jacques Boyer, the first U.S. cyclist to compete in the Tour de France.

An Uncertain Future

But U.S. bicycle racing may still have a way to go before it can really compare to the quality and popularity of its European counterpart. Part of the problem is the lack of a large spectator following for the sport here in North America. The attention of fans draws media coverage, and with that comes the all-important financial contributions of corporate sponsors. It all comes down to money, because without sponsorship a young athlete may be unable to finance his training and buy the expensive equipment it takes to compete. Many promising careers have probably foundered when the demands of getting an education and making a living interfered with the necessity of pursuing a long training program.

Fig. 11-2: Once considered a man's sport only, women have made inroads into racing, though their achievements receive much less recognition. Shown is Connie Paraskevin, three time world sprint champion. *(Dave Black)*

Things are different in many European countries. In Italy, where cycling has long been a way of life and racing is something of a national obsession, bicycle racing is well funded by proceeds from the national lottery. In the Soviet Union and other Eastern European nations, racers are paid professionals, whose education, athletic training, and salary are provided by the state. In all these countries, the best can be assured of getting the training they need to reach the top echelons of bicycle racing.

A SPORT OF STRATEGY AND WITS

American audiences may be uninterested in bicycle racing for a good reason: Most of us simply don't understand racing's subtleties. To the uninitiated, the likely winner of a race should be the cyclist who can outrun all competitors in a mad dash from start to finish. That may be true for the final 200 meters before the finish line (Fig. 11-3). But, what happens over the tens or even hundreds of kilometers before the sprint can make the outcome impossible to predict. Sprinters break from the pack in bursts of speed, only to "blow up" from overexertion and get "reeled in" by the riders behind them. Alliances between rivals and petty rivalries between teammates disrupt carefully laid strategies, making for a constant flux in race leadership. Racing demands intensive effort, it's true, but success also depends upon calculated reason, orchestrated teamwork, and chance.

The enjoyment of racing events, like winning strategy, depends upon an understanding of wind resistance. Wind resistance upon a cyclist's body increases as the square of his speed. So if a rider doubles his speed, he quadruples the wind resistance he has to fight against. Simply put, this means that the lead rider has to work harder to stay up front, while those behind him can use his slipstream to take shelter from the wind and conserve their strength. Good riders learn how to glue themselves to the rear wheels of those in the lead, coming as close as they can without touching. This is called "drafting," and it acts like a tow on the rider who follows behind.

Fig. 11-3: Sometimes the whole race comes down to those few thrilling seconds as everyone sprints for the line. At the far left, Jim Rossi, six-time U.S. sprint champion, is hammering hard to catch his opponents. He came from 12th place to finish second. *(Bicycling Magazine)*

A racer would quickly become exhausted by the effort it takes to "pull" if he tried to hold the lead for long periods of time. If you watch closely during a race you can see riders trading the lead back and forth. Together they can maintain a higher speed than either could alone, a fact that makes for odd alliances at times.

Road races begin in a massed start, with all racers taking off from the line at once. The pack, or peloton as it is called, soon sets a fast pace, with the best riders and strongest teams bunched up in front (Fig. 11-4). Somewhere along the course, one or more of the riders will attempt to "break" from the peloton. When this happens, those in a position to do so may draft off the rider who is making a break, taking a gamble that the lead rider has a good chance of creating and holding a commanding lead. The two, three, or more riders who form the

Fig. 11-4: This race began as a massed start, but the best riders have already asserted themselves at the front of the pack. Good positioning will pay off once the sprint begins.

Fig. 11-5: This is the same race, just seconds later. It's clear that only those who stay near the front have any hope of being in contention. The stragglers were dropped long ago.

breakaway could be bitter rivals, but cooperation may be their only key to success. They will have to take turns pulling each other in order to set a faster pace than the pack. In doing so, they create a gap that subsequent breaks or individuals will not be able to close.

What happens next depends largely on the support of their teams. It's common for teammates to agree before the race to split the prize if one of their members wins. They will let their rider with the best chance to win join in the attack while they attempt to keep others from catching up. The team takes up as much space as it can at the head of the pack and dawdles along, with elbows held out to stop the passage of riders around the side. Blocking is also used in a breakaway, when someone wants to slow its progress and give a hand to a teammate who is trying to catch up. In this case, a rider in second position can let a gap form between himself and the leader, who will have to slow down without someone to pull for him.

Two teammates can try to wear out a rival sprinter by repeatedly pulling away from the break. The sprinter can't afford to be left behind, especially if the end of the race is near. He'll have to jump the gap several times, thereby losing his "snap," the ability to accelerate quickly, as the end approaches. Good sprinters will have strategies of their own, and will try to draft off somebody else until the moment when they can jump for the finish line. A teammate can help with a "leadout," pulling the sprinter along at his fastest pace, which sets up the sprinter for a jump at even greater speed.

With everything that's involved, it's obvious that much of a top rider's success depends upon the strength and cooperation of his teammates (Fig. 11-6). Usually, only the most powerful teams can put a rider across the finish line in first place. At the same time, interteam rivalries between some of the best racers in the world can crop up as they eye an individual chance to win.

This was made clear by the stormy relations between Bernard Hinault and Greg LeMond, members of the La Vie Claire team during the 1986 Tour de France. Hinault, one of three cyclists who have won the Tour five times, was racing his last professional season. It was his final chance for an unprecedented sixth win. But for LeMond, 1986 was to be his year, his best hope to win the Tour himself. Little love was lost between

Fig. 11-6: Racing is one of the most fiercly competitive sports around, but success requires a little cooperation. Belgium's cycling legend Eddy Merckx gets a drink during the Tour of Italy. (UPI)

the two in the process. LeMond publicly leveled barbs at Hinault during the race, charging that the Frenchman had repeatedly joined breaks to win. In spite of the friction, La Vie Claire had a string of victories to its credit, a clear testament to the strength of this powerful racing team.

Watching Road Races

Following the action in a road race can present a bit of a challenge. Road races may cover hundreds of miles, and unless they are televised, it can be difficult to catch anything more than the finish. But, don't be daunted. You can still see plenty of racing action if you do some careful planning. Find the best spots to watch the race and learn the itinerary so you can time your arrivals and departures at a few locations along the route as the riders press on.

Criteriums

Luckily, watching some road races won't require any frenetic activity on your part. The criterium is the most common road race in North America. It's a massed start event, where riders have to complete several laps of a tortuous circuit through city streets. Frequent corners place a premium on a racer's bike handling skills (Fig. 11-7), and make this a race for thrillseekers, whether on the course or at the sidelines. Packs of riders funnel into the corners at breakneck speed and surge out together in a sprint for the next corner. It's not a spectator event for the faint at heart; be prepared to see frequent pileups as riders jostle each other through the turns.

Good criterium riders can negotiate corners at full speed. In the early laps, riders of varying talents will mix up in the pack, slowing down the pace in the turns. The better racers will begin to put some distance between themselves and the pack as the race warms up. Free of the peloton, they can lean harder and pedal farther into each turn without breaking. While other racers are just slowing down to enter the turn, the breakaway group will already be sprinting up the course. They will also

Fig. 11-7: Canadian cyclist Steve Bauer shows the kind of cornering skills it takes to be a successful criterium racer.

build speed and conserve energy by drafting off each other, a practice that's impossible in the chaos of the pack.

To watch a criterium to best advantage, try to find a place with close views of a spot promising fast action and stay there. The racers will pass by with some frequency, depending on the length of the circuit they have to complete. It will help to study the layout of the course ahead of time. Scout it out on foot or bike, and look for overpasses or balconies where you can get an overview of the course below. Get there early, because you will want to be close to the street. Criteriums usually draw boisterous, cheering crowds, adding an element of excitement that is missing from many racing events.

Time Trials

Time trials are held in two broad categories, either for a set distance, such as 40 or 100 kilometers, or for a set time, commonly one or 24 hours. The objective in racing time trials is straightforward: to set the fastest time for the field. Riders start out from the line with a few minutes' break between themselves and the next racer. Depending on the size of the field, this process can take several hours and the race may take much of the day to complete.

Sometimes called the "race of truth," the individual time trial is a lonesome test of athletic prowess. There is no other competitor besides the clock. It's a long-distance endurance race, demonstrating little in the way of strategy. The time trial racer can't use his head to better his position or play off the rivalries of others. He can't stick to somebody else's wheel to take a rest and protect his lead. It takes supreme effort and an ability to ignore the inevitable pain that make for success in the time trial.

Road Races

This is the classic form of the genre, covering a varied terrain over a course that is 100 miles or more in length. Road races can be laid out in one large loop, over several laps of a circuit, or one-way from start to finish, in which case it's called a point-to-point race. Road racing combines the tactics, athletic ability, and skill needed to win all other racing events. A road racer must not only have the superior handling skills of a criterium rider, the endurance of a time trialist, the quick jump of a sprinter, and the power of a good hill climber. Rather, the road racer has to combine all these talents and make up for any deficiencies by using his head. That's probably the main reason such a mystique surrounds the great road racing champions of the world, while many other riders who excel in their own right go largely unnoticed. The champion road racer represents the athletic ideal.

Following a Stage Race: The Tour de France

Often, point-to-point races, criteriums, and time trials are combined in a single event lasting several days, which is called a stage race. The Tour de France is unquestionably the world's most famous example, although none of its stages are criteriums, and most of the races are point-to-point. The Tour de France covers close to 2,500 miles in about 22 stages with only one full rest day thrown in. Little wonder that it is considered the supreme test of racing talent by cyclists from around the world.

When it comes to following a long stage race such as a tour, we are at a disadvantage here in North America because media coverage of bike races is not a common or consistent practice. In Europe, however, the fanatical devotion of thousands of racing fans helps make bike racing front-page news. The Tour de France is a matter of intense national pride, and it is estimated that up to 20 million people, or about one-third of France's population, get out to see part of the race every year. The Tour gets extensive newspaper, radio and television coverage every day for the three weeks it takes to complete.

With all that attention, the commotion and air of festivity that inevitably surround the Tour provide as much reason to see this race as the chance of seeing some of the world's best racers compete (Fig. 11-8). A gypsylike caravan of support vehicles, dignitaries, journalists, and hordes of fans winds its way through the French countryside, descending upon each little town in the Tour's path. The native inhabitants, who have anxiously been awaiting this economic boon for some time, greet the entourage as if the circus has just come to town. The carnival atmosphere runs especially high in the stage towns, where the race finishes each day and the riders try to catch some sleep. These will be some of the best spots to soak up the ambience. After watching the winning sprint into town, you may find a

Fig. 11-8: When the peloton passes by, the whole town is likely to come out to greet it. Here's a scene from the Tour de France. (UPI)

chance to mingle with the racers in the cafés later that night. In the morning, you can catch the excitement of the massed start that begins another day of racing.

The Tour is unbelievably long. It circles the perimeter of the country, from the Atlantic lowlands and the Normandy coast, to the high passes of the Alps and Pyrenees Mountains. It probably won't be possible to see the whole race, but even if you only see part of it you will still be visiting some of the world's most beautiful countryside.

Because of the distances you will have to cover, you should give a lot of thought to how you will travel. Traveling by bike is an obvious choice, because it will get you closest to the action. The race's route tends to be closed off to automobile traffic for several hours before the peloton even makes its appearance. During this time, automobile traffic jams up on either side of the route, while the numerous fans riding bikes are given free access.

The big problem with traveling by bike alone is again the great distance involved. Unless you are a marathon rider yourself, you probably won't have the stamina to finish the average 125 miles that the race covers each day. Happily, the French train system provides extensive service, is inexpensive by U.S. standards, and is accommodating to passengers with bikes. The drawback is that the train will not provide access to many areas that the Tour visits, and some of these may be the least visited and most charming regions of the French countryside. One solution is to rent a car when necessary, and to ride your bike and the train when feasible. If renting a car is too expensive, you can recruit a few companions to split the cost; in the end, it may come more into line with the price of public transportation.

You should study the route thoroughly and decide on good locations to watch the race. Several of the French cycling magazines, and the national sports paper, *L'Equipe*, publish route maps giving detailed information on the race's schedule. From these you can learn what times the peloton is expected to pass certain locations along the way. Next, identify places where you can expect some good racing action. Besides the starts and finishes in the stage towns, there will be other key sites to watch for.

To know where these hot spots are, it helps to know how a stage race is scored. The winner is determined by comparing every rider's cumulative time for the whole series of stages. A race leader is recognized daily as the rider holding the lowest overall time at the end of each stage. In the Tour de France, this rider is awarded a yellow jersey, which he wears until his position is overtaken by another racer. Another element of competition is introduced by awarding bonuses, called *primes* (pronounced "preems"), to riders who win sprints at designated locations along the route. A rider may try for the green points jersey, which is awarded to the one who collects the most primes at these locations. Or, if a strong climber, a rider may attempt to capture the red-spotted mountain jersey by accumulating points at designated areas on the mountain passes.

By studying the route guide carefully, you can find the spots where primes will be awarded. Capturing primes is a focus of fierce competition between the front-runners, so you can expect some exciting sprints at these locations. Mountain passes in general are some of the best spots for viewing the race, because the peloton spreads out as the climb gets tougher, and you can see more than just a flash of the riders as they go by. The long hills give a commanding view of the race, and there is an air of intense excitement as the fans urge the tiring racers on (Fig. 11-9). The sight of unparalleled mountain scenery may alone be worth the trip. For these, as for all other good viewing locations, you must find your spot and stake your claim to it very early. The French take their cycling very seriously; the crush will be tremendous, but well worth it.

Fig. 11-9: When the going gets tough—the fans drive their cars. In a long stage race like the Tour de France, the winner is often decided on the steep mountain passes of the Alps and Pyrenees. (UPI)

How to Watch Track Events

Track racing generally doesn't bring into play the same range of tactics that can make road racing so unpredictable. But, the track still holds mass appeal, since spectators can watch the whole event in one place. Enjoying the track events will take a sharper eye, but once you catch on to the intricacies, you will find the action just as intense as anything the road race can offer.

If you are lucky enough to live near a velodrome (see list on p. 491), you can catch a number of track races every spring and summer. Local tracks will host a variety of events and classes of riders. Races during international events, such as the World Cycling Championships or the Olympic Games, usually get fair to good television coverage. Here's a sample of the track races you can see at these events.

The Sprint

This is something of the aristocrat of cycle racing, requiring tactics more akin to chess than to flat-out athletic performance. In the sprint, two riders (sometimes three at local events) try to beat the other to the end of 1,000 meters, or three laps of a 333-meter track. What makes this race interesting is that the rider's times are recorded only for the final 200 meters of the race.

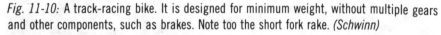

Fig. 11-10: A track-racing bike. It is designed for minimum weight, without multiple gears and other components, such as brakes. Note too the short fork rake. *(Schwinn)*

"What's the sense in that?" you're saying. "Why not just give the riders a rolling start and time them in a 200-meter dash?" You hear the starting gun, and something even weirder happens. These people aren't racing, they are standing on their pedals, trying to hold their bikes still! And why are they staring at each other, as if waiting for something to happen? (Fig. 11-11)

The answer, once again, lies in the principle of wind resistance. Should either rider jump from the starting line at the sound of the gun, he immediately places himself at a disadvantage. The other racer can simply fall into the slipstream behind the leader and get a free ride for most of the race. In the last 200 meters he will jump into a sprint, easily defeating the exhausted front-runner.

A very explosive starter may have an advantage in the sprint if he can immediately establish a lead that can't be closed. Then the other rider can't draft his way around the course. But this requires great endurance on the part of the leader, and good sprinters aren't necessarily strong on endurance. He's also

Fig. 11-11: Two sprinters eye each other warily, each waiting for the other to make the first move. In a short, fast race like the sprint, neither rider wants to start out in the lead, since this would benefit his opponent by breaking the wind for him.

unlikely to get a good time this way, since he's bound to be tired once he reaches the final 200 meters. It's more likely that the two riders will be equally matched, and will try to outwit each other into making a jump, whether by "trackstanding," as described above, or by "soft-pedaling" around the track for a while, until one rider makes his move and the real race begins. Current world record times for the 200-meter sprint are hovering near 45 mph.

The Pursuit

In this event, two riders or two four-person teams start on opposite sides of the track. For 4,000 meters they "pursue" each other around the track, but unless someone dumps their bike, it's not likely that anybody will ever be caught. The real object is to set the best time, and speeds are high from the very start. There's little in the way of tactics or finesse here: it's all-out effort and athletic ability that make the difference (Fig. 11-12). World-record times for the individual pursuit top 30 mph, while the team event is a bit faster, since riders can take advantage of drafting to increase their speed.

Fig. 11-12: The powerful physique of Mark Gorski, an Olympic gold medalist in the sprint, dwarfs a specially designed pursuit bike. Skinsuits, bullet shaped helmets, and radically redesigned bikes have become common as technology is put to the task of shaving seconds from the records. *(Dave Black)*

Time Trials

These races are also a common sight at track events. A typical individual time trial is a 1,000-meter race known as the "Kilo." World-class times for the Kilo are around 1 minute, or a little better than 35 mph. A particularly grueling race is the one-hour time trial, where a cyclist races for one hour in an attempt to cover the most ground he can. In 1984, Francesco Moser of Italy set a world record time of 51.151 kilometers in Mexico City, maintaining an incredible average speed of 32 mph for one hour.

Another brutal test of high-speed endurance is the team time trial. This race is 100 kilometers long, with world-class times approaching 120 minutes. That's an average speed of a little over 30 mph—for two full hours! Racers are able to keep this pace up for so long only through intense concentration and perfectly orchestrated movements. Each rider in a four-person team takes turns pulling for about 30 to at most 45 seconds. He barely assumes lead position before "pulling off" to the side, letting his teammates pass by only inches away. Then he falls back to the end of the line to take a rest (Fig. 11-13). In another

Fig. 11-13: Steve Hegg glues himself to Eric Heiden's rear wheel in this shot of the U.S. men's time trial team. The rider on the left has just "pulled off" the front, allowing Heiden to take the lead. Notice the innovative features of their bikes, including disk wheels, flattened tubing, smaller front wheel, and redesigned frame geometry, all to create the most efficient riding position and aerodynamics possible. *(Dave Black)*

minute and a half he has to be ready to do it again. The movements must be performed flawlessly, since any disruption in the concentration of the group will mean a loss in efficiency and time.

Points Race

This is one of the few massed-start races held on a track. The constant action, the continuous buzz of 30 riders flying around the track in a group, and the potential for crashes make this a more exciting event than other track races. But it's a difficult race to follow because the winner isn't necessarily the first rider to cross the line. Instead, points are earned by placing in a few lead positions each time the pack completes a specified number of laps. The winner is the rider who chalks up the most points by the end. As a rider, keeping track of that tally is a difficult task. For a spectator it's impossible. But, the frequent sprints are sure to bring you to your feet, time after time. You'll just have to enjoy the action, and wait for the end to find out who won.

Other Track Events

These include a massed-start event called the *scratch race*. It follows the same procedure as the points race, without the award of primes. So, the scratch is a simple race to the finish over a course from three to ten miles in length. If the "chase rule" is applied, the competition will intensify. This rule requires all riders leading the pack to take up the chase on a break, or else face being disqualified.

Another massed-start race is the *miss-and-out*, sometimes known as devil-take-the-hindmost. This is an elimination event, where the last rider over the line at the end of each lap, or with the completion of several laps, is dropped from the race. The race continues either to the last rider, or to a sprint between a designated number of survivors.

A remnant of the 19th-century six-day race survives in the *madison*. "Six-day race" is still a common name for this event, but it has been scaled down considerably from the time when racers really did ride continuously for six days without relief, trying to cover the longest distance for the field. These days, the six-day involves teams of two to three riders who relieve each other after every few laps. The relief rider is pushed onto the track from a standing start, and is then shot into the thick of the race by a grasp of the hand and a swing of his teammate's arm. Madisons are run for a set time, rarely longer than a few hours, or for a set distance, usually about ten miles. The madison is a popular race on the European continent, where, owing to its place of origin, it's sometimes called *l'Americaine.*

Racing for the Adventurous

All the races described above form the core of the classic European racing circuit. Purists would argue that membership in the club comes to an end right there. Nonetheless, some superendurance races are finding favor with a new breed of racers, and aficionados swear that these races are the ultimate tests of physical and mental stamina. The purists countercharge that the speed, finesse, and intellectual challenge of road racing are absent in marathon events. They say that this is no sport at all, but rather a plodding, long-distance exercise in self-punishment. Let's take a look at two of these ultra-endurance races: the bicycle marathon, and an even more brutal spinoff, the triathalon.

The Marathon

This race might be thought of as a very long time trial. It's hard to say where road races end and marathons begin, but the 24-hour time trial, a race with record times over 500 miles, is probably as good a place as any to make the distinction. In races lasting more than a full day, the racer's individual talent and his exercise of tactics in the pack bear less and less relationship to the outcome. The longer it goes on, the more a marathon race becomes a measure of raw courage and pure endurance.

Marathon racing can ravage a racer's body and psyche. Perhaps no race illustrates this better than an ultramarathon event called the Race Across America, or RAAM. The RAAM covers over 3,000 miles from Pacific to Atlantic coasts. The average finisher makes the crossing with about two hours of sleep per night, and consumes 8,000 or more calories every day. But many of the starters never even see the Atlantic shoreline. Lack of sleep and physical exhaustion result in a dropout rate of around 40 percent.

For those who do complete it, the RAAM can be a harrowing, even dangerous experience. Many competitors report having vivid hallucinations and late-night conversations with imagined companions, common symptoms of long-term sleep deprivation. Inexplicable accidents have also occurred. Shelby Hayden-Clifton was just 130 miles from the finish line in 1986 when she rode over an embankment and fractured two neck vertebrae. She had just slept for two hours, and reportedly had no idea why she crashed. "It just happened," she said, indicating that she may have had a blackout. Luckily, she fully recovered and is riding again. A Canadian cyclist named Wayne Philips was not so fortunate in the 1985 RAAM. He was paralyzed by a hit-and-run driver near Tucumcari, New Mexico, an accident made doubly tragic by his decision to race without a support vehicle. Philips wanted to show that a rider could finish the race unassisted.

It's now mandatory that all riders be accompanied by a support vehicle in the RAAM. Racers have also adopted high-tech solutions in the quest for faster times. One of the biggest problems with marathon riding is that it fully depletes the body's glycogen, a source of stored energy, forcing it to use fats for fuel. Burning fat is less efficient, and eventually leads to fatigue and a crawling pace. Many RAAM contestants now use liquid food that is high in carbohydrates, in order to replenish blood sugar and ensure continued muscle activity. They have also used the findings of sleep research to determine which is the most beneficial time to sleep each night. Judging by the shrinking record times, the effort is getting results (Fig. 11-14). But, the price of it all is getting a little high. It's estimated that the average contestant in the '85 RAAM spent at least $15,000 dollars in an attempt to split a $20,000 purse.

Triathlons

This is surely one of the most intense athletic events of modern times, bordering on gladiatorial. Those who can summon the reserves to make it to the finish line are as likely to collapse from exhaustion as raise their hands for the victory salute. Those who are champions definitely operate on a different level.

To be fair, you wouldn't have to kill yourself to finish a triathlon. Featuring swims of ½ to one mile, bike races averaging 25

Fig. 11-14: Pete Penseyres may look asleep here, but he actually maintained an average speed of 15.4 mph during the 3,107-mile-long Race Across America in 1985. Penseyres set a record time of 8 days, 9 hours, and 47 minutes for the coast-to-coast marathon. Note the special armrest, which helped to relieve shoulder and neck strain. *(Raleigh)*

miles, and final runs between 5 to 15 miles, most local triathlons are fairly accessible to the average person of good to excellent fitness. But then there are the real gonzo events, such as the Ironman triathlon held in Hawaii every year. The Ironman includes a 2.4-mile ocean swim and a 112-mile bike race, capped off by a 26.2-mile run. All of this happens in 90-degree tropical heat, much of it on a highway that winds through blistering-hot fields of volcanic rock. The champs can do it in nine to ten hours. In case that's not enough for you, there's always the Ultraman. This is a two-day event that starts with a six-mile swim and a 100-mile ride on the first day, and finishes with another 168-mile ride and a 52.4-mile run on the second—definitely not a race for the average fitness buff!

HUMAN-POWERED VEHICLES AND THE CONTINUING QUEST FOR SPEED

Radical change hasn't exactly been a watchword in bicycle design. Few truly dramatic changes have been attempted since the safety bike with pneumatic tires first hit the racks nearly a century ago. Developments in technology, and new, lightweight materials have certainly altered the way the traditional bicycle performs and handles. We can go farther, faster, in greater comfort than ever before. Modifications in design and componentry have also made off-road travel by bike possible. Yet, it looks like the upright diamond-shaped frame with spoked wheels and a chain-driven gear system will be the design of choice for some time to come.

Such longevity and versatility certainly attest to what a simple and sensible machine this really is. But, for everything you can do with a bike, there are still a lot of things you can't do with it, or can't do easily, anyway. Try taking your wash to the Laundromat, or going 60 on the freeway sometime. There are indications, however, that breakthroughs may be on the way. Consider, for example, the following stories of human-powered speed.

On July 20, 1985, John Howard set a new motorpaced speed record of 152.284 mph. Howard is a well-known U.S. amateur cycling champion, as well as a Race Across America veteran and Ironman triathalon winner. He set this pace riding in the slipstream of a race car on the table-smooth surface of the Bonneville Salt Flats. His bike was a $10,000 motorcylelike machine with fat tires and a single 390-inch gear (the average touring bike has around a 100-inch high gear) driven by three sprockets and two chains. Traveling forward 111 feet with each turn of the crank, the bike had to be towed to 60 mph before Howard reached a pedal cadence fast enough to keep it moving. To most people, even 60 mph on a bike would seem a little suicidal. But, Howard was eager for another try after his rear tire suddenly deflated and the bike began to fishtail at 150 mph!

So, you say, how practical is a bike that goes 150 mph, especially when it needs a race car to get it started? Not too practical, I'll admit. But some people are working on alternatives that are more down to earth. In May 1986, a specially designed bike called the Easy Racer reached an incredible speed of 65.484 mph. Its designers collected a $15,000 prize for being the first to surpass the 65 mph mark in a human-powered machine unassisted by a pace vehicle.

The Easy Racer could be the shape of things to come in human-powered transportation. It still rides on two wheels, but the configuration of the traditional bike has disappeared. The rider sits in a semi-prone position, something like sitting in an easy chair. The semi-prone position is more aerodynamically efficient because it reduces the frontal area of the bike. The Easy Racer is also encased with a complete fairing of a synthetic material called Kevlar to reduce drag. Better aerodynamics and a more comfortable seating posture allow a rider to go farther with less energy expenditure and less physical discomfort.

The success of the Easy Racer team represents over a decade of work to set new land speed records for bicycles. This process was given a great boost forward when the International Human Powered Vehicle Association (IHPVA) was formed in 1974. The IHPVA was originally created to provide official recognition for speed records then being set on altered and redesigned bicycles. Many people felt at the time of the IHPVA's founding that the current governing bodies had stifled development through excessive restrictions on design. Presently, the IHPVA holds annual races in order to test and stimulate further developments in human-powered transport.

Early record setters were usually standard racing bikes enclosed inside lightweight fairings. This design took advantage of the more powerful pedal stroke which is possible in the upright posture. However, because of their height and large frontal area, these vehicles were disadvantaged aerodynamically. IHPVA rules stated only that vehicles entered in competition could have no energy source besides that provided by the riders. A very creative process of design and product refinement followed the association's founding.

IHPVA meets tend to be colorful events. The race is unique because it's a design competition as much as an athletic competition. Vehicles of all descriptions, from bikes with fairings to three-person tricycles and quadricycles, compete together. Many vehicles use a prone or recumbent riding position. The Vector (Fig. 11-15), a quadricycle entered in the 1979 competition, used three riders in prone positions who all pedaled with their feet. But, while the front rider steered with his hands, the others turned handgrips attached to the pedals immediately in front of them. It's estimated that this produced 12.5 percent more power than that of cranks turned by foot pedals alone.

Will these innovators develop the human-powered commuter machine of the future (Fig. 11-16)? It's possible, but many problems still have to be worked out. Some form of recumbent bicycle is likely to emerge as the most viable option.

Fig. 11-15: The Vector, a three-person quadricycle, took advantage of hand as well as foot power to record a time of 57.07 mph at the 6th annual IHPVA competition in 1979. This race saw the first successful attempt of a human-powered vehicle to break the 55 mph barrier.

Fig. 11-16. Will this be the shape of commuter transport in the future? Though a design such as this holds promise as a clean and efficient form of transportation, there are still a few bugs to be worked out before most people will be willing to give up their cars for one.

A two-wheeled vehicle is more stable when cornering than either the tricycle or the quadricycle. The semi-prone position is most comfortable, and makes the rider more visible in traffic than a prone-position vehicle. A lightweight fairing is likely too, since reduced drag can increase speed by several miles per hour. The fairing will also protect the rider from the weather and allow cargo to be carried inside, two matters of some importance to the average commuter.

However, use of a fairing has several drawbacks. Side winds can knock the bike on its side. The cyclist also needs assistance to get seated inside. Both problems could be solved by using small outrigger wheels that are dropped or pulled in when necessary. A bigger problem is the vehicle's poor performance in climbing hills. The upright position is still the best for hill climbing, because the rider can apply body weight to the pedals for added power. This and other problems are sure to consume a lot of time and human energy before they can be solved.

Flying Into the Future

In the meantime, another competition is underway in the realm of human-powered aviation. Many will remember Bryan Allen's crossing of the English Channel in the human-powered plane called the *Gossamer Albatross* (Fig. 11-17). That flight not only made aviation history, it also brought the $200,000 Kremer prize for human-powered flight to its designer, Paul MacCready. MacCready and Allen's feat was compared to that of other aviation pioneers, and the *Gossamer Albatross* appropriately took its place beside the *Kitty Hawk* in the Smithsonian Institution.

Fig. 11-17: Bryan Allen pedals into aviation history as he skims above the English Channel in the Gossamer Albatross. It took Allen 2 hours and 49 minutes to become the first person to fly a human-powered plane across the 22-mile stretch of open ocean. (UPI)

But MacCready didn't put his prodigious talent to rest with the *Gossamer Albatross*. He went on to develop several more planes, among them the Bionic Bat, which uses human power along with energy from pedaling that is stored in a battery. The Bionic Bat won another Kremer prize, and MacCready went on to become president of the IHPVA. Later, the *Gossamer Albatross*'s distance record was beaten by a plane called the *Eagle*. The *Eagle*'s MIT designers say it's a forerunner of another human-powered plane named *Daedalus*, after the father of Icarus, whose ill-fated flight is one of the most famous stories in Greek mythology. At the time of this writing, the designers of *Daedalus* are hoping to fly their plane 69 miles from the Greek mainland to the island of Crete.

Whether any of these developments will leave a mark on the future of transportation, or whether inventions like the Bionic Bat and the Easy Racer bike will become the curiosity pieces of some future age, may depend upon our determination to carry the process forward. Reserves of fossil fuels are limited, and, as the growing problem of acid rain shows, we may be forced to reconsider our practice of burning oil and coal long before we can even use these materials up. At least for traveling short distances, we already have the means to create clean, efficient, and healthy forms of human-powered transportation. What's needed now is a vigorous application of human ingenuity.

A WORD TO WOULD-BE RACERS

On the surface, bicycle racing looks like a fairly glamorous activity. Certainly it's a beautiful sport, but also one of the most physically demanding. If by chance my description of bicycle racing has stirred your interest to participate directly, I want to give you one piece of advice. Please don't think that what I have to say here is everything you should know to get started. It's only my intent to stimulate interest in racing for spectators and budding athletes, if I can. For those who seriously want to start racing, I recommend the following books:

Borysewicz, Edward, *Bicycle Road Racing*. Velo-news, Brattleboro, Vt., 1985.

Burke, Edmund, *The Two-Wheeled Athlete*. Velo-news, Brattleboro, Vt., 1985.
Matheny, Fred, *Beginning Bicycle Racing*. Velo-news, Brattleboro, Vt., 1980.

These books provide a complete source of information on racing tactics, training strategies, equipment, diet, and physiology—everything you need to know to pursue this exciting sport—written by the racers and exercise physiologists themselves. If you can only afford to buy one, make it the book by Edward Borysewicz. He's a former coach of the U.S. Olympic cycling team, and perhaps the individual most responsible for the resurgence of world-class cycling in this country. All three are available from *Velo-news*, Box 1257, Brattleboro, VT 05301.

GLOSSARY OF RACING TERMS

Attack—An aggressive acceleration taken to open a lead on other riders.

Blocking—Attempting to slow the progress of the pack in order to assist a breakaway group to create and secure a lead.

Blow up—To be unable to maintain a fast pace due to overexertion.

Break, Breakaway—A rider or group of riders who sprint away from the pack.

Bridge, Bridge a Gap—An attempt to catch up with a breakaway.

Chaser—A rider who tries to bridge a gap.

Drafting—Taking advantage of the slipstream created by another cyclist by riding close to his rear wheel. Also called wheelsucking, sitting-in, and riding in tow.

Field Sprint—A mass sprint toward the finish line by the front of the pack.

Jam—A period of hard pedaling. Also called hammering.

Jump—To accelerate rapidly, as in a sprint.

Leadout—A tactic where one cyclist rides at his fastest pace to help a teammate in tow. The second rider then jumps around the first at an even faster pace to sprint toward the finish line.

Mass Start—A race which begins with all riders leaving the starting line in a group.

Motorpace—A training method where a rider follows a motorcycle or other vehicle which breaks the wind. Also a race where riders are motorpaced.

Peloton—The main group of riders in a race. Also called the bunch, group, and pack.

Prime—A bonus awarded to the first rider to reach a specified point on the course or to the leader at a specified lap during a race.

Pull—To ride at the front of the group.

Pull Off—To leave the front of a group so the next rider in line can take the lead.

Reel In—Action where the peloton overtakes a breakaway attempt.

Snap—The ability to accelerate quickly.

Soft-Pedal—To pedal without applying power.

Trackstanding—A tactic used during sprint races to foil an opponent's attempt to sit-in. Cyclists try to hold their bikes in place until one or both riders break into a sprint. Sometimes called jockeying.

Velodrome—A banked track where bicycle races are held.

VELODROMES IN THE UNITED STATES

The list of U.S. velodromes is still relatively small, but if you live near one of the tracks listed below I encourage you to see what they have to offer. Some of these tracks may be inactive at times. For more information, and to find exact locations, ask around at bike shops or check through local bike clubs.

West

Alpenrose Velodrome, Alpenrose Dairy, Portland, Oregon
Balboa Park Velodrome, Morley Field, San Diego, California
Encino Velodrome, Encino, California
Marymoor County Park Velodrome, Redmond, Washington

Penrose Velodrome, St. Louis, Missouri
Santa Clara County Velodrome, San Jose, California
7-Eleven Olympic Training Center Velodrome, Colorado Springs, Colorado
7-Eleven Olympic Velodrome, California State University, Carson, California

Midwest

Brown Deer Velodrome, Milwaukee, Wisconsin
Dorais Velodrome, Detroit, Michigan
Ed Rudolph–Meadowhill Park Velodrome, Northbrook, Illinois
Madison Velodrome, Harper Woods, Michigan (portable track)
Major Taylor Velodrome, Indianapolis, Indiana
Shakopee Velodrome, Shakopee, Minnesota
Washington Park Velodrome, Kenosha, Wisconsin

Northeast

Lehigh County Velodrome, Trexlertown, Pennsylvania
Kissena Velodrome, Kissena, New York

South

Baton Rouge Velodrome, Baton Rouge, Louisiana
Dick Lane Velodrome, East Point, Georgia

TWELVE

A SHORT HISTORY OF BICYCLING, THE FAD THAT LASTED

Back in 1867 there were only two ways to get around town or the local area: by foot or by horse. Mobile freedom arrived when factory-made bikes in quantity hit the U.S. market around 1867. Heavy, cumbersome, and expensive (Fig. 12-1), they were nevertheless enthusiastically received by Americans. Young people could finally escape from their elders while courting, to the dismay of the clergy, and women as well as men could get around on their own. Millions discovered the joys of this convenient, economical mode of transportation that so quickly took them on pleasant country lanes, did not need to be stabled or fed, and did not require a costly saddle or the attentions of a veterinary surgeon.

Bicycling became an instant fad, an infatuation, virtually a way of life for Americans. By 1885 many factories were working around the clock to fulfill the demand for bicycles. At that time the average price of a bicycle was about $50, the same as the price of a good horse. Bikes were in such demand that the public bought two million of them—one for every 27 people in the United States in 1895—even though the $50-to-$150 price tag was a hefty 12 to 33 percent of the then per capita $420 annual income. In 1902 Henry Ford caused a major depression

Fig. 12-1: This highwheeler, also called an "Ordinary" or "Penny Farthing" has the small wheel in the front to reduce the possibility of an over-the-handlbars "endo" so frequent with these bikes when the big wheel was up front (see Fig. 12-8).

in the bike industry as Americans forsook the two-wheeler for his four-wheel Tin Lizzy. But by 1960 bicycles were again popular as a fun way to good health. In 1974 Americans bought more bikes than cars—11 million bikes versus 9 million new cars. In 1987 they bought an estimated 14 million bicycles as opposed to an estimated 10 million new cars.

Lifestyles, even clothing styles, changed drastically to accommodate this new medium of transportation. By 1895 women were wearing bloomers (Fig. 12-2) and men were wearing knickers and other clothing specially tailored for bicycling. The bicycle also made its mark on social and official activities. By the late 1800s social clubs involved cycling (Fig. 12-3), the military mounted soldiers on bicycles (Fig. 12-4), and police-

Fig. 12-2: Women's clothing styles changed drastically when the bicycle became popular. This young woman is wearing baggy knickers to ride her safety bicycle. (Bettman Archives)

Fig. 12-3: Social clubs were often based on an interest in cycling. Here members of New York's Michaux Cycle Club enjoy the pleasures of indoor cycling in a ballroom atmosphere. *(Bettman Archives)*

Fig. 12-4: These French soldiers of the 1890s carried extra lightweight folding bicycles on maneuvers. Note the rifle strapped to the fork.

men and postmen (Fig. 12-5) routinely made their rounds on two-wheelers. By 1890, men were racing high-wheelers at velodromes (Fig. 12-6), riding them on trails and canal towpaths to the terror of horses and the hostility of bargemen (Fig. 12-7), touring the countryside and occasionally doing an "endo" over the handlebars of their high-wheeler (Fig. 12-8), while women were riding around the country on odd-looking contraptions such as the tricycle in Fig. 12-9. In 1896, Margaret Valentine Le Long rode her bicycle from Chicago to San Francisco, a remarkable feat, considering the primitive roads, two major mountain ranges, and the desert she had to cross between them.

Fig. 12-5: This French postmark commemorates the days when postmen made their daily rounds on a bicycle.

Fig. 12-6: Bicycle races, even on high-wheelers, were as popular in the 1890s as they are today. *(Bettman Archives)*

Fig. 12-7: The sight of a bicycle scared horses and mules. Here mules pulling a barge on the Erie Canal bolt as a cyclist rides by, arousing the ire of the bargemen.

Fig. 12-8: Highwheel bicycles were unstable machines that could propel the rider forward over the handlebars if it hit even a small obstruction.

Fig. 12-9: This woman is sitting inside an Oldreive's tricycle or "iron horse." *(Bettman Archives)*

By the 1890s there were over 400 bicycle manufacturers in the U.S. People spent so much money on new bicycles they had little left to spend on other things, to the consternation of businessmen. For example, in 1896 sales of watches and jewelry had dropped precipitously because the bicycle was a more fashionable status symbol. Piano sales were off as people rode "piano" on their bicycles instead of playing one. A hit tune of the era went this way: "Daisy, Daisy, give me your answer true, for you'd look sweet, upon the seat, of a bicycle built for two." Attendance fell off at theatrical performances, because, I like to think, people were too tired by curtain time from having played around on their bicycles all day.

In 1896, bicycles were big business. To quote from the February 1896 issue of *Outing,* a magazine devoted to the leisure-time interests of the wealthy:

"The cycle trade is now one of the chief industries of the world. Its ramifications are beyond ordinary comprehension. Its prosperity contributes in no small degree to that of the steel, wire, rubber, and leather markets. Time was when the spider web monsters, now nearly extinct, were built in one story annexes to English and American machine shops; now a single patented type of a jointless wood rim, one of the minor parts of a modern bicycle, is the sole product of an English factory covering over two acres of ground. A decade ago the American steel tube industry was unprofitable. The production of this most essential part of cycle construction has, during the past two years, been unequal to the demand, and even now every high-grade tube mill in this country is working night and day on orders that will keep them busy throughout the year.... Prices will be very generally maintained, and the number of riders, of both sexes, will be at least doubled."

However, because metallurgy was not as advanced as it is today, the specifications of the bicycles built during the 1890s called for quite low gearing compared to modern bicycles. To get up to racing speed riders had to wind up to extremely high crank revolutions per minute. A. A. Zimmerman, a famous bike racer of the 1890s, could sustain a cadence of 140 crank rpm's.

Development of the Bicycle

The earliest known depiction of a two-wheeler is in a stained-glass window of a church built in 1637, in Stokes-on-Poges, England (Fig. 12-10). It's hard to believe that this kick-along bike was just a creation from the fertile mind of the artist.

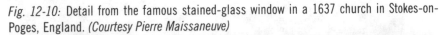

Fig. 12-10: Detail from the famous stained-glass window in a 1637 church in Stokes-on-Poges, England. *(Courtesy Pierre Maissaneuve)*

The first two-wheeler was invented by a Frenchman in 1791. Called a "celerifere" (meaning fast feet), it looked something like the clumsy machine in Fig. 12-11, which I found in the Technical Museum of Milan, Italy.

Baron Karl von Drais of Karslruhe, Germany, made many improvements on the celerifere in 1817, including a better saddle and a steerable front wheel (Fig. 12-12). Called a "Draisene" after its inventor, the rider straddled the saddle, kicked along with his feet like riding a kiddie-car and turned the cumbersome front wheel by leaning in the desired direction.

Fig. 12-11: One of the first bicycles, built around 1791; on exhibit in the Technical Museum in Milan, Italy.

Fig. 12-12: This is the original Draisene push bicycle built by Baron Karl von Dreis in 1817, on exhibit in the Breslau, West Germany, museum.

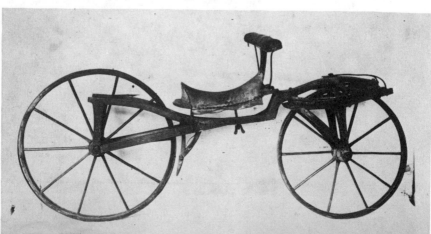

Costly, heavy, and clumsy as it was, the Draisene was taken up by the wealthy (and healthy) of that day. Within a few years, the playboys of Western Europe were kicking their way up and down the boulevards of major cities on what, eventually, came to be known as a "hobby horse." Owners formed clubs, held races, and organized local tours which had to be short, given the hundred-plus pounds of the bicycle.

By 1855, pedals were added to the front wheel of the hobby horse (Figs. 12-13, 14, 15, and 16). Equipped with pedals, the Draisene machine could go even faster than before, without any improvement in shock absorbance, which is why it was so aptly named the "Boneshaker." There were even little cast-iron Boneshakers for children, known today as tricycles (Fig. 12-17).

Fig. 12-13: This "Boneshaker" bicycle with a steel frame, iron tires, and wooden wheels was popular in the 1860s. it was the first bicycle to have pedals.

Fig. 12-14: Another Boneshaker on exhibit at the Technical Museum in Milan, Italy.

Fig. 12-15: This Boneshaker, also in the Milan museum, has a more comfortable saddle and a longer wheelbase than the model in Fig. 12-14.

Fig. 12-16: A detail from the Boneshaker in Fig. 12-13, showing the pedal arrangement on the front wheel.

Fig. 12-17: A child's tricycle of the late 1890s.

A more sophisticated version of the Boneshaker, with an arched spring back that looked vaguely like a modern bike except for the front-wheel pedals, appeared in 1868. Because it was more comfortable than its predecessor it became quite popular in this country.

In 1872, bicycle development took a step backward with the introduction of the highwheeler. You'd think bicycle designers, having built a velocipede frame in 1868 that was similar to that of a modern bike (Fig. 12-18), would now put a simple belt or chain drive on the back wheel. But it didn't happen. Instead, the pedals stayed on the front wheel. To make the bike go faster, the front wheel was made bigger and the small wheel made smaller so the bike could be mounted, as shown in Fig. 12-19. Called the "Penny Farthing" or "Ordinary," the high-wheeler had front wheels sized to fit the rider. Longer-legged riders, theoretically at least, could go faster than shorter-legged riders because they could ride a bike with a bigger front wheel. As you can see in Fig. 12-19, a bigger front wheel meant a bigger frame that placed the rider higher above the pedals. Highwheelers were sized according to the front wheel diameter, which is where the meaningless concept of rating today's bicycle gears in inches instead of gear ratios originated, as I explained in Chapter 4.

Fig. 12-18: This velocipede of 1868 was a lighter, much more comfortable, and more maneuverable descendant of the Boneshaker.

Fig. 12-19: The 1881 standard-model Columbia highwheeler, made by Pope Manufacturing Company, Hartford, Connecticut.

Comfort came to the bicycle in 1888 in the form of pneumatic rubber tires, developed by an Irish veterinary surgeon, Dr. J. B. Dunlop of Belfast. When Dr. Dunlop's son Johnny complained about the harsh ride from his new, hard-tired trike, the good doctor developed pneumatic tires out of rubber sheets and strips of linen that could be filled with air. Dr. Dunlop continued to improve his air-filled tire. One day his friend, William Hume, president of the Belfast Cruiser's Cycling Club, persuaded him to make up a pair for his racing bicycle. With the new tires, Mr. Hume beat the crack racing cyclists of the area in a race on May 18, 1889. The news about the new tires spread fast and soon Dr. Dunlop was in the bicycle tire business. By 1891, bicycles were routinely fitted with pneumatic tires.

By 1895, the bicycle looked much like the bikes of today, complete with chain drive (Fig. 12-20). Tandems were popular but were designed so the woman rode up front and the man in

Fig. 12-20: A Cleveland woman's bicycle of 1895 looks much like inexpensive bicycles of today. Harplike strings on the rear fender help keep flowing skirts from tangling in the spokes.

back could do the steering. For example, in Fig. 12-21 you can see two rods leading from the rear handlebar downtube to the front wheel, so the tandem could be steered by the rider on the rear saddle. The front frame section is designed for a female. It's not clear to me whether gallantry or fear put the woman up front. The sleeker-looking Stearns tandem of 1897 (Fig. 12-22) was also steered from the rear, weighed only 43 pounds (about the same as a high-quality tandem of 90 years later), and sold for around $150.

Fig. 12-21: The woman rode in front and the man in the rear of this 1897 Sterling tandem, but the man controlled the steering with rods attached to the fork.

Fig. 12-22: Another tandem of the 1890s with the same steer-from-the-rear controls as the one in Fig. 12-21.

A few years ago I answered a pounding on my back door to find our local trash collector standing there with a strange-looking, weather-beaten old bike (Fig. 12-23). He had found it that morning on his rounds and wanted to know if I would buy it, since he knew of my interest in bicycles. I gave him $15 for what turned out to be a shaft-drive bicycle made about 1896 by Pierce-Arrow, who later made very elegant and expensive motor cars. Fig. 12-24 shows a close-up of the cranks and worm gear drive casing; Fig. 12-25 shows the rear transmission; and Fig. 12-26 shows the saddle, seatstays, and seattube. Figs. 12-27, 28, and 29 display another make of shaft-drive bicycle.

Fig. 12-23: This 1900 woman's Pierce Arrow shaft-drive bicycle was sold to the author for $15. It's shown in its unrestored condition.

Fig. 12-24: Close-up of the bottom-bracket gear section of the Pierce Arrow shaft-drive bicycle in Fig. 12-23.

Fig. 12-25: Close-up of the rear shaft-drive gear box of the Pierce Arrow bicycle in Fig. 12-23.

Fig. 12-26: The saddle, seat-post, seattube, and seatstays of the Pierce Arrow shaft-drive bike in Fig. 12-23.

Fig. 12-27: A restored 1896 Victor shaft-drive bicycle.

Fig. 12-28: Close-up of the transmission, shaft, and rear gear box of the 1896 Victor shaft-drive bicycle.

Fig. 12-29: Close-up of the transmission of the Victor shaft-drive bicycle.

Technology, like history, sometimes repeats itself. For example, a cam-action brake introduced in 1935 (Fig. 12-30) operated on the same cam principle as a cam-action brake designed by Charles Cunningham a few years ago, which is now made by SunTour for all-terrain bicycles (Fig. 12-31). A two-speed rear derailleur and freewheel introduced in 1934 (Fig. 12-32) has a modern counterpart in the five-speed rear derailleur and freewheel (Fig. 12-33). The front-wheel radial-spoke pattern of a time trial bicycle has its predecessor in the radial spoking of the Boneshaker (Fig. 12-34). The epicyclic gear drive on a tricycle of 1890 (Fig. 12-35) is now used on a bicycle introduced in 1985.

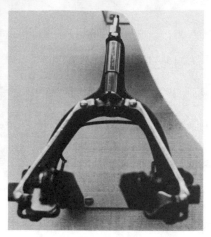

Fig. 12-30: A 1935 cam-action brake.

Fig. 12-31: A 1985 cam-action brake.

Fig. 12-32: A 1934 two-speed derailleur and freewheel.

Fig. 12-33: A 1985 five-speed derailleur and freewheel.

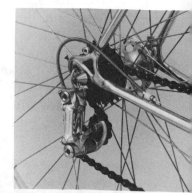

Fig. 12-34: Close-up of the radial spoke pattern of an early Boneshaker.

Fig. 12-35: The epicyclic gear drive of an 1890 tricycle.

Early Lights

By 1890 candle-powered lights were popular (Fig. 12-36) and by 1897 acetylene bike lights were introduced that threw a powerful beam ahead of the cyclist (Fig. 12-37). By 1916, electric lights (Figs. 12-38 and 12-39) lit the cyclist's way as they do today. Oil lamps were also used in the 1890s but their beam was little stronger than the candle-powered lamps.

Fig. 12-36: Early bicycle lights were candle-powered, like the two shown here. Note the "special cycle lamp" candle at bottom center.

Fig. 12-37: Acetylene lamps threw a powerful beam on bicycles of the 1880s. You can still use them.

From L.A.W. Bulletin and Good Roads - 1897

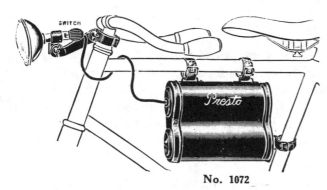

SWITCH

Presto

No. 1072

Fig. 12-38: This stem-mounted electric bicycle light of 1916 used a separate battery pack, which was hung from the top tube.

Fig. 12-39: A self-contained electric light and battery circa 1916, mounts on the stem.

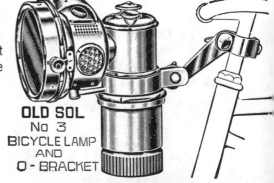

OLD SOL
No 3
BICYCLE LAMP
AND
O - BRACKET

Price $4.25

Materials

Up to the 1930s, most bicycle rims were made of wood and were prone to damage when hitting a pothole. Most bicycle frames were made of mild steel tubing, but some were made of aluminum tubing, such as the Lum-in-num, made in St. Louis, Missouri, and the frame of one make was even made of bamboo.

Hostility in the Early Days

Until large-scale production brought the price of the high-wheeler and safety bicycle of the 1890s within the reach of the general population, cyclists were met with widespread hostility. Farmers took personal delight in blocking the narrow roads of the day with their wagons, and would go as slowly as possible to irritate the faster cyclists behind them. To be fair, bicycles frightened horses (Fig. 12-8), causing them to bolt, throw the rider, or run away, dragging a wagon or surrey behind them. It took a few years for horses to get used to a human on a bicycle.

Country bumpkins delighted in thrusting a stick into the spokes of a highwheeler, which resulted in disaster to the cyclist and guffaws from the pranksters. Horse-drawn vehicles were often deliberately sent careening into groups of cyclists, causing injury to the riders and damage to their bicycles. In the 1880s, English restaurant and tea-shop owners often refused to serve cyclists, particularly females who wore what the owner of one establishment described as "outlandish and shocking costumes."

Early Cycling Clubs

Bicycle clubs of the 1800s were formed for political as well as social reasons. Cyclists wanted improved bicycle trails, revisions of unreasonably restrictive legislation, and protection against wanton attacks by irate citizens.

In 1878 in England, regional cycling clubs joined forces and organized the British Touring Club. The BTC soon began publication of its own magazine, *The Bicycling Times*. In 1883 the BTC changed its name to the Cyclists' Touring Club and its publication's name to *The Gazette*. The CTC is alive and well today, and its publication, now called *Cycle Touring*, is highly respected.

The Gazette was an outspoken and fearless defender of cyclists and cycling in England. Its early pronouncements must have been controversial, because at a national meeting in 1898 its editor was roundly denounced by some of the members, among whom were representatives of bicycle manufacturers. At the same meeting, George Bernard Shaw, an ardent cyclist and lifetime member of the club, arose to defend the editor. He said: "Do you want it [*The Gazette*] to contain fact or fiction? You already have plenty of fiction in the advertising pages . . . I want to raise a strong objection against what has been said as to raising the tone of *The Gazette*. What we want above all things is an abusive *Gazette*. If I wish to read a nice complimentary cycling paper—one that has a good word for everybody, for every dealer and seller, and every sort of kind of invention—I can easily buy one for a penny at any news shop. But we want something quite in the opposite direction in our *Gazette*, even if that publication does sometimes refer to a ladies' article as piffle." [Roars of laughter] "In my view the gentlemen who object to ladies having to stand the same treatment as is meted out to men are the same people who object to ladies cycling together, and therefore I do not think they need be taken very seriously."

Parliament reflected the public's attitude toward bicycling. For example, the Highway and Railway Act of 1878 gave the counties power to regulate the use of bicycles. Local authorities promptly enacted ordinances which forbade cyclists from using public highways, or required them to pull over and stop whenever a horse-drawn vehicle appeared on the horizon.

By 1893 the CTC had grown in size and had so much political clout that it could push the Local Government Act—a.k.a. the Magna Carta of Bicycling—through Parliament. The act abolished the power of the local counties to regulate bicycling. After that, the CTC in rapid order pushed through legislation providing for highway improvements, the safe transport of bicycles on railroad baggage cars, and for recourse in the courts against the antagonisms of the non-cycling public.

For example, a landmark case which drew national attention occurred in Surrey in 1899. Lady Harbeton, a member of the British nobility and an influential member of the CTC, was refused service in the coffee room of the Hautboy Hotel because of her dress. Instead, the hotel's management offered to serve her in the ladies' parlor, an offer Lady Harbeton greeted with much umbrage. The CTC leapt to her defense, took the case to court, and won. The court indicted the owners for "wilfully and unlawfully neglecting to supply a traveller with victuals." A deciding exhibit in this case was a photo of Lady Harbeton which showed, according to the CTC account, "an elderly lady wearing a pair of exceedingly baggy knickerbockers reaching below the knees, and a jacket which came well over the hips and opened sufficiently to reveal the silk blouse underneath."

The League of American Wheelmen

Following a visit to the CTC's Liverpool headquarters, a group of American cyclists formed the League of American Wheelmen in Newport, Rhode Island, in 1880. The summer homes—call them mansions—of many of America's rich and famous were (and still are) located in Newport, which should give you an idea of the social status of cycling at that time.

During its heyday the LAW was a force no politician could afford to ignore. Famous men and women were members, including Orville and Wilbur Wright, who owned a bicycle shop before building and flying the first airplane in the U.S., financier Commodore Vanderbilt, and even Diamond Jim Brady, who once bought his mistress a diamond-studded bicycle.

The League flexed its political muscle in 1884 when it made a test case out of the decision of Haddonfield, New Jersey, turnpike officials who barred bikes from that road. Turnpikes were then state roads used by horse-drawn vehicles (autos were 16 years away). Unless cyclists could use the turnpike system they would be confined to cowpaths or worse (I have run over cow flops on my ATB and I can report that they are hard to clean off, once dried on the bike). With the backing of the League, its Philadelphia chapter sued the turnpike and won, forcing the turnpike authority to rescind its no-cycling stricture.

In another case, the League fought an 1879 restriction by the New York Board of Commissions that outlawed bicycles in Central Park on the grounds that they were an eyesore and a menace to the citizenry. It took eight years of litigation before the governor of New York took matters into his own hands and overruled the board.

Long-Distance Touring in the 1880s

Think what it was like to undertake a cross-country tour back in the 1880s. Few roads, unreliable maps—where they even existed—uncharted territory, locals who were indifferent at best and downright hostile at worst. There were no phones, no stores, nothing by way of medical help for the rider or mechanical help for the bike. Cyclists on their highwheelers were wedged right up against the handlebars (Fig. 12-40), which made the machine hard to steer and maneuver. The rider sat upright on the saddle, which was mounted on a rigid, curved metal tube. The hard saddle and stiff frame did little to absorb road shock, which must have been severe, considering the condition of the roads at the time.

The first person to cross the United States on a bicycle was Thomas Stevens, who rode his highwheeler from Oakland, California, to Boston, Massachusetts, in 1884. "Rode" is hardly the word for this trip; he carried, pushed, dragged and shoved his

Fig. 12-40: On a highwheeler the rider was wedged against the handlebars, which made steering difficult. Braking by the metal spoon on the front wheel was very poor.

75-pound steed through streams and fields, across mountains and deserts.

His was not an uneventful trip. In one bar, rowdy cowpokes forced Stevens to ride around a poolroom, shooting at him as he rode. Once a pack of coyotes pursued him. In one memorable incident, to avoid being hit by a train while he was crossing a deep gorge on a railway trestle, he hung by one hand from the side of the trestle and held his 75-pound highwheeler with his other hand. He forded flood-swollen rivers, barrelled down the Rockies with his metal brake spoons heated till they glowed, was cursed at by boatmen on the Erie Canal whose horses balked and reared when he appeared. Stevens hit paydirt from Chicago on, when the media made him a celebrity by covering his journey from the Windy City to Boston.

There were other equally well-publicized cross-country and even around-the-world bike journeys in the late 1800s. For example, in 1894 a young American, Annie Londonberry, set out one fine July morning to tour the world. She left without a penny, biked throughout the world, and was so successful in publicizing her trip that she returned with over $2,000—not pocket money in those days.

Fannie Bullock Workman and her husband spent ten years touring the world in the late 1890s. Mrs. Workman was the daughter of a governor of Massachusetts and had inherited considerable wealth. Her husband was a physician. Old photos show her mounted on her trusty Rover safety bicycle, clad always in a high-necked blouse, a voluminous skirt, and a pith helmet. The Workmans rode over the Atlas mountains and through the Sahara, which is an unforgettable trip in any era.

Early Bicycle Racing

Men have always turned a hobby into a competitive event, and bicycling was no exception. Starting with the Draisene in 1817, two-wheel racing events quickly became popular. The first official bicycle race involving more modern two-wheelers, held in 1878 over a one-mile course, was won by Will R. Lipton in three minutes and 57 seconds of what must have been an arduous all-out pace, given the heavy, crude bikes of that day.

A bicyclist outran a fast race horse in 1895 when E. F. Lenert pedaled one mile in one minute and 35 seconds. Perhaps the greatest, if not the most notorious bike racer of his day was A. A. Zimmerman. A professional, Zimmerman was king of the wheel in the U.S. and Europe and is still a topic among racing cyclists today. In 1891 he set a new world record for the half mile in one minute, 10¾ seconds—on a 70-pound highwheeler —an accomplishment that made him an instant celebrity.

What made Zimmerman notorious was his training regime, or rather, lack of it. He violated all the rules of training, carousing, and drinking until the wee hours while his teammates slept. In one notable instance he climbed on his safety bicycle after having attended an all-night party and pedaled a paced mile in one minute, 57⅘ seconds at the annual LAW meet in Asbury Park, New Jersey—not a record, but after all, he had been up all night. What seemed to gain him the most notoriety, though, was Zimmerman's laid-back racing style. He never attempted to beat a record or win a race by any more effort or speed than was necessary.

Like today, bike racing in the 1890s was big business. Many pros became wealthy from their winnings. By 1895 there were over 600 professional bike racers in the U.S. alone, and more than that in Europe.

Early track records are impressive even by today's standards. For example, in 1895 Constance Huret pedaled 529 miles, 585 yards in just 24 hours. In 1899, Charles ("Mile-a-Minute") Murphy pedaled a record mile in 57.8 seconds behind a train, riding on a boarded-over section of the Long Island Rail Road. It took six years for a car to break that record; it was driven by former cyclist Barney Oldfield, who pushed Henry Ford's "999" to a mile in 55.8 seconds.

The Bicycle in War

The bicycle was a natural for the military of the 1890s, who saw it as an invaluable tool for advanced scouting, outpost duties, patrols, convoys, and messenger service from the front to the command post. *Harper's Weekly,* in a special bicycle issue of April 11, 1896, noted: "It is in rapidly moving considerable bodies of infantry that the bicycle will find its highest function in time of war. Fancy a force of infantry, independent of roads and railroads moving in any direction, forty or fifty miles in one morning, and appearing on a field not weary and exhausted as after a two-days' march, but fresh and prepared to fight. . . ."

The Italian army was the first to adopt the bicycle to military use. In 1870, each regiment was given four bicycles, each equipped with a brake, lantern, knapsack, rifle support, and a leather pouch for carrying orders. The French army had bikes that weighed only 23 pounds, with a hinged frame so they could be slung over a soldier's back if necessary (Fig. 12-4). In 1885, Austrian soldiers, carrying a full field kit, were said to travel 100 miles per day on bicycles, outdoing the cavalry on horseback.

In America, the first military unit to use bicycles was the Connecticut National Guard. The U.S. Army used two side-by-side bicycles with a "mountain cannon" mounted between them. The Army also used a tandem equipped with rifles, revolvers, and a field pack, and a tricycle fitted with a Colt rapid-fire machine gun.

Between 1890 and 1900 the army taught soldiers how to ride, drill, and conduct field maneuvers on bicycles. The United States Military Wheelmen, a voluntary adjunct of the National Guard, did the same for its volunteers. A Lieutenant Whitney, in 1896, noted: "The balance of power is so nicely adjusted, the chances in the coming conflict will be governed by efficiency in detailed preparation. The bicycle will weigh in the balance."

During the nearly two hundred years since the Celerifere was introduced, the bicycle has progressed from a wealthy man's toy to everyman's vehicle of health and joy. There are faster ways to travel, but few more pleasant than the bicycle.

APPENDIX

ALIGNMENT Applies to the bicycle frame. Dropouts should be parallel; fork blades and stays parallel to the toptube; toptube centered between the stays; the headtube parallel to the fork blades; fork blades parallel to each other; stays parallel to each other; seat tube should be parallel to the bottom bracket sides.

ANKLING Technique of pedaling in which the foot follows through nearly 360 degrees of pedal arc.

BICYCLE COMPUTERS An electronic version of the mechanical bicycle odometer. The computers measure elapsed mileage for the day and total mileage for the trip, cadence, and miles per hour; some can measure pulse rate.

BINDER BOLT Any bolt and nut that holds a part onto a bicycle, such as the binder bolt(s) for saddles, brakes, carriers, lights, generators, computers, derailleurs, cranks, and other bolted-on parts.

BOTTOM-BRACKET ASSEMBLY Spindle, bearings, cones, cups, and locknut. The crank arms are attached to the spindle.

BOTTOM-BRACKET HANGER The short round tube containing the bottom-bracket assembly and to which the downtube, seat tube and chain-stays are attached.

BRAKE BRIDGE A tube mounted between the seatstays to which the rear brake is attached. May also hold fender mount and carrier mount.

BRAKE LEVERS Handlebar mounted levers which control the brakes.

CABLES Flexible steel cables connecting brake levers to the brakes and the shift levers to the front and rear derailleurs.

CADENCE Crank revolutions per minute, a measure of how fast the rider can spin the cranks. A good touring cadence would be 70 crank revolutions per minute.

CHAIN The articulated drive unit connecting the chainwheel gears to the freewheel gears.

521

CHAINSTAYS   The frame tubing from the bottom bracket to the rear drop-outs.

CHAINWHEELS   The toothed gears attached to the bottom-bracket spindle which deliver pedal power to the freewheel gears. Chainwheels may be single, double, or triple.

COASTER BRAKES   A brake mechanism contained in the rear-wheel hub, which is actuated by backpedaling.

COTTER KEY   A key or pin which holds cottered cranks on the bottom-bracket spindle.

CRANK ARM   The long shaft that is attached to the bottom-bracket spindle and to which the pedals are attached.

CYCLOMETER   A mechanical odometer for measuring mileage.

DERAILLEUR   From the French meaning "to derail" or shift. The rear derailleur shifts the chain from one freewheel cog to another, the front derailleur shifts the chain from one chainwheel to another.

DOWNTUBE   The frame tube which is connected to the headtube and to the bottom bracket.

DISHING   Describes truing the rear wheel so the rim is centered exactly between the hub axle locknuts. Necessary because of added width of the freewheel. In dishing, the rear-wheel rim is more toward the right hub flange whereas the front-wheel rim, which is not dished, is centered between the hub flanges.

DROPOUTS   Slotted openings into which wheel hub axles fit. Holds front and rear wheels.

FORK   Consists of the fork blades, fork crown, front-wheel dropouts, and steering tube.

HEADTUBE   The short tube to which is connected the top and down-tubes and which holds the fork with its associated headset bearings, cups, cones, and locknut.

HUB   The front- and rear-wheel units that hold the wheel axle and to which are attached the spokes.

PANNIERS   A fancy word for bike packs and bags.

QUICK-RELEASE   A cam-action lever-actuated mechanism that permits quick and easy removal and installation of a bicycle wheel.

SADDLE   The seat.

SEATPOST   A hollow tube sized to fit into the seat tube, designed to hold and support the saddle. Adjustable so saddle can be tilted as desired.

SEATSTAYS   Two hollow steel tubes attached at one end to the seat tube and at the other end to each of the rear wheel dropouts. With the chainstays (see above) they form the rear triangle of the bicycle frame.

SEAT TUBE   The vertical frame tube attached at its base to the bottom-bracket shell, at its top to the toptube, and to which are attached the seatpost cluster and the seatstays.

STEERING HEAD   Also called a steering tube. A steel tube attached to the fork at the fork crown.

TOECLIPS AND STRAPS   Toeclips, also called rattraps, are metal cages attached to pedals that are designed, along with straps, to keep the foot from sliding off the pedals and to enable the foot to pull up on the upstroke while the other foot is pushing down on the downstroke.

TOPTUBE   Horizontal frame member joined to the headtube and the seat tube.

VARIABLE GEAR HUB   A rear hub containing two, three, or five internal gears and as many gear ratios, shiftable from a handlebar-mounted shift lever.

BICYCLE AND CAMPING EQUIPMENT CATALOGS

Bikecology
President, Alan Goldsmith
1515 Wilshire
Santa Monica, CA 90403-3900
Outside CA: 1-800-282-BIKE, in CA: 1-800-223-BIKE
Catalog of bicycles, frames, parts, components, clothing, exercisers, and more.

CAMPMOR
President, Dan Jarashow
P.O. Box 997-D
Paramus, NJ 07653-0997
Camping gear for the cyclist. Tents, sleeping bags, lights, cookstoves. If it's not here you can probably do without it.

Palo Alto Bicycles
President, Jim Westby
P.O. Box 1276
Palo Alto, CA 94302
Outside CA: 1-800-227-8900, in CA: 415-328-0128
Bikes, parts, and equipment sold by bicyclists. A broad selection of just about everything you need.

Pedal Pushers
Presidents, Ronald and Janis McVay
1130 Rogero Road
Jacksonville, FL 32211-5895
Outside FL: 1-800-874-2453, in FL: 1-800-342-7320
Another excellent catalog, compiled by bicycle enthusiasts.

Performance Bicycle Shop
Garry Snook, President
P.O. Box 2741
Chapel Hill, NC 27514
1-800-334-5471
An intelligently designed catalog of bicycles, bicycle accessories, and clothing. Much help in parts selection.

L. L. Bean
President, Leon Gorman
Freeport, ME 04033
1-800-221-4221
The old standby for high-quality outdoor equipment now sells its own brand of bicycles plus bicycle accessories and of course high-quality camping gear.

Moss Tent Works, Inc.
President, Bill Moss
Mt. Mattie Street
Camden, ME 04843
207-236-8368
High-quality tents for every season and purpose.

REI Cycle Source
P.O. Box C-88125
Seattle, WA 98188-0125
Outside WA: 1-800-426-4840, in WA: 1-800-562-4894
This beautifully photographed and well-designed bicycle catalog comes from Recreational Equipment, Inc. REI also has a bigger catalog on camping and outdoor gear.

Rhode Gear
President, Ned Levine
765 Allens Avenue
Providence, RI 02905
1-800-HOT-GEAR
Many of the items in this catalog such as panniers were designed by Ned Levine. Other high-quality equipment includes a wide range of parts, clothing, and other useful gear.

The Third Hand
President, Jack Moore
P.O. Box 212
Mt. Shasta, CA 96067
916-926-2600
Keep this catalog on your workbench! It has every bicycle tool known to man, plus a wide assortment of spare parts not generally available elsewhere such as derailleur bolts and nuts, seatpost binder quick-releases, and much more. If you do your own repairs and maintenance, you need this catalog.

BICYCLING MAGAZINES

Bicycle Forum
Editor, John Williams
P.O. Box 8311
Missoula, MT 59807
406-728-4497
$14.00 (5 issues)
The publication of the BikeCentennial, the country's premier bicycle organization. There's more about BC in the Tour Guide section of this Appendix.

Bicycle Rider
Editor, Denis Rouse
29901 Agoura Road
Agoura, CA 91301
818-991-4980
$15.98 (9 issues)
Well edited, highly readable, beautifully illustrated, in-depth articles on bicycle touring worldwide.

Bicycle USA
Editor, Dale Adams
6707 Whitesone Road
Baltimore, MD 21207
$22.00 (9 issues)
Official publication of the League of American Wheelmen, the oldest and best cycling organization in the U.S.

Bicycling
Editor, James C. McCullough
33 E. Minor Street
Emmaus, PA 18098
215-967-5171
$15.97 (10 issues)
The oldest living U.S. bicycle magazine. Excellent coverage of all aspects of the sport.

Cycling USA
Editor, Diana Fritschner
1750 E. Boulder
Colorado Springs, CO 80909
303-531-0177
Free to USCF members. $10.00 to non-members (12 issues)
The official publication of the U.S. Cycling Federation, the governing body of bicycle racing in the U.S.

Mountain Bike
Editor, Hank Barlow
Box 989
Crested Butte, CO 81224
303-349-6804
$12.00, one year (12 issues)
Fine articles on off-road bicycle touring throughout the U.S. plus technical data on ATBs.

NORBA News
Denney Griffiths
P.O. Box 1901
Chandler, AZ 85244
602-961-0635
$16.00 (12 issues)
The official publication of the National Off-Road Bicycle Association. Almost 100 percent devoted to off-road racing events.

Outside
Editor, Lawrence Burke
1165 N. Clark St.
Chicago, IL 60610
312-951-0990
$21.00, one year (12 issues)
Macho outdoor adventure articles, usually a major cycling piece per issue. Well written and beautifully illustrated.

Sierra
Editor, Francis Gendlin
530 Bush Street
San Francisco, CA 94108
415-981-8634
$29.00 (six issues)
The Sierra Club Bulletin. If you're a conservationist as well as a cyclist, subscribe to this magazine. Better yet, join the Sierra Club and get the magazine free. Annual dues are $29.00.

Velo News
Editor, Geoff Drake
P.O. Box 1257
Brattleboro, VT 05301-1257
802-254-2305
$18.00 per year (18 issues)
If you like racing you'll love Velo News. *News of upcoming racing events throughout the country, coverage of major races, technical data for the racing cyclist.*

CUSTOM FRAME BUILDERS

F. M. Assenmacher
104 E. May
Mt. Pleasant, MI 48858

Albert Eisentraut
910 81st Avenue
Oakland, CA 94621

Klein Bicycle Corporation
207 South Prairie Road
Chehalis, WA 98532

Steve Potts
105 Montford Avenue
Mill Valley, CA 94041

Scot Nicol
P.O. Box 275
Sebastopol, CA 95472

Charles Cunningham
121 Wood Lane
Fairfax, CA 94930

Bruce Gordon Cycles
1070 W. 2nd Street
Eugene, OR 97402

RRB Cycles
562 Greenbay Road
Kenilworth, IL 60043

Stout Bicycle Manufacturing
3472 South 2300 East #5A
Salt Lake City, UT 84109

Edwins Cycle Company
P.O. Box 81
Owen Sound, Ontario N4K 5P1

BICYCLE TOURS

There are so many bicycle tour operators that space forbids mentioning more than a few of the largest and the most reliable. Here are tour providers in whom I have confidence. You can find dozens of regional tour providers listed in the classified pages of the bicycle magazines in this Appendix that conduct tours in Colorado, Maine, Michigan, Minnesota, Wisconsin, New England, Virginia, Vermont, Canada, the Pacific Northwest, Pennsylvania, Alaska, Oregon, and Washington. Many of the tour providers also offer off-road trail rides for all-terrain bikers. You can find statewide maps and bicycle touring information by writing to the travel or tourism division in the capital of the states you want to visit.

The BikeCentennial
P.O. Box 8308
Missoula, MT 59807
Cross-country, regional, and local tours in the U.S.A. and abroad. A top-quality tour organizer. Has excellent maps (they've been there), clothing, camping gear.

Cycle Vision Tours
1020 Green Valley Road NW
Albuquerque, NM 87107
If you can't go there, the next best tour is via the video tapes from Cycle Vision Tours. Professionally made TV tapes of Vermont in autumn, Yellowstone, San Francisco, and Hawaii, and more to come. These tapes are so good they make indoor bike-exerciser riding fun.

Sobek Expeditions
Angels Camp, CA 95222
Sobek is probably America's premier tour provider, especially for trips abroad. These people are old hands at designing and packaging bicycle tours in Tasmania, New Zealand, Australia, Tibet, and many other out-of-the way places you've ever dreamed about touring with your bike. A few samples: Cycle India, through Bombay, Agra, Goa, Jaipur, Delhi; China Bicycle, 650 miles starting at Hong Kong, to Macao, Beijing, Guangzhou, Guilin; Cycling Eastern Europe, through Zurich, Vienna, Hungary, Transylvania/Romania, Czechoslovakia; Tour de France, from Burgundy to the Bay of Biscay.

American Youth Hostels
P.O. Box 37613
Washington, D.C. 20013-7613
Don't let the "Youth" in AYH fool you. This outfit's for everybody! They have tours throughout the U.S. and overseas. Stay in their hostels, which seem to be everywhere. An inexpensive and fun way to travel by bike! Members get a handbook listing hostels worldwide. The 1987 issue has 242 pages of hostels in every state and in Argentina, Australia, Austria, Belgium, Brazil, Bulgaria, Canada, Chile, Cyprus, Czechoslovakia, Denmark, Egypt, Britain, France, West Germany, and many other countries.

BICYCLE ORGANIZATIONS

American Bicycling Association
P.O. Box 718
Chandler, AZ 85224
One of the two governing bodies of BMX racing.

American Youth Hostels, Inc. (AYH)
P.O. Box 37613
Washington, D.C. 20013-7613
As noted above, the AYH maintains some 254 hostels throughout the U.S. and in cooperation with the International Youth Hostel Federation, 5,000 hostels worldwide. Sponsors organize bicycle tours worldwide. Membership: Senior (age 18–59), $20; over 60, $10; Junior (17 and under), $10.

Association Cycliste Canadienne
BP 2020 Succersdale D.
Ottawa, Ontario
Governing body of competitive cycling in Canada.

British Cycling Federation
26 Park Crescent
London, W.1
England
Governing body of racing in Great Britain. Also offers help to members who wish to cycle-tour. Provides maps, hostel information, accident insurance, and general advice on touring in the British Isles and in Europe.

League of American Wheelmen
P.O. Box 411
Baltimore, MD 21203
The oldest bicycle organization in the U.S. Publishes an excellent magazine, Bicycling USA, which is free to members, who also get a membership roster. Has chapters in all major cities which offer fellowship to cyclists, help with touring, provide maintenance tips. The League is a potent force in promoting bike trails and fending off adverse legislation.

National Bicycling Organization
P.O. Box 411
Newhall, CA 91322
Primarily concerned with BMX bicycle racing.

National Off-Road Bicycle Association (NORBA)
P.O. Box 1901
Chandler, AZ 85244
The governing body of all-terrain bicycle racing. Publishes NORBA News, which lists upcoming racing events throughout the country.

U.S. Olympic Committee
67 Park Avenue
New York, NY 10001
Bicycle racing at Olympic events.

United States Cycling Federation
1750 E. Boulder No. 4
Colorado Springs, CO 80909
The governing body of bicycle racing in the U.S. Allied member of the Amateur Athletic Union of the United States, the U.S. Olympic committee, and the Union Cycliste International (the world governing body of bicycling).

BIBLIOGRAPHY

Alderson, Frederick, *Bicycling. A History* 245 pages. Praeger Publishers, Inc. 1972.

Alexander, Don, and Ochowisz, Jim, *Tour De France '86: The American Invasion* 192 pages. Alexander and Alexander. 1986.

Behrman, Daniel, *The Man Who Loved Bicycles* 130 pages. Harper's Magazine Press. 1973.

Bengtsson, Hans and Atkinson, George, *Orienteering for Sport and Pleasure* 224 pages. The Stephen Greene Press. 1977.

Brandt, Jobst, *The Bicycle Wheel* 149 pages. Avocet Inc. 1983.

Borysewicz, Edward, *Bicycle Road Racing* 180 pages. Velo-News. 1985.

Burke, Edward; Perez, H. R.; and Hodges, Patrick, *Inside the Cyclist* 160 pages. Velo-News Corporation. 1979.

Burke, Edward, *The Two-Wheeled Athlete* 140 pages. Velo-News Corporation. 1986.

Caunter, C. F., *The History and Development of Cycles* 72 pages. British Science Museum Press. 1972.

Contributions by about 25 authors, *Cyclist's Britain* 306 pages. Hunter Publishing, Inc. 1985.

Duncan, David N., *Pedaling the Ends of the Earth* 272 pages. Fireside Books, Simon & Schuster, Inc. 1985.

Farny, Michael H., *New England Over the Handlebars* 174 pages. Little, Brown & Co. 1975.

Ferguson, Gary, *Freewheeling: Bicycling the Open Road* 194 pages. The Mountaineers. 1984.

Fleming, June, *Staying Found* 159 pages. Vintage Books. 1982.

Forgey, William W., M.D., *Hypothermia, Death by Exposure* 172 pages. ICS Books, Inc. 1985.

Forgey, William W., M.D., *Wilderness Medicine* 124 pages. ICS Books, Inc. 1979.

Greenbank, Anthony, *The Book of Survival* 250 pages. The New American Library. 1967.

Grossberg, Milton A., *Family Bike Rides* 112 pages. Chronicle Books. 1982.

Hawkins, Gary, and Hawkins, Karen, *Bicycling in the Western United States* 390 pages. Pantheon Books. 1982.

Hawkins, Gary, and Hawkins, Karen, *Bicycle Touring in Europe* 336 pages. Pantheon Books. 1980.

Hayduk, Douglas, *Bicycle Metallurgy for the Cyclist* 112 pages. Self-published. 1987.

Henderson, N. G.; Armstrong, David; Burton, Beryl; Johnson, Gordon; Porter, Hugh; Watson, John; West, Les. *Cycling Year Book* 128 pages. Pelham Books. 1971.

Higley, Donn C., *Pocketwise Tips on Use of the Compass, Man-Made and Natural* 35 pages. Self-published. 1981.

Hurne, Ralph, *The Yellow Jersey* 255 pages. Simon & Schuster, Inc. 1973.

Jacobson, Michael, *Nutrition Scoreboard* 102 pages. Center for Science in the Public Interest. 1973.

Jones, Phillip N., *Bicycling the Backroads of Northwest Oregon* 192 pages. The Mountaineers. 1984.

Kals, W. S., *Land Navigation* 230 pages. Sierra Club Books. 1983.

Kjellstrom, Bjorn, *Map & Compass* 215 pages. Charles Scribners Sons. 1976.

Kolin, Michael J., and de la Rosa, Denise, *The Custom Frame* 274 pages. Rodale Press. 1979.

Lobeck, Armin K., *Things Maps Don't Tell Us* 160 pages. The MacMillan Company. 1956.

Matheny, Fred, *Solo Cycling, How to Train and Race Bicycle Time Trials* 206 pages. Velo-News. 1986.

Matson, Robert W., *North of San Francisco* 276 pages. Celestial Arts. 1980.

McGonagle, Seamus, *The Bicycle in Life, Love, War and Literature* 142 pages. A. S. Barnes and Company. 1968.

Murphy, Tom A., *50 Northern California Bicycle Trips* 126 pages. The Touchstone Press. 1972.

Paterek, Tim, *The Paterek Manual for Bicycle Frame Builders* 350 pages. The Framebuilders' Guild. 1985.

Platten, David, *The Outdoor Survival Handbook* 160 pages. David and Charles, Inc. 1986.

Savage, Barbara, *Miles From Nowhere* 324 pages. The Mountaineers. 1983.

Selvi, Bettina, *Riding to Jerusalem* 216 pages. Peter Bredrick Books. 1986.

Sjogaard, Gisela; Nielsen, Bodil; Mikkelsen, Finn; Saltin, Bengt; Burke, Edmund R., *Physiology in Bicycling* 110 pages. Movement Publications, Inc. 1982.

Sloane, Eugene A., *Eugene A. Sloane's Book of All-Terrain Bicycles* 285 pages. Simon & Schuster, Inc. 1985.

Sloane, Eugene A., *Eugene A. Sloane's Bicycle Maintenance Manual* 352 pages. Simon & Schuster, Inc. 1981.

Smith, Hempstone Oliver, and Berkeble, Donald H., *Wheels and Wheeling, The Smithsonian Institution Cycle Collection* 104 pages. Smithsonian Institution Press. 1974.

Sterling, E. M., *Trips and Trails Around the North Cascades* 216 pages. The Mountaineers. 1978.

Tobey, Eric, and Wolkenburg, Richard, *Northeast Bicycle Tours* 282 pages. Tobey Publishing Co., Inc. 1973.

Velox, *Velocipedes, Bicycles and Tricycles, How to Make Them and How to Use Them* 128 pages. S. R. Publishers, Inc. 1971 (originally published in 1869).

Watts, Alan, *Instant Weather Forecasting* 64 pages. Dodd Mead & Co. 1968.

Whitnah, Dorothy L., *Point Reyes* 114 pages. Wilderness Press. 1981.

Whitt, Frank Rowland, and Wilson, David Gordon, *Bicycling Science* 364 pages. The MIT Press. 1985.

Wilkerson, James A., M.D., *Medicine for Mountaineering* 365 pages. The Mountaineers. 1975.

Willson, Janet, *Exploring by Bicycle, Southwest British Columbia, Northwest Washington* 100 pages. Gundy's & Bernie's Guide Books. 1973.

INDEX

ABOUT THE AUTHOR

Eugene A. Sloane is the world's foremost authority on bicycles and bicycling. He is the author of *Eugene A. Sloane's Bicycle Maintenance Manual, Eugene A. Sloane's Complete Book of All-Terrain Bicycles,* and the all-time best-selling editions of *The Complete Book of Bicycling,* of which this is the fourth edition. He lives in Vancouver, Washington, and rides his bicycle every day.